FRENCH PROTESTANTISM AND THE FRENCH REVOLUTION

FRENCH PROTESTANTISM AND THE FRENCH REVOLUTION

A Study in Church and State, Thought and Religion, 1685-1815

BURDETTE C. POLAND

PRINCETON, NEW JERSEY
PRINCETON UNIVERSITY PRESS
1957

L.C.CARD: 57-5846

BURDETTE C. POLAND is assistant professor of history at the University of Nebraska. He received his Certificat d'Etudes at the Université de Grenoble, France, and his doctorate at Princeton University. During 1953-1955 he taught as instructor and then as assistant professor at Denison University. This book is an outgrowth of his work at Princeton.

Printed in the United States of America by
Princeton University Press, Princeton, New Jersey

TO NANCY

PREFACE

When Louis XIV revoked the Edict of Nantes, his Huguenot subjects either fled abroad or converted to the Church of Rome. Thenceforth France was ostensibly a nation of Catholics—and unbelievers.

The Revocation of the Edict of Nantes, however, did not strike the death knell of French Protestantism. The emigration and forced conversions of Huguenots to Catholicism notwithstanding, the roots of Protestantism in France were not so easily destroyed. The eighteenth century witnessed a revival of the French Reformed Church which bequeathed to the epoch of the Revolution a well-defined, self-conscious Protestant minority with specific political and religious aspirations. True, they were a small minority, probably no more than 700,000 in number. But to the Catholics who feared them, to the *philosophes* who idolized them, and to the monarchy which valued their presumed economic importance, their significance in 1789 was disproportionate to their numbers. It is the purpose of this study to trace the history of their eighteenth-century revival and, at one and the same time, to relate the impact of the Revolution upon the Protestant community in France and describe the role of the Protestants in that political upheaval.

The history of the Protestants during the last decades of the *ancien régime* has often been told and with the scholarly works of Edmond Hugues, the abbé Joseph Dedieu, and Emile-G. Léonard so readily accessible would scarcely need retelling were it not for its importance to an understanding of the church and community history of the Protestants during the Revolution. A systematic history of the Protestants during the revolutionary period, however, has been attempted only once, by pastor Charles Durand in his *L'Histoire du Protestantisme français pedant la Révolution et l'Empire* (Paris, 1902). Since the appearance of this work, a considerable amount of new material has appeared, making necessary a reappraisal of this period in the history of French Protestantism. Moreover, Charles Durand, writing with the interests of a pastor of the Reformed Church in France, was primarily concerned with the confessional aspects of French Protestantism in this period. The present author, while hoping to do justice to this aspect of the topic, has attempted to meet the need for a fuller treatment of the subject which will take into account the secular history of the Protestants as one of the most important minority groups of France on the eve of the Revolution. What, for instance, was the general attitude of the Protestant population in 1789 toward the impending political reform of the French polity? Were the Protestants more hostile than other Frenchmen toward a monarchy which had sponsored the religious persecutions of the previous century? Can they justifiably be accused of complicity in the revolutionary legislation which destroyed the privileged position of the Catholic Church in France? And when members of their sect were elevated to positions of political importance in the capital and in the provinces, did they abuse their new power at the expense of their Catholic compatriots? This study will attempt to answer questions such as these and to describe the collapse of the Reformed Church during the dechristianization movement of the Terror.

Lest the title of this work be misleading, one point should be clarified. Because persecution played such an important part in shaping the consciousness of this group of French citizens, the author did not feel that a consideration of the French Lutheran minority was a legitimate part of this investigation. More fortunate than their Calvinist counterparts, the Lutherans of France were protected and guaranteed in their religious liberties by the treaties of Westphalia. While they were not totally immune from harassment under Louis XIV and the heirs to his religious policies, the Lutherans were spared the rigors of the Revocation and its complementary legislation. Moreover, ethnically and geographically the Lutherans were a group apart from the Calvinists. Concentrated in the eastern provinces of the kingdom, they were for the most part of Germanic descent and hence differed from the Calvinists, who were thoroughly French and who were liberally scattered throughout the entire southern part of the kingdom.

In closing this introduction, the author would like to take the opportunity to express his gratitude and appreciation to Professor Robert R. Palmer for his generous assistance and advice in the research and writing of this work, and to his fellow graduate students and to members of the faculty at Princeton University who in their graduate thesis seminar patiently and constructively criticized parts of this work during the preliminary stages of the preparation of this manuscript.

CONTENTS

(*The maps were drawn by*)
R. S. Snedeker

FRENCH PROTESTANTISM AND THE FRENCH REVOLUTION

CHAPTER I

Protestantism in France: the Catastrophe of 1685

The Protestants of France are a small minority swallowed up in a sea of Catholics. In a sense this makes them an anomaly, and we should not be surprised to find that they have meant different things to different people. At one extreme there are those who regard them as an inferior species, a disgrace to France, a diseased member which should be severed from the social and political community of Frenchmen. At the other extreme there are those who maintain that the Protestants are the "salt of France."

While writing this book, I stopped a French student who is studying in this country and asked him what he thought about the French Protestant. His reaction was amusing and possibly significant. He screwed up his face, pulled at his nose, thought for a moment, and then said: "Well, you know—" The usual platitudes followed. The Protestant is rich (he said this with what might have been a look of envy); he is clannish, sober, industrious, odd, frugal—and then, as an afterthought (somewhat approvingly), he added that politically the Protestant is really quite progressive.

This reaction might be typical of the average Frenchman's frame of mind with respect to his Protestant compatriot. It reduces itself to the belief that the French Protestant is "different." To whatever extent this is true, the French Protestant invites definition.

Such a definition is not as simple as one might at first suspect, especially when dealing with the French Protestant of the eighteenth century. In the narrowest sense, one is tempted to define him merely as that Frenchman who takes Communion in the Protestant Church, who attends Protestant worship, and who calls himself a Protestant when asked to identify his religious affiliation. However, we are all familiar with the American who calls himself a Protestant, and yet who rarely if ever attends religious services. He may never have taken Communion; he may not even know what Communion is; yet he insists on being called a Protestant. The same is true of the French. In the eighteenth century, some Protestants undoubtedly stayed away from religious services simply because they had what they considered more important things to do. Others living in the northern provinces of France, especially in Normandy and Brittany, could not have attended services if they had wanted to: there were almost no pastors available to administer to them. Hence they were content with a *culte familial* and although not attending formal services or taking Communion they definitely considered themselves Protestants. Moreover, because of stringent legal disabilities imposed upon them, few were willing to admit to anyone in an official capacity that they were Protestant. For the same reasons a large number of them found it expedient to take Communion in the Roman Catholic Church. Many even chose to celebrate their marriages there, and still more presented their children to the parish priest for baptism. Finally, it might be pointed out that in some localities it was not at all uncommon for avowed Catholics to attend Protestant ceremonies—not regularly and out of little more than sheer curiosity, but nevertheless attending and participating.

The first definition—he who attends Protestant worship—is obviously inadequate. It is not only deficient when applied to the *ancien régime*, but it also does not satisfactorily define the French Protestant of the Third Republic or of today. Indeed, even French writers who are themselves Protestant are embarrassed and contradictory when faced with the problem of attempting a definition. Part of their difficulty lies in the fact that they are not content with the strict definition—one who is faithful to the formal exercise of his religion—but insist upon a broader classification. André Siegfried, one of the more prominent contemporary Protestant French historians, measures the Protestant by his tradition, or background, more than by religious beliefs. When we designate a Frenchman as a Protestant, "that does not mean that he has faith, but [rather] that he was born a Protestant and remains one, just as people who are born white remain white."[1] This suggests that the Protestant differs from his Catholic compatriot in something more than religious beliefs. Siegfried would agree; he even goes so far as to suggest that the Protestant "is so distinct from the Catholic, so easy to identify, that one might call him a physiological species."[2] What is it that sets him apart? Any number of things. He considers his religion superior to Catholicism, even if he is not a believer himself. He succeeds in business, Siegfried claims, where a Catholic might fail, because he is

[1] André Siegfried, "Le groupe protestant cévenol sous la IIIe République," in *Protestantisme français*, eds. Marc Boegner and André Siegfried (Paris, 1945), pp. 29-30.

[2] *ibid.*, p. 29.

more active, determined, shows more initiative and spirit. Since the Revolution, his political bent is usually toward the left, regardless of his economic or social position. In short, he does not vote the same as a Catholic. But the greatest difference, one which Siegfried himself unconsciously reveals, lies in his pride in being a Protestant, *his pride in the Protestant tradition and in the Protestant contribution* to the history and civilization of France. "Consequently one can well imagine," says Siegfried, "how different France would be if, in the 16th century, the Reformation had triumphed here."[3]

Not all of Siegfried's coreligionists are as willing as he is to point up the differences which distinguish the French Protestant from the French Catholic. Albert-Marie Schmidt, referring to the thesis that the Protestant is an organism which somehow basically differs from the French norm, feels that "it is important [for us] to dispel the malignant mists of an odious legend. On the basis of certain caricatures excessively confirmed by slanderous evidence, people imagine the Huguenots of yesteryear to have been a seditious cabal of hypocritical and sullen ascetics."[4] By emphasizing the ways in which the French Protestant differs from the average Frenchman, he says, we unconsciously corroborate those who would take the great men in the history of Protestant France and "accuse them of having inoculated the robust body of France with all the venoms of heresy, anarchy, and literary corruption."[5] More timorous than Siegfried, Albert-Marie Schmidt is illustrative of the French Protestant who has been put on the defensive by four centuries of religious stigmatism. Notwithstanding, he is no less eager than Siegfried to demonstrate that the Protestant has left his mark on French history: "Protestant thought, on the whole, has manifested itself . . . with an incomparable diversity. It is evident as a kind of leaven which enables the *génie français* to effect the most auspicious transformations."[6]

But if we turn to Pierre Chazel, we meet a French Protestant with still another interpretation of the role of the Huguenots in French history. "People have talked too much about *la France protestante;* sometimes with the suspicious arrogance of a minority for whom

[3] *ibid.*, p. 55.

[4] Albert-Marie Schmidt, "Pensée protestante et génie français durant les deux premiers siècles de la Réforme," in *Protestantisme français, op.cit.*, p. 60.

[5] *ibid.*, p. 76.

[6] *ibid.*, p. 75.

history should be dated from the St. Bartholomew [Massacre], sometimes quarrelsomely and defiantly, as of a foreign body, encysted with difficulty into the national community. Just the opposite is true. For two centuries—and to the great misfortune of our country—Protestantism has ceased to be a source (*faisceau*) of political, social, and spiritual forces sufficiently strong to inflect by its élan or its resistance the great lines of [development of] our French destiny. It has ceased to be—if it ever was—a state within a state."[7] To Chazel the Huguenot, above all else, is a Frenchman. But in trying to establish this, he cannot refrain from pointing out that perhaps in the final analysis he is something more. For "[religious] credo and attachment to the Church aside, one can detect . . . a certain *climat protestant*, easier to sense than to define, a family air, a 'je ne sais quoi' [characterized by being] parochial, grave and sometimes a little austere."[8]

Where does this leave us? Despite the inherent contradictions present in these views, something can be salvaged by way of a general definition. If we are to accept the opinion of such writers, the Protestant population of France is comprised of more than the communicants. In addition to the latter, there is a group of French subjects who, even if religious skeptics, should be classified as Protestants. For they belong to this *climat protestant*, which is another way of saying that they are conscious of and influenced by a "Protestant tradition."

That this tradition is more secular than religious in its bases was at no time more apparent than during the eighteenth century, when for a variety of reasons few Protestants in France were at all familiar with the nature of the theological differences between their faith and that of the Roman Catholic Church. Yet in spite of their ignorance of the basic tenets of Protestant faith, they were willing to forego their civil rights for what might be called the "privilege" of being Protestants. They were conscious of a "Protestant tradition" and took pride in being a part of it. The relative insignificance of religious beliefs as the determining factor in this attitude was noted by the Moravian missionary Fries, who, after visiting and preaching among the Protestants of southern France in the eighteenth century,

[7] Pierre Chazel, "Génie français et protestantisme dans la France contemporaine," in *Protestantisme français, op.cit.*, p. 77.

[8] *ibid.*, p. 104.

concluded that they were more attached to their religion by an "esprit de parti" than by a "sentiment du coeur."[9] Part of this "esprit de parti" is a feeling of superiority to the Catholics, a trait mentioned by Siegfried. At times it has taken the form of a deep suspicion of the Catholic Church and its ministers. The latter aspect was emphasized by the vicar of Alais, who saw in it the chief factor working against the successful conversion of Protestants to the Catholic faith. Writing in 1737 (?) he maintained that: "Only a few of them are attached to [their religion] out of genuine zeal; most are not even familiar with it. It seems that they have inherited nothing from their ancestors but that venomous hatred of the [Roman] Church and its ministers, which has always characterized the Protestants; the foreign ministers and the preachers who travel around the countryside devote themselves more to inculcating in them a horror of our religion than to instructing them in their own. . . . Most of them cling to their religion only because they sucked in these sentiments with their mother's milk. . . ."[10]

Distrust and fear of the Catholic is part of the Protestant tradition. But it would be unfair to imply that this tradition is nothing more. It also embodies a justifiable pride in the successful resistance of the Protestant Church in France to centuries of religious persecution, as well as pride in the economic and cultural achievement of members of the Protestant sect. To the churchgoers, it includes what André Siegfried calls "a severe aspiration for moral purity" and an "elementary need for direct contact with the word of God" as opposed to simple conformity to ecclesiastical discipline.[11] The French Protestant is under the influence of this tradition. It is a part of him. And, most important, it allows him to entertain the sense of "being different" without interfering with his conviction that he is nevertheless a good Frenchman. We can attempt to show which influences him more—his loyalty to his country or his devotion to the Protestant tradition—but beyond this he defies definition.

The French population is overwhelmingly Catholic, and the

[9] Daniel Benoît, *Les frères Gibert. Deux pasteurs du Désert et du Refuge, 1722-1817* (Toulouse, 1889), pp. 263-264.

[10] "Mémoire au sujet des religionnaires du Bas Languedoc et des Cévennes présenté à la cour par l'abbé de Saint-Maximin, docteur de Sorbonne, prévôt et grand vicaire d'Alais," in Edmond Hugues, *Antoine Court. Histoire de la restauration du protestantisme en France au XVIIIe siècle* (Paris, 1872), volume II, appendix 8, p. 433.

[11] André Siegfried, *op.cit.*, p. 24.

numerical weakness of the Protestant sect explains in part the sensitivity of the French Protestant and his fear of being considered alien, or at best somewhat peculiar. Although figures are available for determining the size of the Protestant minority in France from the time of the Consulate on, it is exceedingly difficult to arrive at anything approximating an accurate estimate of the Protestant population on the eve of the French Revolution. Prior to 1760 Protestants had every reason to conceal their identity. Even as late as 1780 the urban Protestant, in order to circumvent the laws against heretics, frequently led a double life. He celebrated his marriage and baptized his children in the Catholic as well as the Protestant Church and outwardly conformed to Catholicism to whatever extent was necessary in order to obtain a certificate of Catholicity. Consequently a certain amount of ambiguity exists as to the religious identity of such persons. To cite but one example, Félix Bornarel in his biography of Pierre-Joseph Cambon identifies the latter as a Catholic, citing the baptismal records in proof.[12] The Protestants, on the other hand, claim him for their own.[13] Furthermore, those persons in the eighteenth century who were interested in making an appraisal of their numbers more often than not fell into one of two groups: the partisans of the Protestants, who greatly inflated their figures, and their adversaries, who generally tried to create the impression that there were few Protestants remaining in France. Hence there are any number of estimates from which to choose.

Such estimates varied all the way from 400,000 to 3 million, and it was not uncommon for authors to use several different figures according to their interests. But it would appear that the Protestant population of France on the eve of the Revolution lay somewhere between 500,000 and 700,000 persons and hence constituted roughly 2 per cent of the total population.[14] For purposes of comparison, it

[12] Félix Bornarel, *Cambon et la Révolution française* (Paris, 1905), p. 1.

[13] Eugène and Emile Haag, *La France protestante*, 2nd ed. (Paris, 1877-1888), III, 649-656. Note that Cambon is identified as a Protestant in the standard biographical dictionary of French parlementarians: Adolphe Robert, *Dictionnaire des Parlementaires français* (Paris, 1891), I, 561-562. See the *Biographie moderne, ou Dictionnaire biographique de tous les hommes morts et vivans . . .*, 2nd ed. (Breslau, 1806), I, 380, in which the editors likewise identify him as a Protestant. Cases of eighteenth century Protestant pastors, born of Protestant families and yet baptized in the Roman Catholic Church, are not uncommon—Jeanbon Saint-André and Pierre Soulier being cases in point.

[14] See Appendix I.

might be pointed out that proportionately there were no more Calvinists in France before the Revolution than there are Presbyterians in the United States today, or only one-fifth as many in relation to the total population as there are Negroes in contemporary American society. It is important to bear in mind, however, that most eighteenth-century French writers thought the Protestants were far more numerous than they actually were. Even their enemies, in trying to paint them as an insignificant minority lost within the community of French Catholics, grossly overestimated their strength. Consequently, as a political issue on the eve of the Revolution, their importance was disproportionate to their numerical strength. Moreover, the general acceptance of the higher estimates demonstrated how unaware most Frenchmen were of the permanent injury which French Protestantism had sustained as a result of the Revocation of the Edict of Nantes and the religious measures of Louis XIV. If, in the first half of the eighteenth century, before the *philosophes* succeeded in discrediting religious persecution, the government had fully appreciated the real diminution in Protestant strength, it might have been persuaded to show more vigor than it did in trying to extirpate heresy in France. But those Catholics, like the vicar of Alais, who tried to alarm an apathetic and torpid government into concerted action by stressing the resilience of Protestantism in certain provinces, in the long run only convinced the state that the suppression of heresy in France was a Sisyphean task better abandoned and forgotten than pursued.

Where do the Protestants in France live? The French student whom I questioned associated the Protestants of his homeland with Paris, and more specifically with the wealthier residential areas of the capital. This perhaps is where they make themselves most felt today, but it is not their traditional habitat, or at least it certainly was not prior to 1900. While contemporary French Protestants may deny that there is a spiritual or social *France protestante*, there very definitely is a geographical Protestant France. Since the seventeenth century, or even as early as the sixteenth, Protestantism has been reduced to several well-defined areas in France. If we were to take a map and shade in those departments with the largest number of Protestants, a vast semi-circle would appear enveloping the *Massif central* from the east, south, and west. In the east, this semi-circle commences above the city of Lyon and descends the valley of the

Rhône River to the Mediterranean. Moving along the coast about halfway to the Spanish frontier, it then swings in a westerly direction (from about 40 miles north of the Pyrenees) directly across the country to the Bay of Biscay. Thereupon it moves north and comes to an end at the Loire River.[15] Here, in the former provinces of the Dauphiné, Languedoc, Gascogne, Guyenne, and Saintonge,[16] live about fifty per cent of all Protestants (Calvinists and Lutherans) in France today.[17] In the eighteenth century, before the urbanization movement of the 1900's and before the end of religious persecution, this area in the Midi was the stronghold of French Calvinism. A second grouping of Protestants can be found along the German frontier. Most of these are Lutherans, with the exception of the Department of the Haut-Rhin, where Calvinists predominate. The remaining twenty-five per cent of French Protestants are scattered thinly throughout the nation, although prosperous and fair-sized communities exist in the cities of Paris, Le Havre, Rouen, Lille, and Reims.

The concentration of Calvinism in the Midi was not an accident, but rather the consequence of certain historical forces. In the first half of the sixteenth century, the doctrines of the Reformation were preached everywhere in France, and for the most part they were sympathetically received.[18] By 1560, however, it was already apparent that the Reformation had struck deeper roots in certain parts of the nation than in others. In general it was more enthusiastically received in the poorer provinces (parts of Languedoc and the Dauphiné) by the indigent classes and in the wealthier provinces where

[15] See the maps on pages 11 and 13.

[16] The modern equivalent would be the Departments of the Rhône, Ardèche, Drôme, Haute-Loire, Lozère, Gard, Bouches-du-Rhône, Hérault, Tarn, Tarn-et-Garonne, Lot-et-Garonne, Gironde, Charente-Maritime, and Deux-Sèvres.

[17] Pierre Lestringant, "Géographie du Protestantisme français," in *Protestantisme français, op.cit.*, p. 4.

[18] See John Viénot, *Histoire de la Réforme française des origines à l'Edit de Nantes* (Paris, 1926), pp. 43-85, 281-285. Viénot stresses the widespread feeling in France of a need for reform within the Catholic Church and hence feels that the real origins of the French Reformation were indigenous and not a foreign import. "La Réforme a aussi été chez nous un mouvement national. Il y a une Réforme française. L'histoire de la Réforme est donc *un fragment de l'histoire nationale*" (p. 44). Henri Lemonnier, writing in E. Lavisse, *Histoire de France . . . jusqu'à la Révolution*, v, ii, 190-195, 222-227, indicates that the Reformation was initially somewhat stronger in the north, but that the actual establishment of churches took place simultaneously throughout the nation.

Geographic Incidence of Protestantism
Census of 1872

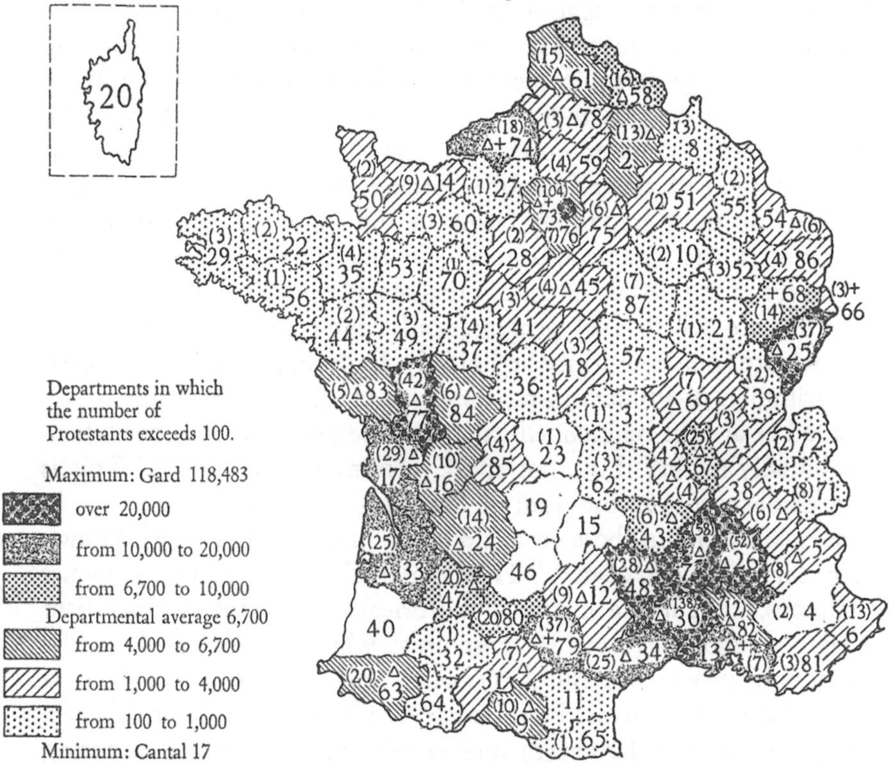

The Departments where the number of Lutherans exceeds 1000 are indicated by the sign +; those where Calvinists exceed 1000 by Δ. The figures given in parentheses indicate the number of pastors.

1. Ain
2. Aisne
3. Allier
4. Basses-Alpes
5. Hautes-Alpes
6. Alpes-Maritimes
7. Ardèche
8. Ardennes
9. Ariège
10. Aube
11. Aude
12. Aveyron
13. Bouches-du-Rhône
14. Calvados
15. Cantal
16. Charente
17. Charente-Maritime
18. Cher
19. Corrèze
20. Corse
21. Côte-d'Or
22. Côtes-du-Nord
23. Creuse
24. Dordogne
25. Doubs
26. Drôme
27. Eure
28. Eure-et-Loire
29. Finistère
30. Gard
31. Haute-Garonne
32. Gers
33. Gironde
34. Hérault
35. Ille-et-Vilaine
36. Indre
37. Indre-et-Loire
38. Isère
39. Jura
40. Landes
41. Loire-et-Cher
42. Loire
43. Haute-Loire
44. Loire-Inférieure
45. Loiret
46. Lot
47. Lot-et-Garonne
48. Lozère
49. Maine-et-Loire
50. Manche
51. Marne
52. Haute-Marne
53. Mayenne
54. Meurthe-et-Moselle
55. Meuse
56. Morbihan
57. Nièvre
58. Nord
59. Oise
60. Orne
61. Pas-de-Calais
62. Puy-de-Dôme
63. Basses-Pyrénées
64. Hautes-Pyrénées
65. Pyrénées-Orientales
66. Haut-Rhin
67. Rhône
68. Haute-Saône
69. Saône-et-Loire
70. Sarthe
71. Savoie
72. Haute-Savoie
73. Seine
74. Seine-Inférieure
75. Seine-et-Marne
76. Seine-et-Oise
77. Deux-Sèvres
78. Somme
79. Tarn
80. Tarn-et-Garonne
81. Var
82. Vaucluse
83. Vendée
84. Vienne
85. Haute-Vienne
86. Vosges
87. Yonne

Based on a map in *Histoire de la population Française avant 1789*, by E. Levasseur, published by Rousseau and Company, Paris.

popular resentment against taxation was most acute (Normandy, Poitou and Guyenne). The sixteenth-century polity of France influenced the geographic incidence of Protestantism; it was more firmly established in those provinces which enjoyed the most independence of royal authority and where the local authorities chose to champion its cause—notably Brittany, Navarre, and Guyenne.

But the most important factor in the minds of Protestant historians is the "non-conformity" or traditional independence of thought of the people in certain regions of France: "There are areas [in France which are] geographically non-conformist, and others which are [non-conformist] ethnically. In dealing with the territorial distribution of Protestantism, the truth of the matter is that it prevailed or at least maintained itself in those peripheral regions which habitually neither think nor speak 'comme tout le monde.' This is particularly true in the Midi of France . . . , in Bas-Poitou . . . , in Normandy and in those areas along the eastern frontier well known for their individualism."[19] This explanation may seem somewhat tenuous,[20] but it is a matter of historical record that Protestantism has been more vigorous in those areas which earlier had been the stamping grounds of the Albigensian and Waldensian heresies. It was also in these areas that discontent within the Catholic Church, as manifested in Jansenism and *richérisme*, was strongest during the eighteenth century.[21] Moreover, the cultural origins of the people living in the Midi differ from those of the French in the north, and this fact, combined with the longer tradition of dissatisfaction with the Catholic Church, would seem to justify the belief that the in-

[19] Emile-G. Léonard, "Les Protestants français au XVIIIe siècle," in the *Annales d'histoire sociale*, II (1940), 9-10. André Siegfried likewise speaks of this regional influence upon the spread of Protestantism in his essay "Le groupe protestant cévenol sous la IIIe République," in *Protestantisme français, op.cit.*, p. 24.

[20] Pierre Lestringant, *op.cit.*, p. 6, denies that the geographic grouping of French Protestantism is the result of the "présence ou l'absence d'affinités humaines particulières" and tries to explain it instead as a consequence of the religious politics of the nation from the sixteenth to the eighteenth centuries. If anything, he argues, Protestantism was initially stronger in the north, but due to the proximity of these provinces to Paris and their subordination to the crown, it was more easily crushed there in the religious wars of the sixteenth century and the policy of suppression which followed.

[21] See the map of the extension of *Jansénisme richériste* in E. Préclin, *Les Jansénistes du XVIIIe siècle et la Constitution civile du Clergé* (Paris, 1929), p. 124. With the exception of the Rhône Valley, it is quite similar to a map of Protestant France.

France, Provinces in 1789

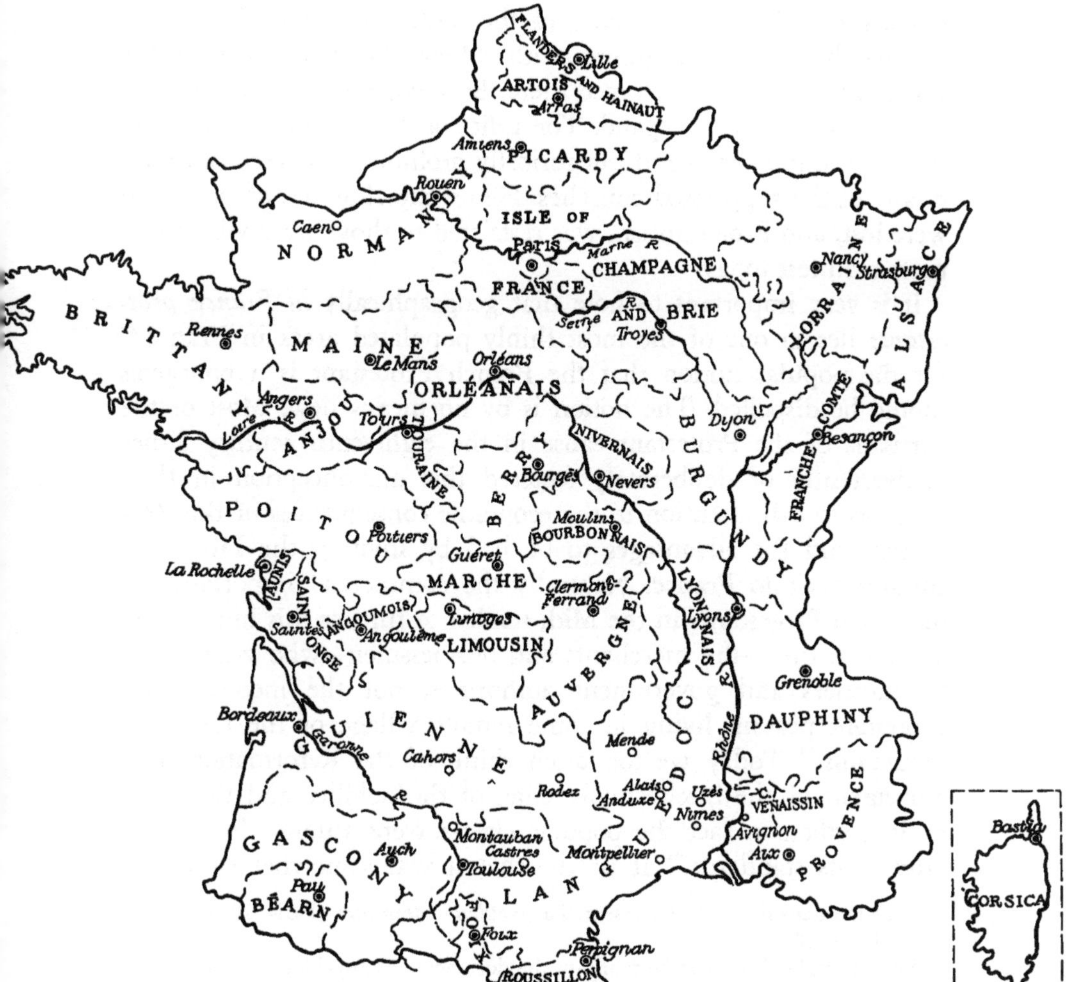

Based on a map in *Shepherd's Historical Atlas*, published by Barnes & Noble, Inc, New York

habitants are traditionally more non-conformist than the average Frenchman. Although prosperous Protestant churches were founded in the north, they suffered more than the others during the course of the Wars of Religion. By the time of the Peace of Amboise (1563) the area above the Loire had been fairly thoroughly cleansed of Protestantism, and a recrudescence of the faith was made all but impossible by the thoroughness with which the edicts against the Protestants were later enforced there. By 1600, French Protestantism had lost its ability to expand. The Edict of Nantes guaranteed only the status quo of 1598 and categorically prohibited the reconstitution of any of the suppressed churches. Hence the churches of the north were lost, and Protestantism was restricted to those areas where it is most manifest today.

It is very important to note that geographically *la France protestante* lies in one of the most thinly populated areas in France,[22] for the popular notion that the French Protestant is a bourgeois should be dispelled. The notion is by no means new. Most of the partisans of the Protestant cause in the eighteenth century either inadvertently or deliberately fostered this misconception in their attempts to call attention to the economic consequences of the Revocation and the advantages to be had by inviting the Huguenot émigrés back to France. Naturally the commercial importance of the urban Protestants in the Midi tended to further this impression, for it was they—the merchants and businessmen—who were noted by travelers and government authorities, not the inconspicuous Protestant peasant living in some remote village of the Cévennes mountains.[23] Today we too often think of the Reformation as a movement of the intellectually elite, of the nobility and the bourgeoisie, when in fact the popular classes were among the first to rally to its standards.[24] It is true that it was somewhat slower in

[22] See the map in Emile Levasseur, *La population française* (Paris, 1889-1892), I, 225 and 224-228.

[23] An example of this can be found in the document "Montpellier en 1768, d'après un manuscrit anonyme inédite. Etat et description de la ville de Montpellier fait en 1768," in the *Archives de la ville de Montpellier*, ed. Jos. Berthelé (Montpellier, 1920), IV, 26. The author, after calling attention to the fact that one-sixth of the city's population is composed of Calvinists, concludes by saying "Généralement parlant, ils sont riches, parce que, ne pouvant entrer dans aucun corps de magistrature, ils sont obligés de se tenir au commerce." The large rural Protestant population in the environs escaped his notice entirely.

[24] See the article by Henri Hauser, "The French Reformation and the French

penetrating the rural areas of France. But by 1560 French Protestantism had cut across all classes, and if any one class was to be more important to the Church than another, it was the peasant. For the nobility were among the last to join the movement, and when Protestantism became a political liability, they were among the first to abandon it.[25] As regards the bourgeoisie, it was far more difficult for them to persist in their faith than it was for a peasant. Living in a town or a city, they were more easily watched by the

---

People in the Sixteenth Century," in the *American Historical Review*, IV (1899), 217-227. Although primarily an attack upon the aristocratic conception of the French Reformation, Hauser's demonstration of the importance of the popular element in its spread also serves to show that it was not the bourgeois movement we sometimes think it was. His explanations for this popular misconception are worth noting. First, it is more usual to study the Reformation in France after 1560 (i.e., the Wars of Religion) when it ceases to be a religious movement to a large extent and becomes a political cause under the tutelage of the nobility. Second, the Catholics do not like to consider the French Reformation in terms of a social movement, for this "would amount to a confession that it was deeply rooted in the national soil, and would make it in the future impossible to regard it as a foreign importation, a superficial or factitious growth" (p. 220). Third, the Protestants themselves are sometimes embarrassed at the social aspects of the Reformation and its more violent manifestations, and would rather think of it as a purely intellectual and spiritual movement. For an illustration of the latter, see John Viénot, *Histoire de la Réforme française* (Paris, 1926), p. 284: "Ainsi un grand nombre de bourgeois apportent à la Réforme une adhésion sincère. C'est l'élite intellectuelle et l'élite morale de la France qui se tourne vers les huguenots." Viénot does, in the next paragraph, mention in passing that the Reformation made a broader social appeal than to the bourgeoisie alone, but he emphasizes the role of the latter.

[25] Most of the Protestant nobility were persuaded to return to Catholicism during the seventeenth century before the adoption of rigorous measures of persecution. A striking example of the success which the Court enjoyed in bringing about these conversions in the Midi can be found in the statistics for the number of *nouveaux-convertis* (i.e., those converting *after* 1680) in the province of Languedoc. See the "Extrait du mémoire de la généralité du Languedoc, dressé par . . . Monsieur de Lamoignon de Basville, Intendant des deux Généralités de Toulouse et de Montpellier," in Henri comte de Boulainvilliers, *Etat de la France . . . ; Estrait des mémoires dressés par les Intendans du Royaume* . . . (London, 1752), VIII, 322. (See Appendix 2.) The fact that only 440 noble families are listed as *nouveaux-convertis* in an area where aristocratic Protestantism had once been strongest in France shows the extent to which conversions had been brought about prior to the Revocation. Furthermore, of those families which had only recently converted, some were on the verge of dying out: "On compte parmi les nouveaux convertis 440 familles de Gentils-hommes, desquels il y en a 109 ou qui n'ont point d'enfans, ou qui n'ont que des filles; de sorte que l'on peut les compter éteints" (pp. 315-316). Also see Charles Weiss, "La conversion de la noblesse protestante au XVIIe siècle," in *Société de l'histoire du Protestantisme français. Bulletin historique et littéraire* (hereafter cited as BPF), I (1852), 46-50.

civil and religious authorities, and it was difficult for them to find a site within a city where many could come together unnoticed for the purpose of worshipping according to their beliefs. If they remained obstinate in their religious beliefs, they had more to lose than a peasant, for Protestants, or those suspected of being Protestants, were barred from all professions except commerce and business. In at least one instance the government tried the rather amazing experiment of attempting to drown out the Protestant element of a town by artificially increasing the Catholic population. In the city of Montauban, the monarchy diluted, with the hope of ultimately destroying, the hitherto sizable Protestant population by moving an *élection*, a *sénéchal-présidial*, a *juridiction consulaire*, a *prévôté*, two *bureaux de direction*, and a *bureau principal de recette* into the city along with all their Catholic personnel and hangers-on.[26] Unless the state could carry the costs of an infinitely complex administration, there were obvious limitations upon the extent to which this means of suppression could be pushed. But it does demonstrate that the government was willing to try almost any means of converting those Protestants who were nearest at hand. Caught like so many fish in a barrel, the Protestant bourgeois either abjured or engaged in a spiritually dangerous dissimulation in order to preserve his material wealth.[27]

The peasant became the most devoted and resolute element in French Protestantism. In part, he came to play this role by virtue of his isolation and relative freedom from ecclesiastical surveillance. In trying to effect the conversion of this dispersed population, the Catholic Church realized that it was faced with a geographical problem. A notable example of this was the diocese of Nîmes in Languedoc, an area which was one of the most heavily populated with Protestants in all of France. In the last decade of the seventeenth century, when the bishop of Nîmes complained that some 50,000 Protestants in the western part of his diocese were too far removed from the seat of his bishopric to be carefully watched, a new bishop-

[26] François Galabert, "Le club jacobin de Montauban. Son rôle politique pendant la Constituante," in the *Revue d'histoire moderne et contemporaine*, I (1899-1900), 128.

[27] Boulainvilliers, *op.cit.*, VIII, 317. Referring to the urban population, Bâville is quoted as saying that "les Huguenots du Languedoc balancèrent quelque temps entre l'amour de leur Religion et celui de leurs biens; mais que le dernier l'emporta et qu'ils restèrent dans le pays."

ric was erected at Alais (today Alès) to remedy the situation.[28] Apparently the experiment was none too successful, for in 1737 the vicar of Alais complained that "the number [of Protestants] is about the same as it was before the Revocation of the Edict of Nantes. Scarcely any families have been genuinely converted, and we have noticed several perversions among those which have been traditionally Catholic."[29]

Hence one of the consequences of the Revocation was to heighten the importance of the peasant element in French Protestantism and to make Protestantism in France basically a rural phenomenon. It has already been pointed out that the Protestant Midi was one of the least populated areas in France before the Revolution. The importance of the peasant element in the Protestant population of this region can best be seen by looking at the population figures for the Departments of Ardèche and Gard. A substantial Protestant minority lives in each of these Departments, but from another point of view they are quite different from one another. The population of Ardèche is preponderantly rural, whereas Gard is among the most urbanized Departments of France.[30] Consider Ardèche first, keeping in mind its rural character. In the middle of the eighteenth century, a detailed list was made of those villages and towns of the Vivarais (i.e., Ardèche) with mixed populations, enumerating the number of Catholic and Protestant families in each (see Appendix 3). In both the largest and second largest towns of the area, the Protestant population was insignificant in comparison with the Catholic; in the largest, Annonay, there were 895 Catholic families versus 90 families of *nouveaux-convertis*, and in Villeneuve-de-Berg 430 Catholic families as compared with 50 Protestant. The only other sizable community on the list is Privas, where the tables turn and the Protestants outnumber the Catholics (277 families to 178). Of the remaining 13 towns with more than 200 families apiece, 7 had Protestant majorities, but the numerical superiority of the Protestants in this group is trifling when compared with the Catholic superiority in the town of Annonay. Finally, the totals for all 98 communities listed show that there were almost as many Protestant

[28] Ernest Roschach, *Histoire générale de Languedoc* (Toulouse, 1876), XIII, 645-646.

[29] "Mémoire au sujet des religionnaires du Bas Languedoc . . . ," in E. Hugues, *Antoine Court*, II, 428.

[30] E. Levasseur, *op.cit.*, I, 329.

families as Catholic in a grand total of 14,290 families. In short, the Protestant population of Ardèche was hardly noticeable in the only two large towns; in the intermediate communities its numerical superiority to the Catholics was of no great consequence; and yet in the area as a whole there were almost as many Protestant families as there were Catholic. The Protestants maintained this ratio only by virtue of their strength in the smallest communities listed.

The same sort of results can be arrived at more quickly in the case of the Department of Gard. According to the statistics compiled from the dioceses of Nîmes, Alais, and Uzès (the present area of Gard) by the Intendant Bâville in 1698 there were roughly 150,000 Catholics and 105,000 *nouveaux-convertis* inhabiting the area. The largest city, Nîmes, had a population of 43,000 in 1787-1789, of whom 13,000 were Protestants.[31] Probably no other city in France had as large a Protestant population and certainly in no other of any size was the proportion of Protestants to Catholics so great. Nîmes, the capital of Protestant France, was two-thirds Catholic, yet in the area as a whole there were only half again as many Catholics as there were Protestants. Here again, as in the case of Ardèche, Protestant strength lay in the rural rather than the urban areas. We can conclude by saying, then, that in the eighteenth century French Protestantism was rural in nature. Indeed, it probably remained rural until the end of the nineteenth century.[32]

Thus we see that the Protestants are a small and relatively self-conscious minority living in the peripheral regions of France. As such, one wonders, as people have for centuries, whether they are really "French." The Protestant himself will admit, even insist, that he is "different." But there are always those who maintain that he is something more, and far worse—those who persist in what Emile Faguet has called "the breaking in of open doors and the storming of demolished fortresses"; those who remain oblivious to the fact that the seditious, anarchic phase of French Protestantism died two

[31] See E. Levasseur, *op.cit.*, I, 227; and the abbé Joseph Dedieu, *Histoire politique des Protestants français, 1715-1794* (Paris, 1925), II, 333. So long as one deals in ratios, there should be no objection to comparing figures of 1698 with others of 1789, for the Catholic and Protestant populations increased in the same degree, and the Catholic Church had little if any success in winning back the Protestant population of this area in the period between the Revocation and the Revolution.

[32] Pierre Lestringant, *op.cit.*, p. 13, points out that the rural nature of French Protestantism did not begin to change until after 1890.

hundred years ago. Consider the verdict of the indomitable critic Charles Maurras: "The Protestants are French by race, language and customs, but their customs and even their race and their language, a little retarded in their development, have received from abroad serious infiltrations and very marked influences. . . . It is true that there exists a Jewish type and a body of Jewish ideas, but much less noticeably than the power and influence of the Jews. On the other hand there is without dispute an *esprit protestant*. He who understands this spirit, he who has studied it cannot possibly conceal his alarm. It not only menaces the French spirit, but more than in the days of Bossuet, it threatens all spirit and all reason, all nations and all states. The prosperity of certain Protestant countries, attributable to a thousand diverse factors, must not confuse us as to the basis of Protestantism: its intellectual tendencies veer toward so perfect an individualism that the title anarchism defines it perfectly. It corrodes societies: it constitutes, following the splendid definition of Auguste Comte, *a sedition of the individual against the species*. . . . The effort of the *Grand Roi* to restore religious unity to France —the least understood and the most poorly judged of all his acts— is nevertheless the one which we understand better and better now that today, through the advantages of Liberty, the yoke of the Protestant minority fastens itself heavily upon all countries."[38]

There are any number of other Frenchmen who share the opinion of Maurras with regard to the Protestants, and some (as we shall have occasion to note later) who express theirs with considerably more venom. Yet nothing stings the French Protestant more than to be thus impugned, or to hear the insinuation that his religion and tradition are foreign to France. Nothing so quickly pushes him to extremes in asserting his sense of belonging to the French nation and to French civilization. Under such circumstances John Viénot, pastor, one-time president of the Société de l'histoire du Protestantisme français, a historian who devoted his life to the study of Protestantism in France, was moved to write: "Calvinism is purely French, not only because it was the Frenchman Calvin who created it, but also because of all Calvin's collaborators, nine out of ten were Frenchmen. . . . Protestant Geneva is a French religious colony. There has been no importation from Geneva to France, but rather

[38] Charles Maurras, *Dictionnaire politique et critique* (Paris, 1933), IV, 197-198, 213.

an exportation from France to Switzerland. There is nothing more French, nothing more 'vieux français,' than the Protestantism of France. . . . French Protestants are so French that truly they are the very salt of France. . . . If Protestantism in France brought about the reform of the Catholic Church, if it produced Gallicanism and evoked Jansenism, which to me seems incontestable, one can say that it has deserved well of France, and in any case one has to admit that it is sufficiently intertwined in the history of France to be recognized as French, traditionally French, as French as conceivably possible. . . . There is no Frenchman more French than the French Protestant."[34] To whom does Viénot dedicate his greatest work, the study which represented a life-time's research? The answer is revealing, both of Viénot and of the Frenchmen whom he represents. He dedicates it "à tous les esprits indépendants qui aiment la France et la liberté."

On 18 October 1685, Louis XIV revoked the Edict of Nantes. Equating national strength with religious unity, and acting in the belief that French Protestantism could not long survive once deprived of its ministers and the right of public assembly, he decreed that all Protestant temples[35] within the kingdom be destroyed immediately, and that henceforth those of his subjects belonging to the "so-called Reformed religion" be forbidden from assembling for the exercise of their religion. All Protestant ministers in France were given two weeks in which to decide either to convert to Catholicism or leave the country. Henceforth all children born to Protestants would be baptized and educated by the Roman Catholic Church. Anticipating the probable reaction of those Protestants living near the frontiers, Louis expressly forbade their emigration from the country under penalty of the galleys for men and of "confiscation of body and goods" for women. Those who had already fled the country were invited to return to the full enjoyment

[34] John Viénot, *Histoire de la Réforme française*, pp. 284-285, quoting Emile Faguet. Faguet, a positivist who attacked all religious intolerance, was born and lived the formative years of his life in Poitou, where the "esprit protestant" is quite strong and undoubtedly left its mark upon him.

[35] Normally the French do not use the word "temple" when speaking of buildings devoted to Catholic worship, but rather the more common word *église*. However, when speaking of the churches of other religions, especially of Protestant churches, they substitute *temple* for *église*, a practice invariably followed by the French Protestants themselves.

of their rights as Frenchmen, with the warning that at the end of four months, if they remained abroad, all their property would be confiscated by the state.

In the preface to the edict, Louis explained his action with the specious argument that his great forebear, Henry IV, had conceded toleration to the Protestants only in order to restore domestic peace and to bring about those circumstances under which the monarchy could work for the ultimate reunion of all heretics with the Catholic faith. To the great misfortune of France and the Catholic Church, according to Louis, Henry had died before he could realize this happy reform. But his heirs had continued the work to the point where "the best and greater part" of the Protestants had "embraced the Roman Catholic Religion." Hence there was no longer any point in maintaining the concession, and Louis felt that he could do nothing better "to blot out entirely the memory of the troubles, confusion, and disasters which the spread of that false religion had occasioned [in France]" than to revoke it entirely.

In behalf of the few Protestants remaining in France, Louis extended a measure of toleration. According to the last article of the edict: ". . . the said members of the so-called Reformed religion, while waiting until it shall please God to enlighten them as He has the others, shall be permitted to live in the towns and countryside of our kingdom, country, and the lands under our authority, both to pursue their commerce and to enjoy their property, without being molested or hindered under pretext [of their religion], on the condition, as aforesaid, that they do not hold services or assemble under pretext of prayers or worship of any kind of the said religion, under the penalties above prescribed of confiscation of body and goods."[36] In short, while the edict destroyed the French Protestant Church as an institution, it ostensibly guaranteed freedom of conscience to those Protestants remaining in France and to those who returned within the allotted time.

This concession had scarcely any meaning. By virtue of the repressive measures against Protestants which the state had employed prior to the Revocation, hardly a Protestant was left in the country who had not been forced to abjure his religion. By so doing he became a *nouveau-converti* and lost any rights belonging to a Prot-

[36] *Recueil général des anciennes lois françaises . . . jusqu'à la Révolution de 1789,* ed. François-André Isambert (Paris, 1822-1833), xix, 534.

estant under the provisions of the edict of Revocation. Any attempt at retracting his abjuration only exposed him to the penalties meted out to relapsers.

And what did it mean—"without being molested or hindered under pretext of religion"? Protestants were still liable to the 400 odd laws, ordinances, decrees, and declarations issued against them by Louis and the Parlements prior to the Revocation. They were free to pursue their commerce, but the liberal professions were completely closed to them: they could not be lawyers, doctors, surgeons, apothecaries, book dealers or printers, surveyors, or even clerks to judges, lawyers, procurators, or notaries. Protestant women could not serve as midwives; hence mothers were to be delivered of their children by Catholics who were empowered by legal statute secretly to baptize the offspring. Protestants could not marry Catholics, and if ill they could not be received into private homes for care. They were forbidden to sell their property without the king's permission. Widows, and wives of men who converted, lost their right to transfer, sell, or bequeath their possessions. Protestants were free to pursue their commerce, but their business credits with other Protestants were forfeited if the latter converted. They could not seek employment as servants in the homes of other Protestants for fear their employers might stand in the way of their conversion; men who violated this restriction were liable to lifetime sentences to the galleys, while women were to be flogged and branded with the fleur-de-lis. Not only were their children to be baptized and educated in the Catholic Church, but when they reached the age of five they were to be surrendered to Catholic relatives to be raised, and in the absence of the latter, to any Catholic family that the local authorities might appoint. The local priest and judge were free, even invited, to render periodic visits to their homes to discuss the advantages of conversion. Freedom of conscience, but at what a price! They were pariahs, to be hounded and "persuaded" by these and a host of similar measures. They were free, but the exercise of this freedom reduced them to the level of second-class citizens.

Alone, deserted by their pastors,[37] suspected by their neighbors,

[37] The pusillanimity of the pastorate, as shown in their precipitous flight, disillusioned and confounded the laity. For an illustration of the despair created by the lack of leadership, see the "Lettre des réformez captifs en France aux ministres refugiez . . . (29 mars 1686)," in BPF, XII (1863), 299-305, part of which reads

bullied by the authorities, separated from their children, living under a cloud of fear and apprehension, how many of them could afford to pay the price for freedom of conscience? And for how long? The altar and the throne were impatient. They could no longer wait upon God to enlighten the recalcitrant. The very word "persuade" disappeared from subsequent edicts against them and was replaced with the frank admission that they were to be "obliged" to convert. Seemingly on the threshold of success, the monarchy would allow nothing to interfere with the completion of its purpose. It was unrelenting against the stalwart, merciless against the hesitant. Within the limits of a life span, there would be no more Protestants in France.

In a burst of energy rare for governments of the time, the monarchy did its uttermost to assure the realization of this end. In August of 1685, the Court had appointed Nicolas de Lamoignon de Bâville as intendant of Languedoc on the merits of his success in effecting mass conversions of Protestants in Poitou. A zealous partisan of the cause of religious uniformity, Bâville took up his new office by staging a grand tour through Languedoc at the head of an army of dragoons and missionaries. At Castres, Montpellier, Sommières, Nîmes, Uzès, Sauve, Anduze, Saint-Hippolyte, Saint-Jean de Gardonnenque—everywhere he and his cohorts passed—the Protestant communities, in awe and fear at the advancing host, bowed before the wishes of their new master. Within eighteen days Bâville and his agents jubilantly claimed to have persuaded 225,000 heretics—as the usual formula of abjuration ran—to "renounce the heresy of Calvin and embrace all the dogmas of the Roman Catholic and Apostolic religion."[38] Results such as these made it possible for Louis XIV to preface the Edict of Revocation with the assertion that Protestantism had all but disappeared from France. In the following months, both before and after the Revocation, similar reports were received at Versailles of the rapid crumbling of the Protestant Church and the Protestant minority throughout the nation. By the end of

"Jugez vous-mêmes, nos très chers pères: que peuvent penser, et que doivent devenir de pauvres malheureux qui se voyent trahi par plusieurs de leurs conducteurs et abandonnez généralement de tous les autres; après de tels exemples faut-il s'étonner sy presque tout a ployé à la fureur des dragons et aux ruses des missionnaires?" For a similar reaction see "Les dragons missionnaires. Fragment des mémoires de Jeanne Terrasson," in BPF, XXVIII (1879), 559-562; XXIX (1880), 27-38.

[38] E. Roschach, *Histoire générale de Languedoc*, XIII, 554-555.

November 1685, all Protestant *officiers du roi* had either converted or abjured. A few months later, the last officer of the military establishment capitulated to the desires of the king, and the soldiers rapidly followed the example. The pastors fled; the temples were razed. In the Dauphiné, Languedoc, and Saintonge, the Catholic churches bulged and overflowed with the newly converted. Louis XIV, ecstatic with the apparent success of his measures, ordered the royal mints to commemorate the victory with medals struck in honor of *Haeresis extincta, religio victrix.*

To be sure, there was resistance. Here and there, in the more remote reaches of the Midi, small assemblies met under cover of darkness to sing hymns and recite psalms. But troops and spies were everywhere. Gradually such acts became increasingly rare. In the Cévennes mountains, the peasants, driven beyond all limits of human endurance by the measures of suppression, took up arms and for two years waged a vicious, savage, and hopeless struggle against the forces of the throne. The wiser, and the majority, bowed their heads in resignation and submission. The few pastors, more resolute than the rest, who remained behind at the time of the exodus, to live in the shadows, hunted and pursued, were helpless in the face of a creeping paralysis of fear and despair that benumbed their former parishioners. Once they had been received into isolated homes with joy and hope; now their arrival created consternation. " 'The terror,' wrote one, 'has so thoroughly established its dominion over the minds of those who might have offered us their help that they no longer even dared open the doors of their homes to offer us their small liberalities; and more than once our meager rations were hurriedly slipped out to us through the cat's hole or other small openings.' "[39] Their own families refused them shelter and turned them away. They were outcasts, hiding in the forests, sleeping in caves, tracked and hounded by bands of archers like predatory beasts —destined, it seemed, to nothing but martyrdom.

In the last year of his reign, only a few months before his death, Louis XIV put the finishing hand to his policy of the extirpation of heresy in France. By the standards of the day, the declaration of 8 March 1715 seemed innocent enough. It merely stated that converted

[39] Edmond Hugues, *Les synodes du Désert. Actes et règlements des synodes nationaux et provinciaux tenus au Désert de France de l'an 1715 à l'an 1793* (Paris, 1885-1886), I, xv.

Protestants who in their last illness refused the sacraments of the Roman Catholic Church should be treated as persons who had relapsed into heresy: their bodies would be publicly desecrated and thrown as so much filth into the common sewer.[40] But the measure closed with a portentous clause: "... the sojourn in our kingdom of those who formerly were members of the so-called Reformed religion and of those born to Protestant parents, since the time we abolished [in France] all exercise of the said religion, is more than sufficient proof that they have embraced the Roman Catholic and Apostolic religion, for otherwise they would not have been either suffered or tolerated here."[41] The line was drawn. There would be no more pretense at "freedom of conscience." Whatever rights a Protestant had enjoyed under the terms of the Revocation were now brushed aside. Henceforth the Protestant had no legal existence. By statutory decree, he did not exist. The Calvinist heresy had been extinguished. Frenchmen were Catholics—or they were apostates.

Or so it seemed. Louis XIV spent the latter part of August 1715 at Versailles. The state of his health was so widely known that in London bets were being placed that he would not live to see the end of the month. It was apparent to all who saw him that his strength and vitality were rapidly ebbing. The prospective regent, the duc d'Orléans, whose salons were normally uninviting and seldom frequented, had suddenly become the center of activity among the courtiers.

Louis sensed that the end was at hand. It was noticed that from time to time he unconsciously referred to himself in the past tense and spoke of the "young king" when he meant the dauphin. He even knew of the London bets. This did not disconcert him. He awaited his death patiently, passing the time reviewing his regiments, listening to his orchestra of violins and oboes, and issuing instructions to his council of state. A pall had fallen over the court, blotting out the usual festivities. The aristocratic sycophants were restless, impatient for the thing to be over so that they could resume their gay diversions. Only a few were moved to sympathy. When the

[40] Which was often enough done; cf. Henri Gelin, "Relevé analytique et alphabétique de tous les procès actuellement connus, intentés aux mourants et aux cadavres protestants sous Louis XIV et sous Louis XV," BPF, LII (1903), 419-456, 573-576.

[41] Isambert, *Recueil général des anciennes lois françaises*, XX, 640.

dying king discovered his *garçons de chambre* in tears at the foot of his bed, he jokingly chided them with "Pourquoi pleurez-vous? Est-ce que vous m'avez cru immortel?"

On the 25th, after a restless night, he requested the viaticum. That evening he received the last sacraments. He began making his official adieux. The doubts and regrets which had hovered in the back of his mind now came to the fore. Of the courtiers, he asked forgiveness for the bad example he had set them. To the dauphin he disclosed his regret at what his wars had done to France and rued the impoverishment of his people. He repented the indiscretions of his earlier life. But to the end he considered his war against heresy one of the greatest achievements of his reign, a permanent and monumental contribution to the glory of the nation and the Roman Catholic Church. He had tried to serve the Church well and found solace in the belief that he had indeed destroyed the last vestige of Protestantism in France. A few days later, in the seventy-third year of his reign, he surrendered his soul "as peacefully as a dying candle."

That same August in Languedoc, while all France awaited the death of their king, the first rays of the dawning sun spilled into a deserted quarry and revealed a small group of somber men, seated on stone and gravel, listening while one of their number quietly discussed the future of the French Protestant Church. Nine men, almost all that remained of the Calvinist pastorate in France, were meeting in what was later to be recognized as the first synod of the "Church of the Desert"—the first French synod since the Revocation. It was here, under the leadership of Antoine Court, that the foundations were laid for the reconstruction of the French Protestant Church.

CHAPTER II

The Eighteenth Century: Persecution and Revival

In the summer of 1716, the following news item appeared in the *Gazette d'Amsterdam*: "Toward the end of last month, the Protestants of Montauban, in imitation of those of the Dauphiné and the Cévennes, assembled in the woods and fields [on the outskirts of the city] in order to pray to God [in the manner of their faith]. Learning of these occurrences, the Intendant repaired to the spot where one of these assemblies was taking place, and upon his arrival the assembly scattered and took flight. However, Monsieur the Intendant succeeded in arresting three or four of their number. . . ."[1] For the next half century, such events took place so frequently as to become almost commonplace. Far from being extinguished, French Protestantism in the eighteenth century provided a seemingly inexhaustible supply of fuel for those who would feed the fires of religious bigotry and persecution.

Louis XIV had destroyed the Protestant Church in France, but he had not destroyed Protestantism. Ordinances and decrees could level the temples, prohibit the assemblies, and exile the pastors, but the spiritual resistance of the laity in many parts of France absorbed the most barbarous complements of that legislation. Threats and violence had brought conversions to Catholicism with surprising facility, but the sincerity of these conversions was still another matter. No sooner had the suppression been completed than discouraging reports trickled back to Versailles. "With the exception of ten or twelve persons, everyone here has converted," wrote the bishop of Grenoble, "but I am very much afraid that with the exception of ten or twelve there is not one genuine convert among them."[2] Similar reports were received from almost all of the southern provinces.[3] And at the same time royal agents noted that the church attendance of former Protestants was anything but exemplary:

[1] Quoted in the *Mémoires de Saint-Simon*, ed. A. de Boislisle (Paris, 1879-1930), xxx, 140.

[2] "Correspondance inédite de l'évêque de Grenoble, Le Camus," BPF, III (1855), 576-587.

[3] "Extrait du mémoire de la généralité du Languedoc . . . par Monsieur de Lamoignon de Basville . . . ," in Boulainvilliers, *op.cit.*, VIII, 317. Also see the "Lettre de M. Julien au Ministre de la guerre (4 mai 1703)," in E. Roschach, *Histoire de*

"With respect to Catholic rites, there are only a very few persons who observe them, and one cannot be too sure of these few, because after giving the appearance of conforming and receiving the sacraments for a certain period of time they then begin to flag more and more until finally they no longer attend church at all. And if by chance you see a few of them appearing there, it is only those who hope thereby to retain an office or an employment and the pensions which they receive from the king, and others who hope to profit from the possessions of those who have emigrated [which are often turned over to those who are considered *bien convertis*], and even these do it with disgust and as seldom as possible. There are even those who, when they are at services and when the priest prepares to perform the sacrifice of the mass, hide their faces in their hats for fear of seeing the act and refuse to look at the altar. And as it is the people of means who have first relaxed from the apparent zeal which they initially showed after their abjurations, the lesser people among them now follow their example."[4]

More and more the partisans of religious uniformity were forced to draw a sharp distinction between the *bien convertis* and the *mal convertis*, between *bons catholiques* and *méchants catholiques*, to compile lists of *nouveaux convertis non convertis*.[5] Yet these distinctions, once made on a wide scale and publicized, further complicated the problem of conversion for the Court and the Church. The Catholic laity as a whole began to treat the new converts with suspicion and scorn and thereby forced them to reconsider their conversions.

Languedoc, XIV, 1739; L.-J. Nazelle, *Le Protestantisme en Saintonge sous le régime de la Révocation* (Paris, 1907), pp. 77-94; E. Arnaud, *Histoire des Protestants du Vivarais et du Velay* (Paris, 1888), II, 16-18; and Jules Chavannes, "Essai sur les abjurations parmi les réformés de France sous le règne de Louis XIV," BPF, XXI (1872), 201-217.

[4] E. Arnaud, *Histoire des Protestants du Dauphiné aux XVIe et XVIIIe siècles* (Paris, 1876), III, 43-44. For a discussion of the pensions and property settlements alluded to in this passage, see C. A. de Janzé, *Les Huguenots. Cent ans de persécution* (Paris, 1886), chapter I; Jules Chavannes, "Essai sur les abjurations parmi les réformés de France sous le règne de Louis XIV," BPF, XXI (1872), 57-72, 105-127; and A. Cans, "La caisse du clergé de France et les protestants convertis, 1598-1790," BPF, LI (1902), 225-243.

[5] See, for example, the "Liste des gentilshommes et principaux habitants nouveaux convertis dans le Languedoc (1686)," BPF, XXIX (1880), 214-224, 349-364; "[Etat des] nouveaux convertis du Vigan, de Sumène, de Bréau et Bréaunèze, et de Meyrueis en 1687," BPF, XLVIII (1899), 638-643; and "Etat exact des familles des nouveaux convertis de la paroisse de Notre Dame de Touraille de Laparade," BPF, LIX (1910), 411-417.

"What are we in the eyes of Roman Catholics?" asked a disillusioned convert. "We are profaners, hypocrites, abominable heretics, candidates for death, hell, and damnation. They are convinced that we have joined their religion only through force, that [in fact] we despise their cult. Their ministers even tell them as much from the pulpit. . . ."[6]

Faced with these obstacles, the government and the episcopate began to doubt that much could be done with the adult *nouveaux convertis*, but they consoled themselves with the expectation that even if all the conversions were insincere, at least the children of the converts could be won to the Catholic faith.[7] In revising their goals in this manner, it was to the children that the State and the Church increasingly directed their efforts. The ecclesiasts in the provinces were instructed to bend every effort in attending to the religious instruction of these children,[8] and the troops in the area were given a free hand in enforcing the observance of these measures.[9] But while the bishops applied themselves industriously to the task of converting the *races futures*, they needed the support of an army of capable, enlightened, and persuasive clerics to insure any measure of success. In all too many provinces, the lower clergy were unequal to the task. The intendants complained of the poor quality of the *curés* and vicars residing in the critical areas, and of the unfortunate consequences of their impetuous proselytizing.[10] When

[6] "Lettre escrite de Vivarets, le 23 de février 1686, sur l'estat des nouveaux convertis de cette province," BPF, XXVIII (1879), 464-470. For a résumé of the confusion within the government caused by the passive resistance of the new converts see Noailles, *Histoire de Madame de Maintenon et des principaux événements du règne de Louis XIV* (Paris, 1849-1858), II, 566-614. The author presents a sampling of the various memoirs of the period which illustrate the measures suggested to best cope with this resistance.

[7] *ibid.*, II, 490-491, 560-561, 567, 605-607. Malesherbes, *Mémoire sur le mariage des Protestans* (s.l., 1785), pp. 7-8, 17-18, 54-55. Mme de Maintenon was of the same opinion: "Toutes les conversions ne sont pas sincères. Mais leurs enfants seront du moins catholiques, si les pères sont hypocrites." Quoted in E. Hugues, *Synodes du Désert*, I, iv-v.

[8] "Réglement pour l'instruction des nouveaux convertis et de leurs enfans," dated 13 December 1698, in Isambert, *Receuil des anciennes lois françaises*, XX, 313-319.

[9] *ibid.*, XX, 3.

[10] E. Roschach, *Histoire de Languedoc*, XIII, 644, 730-731. See Noailles, *Histoire de Madame de Maintenon*, II, 498-500: from Languedoc the intendant Bâville wrote that "Le plus grand, le plus solide, et je puis dire l'unique expédient efficace est de former de bons prêtres pour être curés et vicaires dans les paroisses. Comme elles étaient toutes remplies de gens de la religion prétendu réformée, lors de la con-

missionaries were sent into the provinces of the south, it was sometimes found that many of them could not speak *patois*, and hence their sermons and exhortations were incomprehensible to the population. "Si vous ne savez pas parler le patois," snapped the bishop of Viviers in receiving a group of these missionaries, "que venez-vous faire ici, sots que vous êtes?"[11] Moreover, the populace found many subterfuges for keeping their children out of the reach of these educators. Even when the latter succeeded in compelling the children to attend their courses, the parents could usually undo every evening whatever progress the missionaries had made in the course of a day's instruction. And all too often the instructors were forced to go from house to house in search of their reluctant pupils, a practice which did not enhance the popularity of their courses and certainly impeded the religious edification of the students. In short, this measure was hardly any more successful in achieving sincere converts than the dragonnades had been.

Confronted with a hostile and obstinate population, the government could hope for a successful conclusion of its projects only if it could keep the new converts in absolute quarantine from any residual manifestations of their former religion and could maintain the missionary activities however long it would be before the recalcitrants would realize the futility of their resistance. This was a large task—more than the government could fulfill. It did succeed in driving the ministers out of France and subsequently tracked down most of those who tried to return to their pastorates after the initial slackening of the violent persecution which accompanied the "general conversion."[12] But it never succeeded in stopping assemblies and religious meetings. Throughout this period, small groups met secretly to sing psalms and recite prayers.[13] In the absence of pastors,

version générale, il s'est trouvé de fort méchants sujets pour remplir la plupart de ces places. Si l'on en a ôté beaucoup de mauvais, il faut maintenant y en mettre de bons, et qui sachent prêcher; car toute la dévotion des gens de la religion consiste à entendre la parole de Dieu. On ne réussira jamais auprès des nouveaux convertis, si l'on n'a pas quelques talents pour prêcher."

[11] E. Lavisse, *Histoire de France depuis les origines jusqu'à la Révolution* (Paris, 1900-1911), VIII, part I, 352.

[12] Charles Coquerel, in his *Histoire des églises du Désert depuis la fin du règne du Louis XIV jusqu'à la Révolution française* (Paris, 1841), I, 507-508, lists sixteen pastors executed in France from the time of the Revocation to the death of Louis XIV. All of these were in the Midi.

[13] For an illustration of these clandestine prayer meetings, see "Prière pour se

"prophets" appeared whose activities, even if "fort irrégulière" from a doctrinal point of view,[14] at least provided a measure of inspiration and hope for an oppressed population.

The spiritual resistance of the laity, the inadequacy of the Catholic clergy, the hostility encountered by new converts in the Catholic Church, a growing sense of shame among some former Protestants at the pusillanimity of their conversions—all these combined to produce the materials with which the French Protestant Church could be rebuilt. All that was lacking were the architects—the direction and guidance which only a disciplined pastorate could provide—and a temporary slackening of the government's vigilance. These two conditions were met toward the end of Louis XIV's reign. A noticeable increase in the number of illegal assemblies "in the Desert" (as the Protestants were already beginning to call their clandestine meetings in the countryside) and the appearance of a handful of *prédicants* (unordained preachers) in the Dauphiné and Languedoc probably indicate that as a consequence of military reverses after 1706 in the War of Spanish Succession, the military garrisons which had hitherto been used to enforce the conversion were reduced to a point which seriously limited their effectiveness.[15] At the same time,

préparer le dimanche à la méditation de la parole de Dieu et la lecture d'un sermon," BPF, XXV (1876), 552-556.

[14] Coquerel, *Histoire des églises du Désert*, I, 18. When Coquerel says that the Protestants continued to celebrate their worship "quoique d'une manière fort irrégulière," he is using "irrégulière" in both senses of the word. See Henry M. Baird, *The Huguenots and the Revocation of the Edict of Nantes* (New York, 1895), II, 183-190, for a description of their activities, part of which runs: "[The prophets] would suddenly fall backward, and, while extended at full length on the ground, undergo strange and apparently involuntary contortions; their chests would seem to heave, their stomachs to inflate. On coming gradually out of this condition, they appeared instantly to regain the power of speech. . . . Beginning often in a voice interrupted by sobs, they soon poured forth a torrent of words—cries for mercy, calls to repentance, exhortations to the bystanders to cease frequenting the mass, denunciations of the church of Rome, prophecies of coming judgment. From the mouths of those that were little more than babes came texts of Scripture, and discourses in good and intelligible French, such as they never used in their conscious hours. When the trance ceased, they declared that they remembered nothing of what had occurred, or what they had said." A number of works have been written on this phenomenon, but for more summary treatments of it, see Charles Bost, "Les prophètes du Languedoc en 1701 et 1702," in the *Revue historique*, CXXXVI (1921), 1-36; CXXXVII (1921), 1-31; and Louis Mazoyer, "Les origines du prophétisme cévenol," in the *Revue historique*, CXCVII (1947), 23-54.

[15] E. Roschach, *Histoire de Languedoc*, XIII, 877, mentions that in 1709 as a conse-

the victories of Marlborough and Eugene had a direct affect upon the barometer of Protestant aspirations. Throughout the first half of the eighteenth century, the oppressed Protestants were inclined to interpret French reverses in the field at the hands of the Protestant powers as a promise of renewed international diplomatic efforts to intercede with the monarchy on their behalf. Their hopes were for the most part disappointed,[16] but the very expectation of an impending deliverance from the persecution of the State greatly facilitated the work of the "reorganizers" of the Church.

The new leaders of the Protestants did not come from among the pastors of the Refuge. The clergy which had fled abroad at the time of the Revocation were now old. Their ranks had thinned. They had not resisted the temporal authorities in 1685, and they were certainly not tempted to try it now in the advanced years of their lives. A return to France meant certain death. They knew this perfectly well, and in the comfort and safety of their exile none of them aspired to martyrdom. Rather, the leaders sprang from the people themselves as a spontaneous efflorescence of the *climat protestant.* They were peasants, conspicuous for their lack of training—some even for their ignorance. Jean Vesson had been an *inspiré*, a prophet, a self-appointed *prédicant* from the small village of Cros in Languedoc. Jean Huc (dit Mazelet), the oldest of those attending the first synod of the Desert, at the age of forty could scarcely read or write. A Camisard, he had fled to Geneva following the collapse of that futile rebellion and had "studied" there a short while before returning to France. Within a few years of this first synod, both he and Vesson were to be suspended from their pastoral functions for what

quence of the pressing need for ordnance the government began disarming the bourgeois militia which had been raised almost exclusively for use against the Protestants. Whatever the cause, there was a marked decline in these years of the number of persons sentenced to the galleys: see the list of convicts in Athanase Coquerel fils, *Les forçats pour la foi* (Paris, 1866), p. 262-339.

[16] By this time, the Protestant powers were less inclined than formerly to champion the cause of the French Protestants. Moreover, by the time the negotiations had begun, Louis XIV had succeeded in improving his position militarily and was indisposed to listen to their complaints. See the work by the abbé Joseph Dedieu, *Le Rôle politique des Protestants français, 1685-1715* (Paris, 1920), chapter 12. Queen Anne, however, did effect the release of over half of those Protestants who were serving on the king's galleys; *ibid.*, pp. 276-280; P. Fonbrune-Berbinau, "La libération des forçats pour la foi en 1713 et 1714," BPF, XXXVIII (1889), 225-238. One hundred thirty-six were released in 1713 and 44 more the following year.

we today would call deviationism. Ultimately both were arrested and executed by the government. Pierre Durand, from a family of new converts in Languedoc, attended Catholic services until he was twelve or thirteen years old before devoting himself to the former religion of his parents. At the first synod he was barely fifteen, yet despite his tender age he was already considered a *prédicant.* Two years later he served as moderator of a provincial synod and was authorized to administer the sacraments. In 1732 he suffered martyrdom at the hands of the executioner of Montpellier. Another of these first pastors of the Desert, Etienne Arnaud, like Durand was little more than a boy when he commenced his teachings in Languedoc. He was one of the most promising of the emerging pastorate, but his activities were cut short by his martyrdom at Alais in 1718. Pierre Corteiz and Jacques Roger, neither of whom were able to attend the first synod but who came to play preeminent roles in the restoration of the Church, were also from Languedoc. Corteiz had begun preaching at the age of sixteen or seventeen. Both had studied in Switzerland or Germany before returning to France in the first decade of the eighteenth century to follow their callings. Roger, the reorganizer of Protestantism in the Dauphiné, lived to see the religion of that province well reestablished and in a flourishing condition by the standards of that day before his martyrdom in 1745. Corteiz, condemned to death by default in the same year, miraculously escaped his pursuers time after time and died peacefully in Switzerland in 1767.

And finally Antoine Court—"the scourge of the prophets," "the Restorer of French Protestantism." Born in the Vivarais (Villeneuve-de-berg), he was a typical product of the *esprit protestant.* His parents, although converted, clung obstinately to their former religion. As a child, he attended the numerous clandestine religious meetings which his widowed mother held in their home, where he listened to the reminiscing of better times, of the torments of martyrs, and joined in the hushed singing of songs such as:

> Nos filles dans les monastères,
> Nos prisonniers dans les cachots,
> Nos martyrs dont le sang se répand à grands flots,
> Nos confesseurs sur les galères,
> Nos malades persécutés,

> Nos mourants exposés à plus d'une furie,
> Nos morts trainés à la voierie,
> Te disent (ô Dieu!) nos calamités.[17]

His background and his environment inculcated in him a deep and abiding hatred of the Roman services which he was forced to attend. So outspoken was he in his religious beliefs that he became the butt of his Catholic schoolmates and was jeered at on the streets by adults with "Hé! hé! le fils aîné de Calvin!" The beatings and the bullying only confirmed him in his attachment to a religion he knew hardly more than by name. His education consisted of the primary years in the local Catholic school, where he learned all that his schoolmaster knew and hence could teach: reading, writing, the basic elements of grammar, and a smattering of arithmetic. After three years his formal education came to an end. He had not learned Latin. In spare moments at home he continued his studies, reading the tattered fragments of an old Bible, Drélincourt's *Consolations de l'âme fidèle contre les craintes de la mort* and Baxter's *Voix de Dieu.* Sometime in his teens he discovered that from time to time his mother slipped out of the house for nocturnal meetings with other women to listen to prophets and occasionally to hear an itinerant preacher recite sermons which had been committed to memory. Soon he was attending these meetings regularly. At the age of seventeen he was a preacher himself, delivering sermons of his own composition.

Such were the first pastors of the Church of the Desert, the men who devoted their lives to the resurrection of the French Protestant Church. Many of them were hardly more than boys, unlettered, peasant stock, products of the wild, desolate hills of the Cévennes and the Vivarais. To the staid, educated, comfortable French bourgeois, they were nothing but hillbillies. For these regions were to eighteenth-century France what Harlan and Bell counties are to twentieth-century America. It would be a long time before the townsmen would accept them as their spiritual conductors; some of them never did. But what they lacked in education they made up for in their devotion to their purpose and in an enthusiasm which made them fearless in the face of almost certain death.

It was Antoine Court, still less than twenty years of age, who

[17] E. Hugues, *Antoine Court,* I, 5.

summoned that first synod of the Desert in mid-August of 1715 while Louis XIV lay dying at Versailles. His purposes, as he later described them in his memoirs, were four: "The first was to convoke the people (le peuple) in religious assemblies and to instruct them; the second, to combat the fanaticism which had spread itself everywhere like a conflagration and to bring back to healthier ideas those who had had the weakness to allow themselves to be infected with it; third, to reestablish discipline, the practice of consistories, elders, colloquies and synods; and fourth, to train to whatever extent that I could young preachers, to call ministers in from abroad; and if [the latter] were not up to the vocation of martyrdom and were not disposed to respond to my pressing appeals, to solicit among the foreign powers for sufficient funds to educate and support those young men in whom I might find sufficient courage and will to devote themselves to the service and salvation of their brothers."[18]

The first object—the holding of religious assemblies—progressed with remarkable rapidity. Under the circumstances then existing in the Midi, the very appearance of a pastor or preacher brought the non-conformist population flocking to these pastoral gatherings. Beginning in Languedoc and the Dauphiné, the movement spread westward like a contagion into the provinces of Guyenne, Saintonge, and Poitou. The only fetter to its progress seemed to be the lack of an adequate number of pastors. In some areas the population, impatient for the arrival of their leaders, went ahead on their own account to organize their "churches," elect their consistories, and commence their meetings. As the movement gained momentum, the Protestants showed their confidence by tightening the discipline within the Church. Beginning in 1721, the synods became increasingly adamant that the laity abandon the Catholic Churches, withdraw their children from Catholic schools, marry and baptize their children in the Desert even if it meant "suffering passively the spoliation of their property, the imprisonments, and all the other penalties which might be inflicted upon them."[19]

[18] Quoted in Charles Coquerel, *Eglises du Désert*, I, 25.

[19] E. Hugues, *Synodes du Désert*, I, 29. While opposing marriage within the Catholic Church from the very beginning, the Protestants initially condoned the baptism of children there and recognized the validity of these baptisms: cf. article 3 of the Synod of Languedoc and the Cévennes, 7 February 1718, in Hugues, *Synodes du Désert*, I, 11. By 1721 the policy was reversed. The Synod of the Vivarais, 26 July 1721, ordered that those who married or baptized their children in the

The clergy of the Midi watched the progress of this movement with dismay. For forty years they had worked for the conversion of these people. With the appearance of Court and his apostles, it was patent that most of their labors had been for naught. "Heresy has made more progress," complained the bishop of Alais in 1723,[20] "than in the preceding thirty-five years. In fact, the assemblies which hitherto were quite rare and very secret have become so frequent, so public, and so well attended, that there have been some of more than three thousand persons, and the sound of their psalms has carried as far as the neighboring villages. . . . Our churches which they formerly frequented . . . are now abandoned; there are large parishes where there is scarcely a single Catholic to wait upon the *curés* in their ministry.[21] The fathers and mothers have stopped sending their children to our schools. . . . Those whom we brought up with the greatest of care in the doctrines of the Church soon fall into error and succumb to the caresses or harsh treatment of their parents. . . . It has even come to pass that families dispense with sending them to the church to be baptized; and it appears that there is an increasing tendency among them no longer to receive either baptism or marriage at our hands. . . . But what troubles us most and can have disastrous consequences is the perversion of Catholics of long standing. There is hardly a single town or village where we do not see sad examples of this, and the number increases every day." His fears

Roman Church be suspended from communion; cf. *ibid.*, I, 26. The same year, the Synod of Bas-Languedoc and the Cévennes stipulated the same penalty to those who even attended Catholic mass; cf. *ibid.*, I, 23. These warnings were repeated regularly thereafter. By 1730 the laity were being warned not to send their children to Catholic schools; *ibid.*, I, 94, 99. These provisions were incorporated into the church discipline of 1739; *ibid.*, pp. 372-373, 393-394.

[20] "Réflexions sur l'état présent de la religion dans les Cévennes (19 août 1723)," in E. Hugues, *Antoine Court*, I, 246-250.

[21] See "Les anciens registres catholiques d'une église protestante du Poitou," BPF, XII (1863), 235-238. After 1720 the only persons abjuring their former religion and attending Catholic services were those who sought to legitimize their marriages, creating, in a large degree, a parallel with "occasional conformity" in England at the same time. Also see "Mariages protestants sous le régime de la Révocation de l'Edit de Nantes, 1686-1789," BPF, XLVII (1898), 478-486. It should be pointed out that the alarm of the clergy at the spread of the revival was in many cases more than spiritual; in communities where most of the population was Protestant, the *curé* stood to lose his surplice fees in measure as his parishioners abandoned his church for the Church of the Desert. Cf. the short note by Charles Bost in BPF, 1947, pp. 105-107.

were confirmed five years later, in 1728, by a census taken in the Dauphiné and Languedoc at the request of the Dutch embassy in Paris indicating that in these two provinces alone there were 200,000 Protestants exclusive of those who called themselves Protestants and yet who still attended Catholic mass—an impressive figure, if true, for it represented almost as large a Protestant population as had existed there before the Revocation. This population was grouped around 120 churches under the spiritual guidance of four pastors and eighteen licentiates (*proposants*).[22] The efforts which the government and the Church employed to combat this alarming collapse of the Revocation were largely unavailing. By the 1740's, the attendance at the assemblies often numbered more than 15,000 and some were reported as large as 30,000.[23] The Catholic missions found themselves in hopeless competition with "des zélés uniquement occupés à détruire le bien que nous [the clergy] tâchons d'établir."[24] Conversions to the Roman Church became an increasing rarity.[25]

For his role in bringing about this renaissance, Antoine Court deservedly won the title "Restorer of French Protestantism." He himself, however, took another sobriquet which we have already noted, "the Scourge of the Prophets." For indeed, before the restora-

[22] E. Hugues, *Antoine Court*, I, 324-329.

[23] "Estat des assemblées qui ont esté convoquées dans le département des églises de Nismes (1743-1748)," BPF, XXXII (1883), 361-367. None of the assemblies listed numbered less than 1,000 persons and most of them were well above this figure. In a letter of 8 February 1745, the pastor Paul Rabaut wrote: "L'on me mande de Montauban, que les protestants y donnent des marques extraordinaires de zèle; ils font des assemblées de trente mille personnes. Un dimanche du mois dernier, on y bénit 181 mariages; le dimanche suivant, 60; et celui d'après, 14." Quoted in E. Hugues, *Synodes du Désert*, I, 196. Both Dardier and Dedieu cite assemblies of 30,000 in the years 1744 and 1745; cf. Charles Dardier, "Le centenaire de l'Edit de tolérance de 1787," BPF, XXXVI (1887), 508; and J. Dedieu, *Histoire politique des Protestants français* (Paris, 1925), I, 105. The Protestants and their enemies undoubtedly greatly exaggerated the size of these meetings, but the alarm which they created testifies to their magnitude even if they were not as large as reported.

[24] The bishop of Alais' "Réflexions sur l'état présent de la religion dans les Cévennes," cited above.

[25] See J. Dedieu, *Histoire politique*, I, 78. In 1744 the bishop of Uzès reported that "Nous perdons en moins de deux ans les soins et les peines qu'on a pris pendant cinquante ans pour ramener ces pauvres aveugles." At approximately the same time, the intendant of Languedoc complained to Saint-Florentin that "Ce nouveau mal gagne et augmente tous les jours, au point qu'on compte cent catholiques apostats pour un protestant qui se convertit." See Philippe Corbière, *Histoire de l'église réformée de Montpellier depuis son origine jusqu'à nos jours* (Montpellier and Paris, 1861), p. 418.

tion of orthodox Calvinism could be assured in France, the religion had first to be purged of the radical aberrations which had developed among a Protestant population left thirty years without pastors or the normal guardians of church discipline. The "prophets," "*inspirés*," or "fanatics," as they were alternately called, appeared in the Protestant areas of France on the very morrow of the Revocation. Men, women, and often children of nine or ten years of age, believing themselves to be moved or inspired by the Holy Spirit, wandered about the countryside prophesying in biblical terminology the imminent end of the world, the destruction of "Babylon," the deliverance of the persecuted Church, and the return of Jesus to earth, and imploring the oppressed population to bear their tribulations with patience, to return to the true faith, to repent the hypocrisy of their conversions, and to prepare for the impending cataclysm.

The movement both worried and perplexed the temporal authorities. Consider the experience of the poor bailiff who, through the interrogation of a captured prophet, was trying to get to the roots of the phenomenon. After a frustrating interview with his prisoner, the bailiff was about to leave his cell when he heard a great commotion emanating from the direction of the prophet. Hurrying back, he found his prisoner lying rigid, in a trance, his eyes toward the heavens, furiously beating his hands together and crying out: "Courage my brothers! I tell you, this is the time of persecution. Hold firm! Don't be afraid of losing your property. Manna from heaven will fall upon you, I promise you, my brothers. They say I am possessed by the demon, that I have the devil in my body? No! No! (repeatedly clapping his hands). You will find it written in the New Testament: you must give up your property!"

At this moment, the stupified bailiff collected his wits enough to interject a barbed question: "Written? In which chapter?"

"In chapter . . . , in chapter . . . , ah-h-h . . . I don't remember," sobbed the prophet, who carried on in this manner for another quarter hour. When he revived, he professed to know nothing of what had transpired or of what he had said.[26]

While the bailiff may have enjoyed his momentary triumph over the prophet and have been reassured as to the real nature of these "revelations" (for even a gaoler knows that real prophets should

[26] Charles Bost, "Les prophètes du Languedoc en 1701 et 1702," in the *Revue historique*, CXXXVI (1921), 7-8.

be able to cite their biblical texts), neither he nor others like him were able to fathom the course of the movement or to determine an efficacious way of handling it. They rightly regarded it as infinitely more subversive than orthodox Protestantism. For not only did the prophets keep alive the spirit of religious independence which the State was trying to destroy, but in the climate of religious persecution and severe economic depression which had settled like a plague on the Dauphiné and Languedoc, their activities generated a mass hysteria which promptly led to open rebellion. But in trying to check the heresy through arrests of the prophets, the authorities only worsened the situation, because there was a direct correlation between the intensity of persecution and the activity of the prophets. Each increase in repressive measures only served to draw a populace craving for any measure of consolation or hope more and more into the stream of the movement.

The influence of the prophets upon the population, however, tended to wane with the foundering of several rebellions, with a perceptible relaxation of the persecution after 1707, and with the appearance in the Midi of more conventional spiritual leaders. But Antoine Court still sufficiently feared their pernicious influence to devote a great part of his early activities to undermining their position. Part of this was done through the personal efforts of the pastors themselves, who formed the equivalent of "truth squads" to follow the prophets in their circuits with the purpose of discrediting them in the eyes of their recent audiences.

Yet Court realized that the only sure means of purging the prophets from the Church was to reestablish the disciplinary institutions of the Church itself. By the ancient Discipline of the French Reformed Church, which the churches of the Desert reinstituted with only minor changes, the conduct of pastors fell under the supervision of the consistories of elders and the synods. A consistory had the authority to censure a minister or pastor for improper conduct, and could suspend him from Holy Communion if necessary. With the synods lay the prerogative of examining the learning and doctrinal beliefs of candidates for the ministry and of then investing them with the authority for preaching and administering the sacraments. They served as final courts of appeal in cases dealing with the incompetency of pastors and could depose those found to be justly accused. These powers of and by themselves would not have been sufficient for the task at hand, for in some locales the influence of the prophets was greater than the collective prestige of the entire Church Visible. But in extremities like this, the synods had one weapon which could be used to coerce a rebel's following. Once a pastor was expelled from the Church, those who persisted in attending his services were subject to excommunication by the synods.[27]

This explains in large part Antoine Court's motives in calling the first synod of the Desert (21 August 1715) and in devoting so much of his time and energies to reinstituting the various institutions of the Church—a step which many Protestants opposed as being unnecessary and even undesirable. This and subsequent synods were largely given over to measures designed to destroy the fanaticism within the fold. Elders were appointed and charged with fulfilling the customary functions of their positions. From the very beginning the synods forbade further preaching on the part of women and repeatedly condemned the pretended revelations of the prophets, but it was soon discovered that a certain amount of housecleaning had to be done within their own ranks. Jean Huc and Jean Vesson, two of the original pastors present at the first synod, were found to be irreconcilable in their attachment to the *inspirés*. Huc was dismissed from his functions in 1719.[28] The following year Vesson was put on probation, so to speak, and ordered to preach only those sermons that were first examined and approved by other members of the pastorate.[29] This order he ignored, and in conjunction with Huc led a "schism" which defied the most concerted efforts of the truth squads and lasted until their capture and execution by the government three years later.

Under the circumstances, it was perhaps inevitable that a certain number of persons of dubious morality should find their way into the ranks of the new ministry. Realizing what the effects of this might be upon the young and still fragile Church, Court and the leaders of the Church were forced to turn their attentions to this development almost as much as to the fanatics. Every effort was made to weed out the weaker candidates from a moral point of

[27] Cf. chapters 3, 5, 6, 22, 23 and 26 of the Church Discipline in E. Hugues, *Synodes du Désert*, I, 357-405.

[28] *ibid.*, I, 17.

[29] *ibid.*, I, 18-19.

view before they were accepted into the ministry,[30] and the very breath of scandal subjected the suspected pastor or preacher to the scrutiny of his consistory or synod. Moreover, precautionary steps were sometimes taken to avoid the commission of scandal, such as the provision made by the Synod of Bas-Languedoc in 1720 that "pastors and licentiates are forbidden to enter into houses where there might be the slightest suspicion that they love a girl in a temporal fashion. . . ."[31] Occasional transgressions were not to be avoided. Within a few years of this provision, the preacher Monteil had to be dismissed for seducing a girl,[32] and a similar case against the preacher Boyer in 1731 created another "schism" which lasted for fourteen years and had to be settled in a national synod.[33] Perhaps the most notable disciplinary case which marred the early history of the Church was against one François Dénos (*dit* Chalaye), who was accused, in addition to "fanaticism," of having baptized all his children in the Roman Catholic Church, of having committed the "excesses of a veritable drunkard," of having been seen in a cabaret, knife in hand and in a "frightful rage," wildly threatening his companions with all manner of unpleasant ends, and of several other misdeeds, including a report that he was found in the same cabaret grinding wine glasses to pieces with his teeth. His conduct was deemed by the synod to be unworthy of a candidate for the ministry, and he was forbidden to preach or perform any further ecclesiastical functions.[34]

Such problems might be thought of as the inevitable growing pains of a young Church directed by amateurs. But lest we be contemptuous of these early reformers, we might bear in mind that at least until the twentieth century most revolutions were the work of amateur, not professional, revolutionaries, and that the inexperience of such leaders did not always prevent them from making recognizable contributions to their time. Antoine Court and his associates

[30] For example: Synod of Languedoc and the Cévennes, 7 February 1718, article one: "En premier lieu, l'on ne recevra aucun pasteur dans l'Eglise qu'après un sérieux examen de sa doctrine et de ses moeurs. . . ." *ibid.*, I, 9.

[31] *ibid.*, I, 20. Similarly the Synod of the Vivarais, 26 July 1721, stipulated that "si quelque pasteur se rend familier avec quelque fille d'une manière malséante, on lui défendra d'aller dans la maison de cette fille. Enjoint au pasteur d'obéir." *ibid.*, I, 26.

[32] *ibid.*, I, 34-35.

[33] *ibid.*, I, 112-114.

[34] *ibid.*, I, 68-69.

were in a large sense revolutionaries, undermining and finally destroying one of the more important legacies of the reign of Louis XIV and effecting one of the first breaches in the edifice of the *ancien régime*. For the organization of the Church proceeded apace with the progress of the assemblies. Gradually each important village and town of Protestant France came to have its consistory of elders which actively watched over the conduct of the laity and pastorate alike, checking them in moments of rashness, giving them encouragement in times of adversity. Every six or seven consistories were formed into a colloquy, meeting regularly every half year, where religious questions of general interest to the particular district were considered, and acting as the intermediary between the local consistories and the provincial synods.

At the next level of the Church hierarchy were the provincial synods, to which each consistory deputized its pastor and two of its elders. Here, by majority vote, the general and most important affairs of the Church were dealt with. At first the synods were totally informal as compared with the solemn meetings of the previous century. Their members were "outlaws and vagabonds with prices on their heads, whose descriptions had been circularized by the authorities, unlettered preachers who recited from printed sermons laboriously committed to memory and whose knowledge extended only to the ability to read a few pages of the ancient discipline, [meeting] in the early morning or at night in grottos, woods or isolated houses under the menace of spies, turn-coats and soldiers, to discuss the affairs of the Church, to weigh their reverses against their successes, to take those measures which seemed to them at that critical period to be most propitious for the restoration of their proscribed religion."[35] Beginning in 1715 these synods, however informal, met every year, and through them the affairs of the Church were organized and effectively coordinated. To the three ill-defined "provinces" of 1715-1720 (the Dauphiné, Languedoc, and the Cévennes) were added new provinces as the Church expanded and gained strength. In 1733 among the churches of the Midi a well-defined confederation was organized, the boundaries of the new provinces were drawn, their respective pastors designated, and provisions made for the convocation of annual synods of superior at-

[35] E. Hugues, *Synodes du Désert*, I, liv-lv.

tributes to serve in lieu of the customary national synod in times of persecution.[36] In aiming at the restitution of the sixteen provinces of ante-Revocation days, the pastors directed their attention to the west and north. By 1750 ten provinces had been reorganized (the Dauphiné, Bas-Languedoc, Haut-Languedoc, the Cévennes, the Hautes-Cévennes, the Vivarais, the Montalbanais; Saintonge, Angoumois and Aunis; Poitou, and Normandy) and were holding their synods, consistories, and colloquies with a regularity and precision reminiscent of the days of toleration.

At the top of the ecclesiastical hierarchy, representing the highest authority within the Church, was the national synod. Like the synods of the provinces, they were representative in nature (each provincial synod choosing its delegates from among its own members), they met under the presidency of a minister elected to that post at each meeting, and they arrived at their decisions by majority votes. Although they were supposed to meet every year, this was quite impossible in the eighteenth century, largely because of the risks and difficulties involved in assembling representatives from the various provinces during a time of persecution, and also partly because (as we shall see later) of factional disputes which broke out among the provinces.[37] Nevertheless five were held in the period 1723 to 1748, the fifth composed of representatives from eight provinces, including distant Poitou and Normandy.

[36] Article six of the Synod of Bas-Languedoc, 26 February 1733, in E. Hugues, *Synodes du Désert,* I, 120-121: "Il a été convenu que les églises des Cévennes, Bas-Languedoc et Guyenne seront divisées en trois corps, à chacun desquels seront affectés les pasteurs et prédicateurs sous-nommés. . . , —et que, toutes les années, on tiendra un synode dans une des susdites provinces alternativement, où l'on députera un pasteur et un ancien;—que ce synode tiendra lieu du synode national, seulment tout le temps que la persécution mettra des obstacles à la députation des synods provinciaux du Vivarais et du Dauphiné."

[37] Such disputes were to be settled by the national synod. But the responsibility for calling a national synod was given to each province in turn. A national synod, before concluding its meetings and disbanding, designated which province was to decide the date and place of the next meeting. When this responsibility devolved upon one of the fractious provinces, it could effectively delay the discussion of its difficulties before the supreme tribunal by refusing to call a national synod. The first two national synods were held in 1726 and 1727. The third, in 1730, decided that "On ne s'astreindra pas à tenir un synode national tous les ans, mais qu'on en pourra désormais tenir plus ou moins, selon l'exigence des cas. Pour ce sujet, nous cassons et annulons l'article 23 des articles généraux qui obligeait les églises à en tenir un tous les ans." Cf. E. Hugues, *Synodes du Désert,* I, 107.

The growth of the Church had been impressive. By mid-century, the original three provinces had increased to ten. Consistories regularly collected *deniers* for the relief of the poor. Assemblies met where the attendance occasionally numbered in the tens of thousands. The Church not only forbade attendance at Catholic services, but even felt confident enough to make attendance compulsory at its own assemblies.[38] In some areas almost the entire population of *nouveaux convertis* had been won back to their former religion, and every year saw a further expansion of the revival into still fallow areas.

But the strength of an organized religion is rarely greater than the strength of its ministers. In this respect, eighteenth-century French Protestantism labored under a terrible handicap, one it never overcame. We have already seen that in 1728 there were only four pastors to a reported 200,000 practicing Calvinists in the Midi. The weakness was more than numerical.

Of the "pastors" attending the first synods and directing the *reveil* of French Protestantism, none were ordained. The first to receive formal ordination was Pierre Corteiz in 1718 at the hands of the church of Zurich. In the interim the French churches on their own authority authorized all pastors enjoying the approbation of their elders to perform all the normal functions attached to their positions—preaching, administering the sacraments, and the blessing of marriages.[39] In despatching Corteiz abroad, the Church anticipated that this might become the normal means of consecrating pastors to their ministries. But the experience of Corteiz proved otherwise. Geneva, where he first requested ordination, politely refused to bestow this honor upon him, and Zurich consented reluctantly. Their hesitancy and refusal were partly motivated by a fear of committing an act openly hostile to the French State; but they also were extremely dubious as to the qualifications of these peasants from southern France. Upon the return of Corteiz to France,

[38] See, for instance, the proceedings of the Synod of the Cévennes, 10 August 1730, in E. Hugues, *Synodes du Désert*, I, 95: "Il a été délibéré que les protestants qui refuseront sans en avoir de légitimes raisons, de se rendre aux saintes assemblées, excepté à celles où l'on donne la communion, seront suspendus de la Ste-Cène après leur avoir fait connaître leur tort et le sujet de scandale qu'ils donnent aux fidèles."

[39] *ibid.*, I, 4, 6, 11, 46.

Court proposed that he himself next make the journey to Switzerland. But the synod protested—the season was too far advanced for a trip of long duration and it involved too many risks. Almost certainly the members of the synod suspected their candidate would be refused; rather than risk such an embarrassment and expend the time such a journey would take, they turned to Corteiz. Why could not he, as a fully qualified minister, ordain his friend? This was the course they followed. An untutored Court presented himself before an equally untutored Corteiz for his theological examinations and passed to the satisfaction and delight of all present and concerned.[40] It was in this manner for the most part that the French ministry propagated itself throughout the eighteenth century, candidates for the ministry being examined by the pastors, and elders and in turn consecrated by the synods. In view of the pressing need for pastors, the consequences of this procedure might have been disastrous so far as the calibre of the pastorate was concerned. This was not altogether so, since, with the experience of the "fanatics" and moral-bankrupts so close at hand, the Church resisted the natural temptation of ordaining any and all who presented themselves.

Initially Court had hoped that some of the émigré pastors could be persuaded to return to France to help him in the work of the restoration. Not only did they spurn his pleas, but some of the most prominent pastors tried to dissuade him from resuming the assemblies and even worked actively against him. Part of their scorn and distaste for what Court was doing can be attributed to exaggerated reports which had reached them in their foreign sanctuaries of the fanaticism supposedly inherent in the new religious movement. But it is also quite clear that there were social animosities involved as well. From England, M. de Claris Florian, pastor of the Huguenot church of London, wrote Court in 1719 denouncing the pastors of the Desert as men "sans science, sans une piété bien connue" who seek to "abuser de la simplicité d'un peuple plus lâche que religieux, plus impétueux que fidèle, et moins partisan de la discipline que du désordre." Far from approving of the religious assemblies where lay pastors administered the

[40] Synod of 21 November 1718, in *ibid.*, I, 12-14.

sacraments, he categorically denounced them as "pearls cast before swine."[41] From Switzerland, Pictet, the leading light of the refugee church in Geneva, opposed the assemblies because of the bloodshed and violence they would inevitably precipitate and because he had learned that often "des gens s'y mêlaient de prêcher qui ne savaient pas ce qu'ils disaient."[42] Abbadie and Saurin, the most venerated and learned pastors of the old French church, joined in the disapproval. In Holland, Jacques Basnage, former pastor of Rouen, actually went so far as to write a pastoral letter to the French Calvinists at the behest of the French ambassador. Printed by Cardinal Dubois, the "Instruction pastorale" was widely distributed by the government in the Protestant provinces of France to the great consternation of Court and his followers. "Remember that one of the most important maxims of the Bible," cautioned Basnage, "is that [a true Christian] must obey his sovereign, not only through fear, but also through [the dictates of] the conscience." Their monarch had forbidden their assemblies; they should respect his commandments. Moreover, from a religious point of view, their assemblies were unnecessary, for had not the apostles refrained from public worship when persecuted by the Jews?[43] In 1745 the Court took a similar letter written by the pastor Desmarets and circulated it in Languedoc in an attempt to dampen the popular enthusiasm for the assemblies and to hamstring the progress of the *reveil.*[44] The next year the intendant of Languedoc and Saint-Florentin resurrected the pastoral letter of the now defunct Basnage, reworked it, added a preface, and planted it among the Protestant population for the same purposes.[45]

What advice did these pastors offer the oppressed Protestants

[41] "Lettre de Pierre de Claris à Antoine Court sur les Assemblées," BPF, XXXIV (1885), 71-82.

[42] "Lettre de Pictet à Corteiz sur les assemblées," in E. Hugues, *Antoine Court*, I, 375-378.

[43] Quoted in part by Emile-G. Léonard, "Le problème du culte public et de l'église dans le protestantisme français du XVIIIe siècle," in *Foi et Vie*, 1937, 431-457. Also see his article: "Les assemblées au Désert. Caractères, adversaires et conséquences," BPF, LXXXVII (1938), 470-486.

[44] *ibid.* Also see the BPF, XXVII (1878), 223-231; and J. Dedieu, *Histoire politique*, I, 127-128, 138ff.

[45] The correspondence of the military commander in the Cévennes, the intendant of Languedoc, and Saint-Florentin discussing the plans for planting this letter are reproduced in BPF, V (1856-1857), 192-210.

of France? If they wanted to enjoy the privileges of being Protestant, they must pay the price: *emigrate.* Those who lacked the courage for this, wrote Claris, "should live secluded in their homes, groaning at their cowardice, imploring God for spiritual strength, letting it be known to every single person among whom they live that they are Protestants, they and their children, and suffering joyfully all the trials [which might be inflicted upon them]." Somewhat less poignant was the advice of Pictet and Basnage, who advised the abandonment of the "tumultuous assemblies in favor of small, orderly meetings in private homes—or in other words, a *culte de famille.* In the south, the influence of Court was greater than that of the *émigré* clergy, and the latter's advice was discounted by the population. But in the north, especially in Normandy, their writings delayed the reorganization of the Church on a large scale for a half century, and even then it never regained the vigor which the Protestantism of the Midi had.[46]

While Antoine Court may have doubted from the very outset that any of the pastors of the Refuge could be persuaded to return to France, he had been optimistic in counting upon the charity and munificence of the Huguenot colonies abroad in helping to support the expenses of the French Church. Because of the hesitancy of the bourgeois element to return to the Church until after it became safe to do so (i.e after the mid-point in the century), the Church could not hope to be self-supporting. Not only did Court need funds to educate his pastors; he also had to look beyond France for the money needed to pay his meager pastorate, to purchase the few religious works which were smuggled back into the country, and to relieve the hardships of those imprisoned by the State. In the early years of the revival, Court made several trips to Geneva in search of assistance, and in 1725 the synod of Bas-Languedoc appointed one Benjamin du Plan as their "Deputé auprès des Puissances

[46] E.-G. Léonard's article in *Foi et Vie,* cited above, deals almost entirely with the repercussions of these writings in the province of Normandy. He demonstrates in a convincing fashion that the reluctance of the bourgeois elements in Normandy to participate in the revival of a public cult cost them heavily both in their numerical strength and in their doctrinal beliefs. By remaining content with a private religion, many of them managed to maintain their faith during a century of persecution, but in the process their faith had become more a question of individual opinion, honor, or ancestral tradition than a supernatural, revealed religion. As Léonard puts it: "le culte de famille est devenu le culte de la famille."

protestantes."[47] In their missions abroad, Court and du Plan were warmly received by the foreign colonies and found them keenly interested in the progress of the revival—until the discussion turned to the subject of financial contributions. Most of these émigrés had been separated from France for a half century; some far longer. While they still showed interest in their French coreligionists, it was only with the greatest of persuasion that they could be induced to put their hands into their pockets, and this with discouraging results.

In fourteen years of service to the Churches of France, du Plan may have collected as much as £10,000 from both the Huguenots abroad and from the governments and royal families of the Protestant powers of Europe.[48] The largest part of this sum was allocated to the education of the new ministry. But the problem of finding a suitable school to which the churches could send their divinity students was almost as difficult to resolve as that of financing their studies. In 1726 Jean Bétrine, who had already been preaching in the Churches of the Desert for eight years,[49] was sent to Switzerland as the first candidate for further studies. It had been hoped that the Academy of Geneva would receive him, but the Genevans refused because of their fear of becoming embroiled with the French Resident General. Berne was suggested, but they too refused the candi-

[47] Synod of Bas-Languedoc, 1 May 1725, in E. Hugues, *Synodes du Désert*, I, 38-42.

[48] Daniel Bonnefon, *Benjamin du Plan, Deputy-General of the Reformed Churches of France from 1725 to 1763* (London, 1878), p. 265. The Courts of Saint James, Orange, and the Estates of Holland, Denmark, Sweden, and the Swedish Senate contributed at various times. King Frederick-William I of Prussia refused financial assistance out of respect for his alliance with the Court of Versailles, but he did intervene at Versailles on behalf of Protestants serving on the galleys with favorable results. Of the Swiss cantons, Berne and Zurich seem to have been the most liberal in their support of the French. For the activity of du Plan in raising these funds, see Bonnefon, *op.cit.*, pp. 208-252. In 1754, by comparison, Presbyterians delegated by the Synod of New York in the American colonies were able to solicit £3,200 from friends in Great Britain for the building of what later was to become Princeton University. Cf. Donald Drew Egbert, *Princeton Portraits* (Princeton University Press, 1947), p. 43.

[49] See E. Hugues, *Synodes du Désert*, I, 9. The Synod of Languedoc, 7 February 1718, received Bétrine as a *proposant* to replace Etienne Arnaud, who had been executed fifteen days earlier, and authorized him to preach "le St.-Evangile par toutes les églises où la Providence divine l'appellera." In 1721 he was serving in the Vaunage as a member of the "truth squads" against the heresy of Vesson, the *inspiré*, indicating that he was considered among the most capable of the preachers within the pastorate at that time.

date. Zurich was too far away, and Bétrine did not know German. After much discussion he was directed to the Academy of Lausanne. He could not enroll at the academy, however, because he did not know either Latin or Greek. Hence he received his education, such as it was, under the tutoring of several pastors of the town.

The ignorance of Bétrine (who as a candidate for foreign study probably was considered the most promising and best prepared of the French *proposants*) and that of others like him made it quite clear that French students could not be trained in the regular Swiss academies.[50] Consequently Court turned to the possibility of founding an independent academy at Lausanne for the use of his disciples. By 1729 sufficient funds had been solicited abroad to make this possible. The rewards offered by the French government for the capture of Antoine Court had become so temptingly large, and he had already narrowly escaped capture so many times, that he had just about outlived his usefulness in France. In the summer of 1729 Court left Languedoc for Switzerland and immediately set about establishing his seminary.

The French seminary was entirely independent of the Academy of Lausanne. But the latter loaned members of its faculty to Court and for a time ordained the graduates of the French school. In its first years of operation, the course of instruction was quite short. The need for preachers in France was so great that the provincial synods seldom granted their candidates a leave of absence exceeding eighteen months.[51] In view of the lack of training of those who were sent to the school (the first candidates could barely read or write), its graduates were in many respects "ninety-day wonders" who had acquired a certain familiarity with theological questions but seldom a very profound understanding of them. At this particular stage

[50] Basle, in 1729 and again in 1745, offered to support one student in their academy, but this proved unsatisfactory because the French students lacked sufficient preparation to follow the normal courses of study.

[51] Decision of the Synod of Bas-Languedoc, 21 February 1730, in E. Hugues, *Synodes du Désert*, I, 92. Bétrine had been granted only a year's absence, and when he overstayed his leave, he was summarily recalled and censured by the synod. These restrictions were modified somewhat in the third national Synod, 26-27 September 1730, where it was decided that rather than have the provincial synod limit the time the students could remain abroad, the members of the Academy should decide when the student was sufficiently prepared to return to France: Hugues, *op.cit.*, I, 103-104.

in its development, the French Church did not need theologians so much as it did men who were trained in practical aspects of the pastorate and who might be able to hold their own against the Catholic *curés* in wooing the new converts. In this respect the seminary served the needs of the Church quite well and supplied it with a large part of its pastorate in the succeeding years.

Those who were not fortunate enough to be sent to the seminary in Lausanne were trained for the ministry in *écoles ambulantes* in France itself. As early as 1725 a group of candidates for the ministry would be given an allowance by their synod and assigned to a pastor, whom they followed in his ministerial rounds.[52] Needless to say, this method of instruction was even less formal than the early training at Lausanne had been. One of the few surviving accounts of the conduct of these schools has been left us by Antoine Court:

"I encamped beside a stream beneath the overhanging rocks. . . . Here we stayed for nearly a week; this was our lecture room, these were our grounds, these our rooms of study. To avoid wasting time and to give our candidates practice, I gave them a text of Sacred Scripture to comment upon. It was the first eleven verses of the fifth chapter of Saint Luke (quite appropriately, for it drew the attention of the students to the biblical parallel of their own endeavors, where Jesus befriends the fisherman Simon Peter and tells him "Do not be afraid; henceforth you will be catching men"). They were permitted neither to communicate their views to one another, nor to use any other helps than the Bible. In our hours of recreation, I would sometimes propose a point of doctrine to be explained, sometimes a passage of Scripture, a moral precept. . . . Having proposed the question, I would ask the youngest for his opinion, and then the rest in turn until I reached the eldest. After each one had stated what he thought, I again addressed the youngest, asking him what objections he had to offer to the opinions of the rest, and so from one to the other. After all had expressed their opinions, I gave them my own judgment of the matter involved. When their exercises were ready, a pole was laid on two forked stakes, and this served as our pulpit for preaching. When one of the young men had left it, I asked the others to make remarks, following the system explained above."[53]

[52] "L'Ecole de théologie ambulante," BPF, XXVII (1888), 387-388.

[53] E. Hugues, *Antoine Court*, I, 84-85.

As a means of instruction, this had its disadvantages—not the least of which was the fact that at any moment their courses might be interrupted by an encounter with the troops which were engaged in dispersing the assemblies and occasionally conducting manhunts for the pastors themselves. Moreover, not many of the pastors were sufficiently well trained or educated to impart to their students in these seminars more than the bare formalities connected with pastoral functions. But given the limited abilities of the students and the difficulty of raising funds for studies elsewhere, there seemed to be no other alternative for preparing those students who could not be sent abroad. In 1731 the system was formalized by the synod of Languedoc and steps were taken to establish such schools in each province of the Church.[54]

The *écoles ambulantes* and the seminary in Lausanne functioned throughout the eighteenth century and trained the ministers of the Church until the Revolution. Despite their activity, the shortage of pastors remained chronic. Some three hundred students were given instruction at the seminary in its seventy years of operation, but no records have survived to tell us how many of these were received into the pastorate to serve "under the Cross" in France. The records kept by Antoine Court during his stay at Lausanne do show, however, that the fatality rate—academic, spiritual, and corporeal—among the students was fairly high.[55] Ninety students were received at Lausanne between 1728 and 1753; but of these 90, in 1753, 9 were still pursuing their studies, 9 had died (several at Lausanne), 4 had been killed or executed, 10 had abandoned the ministry and expatriated after periods of service in the Desert of varying durations, 4 had been sent back to the seminary, 6 had given up their desire to enter the pastorate (one of them returning to Catholicism), 3 had emigrated from France, and 1 who had been ordained was subsequently dismissed from the ministry for immorality (Jean Bétrine).[56] Of the 90 students, only 44 were still ministering in the Desert in 1753—and of these 1 was insane.[57] A comparison of the number of pastors serving in France prior to

[54] E. Hugues, *Synodes du Désert,* I, 114.

[55] See E. Hugues, *Antoine Court,* II, 411-419.

[56] Cf. E. Hugues, *Synodes du Désert,* II, 22. He was dismissed in 1747 at his own request, but six years later the Synod of Bas-Languedoc reinstated him.

[57] Cf. *ibid.,* II, 23.

the Revocation with those at the mid-point of the eighteenth century shows even more clearly the handicap of the Church of the Desert. In 1637 there were a reported 647 pastors administering to somewhat over 1,500,000 Protestants in France, whereas in 1756, for roughly 600,000 of the faithful, there were only 65, 17 of whom were not ordained.[58] Only toward the end of the century did the churches acquire anything approaching an adequate number of pastors,[59] and even then the synods frequently complained of "le nombre des protestants de la province, et le petit nombre [de] pasteurs qu'elle a dans son sein,"[60] "le pressant besoin de nos églises,"[61] or "le besoin pressant que la province a des pasteurs."[62]

Notwithstanding the lack of pastors, by the middle of the eighteenth century French Protestantism had experienced a revival and was demonstrating a vitality which stupefied the Church and State. What had happened to make this possible? Before Antoine Court, other pastors had returned to France to thwart the designs of Louis XIV.[63] They had been captured, imprisoned, tried, bound to the wheel, and broken alive. They had failed where Antoine Court succeeded. There are several explanations for this success.

"The seed, the fattening of the Church is the blood of its slain martyrs." The shadow of Tertullian looms large over the history of French Protestantism. Adulation and reverence for martyrs comprise an important element in the composition of the *esprit protestant* and the Protestant tradition. In the eighteenth century it constituted one of the principal strengths of the Huguenot resistance. The memory of those who surrendered their lives for the glory of the Church fortified the laity, strengthened their resistance, and gave them the courage and inspiration they needed to abide by their

[58] Cf. C. Coquerel, *Histoire des églises*, I, 525; H. M. Baird, *The Huguenots and the Revocation*, II, 474-475; and E. Hugues, *Synodes du Désert*, II, 105-106.

[59] In 1763 there were 97 pastors including the *proposants*; by 1787 Baird estimates that there were 125, although this figure seems somewhat high. See Baird, *op.cit.*, II, 475.

[60] Synod of Saintonge, 3-4 August 1768, in Hugues, *Synodes du Désert*, II, 458.

[61] *ibid.*, III, 14: the Synod of the Hte-Cévennes, 8 March 1771.

[62] *ibid.*, III, 380: the Synod of the Dauphiné, 30 September to 1 October, 1783.

[63] For the earlier attempts at the restoration of Protestantism, see O. Douen, *Les premiers pasteurs du désert*, 1685-1700 (Paris, 1879), 2 vols.; and Charles Bost, *Prédicants protestants des Cévennes et du Bas-Languedoc*, 1684-1700 (Paris, 1912), 2 vols.

religion in the face of persecution.[64] Marshall Vauban was one of the first to realize this and to caution his king against the continuation of forced conversions.[65] After seventy-five years of experience, the government eventually came to appreciate the truth of this contention and tempered its policy toward the Protestants accordingly. To the satisfaction of the Protestants? Not to all of them. Writing in 1783, at least one pastor, cognizant of the strength which the Church had gained through oppression, looked back somewhat wistfully to the good old days of persecution.[66]

Another explanation can be found in the abilities and patience of the new leaders which the Church found in the eighteenth century. Protestant historians have tended to attribute the resurgence of Protestantism not only to the fortitude of the laity but in large part to the skill and patience of Court, Corteiz, and the subsequent leaders of French Protestantism in the last years of the *ancien régime*. But just as important, and almost certainly *the* most important explanation lies in the behavior and attitude of the French government after the death of Louis XIV. Confronted with an alarming spread of the Protestant heresy, the Court of Versailles had two alternatives to follow if it sought to avoid inevitable embarrassment: the maintenance of a sustained, energetic, efficient persecution—or outright toleration. It was incapable of either.

With the passing of Louis XIV, the close alliance of the altar and

[64] See Paul de Félice, *Sermons protestants prêchés en France de 1685 à 1795. . . .* (Paris, 1885), p. 20. To the trial sermon preached by Corteiz at Zurich at the time of his ordination, one of the comparatively few sermons printed for distribution in France, Corteiz added a preface calling the attention of the French Protestants under the Cross to the words of Tertullian. "De sorte que les rouës, ni les gibets ne les ont pu détourner, tellement qu'on peut fort bien réciter ici ce que disoit un Ancien Martir aux Payens: Notre nombre croit à mésure que vous le voulez diminuer; le sang des Martirs est la semence de l'Eglise."

[65] See "Le mémoire présenté en 1689 par le maréchal de Vauban, et ses efforts réitérés en faveur des Huguenots," BPF, XXXVIII (1889), 190-209, 243-256, 314-322, 375-388.

[66] The pastor Olivier Desmons, "Mémoire sur la situation actuelle des protestants de France en réponse aux questions qui m'ont été faites par M. Gibert, pasteur réfugié à Londres," (Bordeaux, 1783), reprinted in Emile Doumergue, *La Veille de la loi de l'an X. Etude sur l'église réformée à la fin du XVIIIe siècle* (Paris, 1879), pp. 109-131. Cf. pp. 124-125. Commenting on the *de facto* toleration which the Protestants enjoyed at that time, the pastor Desmons observed that "plus l'Eglise a eu de faveurs de ce côté-là, moins elle a eu de piété. . . . La persécution épure la foi des fidèles, et le sang des martyrs a toujours été la semence de l'Eglise, selon l'expression de Tertullien."

the throne came to an end. In his will, Louis directed that the government be entrusted to a joint regency under his nephew, Philippe duc d'Orléans, and his legitimized son, the duc du Maine. The former was to enjoy the title of Regent, but the duc du Maine, as guardian of the five-year-old heir, was to possess the real exercise of political power. The day after Louis died, his will was discarded. The duc du Maine was eased out of his rightful position and the duc d'Orléans took over the control and direction of the affairs of state.

It at first appeared that the Protestants had much to gain from this coup. The duc d'Orléans, totally unsympathetic with the legislation he had inherited, radically altered the nature of the regime. He had long considered the Revocation an act of madness and deplored its economic and political consequences. Before his marriage, his wife had been a Lutheran. It is quite possible that her sympathy for the plight of the Protestants of France influenced him in his attitude toward the religious problem, for we know from the testimony of Saint-Simon that soon after he came to power he turned his attentions to a project for the recall of the Huguenot émigrés. At the same time, he brought to an end the Jesuit influence over the government. Père Le Tellier, Louis XIV's confessor and the instigator of so many of the anti-Protestant measures, was pensioned and exiled from the Court. The prisons were opened and the Jansenists freed. The new president of the *conseil de conscience* and the keeper of the seals were Jansenists themselves. Lamoignon de Bâville, who as intendant of Languedoc had zealously executed the anti-Protestant legislation for thirty years, was recalled and retired from active service. Even the foreign policy was reversed. The Protestant powers, against whom Louis XIV had warred so often and so long, now became the allies of France. In the interests of these alliances, it was deemed wise to avoid making an issue of the French Protestant problem.[68] Moreover, the king of England was a descendant of a Huguenot émigré, and it was hoped by some that new efforts would be made by the Court of Saint-James to alleviate the sufferings of the French Protestant population.

[67] Cf. the *Mémoires de Saint-Simon*, ed. A. de Boislisle, xxx, 140-148.

[68] To Saint-Simon, this seemed the best explanation for the Regent's toying with the idea of recalling the refugees. Cf. Saint-Simon, Mémoires, *op.cit.*, xxx, 142: referring to the Regent's project for a recall of the Huguenots, Saint-Simon wrote "Je ne veux accuser personne d'avoir suggéré au Régent une telle pensée,

However hostile he was to the legislation of his predecessor, the duc d'Orléans feared to alter its letter. The project for the recall of the émigrés was dropped. The hundred-odd laws against the Protestants remained on the statutes. "Je maintaindrai les édits contre les religionnaires," he is reported to have said, "mais j'espère trouver dans leur bonne conduite l'occasion d'user de ménagements conformes à ma clémence."[69] This meant in practice that the policy of the Regency was to be one of indifference. The Protestants would not be pressed so long as they remained unobtrusive. Thus when the Cardinal de Noailles complained to the Regent of large numbers of Frenchmen attending services at the chapel of the British embassy in Paris, the duc d'Orléans turned his back on the affair. Only when the protests of the Parisian clergy became too loud and numerous to be ignored were any arrests made, and the victims were soon released.[70]

It should be made clear, however, that indifference did not mean toleration. In adopting this policy, the duc d'Orléans had not anticipated the sudden mushrooming of assemblies under the stimulus of the pastors of the Desert. This constituted a license which could not be overlooked. Disturbed at the growing restlessness in the Midi, the Regent permitted the intendants to employ their troops against the assemblies, and at the same time appealed to the pastors Basnage and Pictet to use their influence to check the meetings. Thus on the one hand the government distributed pamphlets to the Protestants recommending private worship of their religion, and on the other hand sent the army against those who refused to comply. A number

parce que je n'ai jamais su de qui elle lui étoit venue; mais dans l'extrême désir où il n'avoit cessé d'être de s'allier étroitement avec la Hollande, surtout avec l'Angleterre . . . les soupçons ne sont pas difficules. Il croyoit par ce rappel flatter les puissances maritimes, leur donner la plus grande marque d'estime, d'amitié, de complaisance et de condescendance, tout cela paré de la persuasion de ranimer, d'enricher, de faire refleurir le royaume en un instant."

[69] J. Dedieu, *Histoire politique*, I, 11.

[70] *ibid.*, I, 12-13. During the first years of the Regency, the Protestants of Paris frequently used the chapels of the embassies of Great Britain, Sweden, and Holland. See BPF, XIII (1864), 8-10. The *Mercure* reported the incident as follows: "Le 12 [mars 1719] on enleva par ordre de la cour dix-sept personnes de l'un et l'autre sexe au sortir des hôtes des ambassadeurs d'Angleterre et de Hollande, où elles étoient allées entendre le prêche. On les conduisit en prison, d'où elles ont été élargies quelque temps après." Quoted in *Journal du Marquis Dangeau*, ed. F. de Conches (Paris, 1854-1882), XVIII, 16.

of assemblies were surprised, a few unfortunates were killed in the encounters, prisoners were taken, and at least twenty-four men were sentenced to the galleys.[71] This was certainly not toleration, but neither was it a very effective way of conducting a persecution. Intermittent and vacillating, it made it possible for the Protestants to reorganize and rebuild their Church. It was sufficiently intense to provide them with martyrs, but not so severe as to cripple their revival.

Given the confusion, hesitations, contradictions, and gross inefficiency of the *ancien régime* in the last century of its existence, it is extremely difficult to make any generalizations about the overall policy which the government followed with respect to the reawakened Protestant minority. In general, the State did not want to be bothered with the Protestants. It had no desire to persecute them, for it was no longer interested in establishing the religious unity which Louis XIV had held so dear. It was far too occupied with other matters to concern itself with such high-flown schemes. To whatever extent the behavior of the Protestants and the pressure of the Roman episcopate would allow, the Court of Versailles was willing to forget the Protestants.

Throughout the greater part of the period of the reorganization of the Church, the responsibility for executing the policy of the government with respect to the Protestants was left to one man, the secretary of state in charge of the *département des affaires générales de la religion prétendue réformée*. For fifty years, from 1725 to 1775, the inept, confused, and timid Saint-Florentin tried his best to handle a hopeless situation. His policy, to the extent that he had one, was essentially the same as that of the Regency—one of cautious containment. To the inquiries of intendants seeking to be enlightened on how to behave toward the increasing activity of the Protestants, the answer was generally to act "avec sagesse" and avoid any scandal,[72] to "fermer les yeux" on the increased number of baptisms in the Desert,[73] advising that "il est encore prudent de dissimuler,"[74] cautioning the officers that "l'usage exact des ordonnances serait

[71] Athanase Coquerel, *Forçats pour la foi*, pp. 339-340, lists nineteen persons condemned to the galleys during the Regency, to which should be added five additional persons cited in E. Arnaud, *Histoire des Protestants du Vivarais*, II, 412.

[72] J. Dedieu, *Histoire politique*, I, 42.

[73] *ibid.*, I, 67.

[74] *ibid.*, I, 74.

fort dangereux."[75] In preparing the instructions for the last intendant sent into Languedoc with orders to "persecute," Saint-Florentin expressed his disapproval of being over-indulgent with the Protestants, but still conceded that "the rule to which you must hold in regard to the *religionnaires* should be one of firmness tempered by condescension. You must restrain them without forcing them to revolt, using your authority without compromising that authority, dissembling opportunely, threatening rather than punishing. . . ."[76] Rewards for the capture of pastors were still outstanding, but most officials fervently hoped that none would be caught because of their fear of the embarrassing consequences.[77] In place of mass arrests and dragonnades, the government increasingly turned to the use of collective fines levied against entire communities—which the Protestants soon accepted as toleration in return for tribute.

The government could never have followed so temperate a policy had the Huguenots of the eighteenth century behaved in the manner of their ancestors. Certainly one reason for proscribing them in the seventeenth century had been their position as a strong and potentially disloyal minority within the realm. In the eighteenth century, the Huguenots were no longer strong. Moreover, from the revolts of the previous century and the rebellions of the Cévennes in the last years of the reign of Louis XIV, they had learned a bitter lesson. They could never hope to be tolerated if they continued to be seditious. No one realized this more than Antoine Court and his associates. His success in reorganizing the Church is partly due to his recognition that from a political point of view Protestantism would have to be made respectable.

In directing the affairs of the Church, its leaders were chary of any acts which might have disquieted the government unnecessarily. Du Plan in preparing for his missions abroad, warned that regardless of the desperate need for pastors in the Desert, it would be dangerous to seek the assistance of foreign ministers. In a letter to his colleagues in France, he pointed out that "if foreign ministers came to our succor, the fact would at once be discovered; . . . the

[75] *ibid.*, I, 91.

[76] "Mémoire lu et approuvé au conseil, pour servir d'instruction à M. le Maréchal de Thomond, dans la conduite qu'il doit tenir à l'égard des Protestants du Languedoc, 7 janvier 1758," BPF, XVIII (1869), 429-435.

[77] For illustrations of this, see J. Dedieu, *Histoire politique*, I, 135-138, 239, 362-363.

Court would suspect a revolt, and this above all things it is necessary to avoid."[78] Among the first resolutions passed by the first national synod of the Desert was the regulation that: "All pastors, *proposants,* elders and all persons subject to our regulations shall remain inviolably submissive and obedient to the superior powers in all matters where God and the conscience are not offended; more specifically [they shall obey] the king Louis XV, our Sire, his legitimate successors, his governors, commanders, intendants, magistrates, and other persons established [in authority] by him; they shall make public and specific prayers for his august person, for the princes and princesses of the royal family, and for all those who exercise police and magisterial powers in his name; and they will favor no traitor, rebel, or disturber of the public tranquillity; and if anyone should be wicked enough to refuse to fulfill so important a duty of divine institution, he will be prosecuted by all the means at the disposal of the Church."[79]

The ministers of the Church were ordered to exhort the laity "to be faithful to the crown and to do nothing which might cause the least suspicion of rebellion" on the part of the Protestants.[80] These sermons were printed and distributed among the faithful; they constitute the largest part of the printed sermons which have survived to this day.[81] The laity were forbidden to carry weapons to assemblies.[82] "In order to give proof of their affection, their fidelity, and their submission to the edicts of his Majesty," they were threat-

[78] In a letter to Antoine Court, November 1725, quoted in D. Bonnefon, *Benjamin du Plan*, pp. 116-117.

[79] Article 2 of the proceedings of the First National Synod, 16 May 1726, in E. Hugues, *Synodes du Désert*, I, 54.

[80] *ibid.*, I, 22, 24-25.

[81] See the bibliographical essay by P. de Félice, *Sermons protestants prêchés en France de 1685 à 1795* (Paris, 1885) and the article by E. Arnaud, "Quelques sermons du Désert de France," BPF, XXXV (1886), 516-524. The Church's insistence upon submission to the Crown was so comprehensive as to be virtually incomprehensible to a twentieth-century student of the period. G.-Edouard Guiraud, in one of seven theses of a dissertation submitted to the theological faculty of the University of Geneva, expresses his bewilderment at their behavior and (although he does not develop the point) seems almost tempted to treat it as a deviation from Calvinist orthodoxy. Cf. G.-Edouard Guiraud, *Le Séminaire de Lausanne et le Pastorat en France pendant la période du Désert, 1715-1787* (Geneva, 1913).

[82] E. Hugues, *Synodes du Désert*, I, 22, 77-78. Apparently this was not faithfully observed, for it seems that in a number of the encounters between the troops and the assemblies the Protestants fired upon the men sent against them.

ened with excommunication if they refused to pay their taxes or engaged in contraband.[83] Although the Church appointed a Deputy General to represent them "auprès les puissances protestantes," he was carefully instructed by the national synod to "observe religiously [the rule of] doing, saying, or favoring nothing against the sovereign powers and in particular against our king and his legitimate government . . .; to limit himself exclusively to demonstrating respectfully, and always in a humble and submissive manner, the justice and equity of according us . . . the free exercise of our communion according to the word of God."[84]

For the person of the king, the Protestants had the utmost respect. When news arrived that he had fallen ill at Metz (1745), prayers were offered in Protestant assemblies throughout the nation for his speedy recovery and for the success of his armies against the enemies of France.[85] In the summer of 1778, the Synod of Saintonge resolved that "the company, . . . happy at the successful pregnancy of our Queen, which gives us the hope of seeing the glorious name of Bourbon perpetuated in this kingdom, our *patrie*, orders . . . the preparation of a pastoral letter inviting all of our churches to dedicate one day to ardent prayers on this subject."[86] Far from attributing their suffering "under the Cross" to the madness of a tyrannical king, they accepted it rather as "the wrath of God visited upon us because of our disobedience to His divine commandments."[87] The Protestants of eighteenth-century France spurned the teachings of Hotman and Beza and looked instead to Matthew and Saint Paul.

The pastors of the Church, while striving to keep the masses obedient to the civil authorities, also sought to convince the govern-

[83] *ibid.*, I, 112, 127, 391. Yet one qualification was made in this: "L'assemblée ne comprend point dans cet article la contrebande des livres de religion qui ne porte aucun préjudice ni au Roi ni à l'Etat."

[84] *ibid.*, I, 76-77.

[85] *ibid.*, I, 189, 193, 199, 212, 225-228 note, 235, 255; and II, 109 on the occasion of the attempt on the king's life by Damiens. For an illustration of the sincerity of these professions of fidelity and respect for their sovereign, see the letter of the pastor Pomaret to the pastor Desmons, quoted in Hugues, *Synodes du Désert*, III, 83-84 note: "Nous avons perdu un bon Roi en perdant Louis XV; les prisons, les galères, tout regorgeait de nos confesseurs, quand il monta sur le trône, et quand il l'a quitté, il ne s'est trouvé aucun de nos frères en captivité. Ce bon prince a eu ses faiblesses, même ses vices. Eh! quel homme ne les a pas!"

[86] *ibid.*, III, 256. A listing of such sermons is given by P. de Félice, *op.cit.*, pp. 30-39.

[87] *ibid.*, I, 84, 87 note, 117-118, 119, 152, 157, 161, 173, 199, 208-209 note, 218, 223-224 note, 224-225, 233, 243, 258, 269, 288, 290, 348, 349 note; III, 450.

ment that Protestantism no longer stood for anarchy, but for order. Time and again they addressed personal appeals to the local commanders, to the intendants, and to the Court itself, professing their loyalty and submission to the State.[88] But the authorities, rather than accept the professions of good faith on the part of unknown and outlawed pastors, based their opinions of the political nature of Protestantism on the actions of the Protestant population as a whole. On several occasions they fully expected the Protestants of the south to rise in rebellion in league with the Protestant nations allied against France. Instead, the Midi remained quiet. Whatever tendencies there were for revolt were held in check by the pastors. The officials were impressed. In 1741, with the entry of France into the War of Austrian Succession, the intendant of Languedoc, although still wary of what the Protestants might do, apprised the Court that in the Vivarais, one of the traditional centers of Protestant unrest, there were no indications at all of any subversive movements. "We still see nothing which would indicate that their hearts are not completely tied and submissive to the king. . . . (Although we know they possess quantities of weapons,) they pay without a murmur all the taxes imposed upon them. . . . I am convinced that whatever attempts foreign emissaries might make among them to incite them [to rebellion] will not succeed if M. de Ladevèze were to have three or four battalions at his command."[89]

[88] See, for example, the "Lettre du nommé Court . . . écrite à M. de La Devéze," reprinted in E. Hugues, *Antoine Court*, II, 447-453 where Antoine Court summarizes the efforts of the pastors to that date in keeping the Protestants submissive and of earlier appeals to the authorities. Also: "Lettre du pasteur Jean Pradel à l'intendant du Languedoc, Lenain," BPF, IX (1860), 81-84; "Lettres inédites de 13 pasteurs du Désert à l'intendant Le Nain," BPF, IX (1860), 236-252. Such appeals were sometimes made collectively through the synods or colloquies; for instance, see the letter addressed to M. de Ladevèze, 3 July 1744, by the Colloquy of Haut-Languedoc in E. Hugues, *Synodes du Désert*, I, 178-179 note.

[89] J. Dedieu, *Histoire politique*, I, 67. Similarly, during the Seven Years War, the British, contemplating a descent at Rochefort, where the personnel of the coast guard were almost all of Protestant descent, made enticing promises to the Protestants of the region in an effort to enlist their support. These advances were spurned, however, much to the satisfaction of the maréchal de Senneterre, the governor of Saintonge, who had been more than dubious as to the loyalty of the local population. In gratitude for their loyalty, he praised them publicly and spoke to the king of their fidelity, promising the Protestants at the same time that he would henceforth serve as their protector. Cf. A. Salomon, "P.-C. Fries, émissaire morave en France," BPF, LXXXI (1932), 29-34.

Repeated demonstrations of their loyalty began to take effect. Intendants charged with executing the legislation against the Protestants found their duties increasingly repugnant.[90] As they came to appreciate the valuable role the pastors were playing in keeping the populace quiet, first local officials and ultimately the government itself began to establish liaisons with the pastors of the Desert. In 1746, fearful of repercussions in the Midi following the French defeats at the hands of Marshal de Saxe, the intendant Lenain instructed a Protestant merchant of Montpellier to contact the principal ministers and preachers of the province and win assurances from them for the maintenance of peace. The latter were only too happy to cooperate and in a letter to Lenain assured him that "we have exhorted and we propose to continue to exhort our flocks on every occasion to remain submissive to their sovereign, to be patient in their afflictions, and never to depart from the practice of this precept: *Craignez Dieu et honorez le roi.*"[91] Lenain was so impressed with these and other examples of their patriotism and loyalty that he communicated to the synods of the Church a project for the formation of volunteer battalions of Protestants to serve on the frontiers in defense of the country.[92] Again in 1755 the intendant contacted the Protestants of Nîmes and concluded a "treaty" with them, promising that the government would close its eyes to the activities of the Protestants if they in turn would not receive any foreign emissaries who might be sent among them and if they could bring themselves to hold their assemblies less frequently and with a little

[90] Note, for instance, the protest of the intendant Saint-Priest to Saint-Florentin in 1751: "Je ne dois pas vous laisser ignorer, Monseigneur, que c'est avec répugnance extrême qu'il m'arrive de condamner des particuliers pour fait de religion. Je vois qu'en toute autre matière les N[ouveaux] C[onvertis] ne cedent pas aux autres sujets du Roi pour la fidélité et pour l'obéissance." E. Hugues, *Antoine Court*, II, 368.

[91] E. Roschach, *Histoire de Languedoc*, XIII, 1079-1080; J. Dedieu, *Histoire politique*, I, 145-146; "Lettres inédites de 13 pasteurs du Désert à l'intendant Le Nain," BPF, IX (1860), 236-252. The hope of the Protestants in making such appeals was expressed by the closing words of a memoir addressed to the Marquis d'Argenson by the pastor Paul Rabaut the same year: "Craindre Dieu, et honnorer le Roy, c'est la devise des Réformés de France: ils osent espérer que lorsque Sa Majesté sera informée de leur triste état, et qu'elle connoîtra leurs sentimens, elle daignera les honnorer de sa bienveüilance royale, et ordonner qu'on les traite, non plus comme ses ennemis, mais comme étant ses sujets et ses enfans." Cf. BPF, XLIV (1895), 126-153.

[92] E. Hugues, *Synodes du Désert*, I, 229-230.

less *éclat.*[93] Thereafter it became customary for intendants of the south to establish working agreements with the pastors. These steps were taken at the initiative of the officers themselves and not always with the approval of their superiors. But finally the Court itself came to realize that this was the most effective way of working with the Huguenots. In 1775, at the time of bread riots in Paris and of acute shortages of food throughout the country, the controller general dispatched circular letters to the *curés* of the kingdom, urging them to preach to their flocks on the necessity of calm and patience in the period of crisis. By the letter of the law there were no Protestants in France; nonetheless the message was sent to the pastors of the Desert as well.[94] It represented the first official *démarche* of the government to the outlaw ministers of the French Reformed Church in the eighteenth century. The granting of a fuller toleration seemed to be merely a question of time.

By 1757 the government of France had renounced once and for all the policy of active persecution inherited from Louis XIV. Indeed, it had never persecuted with much vigor since Louis' death, and as a consequence of what M. Georges Pagès calls the "déformation de la monarchie d'ancien régime" it is doubtful that it ever could have to any great degree. So encumbered with ancient carryovers had the French administrative system become that a uniform, concerted, and prolonged execution of government policy was scarcely possible in the provinces of France. With local officials enjoying a fairly large degree of autonomy and independent action, their own impressions of how to deal with the Protestants, rather than their orders from Paris, usually determined the measures taken against the *religionnaires.* When their instructions seemed inept, they disobeyed them.[95]

This was true of the courts as well as of officers in the administra-

[93] E. Hugues, *Antoine Court,* II, 324-325; BPF, XVIII (1869), 430. A similar arrangement was made again in 1759 by the Maréchal de Richelieu: cf. Rabaut le Jeune, *Annuaire ou répertoire ecclésiastique à l'usage des églises réformées et protestantes de l'Empire français . . .* (Paris, 1807), p. 53.

[94] "La première démarche officielle du gouvernement de Louis XVI auprès des pasteurs du Désert du Bas-Languedoc," BPF, IX (1860), 457-458; C. Coquerel, *Histoire des églises,* II, 529-530; J. Dedieu, *Histoire politique,* II, 170-171.

[95] For illustrations of how officials ignored their orders to intensify the persecution, see J. Dedieu, I, 31-32, 42-43, 46-47, 50-52, 54-55, 72-73, 202-207, 213-214, 219-221, 276-277, 304-312, 322-324, 363-364; II, 85-89, 91-96.

tion. A case in point is that of Madame Pratviel, which took place in 1739 in the city of Castres, Upper Languedoc. This lady declared on her death bed her intention of dying in the Protestant faith. She recovered, however, and was brought to trial charged with having relapsed into heresy. Ignoring the edicts, which were quite clear as to what should be done in such cases (perpetual banishment and confiscation of her entire estate), the court dismissed the case.[96] Later in the century, the Parlement of Toulouse was equally indulgent with the Protestants. One Madame Ponce died childless and willed her entire estate to her husband, a Protestant minister. The deceased's brother attacked the legality of the will, arguing that his sister had married Monsieur Ponce "in the Desert" and without the formalities of the Roman Catholic Church; hence it followed that the "marriage" of M. and Mme Ponce constituted nothing more than simple concubinage and that the brother was the legal heir. The legatee proved his marriage to the court by presenting a certificate stamped by the seal of a pastor of the Desert.[97] Another anecdote tells clearly what sometimes happened to the anti-Protestant legislation in the hands of local authorities:

"While staying at a hotel of a large commercial city of the kingdom, I saw a personage dressed in court robes arrive, a book in his hand and accompanied by a number of men and women paired off as if for a ceremony. If it hadn't been for the air of festivity, I should have taken this man by his costume and his gravity to be an officer of justice come to serve writs. But someone told me that this was a Protestant minister who had come to perform a marriage. He fulfilled his functions toward noon in the room beneath mine. The proprietors of the hotel, both Catholics, attended the ceremonies without any scruples. I expressed my astonishment at this ceremony and at the connivance of the proprietors. They answered: it is true, Monsieur, that according to the police ordinances we should be fined for this. But our magistrates have a secret understanding with the Huguenots, and besides the minister recited the prayers just like we do. Isn't it just as good this way?"[98]

In the three instances when the government momentarily em-

[96] *ibid.*, 64-65.

[97] L'abbé J.-B. Bonnaud, *Discours à lire au conseil en présence du roi . . .* (s.l., 1787), pp. 143-145.

[98] *ibid.*, p. 138.

barked on activity bordering on real persecution—1724, 1745, and 1752—its measures were found to be futile. It was a simple matter to disperse the assemblies and drive the pastors into hiding, but no sooner was the pressure relaxed than the assemblies and pastors would immediately reappear. The intendants in the provinces simply never had enough troops at their disposal to maintain an effective suppression for any length of time. On more than one occasion the effectiveness of their descents upon assemblies was jeopardized by Protestants serving within the ranks, who warned their coreligionists in time for them to save themselves.[99] The intendants, to spare themselves embarrassment with their superiors, had few alternatives but to turn to the Protestants themselves and seek some sort of agreement with them advantageous to both. Moreover, Saint-Florentin, after ordering an intensification of the persecution in 1752, was infuriated at the consequences. When it appeared that the government was serious in embarking upon acts of repression, the Protestants began making preparations on a large scale to accept the long-standing invitation of the foreign powers to receive them. This was just what the Court wanted to avoid. These industrious, skilled, and wealthy citizens had to be kept in the country at all costs; there could be no repetitions of the exodus of 1685. Saint-Florentin frantically wrote the intendant in charge of the persecution: "I am exceedingly displeased, Monsieur, to learn . . . of the measures which foreign nations are taking to attract our *religionnaires* and to steal from us the workers of our manufactures. It is of the utmost importance that you try to prevent, by all possible means, the loss which our state might suffer from this. . . . Indulgence toward the Protestants and all the assuagements which are at all possible of being accorded to them . . . are the surest means of keeping them here."[100]

[99] "Mémoire sur la manière de se conduire relativement au rétablissement de l'ordre dans les matières de religion, 10 Septembre 1753," BPF, x (1861), 284-305; the memoir speaks of "des officiers et soldats protestans qui, par esprit de religion ou par commisération, ont donné des avis aux nouveaux convertis."

[100] "Lettre de Saint-Florentin à Saint-Priest sur l'émigration," in Hugues, *Antoine Court*, II, 479-480. The emigration of Protestants from France in the eighteenth century was insignificant. A handful left the country after the publication of the edict of 1724; the persecution of 1750-1752 caused 218 to expatriate. Cf. A. Picheral-Dardier, "L'émigration en 1752, documents inédits," BPF, XXV (1886), 241-251, 289-306, 337-351, 385-405, and the "Mémoire sur la population protestante du

The government found the loyalty of the Protestants disarming. Under the circumstances, it was disinclined to persecute them. Why, then, did it not grant them legal toleration? It sometimes wanted to, but it could not.

One of the last recorded statements by the dying *Grand Roi* was the final appeal to the ministers huddled around his death bed: "I hope you will do your duty and that you will remember me sometimes."[101] The memory of Louis XIV cast a long and awesome shadow over the history of eighteenth-century France. Many of his acts were exceedingly unpopular, some were patently inapplicable. But by tradition the king and the Court were bound to respect, if not to execute, the work of their predecessors. The Edict of Revocation was a case in point. Its author had declared it to be "perpetual and irrevocable." Hence it was inviolable.[102] For any who might have thought otherwise, the Gallican Church reminded them that the memory of Louis XIV must not be offended.

If the Revocation could not be undone, the government's only solution to the Protestant problem was to make the edict workable. Here the secular authorities collided head on with the Roman Catholic Church. Beginning in 1732 the clergy began to have serious qualms about admitting the new converts to its sacraments. Experi-

---

diocèse de Nîmes avant et après la révocation," BPF, XXIX (1880), 188-192. Those who left in 1752 settled in Ireland at the invitation and expense of British landholders. It is even possible that the emigration during the eighteenth century was offset by the return of some of the émigrés during the first years of the Regency. Because of the apparent toleration in France, "dès la première année de la régence, un assez grand nombre de protestants avaient quitté l'étranger et étaient venus grossir le nombre de ceux qui voulaient braver les persécutions de l'intérieur," Coquerel, *Histoire des églises*, I, 122. Coquerel apparently was using Saint-Simon for his source of information in this (cf. Saint-Simon, *Mémoires, op.cit.*, XXX, 140), who attributed the appearance of assemblies in the Midi to the increased boldness of those Protestants who had remained in France as well as to those who had returned. But since persons at this time generally overestimated the size of the emigration and the completeness of the conversion, the assemblies may not so much indicate a return of the Huguenots as the shortcomings of the conversion.

[101] From the description of Louis' last hours in the *Journal du Marquis de Dangeau*, ed. F. de Conches (Paris, 1854-1882), XVI, 128.

[102] See BPF, XIII (1904), 94-95. When asked at the beginning of his reign by Malesherbes to render toleration to the Protestants, Louis XVI answered: "Oui, je conviens avec vous que l'humanité réclame la tolérance. La persécution ne convertit point. . . . Mais la loi qui statue sur le sort des protestants est une loi d'Etat. Louis XIV en est l'auteur. . . . Ne déplaçons pas les bornes anciennes; la sagesse les a posées."

ence had shown that the vast majority of the Converts never again set foot in the Church once they had legitimized their marriages there. The holy sacraments were being profaned a thousand times over. This could not be permitted to continue. Hence the system of *épreuves* was instituted. The system varied from diocese to diocese, but in general those converts desiring to be married had first to pass a probationary term of regular attendance at Catholic ceremonies followed by the signing of a written abjuration of their former religion. The duration of this probationary term usually varied from four months to a year. But in some cases over-scrupulous *curés* demanded observance for two, three, or four years, and in some exceptional cases as long as from eight to twelve years.[103] Needless to say, this delay caused a certain amount of inconvenience to anxious fiancés. The government, seeking an explanation for the failure of the Edict of Revocation, seized upon the *épreuves.* The clergy, instead of working for the conversion of former Huguenots, were impeding it. They were driving them from the Church and into the Desert with their ridiculous scruples. Skeptics and nonbelievers had no difficulty in receiving the sacrament of marriage, and the early Church had welcomed heretics to its bosom as an opportunity for bringing about their conversion. By insisting upon *épreuves* for new converts, the clergy were being unreasonable, discriminatory, and short-sighted.[104]

Convinced that the converts frequented the Desert not so much out of love for their religion as because of the refusal of the *curés* to admit them to the sacraments,[105] the government came to feel

[103] Janzé, *Les Huguenots,* pp. 83-84.

[104] In a letter of 19 May 1750 from Saint-Florentin to Saint-Priest, the secretary confessed that "J'ai toujours pensé comme vous que les mariages et les baptêmes sont la grand difficulté, que la rigueur que MM. les évêques y apportent ne sert qu'à rebuter les protestants, à procurer des assemblées, à multiplier les évasions. . . ." BPF, IX (1860), 442-443. A year later (29 October 1751) Saint-Florentin again wrote to Saint-Priest that the Protestants "se plaindrent que dans le cas où il n'y a contre la plupart d'entre eux que des présomptions tirées de la naissance ou de la non-fréquentation des églises, on les traite plus durement qu'une multitude d'impies et de déistes déclarés dont le royaume est rempli, et de qui on n'exige ni les professions de foi en les mariant, ni une pratique extérieure de notre religion après le mariage." Cf. Philippe Corbière, *op.cit.,* p. 580.

[105] In some cases, Protestants arrested for having attended assemblies in the Desert did not hesitate to complain to the government that they did so only because the *curés* refused to marry them in the Catholic Church. For example, eighteen inhabitants of Bergerac convicted by the Parlement of Bordeaux "pour crime

that it was the Church, not the Protestants, who were responsible for the shortcomings of the Revocation. If the Church could be persuaded to demand nothing more by way of *épreuves* than three months' attendance at Catholic services, and if *curés* would record the births of the progeny of the earlier marriages consecrated in the Desert without stigmatizing them as illegitimate, "there would be every reason to believe," wrote the intendant of Languedoc to Saint-Florentin, "that most of these [earlier] unions would be rehabilitated [in the Catholic Church], and the new converts would desist from going into the Desert."[106]

Conferences with the bishops of Languedoc had been initiated by the intendant of that province (with the approval of the king) in 1738, and were carried on in a desultory fashion until 1741. But nothing came of them. They were resumed in 1752. The bishops at first remained obdurate, maintaining that the responsibility for the Protestant revival lay with the civil authorities, who had relaxed the severity of the anti-Protestant legislation. It was only with the greatest of difficulty that they were persuaded to accept the government's program, and as their *quid pro quo* they demanded that the government take every possible action to disperse the assemblies and cleanse the area of pastors. The plan was adopted and applied to Languedoc in 1754, but the results were discouraging. The assemblies, momentarily forced to cease their functions, soon reappeared. By 1756, with the outbreak of the Seven Years War, there were no longer enough troops available to maintain the vigilance and pressure against public assemblies. Moreover the intendant charged with the execution of the persecution had in the meantime entered into amicable relations with those whom he was supposed to be perse-

---

d'exercice de la religion prétendue réformée" petitioned the king, arguing that they had repeatedly tried to be married in the Catholic Church (some for as long as six years) and had repeatedly been refused the sacrament by their *curé*. Hence they were forced to seek out pastors in the Desert, and if this was a crime, the *curés*, not they, were responsible. See G. Charrin, "Les jurades de la ville de Bergerac," in *La Révolution française*, XLVII (1904), 90-91. Also see the "Requête des protestants de Clairac, Tonneins, Castelmoron, Nérac au Roy, 12 janvier 1755," BPF, XXXI (1882), 541-547.

[106] "Mémoire de Saint-Priest à Saint Florentin sur la question des mariages," (30 April 1751) in E. Hugues, *Antoine Court*, II, 480-495. M. le comte de Moncan, military commander in Languedoc, was of the same opinion in his "Mémoire sur la manière de se conduire relativement au rétablissement de l'ordre dans les matières de religion," (10 September 1753) BPF, X (1861), 284-305.

cuting.[107] The plan was abandoned and the ecclesiasts resumed the practice of *épreuves.* Its abandonment marked the last serious attempt on the part of the government to enforce the Edict of Revocation in conjunction with the Church. Thereafter, although the Church repeatedly called upon the State to reassume its role as the defender of the faith against the hydra of heresy, the appeals went unheeded. The State, on the verge of confessing to the futility of its half-hearted attempts at consummating the Edict of Revocation, began drifting instead toward a new settlement of the Protestant question—a settlement of its own, independent of the Church.

In the succeeding years the Protestant Church enjoyed a measure of toleration quite unlike anything it had experienced since the early years of the reign of Louis XIV. The letters of pastors and the proceedings of the synods reflected a new feeling of hope, an increasing sense of optimism. The sixth national synod (1756) ordered all provinces still holding their assemblies at night to conform to the practice of those where they were held in open daylight.[108] By the end of the decade, the assemblies were moving closer to the towns—and then into the towns themselves. Saintonge in 1763 boasted of twenty-seven "temples" furnished with benches where the faithful assembled in full view of everyone.[109] From Maz-d'Azil, the elders of the church could happily report that "every day we see our pastor fraternizing with the *curés,* carrying children in the middle of the day to be baptized at the prayer house, our church in the middle of the town, directly across from the cathedral, separated from it by no more than the market place, on one side of which you can hear psalms sung in French, and on the other in Latin—in short as if we possessed full liberty."[110] Everywhere re-

[107] To the annoyance of Saint-Florentin, who seemed powerless to control his subaltern. For the expression of his disapproval, see the "Mémoire . . . pour servir d'instruction à M. le Maréchal de Thomond dans la conduite qu'il doit tenir à l'égard des Protestants du Languedoc," BPF, XVIII (1869), 429-435.

[108] E. Hugues, *Synodes du Désert,* II, 85.

[109] *ibid.,* II, 340-341 note.

[110] *ibid.,* II, 315 note. The toleration was so open that even the occasional traveler took note of it. Cf. *Archives de la ville de Montpellier, op.cit.,* IV, 26: "Depuis quelques temps, ils (i.e. the Protestants) vont assés publiquement à leurs assemblées, qui se tiennent, tous les dimanches, à une certaine distance de la ville et à la campagne, où des Ministres viennent prêcher, donner la Cêne, publier les bans, marier et baptiser les enfants: c'est ce qu'on appelle marier, baptiser au desért. Il y a bien de ces mariages dans la ville, sur lesquels on ferme les yeux."

ports were made of an unaccustomed freedom: letters from Provence spoke of the "paix profonde"; from Haute-Languedoc, of "presque entière liberté" where "les baptêmes et les mariages se célèbrent publiquement et sans crainte"; the Vivarais basked in a "tranquillité [qui] ne saurait être plus grande."[111] With the cessation of man-hunts for pastors, the churches instructed their ministers to give up their ambulatory ministries and take up permanent residences close to their churches.[112] In Paris, the Protestants once again began attending the services of the embassy chapels; the police watched them closely and compiled lists of those attending, but made no attempt to interfere.[113] From the west (July 1773), the pastor Desmons, in a letter directed to Geneva, described in glowing terms the freedom which the Protestants now possessed:

"This province enjoys a liberty unknown to the Protestants of France since the Revocation. Saintonge and Angoumois have temples in every burg and town of any importance. . . . Last month I visited these various churches and saw with astonishment that our faithful are just as free as you are in your happy clime. They assemble regularly twice every Sunday. . . . The temple of Marennes is as handsome . . . as most of those I have seen in your villages. It has its rostrums, its benches, a walnut pulpit skillfully sculptured and suspended, and on the door they have prominently inscribed the passage by Saint-Paul: *Craignez Dieu et honorez le Roi.* Would you imagine that after the horrors of all the persecutions which our churches have endured that now we would see Catholics in our temples applauding our sermons—they who not long ago would have soaked their homicidal hands in the blood of their fellow citizens, and that the government, which denied us a liberty which nature accords to all men, would allow us to erect the temples which formerly they had demolished. . .?"[114]

At the same time the assault of the *philosophes* upon the citadels of superstition began to show in the attitude of intelligent people toward the Protestants. Those officials who still took action against the Protestants often did so apologetically. In the comté de Foix

[111] "Lettres écrites de 1763 à 1776 aux églises du Béarn par les églises des diverses provinces," BPF, v (1856-1857), 259-264.

[112] E. Hugues, *Synodes du Désert*, II, 453, 471.

[113] "L'église de Paris en 1766," BPF, XXXV (1886), 505-511.

[114] E. Hugues, *Synodes du Désert*, III, 77-78 note.

the military commander, badgered by the clergy to close down one of the Protestant schools that were springing up in many parts of France, could not hide his sympathy for the guilty schoolmasters. "You are attached to your religion," he told them; "you wish to transmit it to your children; *cela est bien raisonnable.* But instruct them in your homes. Try not to affront the Ignorantines."[115] In Paris, Court de Gébelin, the son of Antoine Court, served as the "correspondent of the churches," openly representing the interests of the French Protestants, bombarding the various ministries with projects for toleration—even to the point of personally presenting his views to Saint-Florentin in a stormy interview. His religion did not bar him from the Court of Versailles, where, as the author of a philosophic work, he attended the audiences and in 1774 was admitted to present his work to the king and queen in person.[116] In 1781, six years before the Edict of Toleration and eight years before Protestants were officially admitted to civil employments, he was appointed to the office of *censeur royal.* At the local level the ban against Protestants entering political offices was slowly raised. When the Protestants of la Rochelle elected coreligionists to the *hôtel de*

[115] *ibid.*, II, 385 note. A similar incident has come to light in correspondence published in BPF, XLV (1896), 328-331. In a letter of 29 December 1767, the bishop of Uzès complained to the Prince de Beauvau that a pastor (Bruguier) and his wife had taken up residence in the center of the town of Saint-Ambroix; "quoique connu de tout le monde pour ce qu'il est, il paroit en public avec autant de liberté que toute autre personne." This was more than the bishop could tolerate, and he asked the Prince de Beauvau to have the pastor removed from the town. The request quite obviously annoyed the Prince, who answered the bishop by demanding if it would not suffice to have the pastor asked to remain unobtrusive. When the bishop replied in the negative, the Prince reluctantly took measures to have the pastor removed to a neighboring village. Again in 1782 the bishop of Castres denounced to the comte de Périgord the pastor Bonifas-Laroque for having celebrated a marriage in the Desert. The comte de Périgord was willing to oblige the bishop and issued orders for the arrest of the delinquent pastor; but at the same time he took the pains of warning "le coupable" of his impending arrest, thereby giving him the opportunity of escaping. Cf. BPF, XXXVIII (1889), 342. Even minor officials were reluctant to execute the orders of church authorities, as is shown by the incident narrated in the "Lettre inédite de Rabaut Saint-Etienne à Court de Gébelin, 27 septembre 1765," BPF, XLVI (1897), 545-547. Also see BPF, LXXXI (1932), 30.

[116] Cf. J. Dedieu, II, 96-116. Dedieu has noted that among the subscribers to Gébelin's *Le monde primitif analysé et comparé avec le monde moderne* were the king, the archbishop of Paris, Monseigneur de Beaumont, the bishop of Agde, a number of ministers and intendants, and members of the royal family, including the counts of Provence and Artois, the Duke of Chartres, and Mme Adélaïde.

ville in 1779, the government took no action to annul the act—a significant concession in view of the impending war with Great Britain and the notorious reputation of the Rochelais.[117] Four years earlier the last of the Protestants serving on the galleys at Toulon had been delivered from their chains.[118] In 1775, the Parlement of Paris decreed that in the future judges levying fines against parents who refused to baptize their children in the Catholic Church and seizing the children to have them forcedly baptized would themselves be fined 1,000 livres. A similar measure was rendered in favor of the Protestants of the Ile de Ré five years later.[119] The law dating from the period of the Revocation, which in order to prevent the emigration of the new converts forbade them to sell their property without the permission of the king, was allowed to lapse in 1781. In short, the Protestant was becoming socially and politically acceptable. His religion no longer stigmatized him in the eyes of many of his compatriots. More and more he was taken for what he was: a Frenchman.

In 1785, Lafayette wrote his friend General Washington: "Protestants in France are under [an] intolerable despotism. Altho' oppen [sic] persecution does not now exist, yet it depends upon the whim of king, queen, parliament, or any of the ministry. Their wills have no force by law, their children are to be bastards, their parsons to be hanged."[120]

While open persecution had been abandoned and the status of the Protestants greatly ameliorated, neither the Protestants nor the government could long be content with merely *de facto* toleration. The divorce between reality and the letter of the law had not been mended. The barbarous code of Louis XIV was still intact. By the Declaration of 8 March 1715, Louis had declared the general conversion complete. The legal fiction had been adopted and maintained despite all evidence to the contrary that there were no longer

[117] *ibid.*, II, 119, 227-228, 242-243.

[118] "Les deux derniers galériens protestants," BPF, I (1852), 176-183, 320-323.

[119] Olivier Desmons, "Mémoire sur la situation actuelle des protestants. . . ," in Emile Doumergue, *op.cit.*, pp. 116-118.

[120] And like a true soldier, he proposed to fly to the ramparts of their defense—for he goes on to say: "I have put it into my head to be a leader in that affair, and to have their situation changed." *The Letters of Lafayette to Washington, 1777-1799*, ed., Louis Gottschalk (New York, 1944), p. 296.

any Calvinist subjects of the crown; Frenchmen were either *anciens catholiques* or *nouveaux-convertis*. In harmony with this declaration, the amorphous mass of seventeenth-century legislation concerning Protestants was recodified in 1724.[121] The terms of the Revocation were reaffirmed by the provision that the Apostolic and Roman Catholic religion was the only religion to be exercised in the realms of the French crown, and any Frenchman (viz. any new convert) apprehended in the act of worshipping according to the rites of any other religion was to be sentenced to the galleys *in perpetuum* and his property confiscated. The death penalty was stipulated for any minister of the Reformed Church who "returned" to France to conduct assemblies, as well as for any persons attending these meetings who were arrested bearing arms. The new converts were instructed to baptize their children in the Catholic Church within twenty-four hours of their birth. The Church exercised a complete monopoly over the education of these children, and their parents were held responsible for seeing to it that they received the benefits of this instruction until they reached the age of twenty-one. Should any subject in his last illness refuse the sacraments of the Catholic Church, his body was to be publicly desecrated, or, if he recovered, he was to be condemned to perpetual banishment and his estate confiscated by the State. Inasmuch as all French Protestants had long since been barred from public office, the new declaration excluded the new convert from all offices and public functions, made him ineligible for the degrees of medicine and law, and excluded him from the liberal professions unless he could present a "certificate of Catholicity" signed by his *curé* attesting to his general conduct, morals, and faithfulness in attending the ceremonies of the Roman Catholic religion. Finally the only marriages enjoying legal recognition were those celebrated in the Catholic Church.

True, these laws had for the most part become *lettres mortes,* but they were still there. As the pastor Desmons rightly observed in 1783, "the most insignificant procurator, the most insignificant fanatical *curé*, has only to arm himself with the barbarous code of Louis XIV and the even more barbarous declaration of 1724 to

[121] Déclaration concernant la religion, Versailles, 14 mai 1724: Isambert, *Recueil général des anciennes lois françaises,* XXI, 261-270.

put any family or jurisdiction in the greatest anxiety and alarm. Nor is this without example, for even now I am every day occupied with defending the oppressed [against this sort of tyranny]."[122] This is what Lafayette meant by an "intolerable despotism." The Protestants were tolerated, but they lacked any concrete assurances that the toleration of today might not become a pogrom of tomorrow. Their king, by his coronation oath, was still pledged to wage the war against heresy; the Church still urged him "to consummate the work which *Louis le Grand* had undertaken and *Louis le Bien-Aimé* has continued."[123] They still pressed for the rigorous enforcement of the Declaration of 1724.[124] The Protestants were justified in their uneasiness. Their only shelter from the storm of persecution was the enlightenment of their epoch. As the pastor Desmons went on to say, this would scarcely protect them "if the government were to change its system. All our hopes lie with a tolerant prince. Such is he who governs us now; but if his confessor or his ministers were ambitious or fanatics, everything could change in a moment. [What guarantee have we that our monarch will not one day command] 'Tirez dessus, la messe ou la mort.' "[125]

[122] Olivier Desmons, *Mémoire sur la situation actuelle des protestants de France* . . . (Bordeaux, 1783), reprinted in Emile Doumergue, *La Veille de la loi de l'an X* (Paris, 1879), pp. 109-131.

[123] "Remontrances sur les entreprises des Protestants," in the *Collection des procès-verbaux des Assemblées-Générales du Clergé de France*, VIII, 2nd part, pièces justificatives, pp. 711-714 (for the General Assembly of 1775), part of which reads: ". . . achevez l'ouvrage que *Louis le Grand* avoit entrepris, et que *Louis le Bien-Aimé* a continué: il auroit eu la gloire de le finir, *si les ordres, qu'il ne cessoit de donner*, avoient été mieux exécutés. . . . Il vous est réservé, SIRE, de porter ce dernier coup au Calvinisme dans vos Etats. Eh! qui pourroit douter de votre volonté, sur un point que le feu Roi et son auguste Bisaïeul, regardoient, avec raison, comme un des plus importants pour le bien de leurs Peuples?"

[124] For the protests of the French clergy with respect to the spread of the Calvinist heresy as registered in the General Assemblies of the dates indicated in parentheses, see the *Collection des procès-verbaux des Assemblées-Générales du Clergé de France*, VII, 2016-2026 (1745); VIII, 339-347 (1750); 656-657 (1758); 1048, 1052-1053 (1762); 1405, 1415, 1437-1438, and pièces justificatives: 459-462, 477 (1765); 1816-1817, and pièces justificatives: 566-568 (1770); 2029 and pièces justificatives: 685-687 (1772); 2225-2228, and pièces justificatives: 711-714 (1775). Also see the "Mémoire sur les entreprises des Protestants présenté au Roi par l'Assemblée du Clergé de France en 1780," reprinted in J.-J. Bonnaud, *Discours à lire au conseil en présence du Roi par un ministre patriote* (s.l., 1787) pp. 344-355; and "Le clergé catholique et les protestants français en 1775, 1780, et 1788," BPF, XXXVI (1887), 531-539.

[125] Desmons, *Mémoire sur la situation actuelle*, pp. 120-121.

The precariousness of their position was matched by the embarrassment of the government's. The *philosophes* had convinced a small but vocal part of the population that the laws against the Protestants were an insult to French civilization. The laws were bad enough. The fact that they were seldom enforced cast a dubious light on the nature of French justice as a whole, suggesting that other laws were equally absurd and equally liable to infractions. But the greatest source of embarrassment was the question of an *état civil* for the Protestants. Their lack of civil rights led to a number of complications. To say nothing of litigation over contested wills, the law courts had been vexed with cases where persons had apparently used the Church of the Desert to perform "marriages on trial"—a subterfuge which often proved disadvantageous to the bride, for the marriage could be dissolved at the convenience of the groom before any court so long as marriages celebrated outside the Roman Catholic Church were invalid.[126] If this practice were allowed to continue, the morality of the people would surely be undermined. Or, again, the militia in France were recruited from among bachelors by means of a *tirage au sort* (lottery). Since most Protestants by the end of the century were celebrating their unions in the Desert, husbands were frequently drafted to the colors in spite of their protests of ineligibility. They made poor militiamen, and on some occasions their families and friends were sufficiently agitated to take up arms in their defense.[127] And finally, as Rulhière, Malesherbes, Condorcet, and Lafayette delighted to point out, in France—the mirror of the enlightenment and of civilization—in France, one to two millions of the subjects were legally and officially outright bastards. For an entire century Protestants had been victimized by brutal laws and stupid priests. The State had insisted that they marry in the Catholic Church. The Church drove them out, and then turned around and asked the State to drive them back in. An absurd state of affairs, one that cried out to all humanity for remedy.

[126] See Pierre Taillandier, *Le mariage des protestants français sous l'ancien régime* (Clermont-Ferrand, 1919), p. 74, 82.

[127] Saint-Priest complained of this to Saint-Florentin in a letter dated 12 April 1754; cf. E. Roschach, *Histoire générale de Languedoc*, XIV, 2223. Similarly, Paul Rabaut complained of it in a memoir of 1752: cf. "Les protestants du Languedoc et leurs persécuteurs en 1752. Texte inédite du mémoire que Paul Rabaut remit à M. Paulmy d'Argenson," BPF, XLIV (1895), 145. For a further discussion of the problem, see BPF, L (1901), 200-201, 251-256, 468-471.

When laws become distressingly obsolete, as the anti-Protestant legislation had, they are usually rescinded. But the *ancien régime* followed no such convention. For most of the century it had tried to ignore the Protestants, and on those occasions when this was impossible, it had made haphazard attempts at solving the religious question within the framework of the existing legislation. Only once did the monarchy show signs of shaking itself from its studied indifference. In 1764 Saint-Florentin had charged the lawyer Gilbert de Voisins with the preparation of a draft in favor of the Protestants. The work lagged. Gilbert died in 1769 with nothing to show for his labors but a memoir on the subject, which was not published until 1787, when the struggle for toleration had been all but won.

Much of this changed after 1775. Saint-Florentin—old, harried, and exhausted, unable to establish favor with the new king—was retired from his office. In his stead appeared a coterie of officials with philosophic leanings: Malesherbes, Amelot, and the baron de Breteuil. As the successive secretaries in charge of the religious problems of the kingdom, they did far more than their predecessor in drawing the teeth from the anti-Protestant legislation. But they were singularly unable to bring to the fore a concrete and constructive plan for reform.

In the atmosphere of an increasing awareness of the need for reform, a conspiracy of frustrated reformers had come together by the middle of the 1780's: Malesherbes, Breteuil, Lafayette, Rulhière, and a young pastor from Nîmes, Rabaut Saint-Etienne.[128] With respect to possible plans for extending civil rights to the Protestants, the conspirators had any number from which to choose. Since 1750 the devising of such legislation had become a professional pastime for enlightened legists. Some one hundred memoirs on the subject had appeared in print.[129] What was needed instead was a suitable device for convincing Louis XVI and the Court that a reform was both desirable and necessary. They correctly appraised the hesitancy of the throne as due to respect for the Church on the

[128] For the steps taken to get Rabaut Saint-Etienne involved in the conspiracy and for the preparations of his trip to Paris, see "Correspondance de Lafayette, Paul Rabaut, Rabaut Saint-Etienne, de Poitevin," BPF, III (1855), 330-344.

[129] See the bibliographical essay by A. Lods, "Les partisans et les adversaires de l'édit de tolérance," BPF, XXXVI (1887), 551-565, 619-623.

one hand and the weight of tradition on the other. Malesherbes was the first to succeed in driving a wedge between the two. With his two *Mémoires sur le mariage des protestans* (1785 and 1786) he began by adducing the various utilitarian arguments in favor of toleration: the inexpedience of having a large number of discontented subjects within the kingdom; the irreparable harm done to the commerce, industry, and population of the country as a consequence of the Huguenot emigration, which he mistakenly asserted still went on. But the weight of his argument rested with moral and personal considerations. If anyone could contend that Louis XIV had tried to achieve the conversion of his subjects by means of force, surely no one could still maintain that these measures had succeeded. If anything, persecution had hindered sincere conversions. Force had bound the heretics all the more closely to their beliefs, as well as inculcating in them a fierce hatred of the religion they were required to adopt. With the exception of those who had emigrated, there were still as many Protestants in the kingdom as there had been before the Revocation (again he was mistaken). By persecution, "the king has lost subjects, without the Church having acquired any Catholics."[130] Malesherbes then went on to point out delicately to Louis XVI that "if Louis XIV, the most feared and the best obeyed of all kings, the most resolute in his principles, the most constant in his resolution, and whose reign has been longer than any other, if he was unable to operate the conversion which he held so dear, it is clear that no one should flatter himself by hoping to achieve it by the same means."[131]

And what of Louis XIV's *real* intentions? Is it possible that posterity has misunderstood them? "Neither justice, humanity, nor reason can condone the condemnation of an entire people to bastardy simply to punish them for the heresy of their forebears."[132] Louis XIV was an infinitely reasonable king. In revoking the Edict of Nantes, it had never been his intention that his Protestant subjects should have a civil status in any way different from that of his Catholic subjects. Those who converted were to be married in the Church and hence would enjoy the full rights of a French citizen. But what of the *opiniâtres,* those who persisted in their faith? By

[130] *Mémoire . . . fait en 1785*, p. 6.
[131] *ibid.*, pp. 6-7.
[132] *ibid.*, p. 4.

a masterful sleight of hand, Malesherbes presented his audience with the long-forgotten *Arrêt du conseil* of 15 September 1685. Here was conclusive proof that Louis had never intended to condemn his subjects to civil death. Promulgated when the Edict of Revocation was already being prepared, it provided that any Protestant living in a province from which the pastors had already been excluded could celebrate his marriage or baptize his children at the hands of a Protestant minister; he had only to petition his intendant, who in turn would procure the pastor elsewhere and authorize the ceremony to take place in his presence.[133] Neither the Edict of Revocation nor any subsequent legislation annulled this provision. Indeed, the Revocation had specifically stated that Protestants were to have full enjoyment of their property without interference under pretext of religion. Until 1715, then, every Protestant in the kingdom was legally entitled to have his marriages and baptisms blessed by a minister of his own religion.

How had it come to pass that the legislation of this wise monarch had condemned more than a million Frenchmen to bastardy? Louis XIV had been duped by his confessor and betrayed by the Church. The *Arrêt du conseil* of 1685 had been invalidated by the legal fiction in the Declaration of 8 March 1715 to the effect that there were no longer any Protestants in the kingdom. At the time this measure was taken, Malesherbes hastened to explain, Louis was old and infirm. Its real author was Père le Tellier, his confessor, who exercised absolute power over the king's conscience. Indeed, it is most probable that Louis never even saw the preamble into which the legal fiction had been incorporated.[134] By this coup, le Tellier had deprived the Protestants of their legal heritage, the heritage which Louis had tried to guarantee to them. But even more disastrous was the change in attitude on part of the Church. By refusing to marry or baptize the new converts except under intolerable conditions—a step which Louis XIV could never have foreseen—the Church had deprived more than a million Frenchmen of their natural rights.

The gist of Malesherbes' argument was clear. The pious plans of Louis le Grand had been mutilated by his lieutenants and mis-

[133] *ibid.*, pp. 48-49. In Isambert, *Receuil générale des anciennes lois françaises*, XIX, 529.

[134] *Second mémoire sur le mariage des protestans*, pp. 42-43.

understood by posterity. The point which Louis XVI could scarcely overlook was the overpowering suggestion that if Louis XIV still lived, he, too, would deplore the plight of eighteenth-century Protestants and immediately take steps to remedy it. From this point the conspirators pressed home their attack. An investigation into court records turned up evidence which corroborated their theses. Nowhere could they find evidence of a single Protestant marriage having been broken by the courts until the reign of Louis XV. Breteuil was the next to try to interest the king in the possibility of reform. His *Rapport général sur la situation des Calvinistes*[135] repeated the arguments presented by Malesherbes. He went on to demonstrate that Louis XIV had never intended to use force in effecting the conversions. The dragonnades had been the invention of an over-zealous lieutenant, M. de Louvois, and were a method of which the king had thoroughly disapproved, but which was furtively continued in spite of his disapproval. In the present state of affairs, the *religionnaires* were being subjected to an even more iniquitous form of coercion, the denial of all civil rights. Thus, the argument went, Louis XVI should regard an edict of reform as a complement to the Edict of Revocation. Protestantism, as a state within the State, had been destroyed. This had been the principal purpose of the Revocation. All that now remained was to render to the Protestants the legal rights which had maliciously been taken from them. Far from being a violation of the legacy of his great forebear, an edict of toleration would be the fitting capstone to the work of Louis XIV.[136]

The theater of the movement for toleration widened. In February

[135] *Rapport général sur la situation des Calvinistes en France, sur les causes de cette situation, et sur les moyens d'y remédier* (Paris, 1786) in Claude-Carloman de Rulhière, *Eclaircissemens historiques sur les causes de la Révocation de l'Edit de Nantes et sur l'état des protestans en France* (Geneva, 1788), II, 15-82.

[136] The same tack was taken by Rabaut Saint-Etienne in a memoir prepared, it seems, for the benefit of those preparing the Edict of Toleration. He advanced the specious argument that Louis XIV revoked the Edict of Nantes only because he believed there were no longer any Protestants in his kingdom: ". . . il donne ce motif expressément, d'ou il suit que s'il eût cru qu'il y en eût trois millions, il ne les eût pas privés des privilèges des sujets." In granting an edict of toleration, "on ne ferait donc . . . que ce que ferait Louis XIV lui-même, s'il régnait. . . . [Le Roi] en serait le parfait imitateur, et qu'il agirait et parlerait comme Louis XIV lui-même." See Gustave Fabre, "Trois manuscrits de Rabaut Saint-Etienne," in the *Mémoires de l'Académie de Nîmes,* VIIe series, XVI, 193-240.

1787 Robert de Saint-Vincent addressed a long and eloquent appeal to the throne from the Parlement of Paris in favor of the Protestants.[137] A few weeks later the appeal was renewed in the assembly of Notables, first by Calonne and then by Lafayette. A motion by Lafayette was approved and submitted to the king. Louis wavered under the logic and pressure of these blandishments and then conceded. By the end of the year (November 1787) he appended his signature to an edict drafted by Malesherbes with the assistance of Breteuil, Lafayette, and Rabaut Saint-Etienne. Registered by the Parlement of Paris, on 19 January 1788, the Protestants of France were granted the long-overdue and long-awaited Edict of Toleration.

In the wording of the Edict, the authors had done their best to make it as much in harmony as possible with the spirit and actions of earlier reigns. In the preamble,[138] the king declared that the State was still inextricably bound to the Catholic faith and would favor that religion insofar as possible: ". . . we shall always favor with all our power the means of instruction and persuasion which tend to tie together all our subjects by the common profession of the ancient faith of our kingdom." But as a means of attaining the desired unity of faith among French subjects, the throne now renounced the use of violence as contrary to reason, humanity, and the true spirit of Christianity. "A rather long experience has shown us that these rigorous trials have proved unsuccessful in converting [our non-Catholic subjects]." Thus, "while we wait upon Divine Providence to bless our efforts and to work this happy revolution, our justice and the interest of the kingdom no longer permit us to exclude from civil rights those of our subjects . . . who no longer profess the Catholic religion. . . . We can no longer allow our laws to punish them fruitlessly for the misfortune of their birth by depriving them of the rights which nature itself never ceases to demand in their behalf."

The spirit of the Edict of Revocation seemed not to have changed: the State still officially worked for the religious unity of all Frenchmen. Nor were the basic provisions of the revocatory edict altered. "The Catholic religion, which we have the good fortune to profess, will alone enjoy in our realm the rights and honors of public

[137] The entire address is given in BPF, v (1856-1857), 423-444.

[138] The entire edict can be found in Isambert, *Receuil général des anciennes lois françaises*, XXVIII, 472-482.

worship; while our other non-Catholic subjects . . . will obtain from the law only what natural justice does not permit us to deny to them—namely, the authentication of their births, marriages, and deaths."

What specifically did the Protestants gain by the Edict? The main body of the law began with a paraphrasing of the last article of the Edict of Revocation: ". . . nevertheless we shall permit our subjects who profess a religion other than the Roman Catholic religion . . . to enjoy all the benefits and rights which can or should appertain to the title of possession and inheritance, and to exercise their businesses, arts, trades and professions without being disturbed under pretext of their religion." In short, it reaffirmed the freedom of conscience which the Edict of Revocation had ostensibly guaranteed. The only innovation was the initiation of a civil form of marriage. Those subjects who had already married outside the Church could legitimize their unions and their children by appearing before a *curé* or royal judge within one year of the publication of the Edict to declare the date of the marriage, the number, age, and sex of their children. With respect to the future, non-Catholics desiring to be married could either present themselves to the *curé* of their parish or, if they preferred, before the royal judge of their town. In either case their bans were to be published at the door of the parish church at the conclusion of the mass without any mention of the religion of the contracting parties. The *curé* or the judge then declared the couple legally married and recorded the marriage in the appropriate registers.

The monarchy granted its Protestant subjects the rights of marrying, dying, and bequeathing their estates outside the pale of the Catholic Church. That was all. Certainly the Protestants had hoped for far more. The Edict recognized their religion only in a most negative manner. In the entire body of the Edict, the word "Protestant" appeared only once—and then only in the preface.[189] Otherwise the Protestants were everywhere referred to as "our other non-Catholic

[189] When the Parlement of Paris inquired of the king whether it was his intention that the Protestants were to be allowed the liberty of public cult, he responded: "Avant la révocation de l'édit de Nantes, les protestants avaient une existence religieuse, mon édit ne leur en donne aucune, les protestants n'y sont pas même nommés." Cf. Jules Flammermont, *Remontrances du Parlement de Paris au XVIIIe siècle* (Paris, 1888-1898), III, 701.

subjects." Moreover the Edict specifically denied their religion the right of public worship. It denied the existence of their pastors; or, more accurately, it categorically prohibited "those who pretend to be ministers or pastors of any religion other than the Roman Catholic to assume the said status by any act, to wear in public clothes different from those of others of the same religion, or to assume any prerogatives or distinctions." The civil authorities were not to accept a certificate of marriage, birth, or death signed by any such persons, for they were of absolutely no legal value.

The monarchy conferred on the Protestants the rights of citizenship, but it left them second-class citizens. They incurred all the responsibilities that went with citizenship, even to the extent of sharing equally with their Catholic compatriots in the support of the parish church, its institutions, and its ministers. But they remained ineligible for offices in the judiciary, the municipalities, and the universities. [140] There was no indication that the State was contemplating a restitution of the wealth it had accumulated over a century of persecution through the confiscation of the property of émigrés and fines levied upon Protestants.[141]

Consequently the Protestant reception of the Edict was mixed. The synod of Bas-Languedoc warmly expressed its gratitude to the monarchy and enjoined the faithful to comply scrupulously with the provisions of the Edict.[142] The churches of Béarn, while "pénétrées de reconnaissance," could not conceal their hope that the Edict seemed to promise them "encore de meilleurs choses."[143] Haut-Languedoc felt it necessary to "modérer la joie indiscrète des uns

[140] Although Rabaut Saint-Etienne interpreted their exclusion from these offices specifically to mean that those forbidden professions that were not mentioned were now open to them: viz. the professions of lawyers, surgeons, doctors, apothecaries, notaries, and positions in the guilds. Cf. "Observations de Rabaut Saint-Etienne sur l'édit de Louis XVI restituant l'état civil aux non-catholiques," BPF, XIII (1864), 342-352.

[141] It is interesting to note that even before the Edict of Toleration some officials, either through sympathy for the Protestants or misinterpretation of the laws, had restored some of this confiscated property to Protestants and/or their descendants. Cf. the *Archives parlementaires*, XVII, 35: during the debates in the Constituant Assembly on the question of the restitution of Protestant property, M. d'Estournel observed that "pendant que j'étais député des Etats d'Artois à la cour, en 1786, j'ai fait rendre, par la régie, des biens des réligionnaires."

[142] E. Hugues, *Synodes du Désert*, III, 543-544.

[143] *ibid.*, III, 562.

et réprimer le mécontentement des autres," and in stipulating how the laity should observe the provisions of the act adopted a wait-and-see attitude until it should become clear what policy the government might take with respect to the exterior forms of their religion.[144] The churches of Poitou and the Vivarais mentioned it only in passing; those of the Hautes-Cévennes did not even mention it.[145] Anticipating an adverse reaction to the Edict, Rabaut Saint-Etienne cautioned the pastors of Languedoc to avoid speaking about it from the pulpit lest the laity be given exaggerated ideas about what it promised them, and recommended instead that they and the elders privately point out to the people that however limited the concessions were, the Protestants would at least no longer live under the uncertainty of renewed persecution.[146]

On the whole, the Protestants were grateful for the rights which the government had given them, even if they felt, as Rabaut Saint-Etienne was later to declare from the floor of the National Assembly, that the "non-catholiques n'avaient reçu de l'Edit de novembre 1787 que ce que l'on n'avait pu leur refuser."[147] The Edict reinforced the belief that further concessions were in the offing. The Protestants could look forward into the future with anticipation—with the hope for a religious liberty which was still denied them, for equality with their fellow citizens, and for the development of a sense of fraternity which would see them accepted as Frenchmen not only legally but socially as well. In 1788 there was nowhere in France so sizable a group of people who had more to gain from changes in the structure of French society or the French polity. Persecution lay behind them; revolution was ahead, with its bright promise of a new freedom.

[144] *ibid.*, III, 556-558.

[145] *ibid.*, III, 550-552, 554, 564-565.

[146] "Instructions de Rabaut Saint-Etienne aux pasteurs du Languedoc au sujet de l'édit de tolérance," BPF, XXXVI (1887), 548-551.

[147] At the time of the drafting of the Edict, Rabaut Saint-Etienne had hoped that the Protestants might be granted full toleration. For an expression of his initial disappointment when he discovered that this was not to be the case, see "Lettre de Rabaut Saint-Etienne sur l'édit de tolérance, 6 décembre 1787," BPF, XXXIII (1884), 360-364.

CHAPTER III

Emancipation and Conflict: 1787-1791

Dans un cantique solennel
Offrons chacun à l'Eternel
Notre vive reconnaissance;
Chrétiens, sa droite a fait vertu,
Il a pour jamais abattu
Le monstre de l'intolérance . . .
Après l'orage, qu'il est doux
De voir enfin lever sur nous
L'aurore des jours plus prospères.[1]

Thus, to the tune of the Twenty-fourth Psalm, did the Protestants of France sing forth their thanks for the Edict of Toleration. Proscription, persecution, even intolerance itself, melted before the "dawn of more prosperous days"—days which saw the Protestant population of the nation flock to the royal judges to register their marriages and the births of their children. The aged and the infirm who appeared to establish not only their own civil status, but that of their children and grandchildren as well, testified to the duration of the senseless persecution. The joy of these people was expressed by the pastor of Sainte-Foy in exulting that "henceforth one can be a Frenchman without being a Catholic."[2] Throughout the year and into the next the officials of the Crown patiently recorded the records of these lost generations. As late as February 1789 Rabaut Saint-Etienne noted in a letter to the pastor of Saint-Hippolyte that in Nîmes "the office of the magistrate is filled with a clamorous and eager multitude" of Protestants.[3] In order to accommodate the hundreds of thousands who sought to comply with the provisions of the Edict, the period of grace had to be extended to January of 1791.[4]

[1] "Discours [de Rabaut-Pomier] fait à l'occasion de l'édit du roi qui regarde les Protestans . . . ," BPF, XXXVI (1887), 596-604.

[2] Louis Mazoyer, "L'Application de l'Edit de 1787 dans le Midi de la France," BPF, LXXIV (1925), 151.

[3] *ibid.*, 157.

[4] Lettres patentes du roi, 13 décembre 1789. See A. Lods, *La législation des cultes protestants. Recueil complet des lois, ordonnances, décrets . . . relatifs aux églises protestantes* (Paris, 1887), pp. 16-17.

"Our king has torn asunder the clothes of mourning which we wore so long and has transformed them into those of rejoicing."[5]

It has already been noted, however, that the Protestants—or many of them—had hoped for more from the government than simply the recognition of their civil status. The Catholic Church was not unaware of these aspirations and from time to time had cautioned the government that concessions to the heretics would only embolden them and serve to encourage them in demanding further concessions. These fears were now realized. For, while the majority of the Protestant churches remained cautious and waited to see what the future would bring, others began to show courage and recklessly magnified the extent of their newly won toleration. At Ruffec the Protestants demanded the return of their old cemetery; at Villarson they suddenly refused to contribute to the support of the Catholic Church. At Castres, La Portanelle, Chatillon-sur-Loire, Villegordon, Bérangers, Vauvert, and Ganges they boldly began holding their assemblies inside the towns with no pretense at secrecy. More than once the Comte de Périgord had to remind Paul Rabaut that his coreligionists were not authorized to open their schools or hold public meetings. Their boldness taxed the patience of the more tolerant priests. The *curé* of Montbrehain was scandalized by their conduct: "I received the edict of the king with joy," he wrote. "I should be pleased if all Protestants were to conform with it, but I see, with the greatest concern, that far from obeying the orders of His Majesty, they prevaricate them more than ever before."[6]

The last General Assembly of the Clergy of France (1788) afforded the chagrined ecclesiasts the opportunity of multiplying such complaints many times over.[7] Their *Remontrances* presented

[5] Mazoyer, "Edit dans le Midi," BPF, LXXIV (1925), 151-152.

[6] Dedieu, *Histoire politique*, II, 280.

[7] See Charles-L. Chassin, *Le génie de la Révolution* (Paris, 1865), II, 177-185. The clergy protested that since November "il se manifeste des mouvements extraordinaires dans les diocèses. . . . Les religionnaires publient hautement que la liberté est rendu à leurs ministres; qu'ils peuvent tenir des assemblées; que la pompe d'un culte solennel et national est seulement réservée à la religion catholique." They reminded the king that the unity of religion "est analogue aux moeurs et au caractère des Français, essentiellement amis du roi et de l'autorité monarchique. . . . Sire, vous le savez la religion catholique tient aux racines de la monarchie française; elle n'a point cessé, depuis treize cents ans, d'être la religion de l'Etat. . . .Chaque nouveau souverain promet solennellement [le jour de son sacre] à Dieu et à son peuple, de maintenir la foi catholique, et d'écarter l'hérésie

to the king 27 July 1788 and subsequently printed protested against the manner in which toleration had been extended: "Without consulting the sovereign pontiff, or the bishops of France whose assembly had already been convened, all the curates of the kingdom have been delegated, along with the magistrates, to publish the bans of the non-Catholics, to marry them in a purely civil ceremony, with the obligation of expressly and publicly declaring to the contracting parties that they are united in legitimate marriage."[8]

In summing up their demands, they made it clear that they expected the king to maintain their jealously guarded privileges in the kingdom. Ostensibly applauding the charity and justice of the measures taken to insure to the Protestants their civil rights, they hastened to opine that henceforth: ". . . less severe ordinances more faithfully executed will proscribe any religion other than the Catholic religion, and the pastors [*prédicants*] will disappear, the assemblies will cease, and the non-Catholics will remain excluded from the exercise of the rights of patronage and the possession of offices and employments connected with the public order."[9]

The same stand was taken by the archbishop of Narbonne in his address to the king at the closing ceremonies of the Assembly. He expressed the satisfaction of the Church with the Edict of Toleration, but with the recent disturbances in the Protestant areas in mind, reminded the sovereign that "to the [Catholic Church] alone belongs the right of religious instruction in the kingdom; it alone has ministers, temples, rites, and ceremonies; it exercises a legal jurisdiction; the officers of Your Majesty are charged with seeing to the execution of its judgments. . . ."[10]

---

des terres de sa domination. . . ." They went on to warn that "les conversions vont devenir plus rares, et les apostasies plus fréquentes. Dans les campagnes, un peuple grossier, voyant toutes religions tolérées, croira pouvoir, en se rangeant sous d'autres étendards, s'affranchir des devoirs pénibles de la catholicité, du poids de la confession et du joug de l'abstinence. Combien la révolution sera plus prompte encore dans les villes, au milieu des progrès effrayants de l'irréligion et de l'Immoralité! etc., etc. . . ."

[8] "Le clergé catholique et les Protestants française; 1775, 1780, 1788," BPF, XXXVI (1887), 537.

[9] *ibid.*, 538.

[10] *Archives parlementaires*, 1st series, I, 386-387. The king tried to reassure them by saying: "Je vois avec satisfaction qu'il [i.e. the archbishop of Narbonne] rend hommage aux vues humaines et religieuses qui ont dicté mon édit concernant les non-catholiques; en leur accordant l'état civil, j'ai eu soin de maintenir l'unité

Closing its Assembly in this vein, the French Catholic Church showed that it had no intention of relinquishing its privileged position in the French State. The Protestants—whatever their aspirations—could hardly have thought otherwise. Nevertheless there were undercurrents of hostility which led the pastor Gal-Pomaret to observe that "in taking us from between the teeth of the lion which held us in his jaws, the Parlement seems to desire that to a certain extent we be left between his claws."[11] Indeed, the Parlement of Paris had been most reluctant to accept the Edict in the form in which it was presented to them[12] and finally registered it only under considerable pressure from the king and with his solemn assurances that he would always maintain "the holy religion into which by God's grace I have had the fortune to be born," and the promise that he would "not permit it to suffer the slightest diminution of strength in my kingdom."[13]

The hesitance of the Parlement of Paris to register the Edict had an adverse effect upon the provincial parlements, encouraging them to resist it as well. The Parlement of Rennes at first insisted upon the same modifications demanded by their counterparts in Paris, and at Besançon the Parlement acted only under the coercion of the intendant and commander of the Franche-Comté. The Parlement of Toulouse resolved to alter the text of the Edict by specifically excluding the Protestants from the offices of mayor, lieutenant-mayor, town-councillor, jurats, and sheriffs. Although the Comte

---

du culte public dans mon royaume. La foi que j'ai reçue de mes pères sera toujours la foi nationale et dominante dans mes Etats."

[11] Mazoyer, "L'Edit dans le Midi," BPF, LXXIV (1925), 169.

[12] The reaction of the Parlementarians, as described by a contemporary witness, is described in the BPF, XXXVI (1887), 543-546. The nature of their objections—the same in most respects as those of the Church—can be found in the "Remontrances sur l'édit donnant un état civil aux non-catholiques, 20 janvier 1788," *Remontrances du Parlement de Paris au XVIIIe siècle*, ed. Jules Flammermont (Paris, 1888-1898) III, 694-702. The members of the Parlement were not totally unsympathetic to the interests of the Protestants, however, for they anticipated that the Protestants would encounter considerable expenses and loss of time in having to have their civil status acted upon by the royal judges in the *chef-lieux* of the *sénéchaussées* instead of by the *juges des lieux*, and recommended that the latter be empowered to serve the needs of the Protestants.

[13] E. Roschach, *Histoire générale de Languedoc,* XIII, 1342-1344. Even under the pressure of the king, eight members absented themselves during the registering to avoid associating themselves with the measure and twenty-four other members proposed making a further remonstrance against it.

de Périgord compelled them to comply with the king's desires, they proceeded to raise constitutional questions pertaining to the right of provincial parlements, based on "un principe constitutif de la monarchie française," to verify all ordinances of the king.[14] Such opposition clearly demonstrated that the Parlements and their personnel had not befriended the Protestants in the past and demanded a reform of the penal legislation against them out of an adherence to the principles of religious toleration as much as out of their desire to see an antiquated legal system overhauled and simplified. In such circumstances, the Protestants were perhaps justified in their concern over the "claws of the lion of intolerance."

To the unfriendliness of the Church and the Parlements were added the inevitable confusions and complications in the actual application of the Edict. The bishop of La Rochelle, whose diocese included most of Bas-Poitou, sternly ordered his curates not to lend their services in any way to the execution of the Edict.[15] The magistrates were often bewildered by the provisions of the Edict and delayed its execution with such inquiries as how the civil status of orphans was to be recognized and what attitude was to be taken toward mixed marriages between Catholics and Protestants. The Protestants in turn complained of the expenses incurred in traveling to the seats of the royal judges, of delays which meant, in addition to loss of time, hotel and food expenses which many of them could scarcely afford, of the fees demanded for the registering of their marriages. Louis Mazoyer, in an excellent essay on the application of the Edict in the Midi, was more impressed with the shortcomings of the measure than with its advantages. "In short, the Edict of 1787," he wrote, "was in no manner a happy solution to the Protestant question. It embarrassed the functionaries, irritated the ecclesiasts, unnerved the Protestants. It displeased the Catholics, less jealous of the yearning which it appeased than disquieted at the appetites which it risked arousing; it displeased the Protestants whose aspira-

[14] Dedieu, *Histoire politique*, II, 290-294.

[15] "Mandement de Mgr. l'évêque de La Rochelle," BPF, VI (1858), 157. See A. Lods, "L'Attitude du clergé catholique à l'égard des protestants en 1789," *La Révolution française*, XXXIII (1897), 128-137; and L. Merle, "L'Edit de 1787 dans le Bas-Poitou," BPF, LXXXI (1932), 132-158. The instruction was quashed by an arrêt du Conseil du Roi, but nevertheless the curates seem to have followed the instructions of their bishop, for no records of Protestant civil statuses appeared on the parish records until 1791.

tions, whetted by long expectation, it could not satisfy. In the eyes of the partisans of tolerance, it was not sufficiently bold; in the eyes of the fanatics, it was too audacious. Its justice—tardy, incomplete, hesitant, and almost hypocritical—gave birth among the former to a disdainful sulkiness and among the latter to a jealous disquietude."[16] In short, it was one more example of the clumsiness of the old regime, and of the obstacles which that regime faced in any effort to save itself through reform.

If, as M. Mazoyer suggested, the "partisans of tolerance" were disappointed with the Edict of 1787 and the Protestants disquieted at its limitations, we should expect to find in the *cahiers de doléances* of 1789 expressions of both these moods. The provisions for the summoning of the States General provided the Protestants of France with an admirable opportunity for expressing their grievances and for petitioning for an amelioration of their status. True, the would-be reformers of the French polity, many of whom might be expected to fall under Mazoyer's category of "partisans of tolerance," continued to urge further reforms in favor of the French non-Catholic minorities. Miss Beatrice Hyslop, in her study of the general cahiers of 1789,[17] by drawing up a list of the authors of fifteen common pamphlets written on the eve of the electoral campaign, has noted that four of these authors called for one of the more radical of reforms which the Protestants could desire: religious toleration.[18] Significantly, however, Rabaut Saint-Etienne, one of the fifteen authors selected by Miss Hyslop, made no such demand in his tracts—a surprising omission on his part in view of his position as an ordained Calvinist minister, his active role in championing the cause of French Protestantism, and his own dissatisfaction with the Edict of Toleration which we have already noted.[19] In

[16] Louis Mazoyer, "L'Application de l'Edit de 1787 dans le Midi de la France," BPF, LXXIV (1925), 149-176.

[17] Beatrice Frye Hyslop, *A Guide to the General Cahiers of 1789*, Columbia University Press: New York, 1936.

[18] *ibid.*, pp. 66-67—the writings of Nicolas Bergasse, Condorcet, the abbé Siéyès, and the Délibérations du Tiers de Rennes des 22-27 décembre 1788.

[19] See above, chapter II, p. 82. The pamphlet referred to is his "Considérations très importantes sur les intérêts du tiers état . . . ," which can be found in the *Oeuvres de Rabaut Saint-Etienne*, ed. Collin de Plancy (Paris, 1826), II, 237-324. This pamphlet, which called for preponderant representation of the third estate in the impending States General, went through a number of editions both in the

view of the readiness of the ultra-reactionary fringe of the Catholic historians of the Revolution to depict the Protestants as monsters who seized the opportunity presented by the crumbling of the *ancien régime* to further their own interests at the expense of the Catholic religion, this omission calls for investigation.

The truth of the matter is that however much the Protestants desired complete equality with Catholics, their responsible leaders —those who had had the opportunity of sampling public opinion at the time of the struggle for the Edict of Toleration—realized that the moment was not yet propitious, the *philosophes* and the Enlightenment notwithstanding, for advancing their demands. Proof of this can be found in a memoir written by Rabaut Saint-Etienne shortly before the drafting of the Edict of 1787.[20] Rabaut Saint-Etienne began by assuring the ministers charged with the preparation of that measure, and hence by indirectly assuring Louis XVI, that if the king were to restore the Edict of Nantes, "he would be the perfect imitator of [his great forebear, Louis XIV]." However, this did not seem to him to be the perfect solution. What was needed was a "more simple edict more suitable to our [present] circumstances and customs." Expanding on this point, he cautioned that "in according [all non-Catholic sects] a liberty of public cult, one must distinguish between liberty and publicity, and maintain the respect due to the national religion." His demands, then, were surprisingly modest: "It is enough to concede to them a non-public cult, and their prayer houses should be permitted to have no exterior decorations, these belonging to royal and national buildings alone." Their religious services were to remain private, and as for their pastors the state "must not recognize them as ministers, but simply as citizens. . . . It would keep them under surveillance as citizens and forget them as ministers."

Rabaut Saint-Etienne's demands were by no means radical, and his timidity was shared by another pastor of the Midi, Jeanbon Saint-André, future Jacobin and member of the Committee of Public Safety. Writing prior to the Edict of Toleration, he, too, confessed that the Edict of Nantes had been too favorable to the Protestants—

provinces and in Paris. It is briefly summarized in Mitchell B. Garrett, *The Estates General of 1789* (New York, 1935), pp. 91-93.

[20] Gustave Fabre, "Trois manuscrits de Rabaut Saint-Etienne," *Mémoires de l'Académie de Nîmes*, 7th series, XVI (1893), 193-240.

too easily exploited by "les grands" (the higher nobility) and used in a fashion which no state could have tolerated.[21] In preparing a new law to regulate the liberties of the non-Catholics, the state should simply recognize and concede what in fact the Protestants already enjoyed by virtue of the unofficial toleration of their Church of the Desert—a Church "with no exterior pomp which would call attention to its existence," one which "in its obscurity must even be subject to a police which would keep it from overstepping the limits assigned to it."

If the Protestant Church were to have pressed actively for a fuller recognition of its status in the nation, one would have expected it to have done so through its own official organs. In spite of the specific prohibition in the Edict of Toleration against the Protestants' petitioning the government as a collective group within the nation, the Church, through any of its synods and best perhaps through a national synod, could very readily have drafted a plea to the throne to be presented by any one of their supporters in Paris. Similar actions had been taken in the past at a time when the law refused to recognize the existence of any Protestants in the realms of the French king. The only agency which could speak for the Protestants as a whole was the national synod, which, it will be remembered, had not met since 1763. Cognizant of the lamentable state into which the Church organization had fallen since that time, the Synod of Saintonge, meeting in June of 1787, charged the pastor of Bordeaux, Olivier Desmons, with preparing a memoir "to show with the most forceful reasoning the need of convoking" a national synod.[22] Desmons, who perhaps more than anyone else had become alarmed at the anarchy into which the Church seemed to have fallen as a consequence of its lack of a central organ of leadership, subsequently prepared such a memoir.[23] But its conclusions were quite different from what they might have been because of the intervening announcement of the Edict of

[21] "Considérations sur l'organisation civile des églises protestantes . . . ," quoted at length by Léon Lévy-Schneider, *Le Conventionnel Jeanbon Saint-André . . . , 1749-1813* (Paris, 1901), I, 33-39.

[22] Article 21 of the Synod of Saintonge, Angoumois et Bordelais of 20-23 June 1787 in E. Hugues, *Synodes du Désert*, III, 534.

[23] "Mémoire à communiquer aux provinces sur la nécessité de convoquer des synodes nationaux . . . ," in Emile Doumergue, *La Veille de la loi de l'an X*, pp. 13-28.

Toleration and the more momentous announcement of the summoning of a States General. Rather than seizing the opportunity for pressing their demands on the State, Desmons evidenced the same caution and timidity that his fellow pastors had two years earlier. A national synod, he felt, would draw attention to the Protestants at a time when everyone was anxiously awaiting political developments in Paris. Hence he concluded it would be safer for the Church to wait until after the States General had met and the nation had returned to a more tranquil state of mind. The synod of Saintonge was of the same mind, and in approving his memoir at its convocation of May 1789 took no further action toward calling together the synod beyond having Desmons' memoir printed and circulated among the provinces of the Church.[24]

In the two years 1788-1789 neither the synods of the Church nor its pastors were of a mind to press too actively for an extension of the Edict of Toleration. But if the spokesmen for the Church were hesitant to draw attention to their needs, the laity as a whole were not. The request for religious freedom appears infrequently in the cahiers of the third estate, but where it does appear it was in almost all cases from areas with large Protestant populations. The *tiers* of Montpellier, for instance, asked "that the king be thanked for the Edict of 1787 in favor of the non-Catholics as being a monument to his wisdom, and that he be most humbly entreated to give them its complement which the nation expects of the superior views of his justice and beneficence."[25] That of the city of Nîmes was cast in a more philosophic tone: "[We ask] that it be very humbly represented to His Majesty that freedom of thought is one of man's dearest possessions, especially in matters of religious opinions; that consequently nothing could be more worthy of his wisdom than to have permitted the free expression of all religions based on sound morals, the sole means of procuring the instruction of the people and of giving an inner sanction to the principles which direct their conduct; a work wisely begun by the Edict of November 1787, but one which awaits its complement from His Majesty's superior insight into justice, and from the advancement of the civilization of the Nation."[26] Another plea

[24] *ibid.*, III, 590-591.

[25] *Archives parlementaires*, 1st series, IV, 55.

[26] E. Bligny-Bondurand, *Cahiers de doléances de la sénéchaussée de Nîmes*

often cited because of its similarity with the statement of religious toleration incorporated into the Declaration of the Rights of Man and the Citizen was that of the *tiers* of Mont-de-Marsan in the southwestern corner of France (present Department of Landes)—"that every man should enjoy the most perfect freedom of conscience; that no one be punished or disturbed unless, under pretext of religion, he himself disturbs the peace, tranquillity, and security of society."[27]

Such were the spontaneous demands of the Protestants in those areas where they were numerically strong enough to make their desires felt.[28] While it is often pointed out that the liberal tone of such cahiers was set by the efforts of one or two ambitious leaders of the Protestants, this by no means indicates that these supposed leaders were imposing their wishes on an apathetic or hostile populace.[29] This is particularly true of the *sénéchaussée* of Nîmes, the stronghold of French Protestantism at the close of the eighteenth century, where Rabaut Saint-Etienne is reputed to have exercised a disproportionate influence in the drafting of the cahier. Miss Hyslop, qualifying this contention, has pointed out that whatever Saint-Etienne's influence may have been, the text of the cahier was read aloud twice in the assembly responsible for its preparation and discussed before being adopted. "If, therefore, the general

---

pour les Etats Généraux de 1789 (Nîmes, 1908), I, 570. The same article was incorporated in the general cahier for the *tiers* of the *sénéchausée.*

[27] *Archives parlementaires,* 1st series, IV, 34.

[28] Mont-de-Marsan would be an exception. The Department of Landes is among the least populated with Protestants in all of France, and however many Protestants inhabited the area were apparently in too small number to merit the establishment of a consistorial church under the provisions of the reorganization of the Church during the Consulate.

[29] Examples of this hypothesis are not hard to find. E.-G. Léonard attributes the request for the perfecting of the Edict of Toleration in the cahier of the *tiers* of the bailliage of Caen to the efforts of one of the elders of the Protestant church in the city: cf. his article in *Foi et Vie* (1937), 452. L. Merle makes the same point of the doctor Gallot in the cahier of the third estate of Poitou: BPF, LXXXI (1932), 151-152. L. Mazoyer says the same of Rabaut Saint-Etienne with respect to the cahier of Nîmes, and of Montpellier he wrote: "il en est de même à Montpellier, où le pasteur Soulier . . . a contribué à la rédaction des voeux du Tiers et où [le pasteur] Rabaut-Pomier exercé une influence prépondérante." Cf. L. Mazoyer, "La question protestante dans les cahiers des Etats Généraux," BPF, LXXX (1931), 41-73. Bligny-Bondurand similarly attributes the philosophic tone of the cahier of Nîmes to the work of Rabaut Saint-Etienne; cf. Bligny-Bondurand, *op.cit.*, I, XXX-XXXI.

cahier of the third estate of Nîmes expressed the ideas of Rabaut Saint-Etienne, it did so with the full knowledge and approval of the assembly, and we may conclude that the cahier represents faithfully the collective opinion."[30] Moreover it is worth noting that the same demand was made in seventeen of the preliminary cahiers of the area, and that while models seem to have been utilized in their preparation, the wording is totally different from that of Nîmes.[31] In asking for religious toleration, the inhabitants of these villages were not parroting the views of Rabaut Saint-Etienne, but giving expression to one of their fondest desires.

In addition to religious freedom, the Protestants wherever they could gave expression to their other wishes. One of their more frequent demands was for an extension of the Edict of Toleration to a full recognition of their civil rights. The *tiers* of Bagard (*sénéchaussée* of Nîmes) observed "that in certain areas, like the Cévennes . . . , it is difficult and often impossible to find enough Catholic citizens to exercise public offices," and although the latter are noted for their "probity, they have neither the ability nor the knowledge which such positions demand"; hence the Protestants requested that they be admitted to all offices, "at least in those towns and communities where the number of Catholics does not balance the Protestants."[32] The third estate of the *sénéchaussée* of Castelnau-

[30] B. Hyslop, *op.cit.*, p. 56.

[31] The wording of the demand in the cahier of Garrigues is the same as for Colorgues; in Brignon, Castelnau, and Saint-Bauzély the same as for Saint-Geniès de Malgoirès; Mus, Uchau, and Codognan as for Vergèze. The wording for the first two of these may very well have been taken from one of the many pamphlets in circulation at this time, for they are similar to those of other regions of France. That of Vergèze, Mus, Uchau, and Codognan very definitely sprang from the nature of the local situation, for rather than appealing to the inalienable rights of man, the inhabitants point out "que cette communauté, ayant éprouvé une émigration des sujets non catholiques de Sa Majesté, par l'effet de la révocation de l'Edit de Nantes en 1685, et ceux qui y restent desdits sujets non catholiques, qui sont en grand nombre, ayant reçu une marque particulière de la protection de Sa Majesté, par son édit du mois de novembre 1787; les habitants de cette communauté, en portant au pied du trône la respectueuse reconnaissance qu'ils partagent avec le reste des Français, ne peuvent s'empêcher de supplier Sa Majesté d'étendre ses bienfaits jusqu'à revoquer entièrement les exceptions portées par le susdit édit. Il ne peut résulter qu'un très grand avantage pour tout le royaume de la suppression de ces exceptions, que l'équité [et] le droit naturel ne doivent plus laisser subsister." Bligny-Bonduarand, *op.cit.*, I, 233-234.

[32] Bligny-Bondurand, *op.cit.*, I, 91-92. The same or similar demands were made by the communities of Corbès, Tornac, Codognan, Mus, Saint-Dionisy, Uchau, Vergèze, and Vialas.

dary asked that non-Catholics be admitted to the offices of consular jurisdictions, the administration of hospitals and charities, "and to all other posts for which the qualities of compassion and feeling alone should determine any preference."[33] But more important and more frequently expressed was their hope for a restitution of the confiscated property of Protestants which the State still held. In the *sénéchaussée* of Nîmes, the community of Calvisson along with several others pointed out that "there are a considerable number of religionnaires in this region and the largest part of their properties are held by the administration of taxes," and asked His Majesty that he accord a definitive restitution of this wealth to the legitimate owners.[34] This plea was made in at least eleven general cahiers of the third estate which were subsequently sent to Paris.[35]

In like manner the nobility took the occasion to express their views on the Protestant question. In fourteen of their cahiers they expressed their satisfaction with the Edict of Toleration, and ten others asked for its revision in a sense favorable to the non-Catholics.[36] Two asked for the formal recognition of complete freedom of conscience,[37] and an occasional demand was made for the return of confiscated Protestant property.[38] The demand peculiar to their class was that of equality with Catholics in the army. Since the Revocation, native-born Protestants had been forbidden to hold commissions in the French military establishments. A number of them nevertheless had served as officers rising to ranks as high as *maréchal de camp,* and despite the prohibitions a few of them seem to have professed their true religious beliefs quite openly.[39] But their religion barred them from the order of Saint-Louis, a reward extending pensions and privileges to retired officers, but one which demanded a formal statement of Catholicity on the part of the

[33] *Archives parlementaires,* 1st series, II, 561.

[34] Bligny-Bondurand, *op.cit.*, I, 177—similarly demanded by the communities of Cruviers, Lédignan, Saint-Ambroix, Saint-Bénézet, Uzès, and Saint-Bonnet.

[35] Aix, Castres, Cotentin, Forcalquier, Montargis, Montpellier, La Rochelle, Nérac, Nîmes, Périgord, and Poitou.

[36] L. Mazoyer, "La question protestante dans les Cahiers des Etats Généraux," BPF, LXXX (1931), 52-53.

[37] The nobility of Montargis: *Archives parlementaires,* 1st series, IV, 23; and Charolles: *ibid.*, II, 616.

[38] For instance Paris and Nîmes.

[39] See the interesting article by E.-G. Léonard, "L'Institution du Mérite militaire," BPF, LXXXII (1933), 297-320, 456-481.

applicant, something which not a few officers declined to make as being incompatible with their true beliefs. To extend similar rewards to non-Catholic foreigners serving in the army, Louis XV had created the order of the *Mérite militaire*. Hence in certain localities the nobility asked that they be admitted to the *Mérite militaire*, or that a similar order be established for them—the nobles of La Rochelle, for instance, asked that: "His Majesty be asked to accord a military decoration to those of his French, non-Catholic officers who have merited this favor by the length of their services or their distinguished actions in time of war. It would be worthy of the greatness and justice of the best of kings to bring to an end those distinctions which only tend to perpetuate a feeling of apartness among his subjects who, after such a long period of misfortune, have arrived at the happy epoch where they shall all live together as a single family. It would be worthy of his generosity to reward a segment of officers whose ancestors have perhaps greatly contributed to the recognition of the rights of the august family of the monarchy and who have served under him with glory and fidelity."[40]

What did the Protestants want, then? Judging from the cahiers of 1789, a Protestant on the eve of the Revolution might have answered: "To be a Frenchman—to share with our Catholic compatriots the full enjoyment of the rights of citizenship." This would seem to have been a reasonable demand, especially in an age noted for its espousal of the cause of tolerance. But how did the rest of the nation feel? Was the average Frenchman sympathetic to the entreaties of his non-Catholic countrymen? Was he hostile to their aspirations? Those who have studied the problem conclude that he was neither.[41] His attitude can best be described as one of indiffer-

[40] *Archives parlementaires*, 1st series, III, 476. The same request was made by nobility of the Agenais, Béziers, Annonay, and Villeneuve-de-Berg.

[41] Edme Champion, *La France d'après les Cahiers de 1789* (Paris, 1911), 4th edition, treats the question only in passing. Two good summaries of the problem are Louis Mazoyer, "La question protestante dans les Cahiers des Etats Généraux," BPF, LXXX (1931), 41-73; and A. Denys-Buirette, *Les questions religieuses dans les Cahiers de 1789* (Paris, 1919), pp. 414-427. The attitude of the clergy toward the Protestants is examined by A. Lods, "L'Attitude du clergé catholique à l'égard des Protestants en 1789," in *La Révolution française*, XXXIII (1897), 128-137, which treats the matter through the medium of the General Assembly of the Clergy of 1788 and the electoral campaign at Lyon more than through the cahiers; and Charles-L. Chassin, *Le génie de la Révolution* (Paris, 1865), II, 119-204, an extremely anti-clerical study of the problem, and not always an accurate one.

ence. Of the *cahiers de bailliage* studied by L. Mazoyer in the *Archives parlementaires,* only 35 per cent treat the Protestant question in any manner at all. Excluding those of the clergy, the percentage falls below twenty. And of the three orders in French society, the third estate dealt with it less frequently than either of the two other orders.[42] Judging on the basis of the preliminary cahiers (*cahiers de paroisse*) published in the same collection, Mazoyer doubts that any more than one per cent of all the preliminary cahiers took the Protestant question into consideration.[43]

Among the cahiers of the third estate, expressions of outright hostility were rare. The preliminary cahier of the parish of Livré (*sénéchaussée* of Rennes) reflected the last embers of sectarian hatred remaining from the religious wars of earlier centuries by pointing out that religious toleration always provoked "des désordres affreux" and asked that the Edict of 1787 be revoked. Likewise the parish of Champs in Auvergne maintained that "its most important request, the one dearest to its heart," was the revocation of the Edict, for "a mixture of heretics with Catholics is all too likely to alter little by little the true principles of the faith and of the true religion."[44] The same animus was expressed by the parish of Rhodes in Lorraine, but these were isolated cases and may have reflected more the influence of a local *curé* in the assemblies charged with their preparation than the sentiments of the local population. The *tiers* of Franche-Comté hoped that the Edict would not be applied in its province, but did not actually call for its abolition.[45] Carcassonne asked that the Catholic Church enjoy the rights of public worship "to the exclusion of all other sects," and while they approved of the admission of Protestants to economic employments which hitherto had been closed to them, they felt that under no circumstances should this relaxation of the law be extended "to the exercise of justice or police [functions] anywhere in the kingdom,

[42] Mazoyer found that out of 438 *cahiers de bailliage* in the *Archives parlementaires,* 152 took up the Protestant question: 85 cahiers of the clergy, 32 of the nobility, and 35 of the *tiers.*

[43] Only 757 such cahiers are printed in the *Archives parlementaires,* whereas according to Miss Hyslop about 20,000 still survive.

[44] L. Mazoyer, "La question protestante . . . ," BPF, LXXX (1931), 61-62.

[45] *Archives parlementaires,* 1st series, II, 338: "La province de Franche-Comté sera conservée dans la religion catholique, apostolique et romaine à l'exclusion de toutes autres, Sa Majesté étant suppliée de ne point y envoyer l'édit des non catholiques."

nor to public instruction."[46] On the other hand, thirteen general cahiers expressed their satisfaction with the Edict, three of them (Amiens, Evreux, and Auxois) asking that it be sanctioned by the States General "in order that the liberty of citizens can never again be compromised by a revocation of the law."[47] It was noted above that eleven *cahiers de bailliage* requested the return of the confiscated property of the Protestants, but three of these (Montargis, Castres, and Poitou, the latter two in regions with sizable Protestant populations) showed a lack of sympathy for the religious ambitions of the Protestants by asking that Catholicism remain the dominant religion in the kingdom. Six *bailliages* outside the geographical limits of *la France protestante* asked for the restitution of the Edict of Nantes or its equivalent in the guarantee of religious freedom for the Protestants.[48]

In summary, out of 164 *cahiers de bailliage* for the third estate, only 35 were moved to take the Protestant issue into consideration, and not all of these in a favorable light. If we were to put aside those emanating from Protestant areas, the degree to which the French Catholic was moved to compassion for his Protestant fellow countryman would seem to have been slight indeed. The silence of the other cahiers, which after all were largely expressions of "grievances," would seem to indicate that the common man in France passively approved of the extension of civil rights to the Protestants, while his loyalty to the Catholic religion—often expressed in the cahiers—cast an unfavorable light on Protestant hopes for freedom of public worship.

The relative neutrality of the third estate was in sharp contrast to a hostility which the clergy rarely concealed. The concessions already made in favor of the non-Catholics, combined with the bold actions of the Protestants in some areas, engendered a fear among the clergy that the State might soon bow to the demands

[46] *ibid.*, II, 532.

[47] Mazoyer, "La question protestante . . . ," BPF, LXXX (1931), 57.

[48] Théatins, Châteauroux, Aunay, Bellocq, Saint-Louis-la-Culture, and Aurons. Cf. *ibid.*, p. 60. The demand of the *tiers* of Châteauroux is worth noting for the light it throws on the attitude of its authors toward the absolutism of Louis XIV: "Les Etats généraux accorderont aux non catholiques sans exception une existence solide et un état civil sans aucune restriction, en les rétablissant dans les droits qui leur étaient accordés par l'édit de Nantes, rendu d'après le voeu de la nation et révoqué sans sa participation." *Archives parlementaires*, 1st series, II, 326, article 12.

for a "tolérance universelle." Hence out of 131 cahiers of the clergy, 64 categorically refused to share the rights of public worship with the non-Catholics and requested that the States General enact a fundamental law to this effect.[49] The clergy of Besançon went beyond this and asked its deputy to the States General: ". . . to vigorously demand with all possible zeal . . . the maintenance of the [Roman Catholic] religion in all its purity; he will represent to the king that the most essential article of the capitulation which united this province (Franche-Comté) to the crown concerns religion; that the predecessors of the king expressly and formally promised never to permit a sect contrary to the Roman Catholic and Apostolic religion to introduce itself into this province; he will support his demands with those of the Parlement of Franche-Comté, which has rejected the edict of the non-Catholics as contrary to our privileges and capitulations; he will ask that this edict not be presented again for enregistering and that articles 12, 13, and 14 or the declaration of 14 May 1724 (excluding non-Catholics from government posts and the liberal professions) continue to be executed." After spelling out in detail the nature of these articles, the clergy concluded by instructing their deputy to demand "finally that the non-Catholics be excluded from all public and private education . . . , and that at the death of each Protestant minister in the *quatre terres* [belonging to the House of Wurtemberg and enjoying by special grant religious freedom] a Catholic minister be substituted in his place."[50]

Demands on the same order as this were made by other assemblies in the provinces of Franche-Comté, Flanders, and Alsace. Furthermore, in 29 cahiers the clergy called the attention of their deputies to the Remonstrances of the General Assembly of 1788 and instructed them to seek modifications and corrections to the Edict of Toleration in harmony with those Remonstrances. Twenty-five asked that non-Catholics, who by virtue of seignorial possessions enjoyed the right of patronage to ecclesiastical fiefs, not be allowed to exercise these rights. Although none of their cahiers asked for a renewal of the persecutions of old, several called attention to the assemblies and illegal activities of pastors, asking that

[49] Mazoyer, "La question protestante . . . ," BPF, LXXX (1931), 46.
[50] *Archives parlementaires,* 1st series, II, 333-334.

they be repressed.[51] Only three of their cahiers asked for the complete withdrawal of the Edict of Toleration (Metz, Puy-en-Velay, and Bordeaux).[52] If the rest somewhat grudgingly acquiesced to the extension of civil rights to the Protestants, they were alarmed at the manner in which the Protestants were interpreting it and fearful of what the future might bring. Perhaps the best example of their attitude was expressed by the Clergy of Puy: "We must annihilate forever the new pretentions which our brethren have already revealed; to be sure they are unfortunate, but they do not have the right to involve us in their misfortune."[53]

Perhaps the two phenomena most worthy of note in the Protestant areas of France on the threshold of the Revolution were the spirit of fraternity among the Catholic and Protestant populations despite the guarded attitude of the Catholic clergy, and the political activity of the newly emancipated Protestants in the first stages of the political upheaval. The indifference of the third estate in its cahiers to the Protestant question and the almost total absence of expressions of surprise or indignation at the Edict of 1787 would seem to indicate that few Frenchmen were conscious any longer of a "péril protestant," that the French Calvinist was accepted as a compatible, integral element in French society. Certainly he was no longer regarded (as once he had been) as a seditious, troublesome, undesirable ulcer within the national community. This new sense of fraternity, unusual when compared with the widespread suspicion of Protestants in the latter part of the seventeenth century and at intervals of the nineteenth, was a consequence of the peaceable behavior of the Protestants during the reigns of Louis XV and Louis XVI and of the decline of interest in dogmatic contro-

[51] For instance the clergy of Caux asked the king to "réprimer les assemblées illégales; de mettre un frein aux abuse occasionnés par cet édit. . . . D'ailleurs les protestants se sont arrogés l'exercise le plus entier de leur religion, telle que l'administration d'un baptême, souvent défectueux, et l'érection de temples où ils se rassemblent au son des cloches qui appellent les catholiques à l'église." *ibid.*, II, 574.

[52] The clergy of Bordeaux, for instance, resolved to request their deputies to demand "la suppression de l'édit concernant les non catholiques, qui donne aux curés la faculté de publier les bans des non catholiques, l'ordre du clergé déclarant ne pouvoir pas prêter son ministère pour des mariages autres que ceux qui sont contractés suivant le rit catholique." *ibid.*, II, 393.

[53] Mazoyer, "La question protestante . . . ," BPF, LXXX (1931), 50.

versies. The patriotism and loyalty, obedience and submission of the Protestants throughout the course of the eighteenth century had made it possible for the people of France to forget that their Protestant neighbors had in the past sometimes betrayed their country to its enemies, that with torch and sword they had once seared the breast of France with the agonies of religious war.

While memories of Protestant seditions faded into the background, the concern of Frenchmen for the doctrinal controversies which had been their cause also waned. Their interests turned in another direction, one in which they could meet on common grounds, forgetful, almost unconscious, of their differences. A contemporary observer of the city of Montpellier, once the seat of fierce sectarian controversies, noted the change in this way: "As to the philosophical spirit of the city, it is no longer a question of disputes over Calvinism, Molinism, and Jansenism. One cannot but agree that in their place the reading of philosophic books captivates the minds of most people to such an extent, especially among the young, that one has never seen so many deists as there are here today. They are peaceful in this, to be sure, and adopt the cults of any kind of religion whatsoever, without really embracing any, believing that it is enough to practice moral virtues in order to be a virtuous man [*un honnête homme*]."[54]

Thus apparently the theological decline in both the Catholic and Protestant churches had reduced the former religious enmities to a point where Protestant and Catholic could together taste the fruit of the tree of the Enlightenment. But this accord was known by people of means, education, and culture, whereas religious fanaticism more often than not breeds itself among the poor, the uneducated, those who in their isolation remain cut off from the ideas of others and become obstinately intolerant in their ignorance. What of these? The records kept by an inconspicuous clerk in the village of Aubais (Languedoc) tell a surprisingly similar story. The Protestants of Aubais, who comprised almost half the population, enjoyed the tolerance of a Catholic seigneur. The latter closed his eyes to the assemblies of the Calvinists and was even known to offer his hospitality to an occasional pastor who passed through the area—to men with prices on their heads. The people themselves did not

[54] "Montpellier en 1768 . . . ," *Archives de la ville de Montpellier*, ed. Jos. Berthelé (Montpellier, 1920), IV, 27.

form two separate clans, Catholics and Protestants. They got on well with one another, Catholics on at least one occasion joining in the assemblies of the Protestants, and Protestants not disdaining to listen to and even to praise the better sermons of the *curé*. Frequently they intermarried, a course which usually entailed the abjuring of one or the other—something which in other times might well have led to bloodshed.[55]

Was this the norm? More than likely it was. To be sure, there were times when inordinately large assemblies of Protestants in the Desert seem to have created anxiety among the Catholics, raising fears of the renewal of civil war. But such fears were groundless. The resistance of the Protestants in the eighteenth century was no longer that of the sword; it was passive, ductile, yielding like a willow before the storms which sought to uproot it. For those who would point to occasions of alarm, other incidents can be cited to balance their arguments. What of the pastor, Paul Vincent? Surprised by dragoons as he was preaching to an assembly in the Desert, he was befriended by the local *curé*, who rushed to his aid, offering him shelter and security in his own dwelling, even tendering asylum in his church—an act of charity and compassion which saved the life of the pastor.[56] And what of the words of the pastor Rabaut Saint-Etienne, rendering a eulogy as a Protestant pastor to the memory of the Catholic bishop of Nîmes: "As for me, an obscure citizen, who knew you only by name and by your virtues, venerable shadow, if I have paid tribute to your ashes, a tribute owing to a man of goodness, I was only surrendering to an irresistible impulsion from my heart. Let the earth be covered with men of your justice and beneficence, and I shall bless the Creator for having given me life!"[57] Where were the passions of religious intolerance? Time had quenched their flames; few of the embers could be seen.

Manifestations of this concord, traces of the oblivion into which religious rivalries had fallen, were present in the opening days of the

[55] Emile-G. Léonard, *Mon village sous Louis XV, d'après les Mémoires d'un Paysan* (Paris, 1941), pp. 239-284.

[56] An incident reported to have taken place near the village of Canaules (diocese of Alais) in 1760. Cf. A. Borrel, *Histoire de l'église réformée de Nîmes . . .* (Toulouse, 1856), 2nd edition, p. 422.

[57] "Hommage à la mémoire de l'évêque de Nîmes (1779)," *Oeuvres de Rabaut Saint-Etienne*, ed. Collin de Plancy II, 115-133.

Revolution. Generally, as we have seen, the clergy of France took the opportunity afforded by the convocation of the States General to register their dissatisfaction with the Edict of Toleration and their fears for the future of the Catholic religion. Yet one of the only two cahiers of the clergy to give expression to pro-Protestant sympathies was that of Castres, an area which had experienced the earliest stirrings of the Protestant revival in the eighteenth century.[58] In Nîmes, the capital of French Protestantism at this time, the cahier of the clergy made no mention of the Protestants, none of the Edict of Toleration, and no plea that the monopoly of the Catholic Church to the privilege of public worship be safeguarded by the State. The absence of such demands made their cahier unusual, especially in view of the vigor of Protestantism in that region.[59] The cahier of the clergy of Montpellier was almost as temperate as that of Nîmes and certainly more moderate than the norm, for they asked nothing of the king with respect to the Protestants except that he give "attention to the Remonstrances of the last assembly of the clergy on the Edict of the non-Catholics, remonstrances as much in conformity with the rules of prudence as with the spirit of charity with which the Clergy will always be animated in their dealings with their separated brethren."[60]

To judge from the cahiers of the third estate, it does not appear that the Protestant communities were any more hostile to certain institutions of the Catholic Church than what might be considered normal for France at that time. Of the thirty parishes in the *sénéchaussée* of Nîmes which asked for an amelioration in the lot of the Protestants, seven asked for the abolition of the ecclesiastical tithes.[61] For these communities, this was above the percentage

[58] *Archives parlementaires,* 1st series, II, 562-565. Although their cahier began with the customary plea to His Majesty to "arrêter les progrès de l'irréligion et s'opposer au projet de l'établissement d'une tolérance universelle, et qu'à cet effet, il veuille bien réformer son édit de novembre 1787 . . . le tout conformément aux sages remontrances de la dernière assemblée du clergé de France," in the next breath they asked for the restitution of Protestant property: ". . . et le supplier de nouveau d'accorder aux successeurs naturels des anciens fugitifs [most of whom would still be Protestants] la mainlevée des biens qui sont encore en régie." Aside from Castres, the clergy of Cotentin were alone in asking that the Edict of 1787 be modified in a sense favorable to the Protestants. Cf. Mazoyer, "La question protestante . . . ," BPF, LXXX (1931), 46.

[59] Bligny-Bondurand, *op.cit.,* II, 573-579.

[60] *Archives parlementaires,* 1st series, IV, 44.

[61] Bligny-Bondurand, *op.cit.,* I, 92-94, 158, 164, 194, 357; II, 319, 442.

considered to be average for France as a whole,[62] but this does not necessarily indicate a more deeply rooted hostility to the Catholic Church. The inhabitants of Saint-Médier, for instance, in making this demand, explained that "since times immemorial" they had had neither priest nor church in their village; moreover they did not feel the need for either, because all the inhabitants were Protestants.[63] Under such circumstances the demand was certainly a reasonable one. As for the suppression of the religious orders, only two of the communities requested it.[64] Moreover, some Protestant communities did not hesitate to show their sympathy for the Catholic Church in various ways, Anduze, a sizable town, four-fifths of whose inhabitants were Protestants, asking that the *portions congrues* of the *curés* and vicars in the diocese be increased.[65]

The "vive émotion" created by the announcement of the impending States General gave all Frenchmen a higher cause toward which to direct their attentions. The atmosphere of expectancy and optimism, the fierce hope that better days were dawning, made

[62] Denys-Buirette, *op.cit.*, p. 238. After consulting 2,375 parish cahiers, the author found that 5 to 6 per cent demanded the suppression of the tithes.

[63] Bligny-Bondurand, *op.cit.*, II, 319.

[64] *ibid.*, II, 149, 216. Saint-Geniès de Malgoirès, a community of 264 hearths, made the demand as follows: "Il est dans le royaume différents ordres religieux absolument inutiles à l'Etat, et qui possèdent des richesses inappréciables. La suppressions de ces ordres serait pour l'Etat une ressource à ses besoins actuels. Elle l'empêcherait d'être privé, à l'avenir, de plusieurs citoyens utiles. Sa Majesté doit être suppliée de faire cette suppression." Saint-Bauzély, comprising only 45 hearths, did not prepare a cahier of its own, but instead adopted that of Saint-Geniès. Denys-Buirette, *op.cit.*, p. 349 estimated that roughly two per cent of the cahiers made such demands.

[65] Bligny-Bondurand, *op.cit.*, I, 43. J.-A. Blachon, in his *Recueil de discours ou fragmens de discours relatifs à diverses circonstances de l'Etat prononcés par J.-A. Blachon en sa qualité de pasteur de l'église réformée à Bordeaux, puis à Anduze* (Nîmes, 1804), p. 97, note 1, put the population of Anduze at 5,263, of whom 4,607 were Protestants. The solicitude of the latter for the lower clergy carried over into the realm of politics. At the general assembly of the three orders of the *viguerie* of Anduze in December, 1788—a meeting called to discuss the form of representation in the approaching States General—the representatives, preponderantly Protestant, resolved that the representation of the *curés* should be increased, describing the *curés* in their official resolution as that class of men "qui seule prend les hommes au berceau, les soutient, les aide et les console dans les événements fâcheux dont leur vie est parsemée, qui enfin les accompagne au tombeau, après avoir adouci et partagé l'horreur de leurs derniers moments. . . ." The same measure was adopted by the general assembly of Nîmes. Cf. Albert Durand, *Histoire religieuse du Département du Gard pendant la Révolution française* (Nîmes, 1918), pp. 11-18.

religious differences seem trifling and of little consequence. Expressions of an awareness of these differences were conspicuously lacking in the cahiers of all but the clergy, and the *tiers* of Chamborigaud (*sénéchaussée* of Nîmes) could note with obvious satisfaction "that happily harmony reigns in the nation and in general we no longer see that spirit of fanaticism which used to disunite our citizens by force of prejudices and the differences of [religious] sentiments. . . ."[66] In the primary assemblies which began meeting everywhere in France early in 1789, the Protestants seem to have been accepted as equals by their Catholic compatriots. The one exception was at Lyon, where a Catholic merchant, as much out of legal scruples it seems as out of religious bias (for the full extent of the civil rights of the Protestants still had not been clarified), penned off a pamphlet the argument of which was that the Edict of Toleration had not granted the full rights of citizenship to Protestants and, since they were still excluded from a number of public offices, they had no right to participate in the electoral assemblies or to be elected to the States General.[67] His argument, however, was immediately contested by his fellow Lyonnais without regard to religion and at least one Catholic was sufficiently unconvinced by the legality of his arguments to implore that "in these blessed days, it must not be our city—alone among all others—which sets the odious example of clinging to hideous memories of the past."[68] The dispute was brought to an abrupt end by the regulation of 24 January 1789 relating to the convocation of the States General, which set no religious qualifications for participation in the elections of deputies to the "grande et solennelle assemblée." The electoral assemblies proceeded to show that they felt no animus for their Protestant compatriots. In the *sénéchaussée* of Nîmes, in spite of opposition from the clergy, Rabaut Saint-Etienne was the

[66] Bligny-Bondurand, *op.cit.*, I, 222.

[67] See Armand Lods, "L'Attitude du clergé catholique à l'égard des protestants en 1789," *La Révolution française*, XXXIII (1897), 128-137. The clergy in their cahiers did not go as far as this. The one case where the matter was taken up—the cahier of the clergy of Saint-Paul (Paris, intra muros)—they demanded "que l'état civil des non catholiques soit favorisé; avec cette restriction néamoins que, dans aucun cas, ils ne puissent être admis dans les administrations municipales et de judicature, ni concourir que médiatement à la confection des lois qui intéressent les trois ordres, et qu'à cet effet ils soient électeurs et non-eligibles aux Etats généraux." *Archives parlementaires*, 1st series, v, 270.

[68] A. Lods, "L'Attitude du clergé . . . ," *La Révolution française*, XXXIII (1897), 132.

first of the deputies to be elected, and of seven additional representatives chosen there, five were Protestants.[69] Altogether, Protestants and Catholics joined in bestowing upon some twenty Protestants the honor of representing them in their first States General in 175 years.

In view of the reforms which the Protestants still thought were owed them, it is not surprising that they should have been enthusiastic in their reception of the Revolution. On 24 December 1789 the French National Assembly passed a law admitting Protestants to all degrees of the administration and to all civil and military offices, granting in effect the final completion of the Edict of Toleration with respect to their civil rights. A subsequent address of the non-Catholics of Montauban to the legislators of France, thanking them for their measure, is revealing for the light it throws on the psychology of the Protestant on the eve of that Revolution and of his attitude toward the *ancien régime*:

". . . Foreigners in a land which saw us born, proscribed by laws whose inconsistency was equalled only by their barbarity, we carried for more than a century, stamped on our foreheads, the sign of the most humiliating and least deserved of reprobations. In vain we gave our country our tender love; vainly we consecrated all our labors to its prosperity; . . . in vain did the experience of two centuries show that we aspired to nothing beyond the honor of being faithful subjects and peaceful citizens;—unnatural mother, our country treated us harshly. Crueler even than if she had torn us from her breast, she held us there only to steep us with afflictions, to make us savor, as it were, all the horror of the disgust with which she overwhelmed us.

[69] Cf. Charles-H. Pouthas, *Une famille de bourgeoisie française de Louis XIV à Napoléon* (Paris, 1934), p. 83, note 2. Shortly after the election of Rabaut Saint-Etienne, his father, Paul Rabaut, wrote to a friend in Geneva: "Monsieur, vous avez sans doute appris la députation de mon fils Saint-Etienne pour les Etats généraux. Elle se fit à la très grande pluralité, nonobstant les cabales, soit des gens d'affaires, soit du clergé; il y eut entre autres grand nombre de députés de la côte du Rhône, tous catholiques, qui votèrent pour lui. . . . Dans la plupart des provinces, on a député beaucoup plus de prêtres que d'évêques. L'évêque de Nîmes, et celui d'Uzès, qui désiraient tous les deux d'être nommés, ont leurré leurs prêtres en leur disant qu'attendu la réputation et l'éloquence de M. Saint-Etienne, la Religion catholique était en péril, et qu'il fallait nommer des hommes qui pussent leur faire tête, c'est-à-dire des évêques, et ils ont eu la faiblesse de les croire." See *La Révolution française,* xxxv (1898), 88-89.

". . . [Henceforth] our fidelity to the laws will only be equalled by our attachment to the sacred person [of our citizen king], and we shall strive to prove ever more by this means that this religion, our devotion to which was so long made a crime,—that this religion, if it is favorable to liberty, is at the same time the declared enemy of insubordination and license. Continue, *Nosseigneurs*, to work with ardor for the regeneration of our kingdom. . . ."[70]

Scarcely any other document better illustrates the tenor of Protestant thought in the opening stages of the Revolution—the Protestant awareness of the injustices with which the *ancien régime* had burdened them, "foreigners in their own homeland." Nothing could better explain the joy and hope created by the announcement that the king was about to call upon his people—all of them, without distinction to religious differences—to help in the regeneration of the kingdom. Giddy with expectancy, pastors mounted their pulpits and animated their flocks with sermons devoted to the dawning era. At La Rochelle, the pastor Dugas *fils* spoke to his congregation on the "sentiments which should actuate a good Frenchman and on the duties which he is called upon to fulfill in the present circumstances," basing his address on the passage from Romans which reads: "the night is far gone, the day is at hand. Let us then cast off the works of darkness and put on the armor of light."[71] At Montauban, Jeanbon Saint-André, preaching on the new liberty and the obligations which it imposed, appropriately took as his text the passage in Galatians: "for you were called to freedom brethren; only do not use your freedom as an opportunity for the flesh, but through love be servants of one another." In the Quercy, on the day that the bourgeois militia were called to take their oath, the pastor Fonfrède de Robert used the occasion to speak to them on the love of one's country.

In the synods of the Church, the same patriotic sentiments were given expression. The synod of Saintonge in April of 1789 instructed the pastors of its province to pray at every service for God's blessings and guidance for the legislators of France in dealing with the prob-

[70] François Galabert, "Les sentiments des Protestants au début de la Révolution; Adresse des non-catholiques de Montauban à l'Assemblée nationale," BPF, LI (1902), 151-157.

[71] For this and subsequent sermons cited, see Paul de Félice, *Sermons protestants prêchés en France de 1685 à 1795 . . .* (Paris, 1885), pp. 40-44.

lems of state.[72] The proceedings of the Synod of Bas-Languedoc (6 May 1790) noted that the "assembly began by the offering of ardent thanksgivings to the Supreme Being for the prosperity which an auspicious constitution of the kingdom promises to all Frenchmen." Thence all the members of the synod took the civic oath, "all swearing to be faithful to the Nation, to the Law, to the King, and to the Constitution decreed by the National Assembly and sanctioned by the king."[73] For the Protestant Church, the memory of the fall of the Bastille soon came to stand for something more than a civic holiday; it was officially declared a religious holiday which the faithful should commemorate by offering their thanks for the blessings which Divine Providence had showered upon them.[74]

At the same time a number of Protestants in the Midi distinguished themselves by their patriotic fervor. In the fall of 1788, in the midst of the pamphleteering campaign which everywhere in France stirred the emotions of the people, Rabaut Saint-Etienne plunged into the political fray with his *Considérations sur les intérêts du tiers état.* Beware, he cautioned the citizens of France, clearly seeing the basis of the conservative defense against radical reforms—beware of those who would defend the existing political order by appeals to the ancient constitution of the nation. Such laws, such a constitution if it exists, is not at all inviolable as they would have you believe. "The nation, assembled and consulted by its king with the object of regenerating the kingdom, has the perfect right of taking these laws and fundamental maxims under examination, laws which by themselves have prevented everyone from bringing about reforms." The people of France must not be duped by the arguments of those legists who defend the *status quo.* If at the whisper of the word "reform" they cry out in anguish at the attack upon a hallowed constitution, it is not the constitution they wish to defend, it is their privileges. France can never be remade if the people are to cringe before such selfish interests. Privilege must be uprooted. The only just and reasonable basis for laws is

[72] E. Hugues, *Synodes du Désert,* III, 591-592.

[73] *ibid.,* III, 603.

[74] Synod of Saintonge, 11-13 August 1791: "L'époque de notre liberté civile devant être pour tout bon Français un jour destiné à témoigner à l'Etre suprême notre reconnaissance, il a été arrêté que l'anniversaire du 14e juillet serait célébré dans nos églises par un service solennel." E. Hugues, *Synodes du Désert,* III, 640.

the maxim *salus populi, suprema lex esto*. And the people themselves must be the judge of what constitutes the common weal.

Who are the people? It would be better to ask, what is the third estate? Rabaut Saint-Etienne's answer was a bold challenge to the privileged orders of French society: "[The third estate] is the nation minus the clergy and the nobility. The clergy is not the nation; it is the clergy, that is to say, an assemblage of two hundred thousand nobles and commoners consecrated to the service of the altar or of religion. The nobility is not the nation, but only the decorated part of the nation. It is a certain number of Frenchmen to whom certain hereditary honors and prerogatives have been accorded. Remove by supposition the two hundred thousand clergy and you still have the nation. Remove by supposition all the nobles and you still have the nation; for a thousand nobles can be created in a day, as was done after the Crusades. But remove the twenty-four million Frenchmen who constitute the third estate and what will you have left? Nobles and clergy, but not the nation."

And finally the question which was uppermost in the minds of all politically minded Frenchmen at this time: how should, nay how *must*, the third estate be represented in the impending States General? Again, Rabaut Saint-Etienne warned, beware of appeals to tradition: "Do not open your books, there you will find all the contradictions [of the past]; do not consult the example of your ancestors, they had no principles at all and consequently they were debased; do not bother to ask what was done in the past, for you know very well that you were sacrificed. For guidance, consult nothing except your common sense . . . and natural law, the basis of all rights in all ages and climes." Then how shall the third estate be represented? "We have already supplied the answer; since there are diverse interests and diverse orders in our society, each order must send its deputies in proportion to its interests." Since the third estate is the nation, its representation should be preponderant, its representatives should be chosen from among their own number, and as for the means of choosing them, "there is only one: it is to elect them yourselves—every tax-payer is eligible, every tax-payer is an elector."

In the province of Guyenne, the same problems occupied the minds of an excited population. When the nobility of the province in collusion with the Parlement of Bordeaux tried to seize the initiative in the coming electoral campaigns by having the public reunions of the three orders approve their plan for the maintenance of the vote by order and unanimity of orders in the States General, it was another Protestant, Laffon de Ladébat, the leader of the liberal faction of the nobility, who sounded the alarm and led the defense of the interests of the *tiers.* The general assembly of the third estate, meeting in December of 1788, chose as the statement of its position on the electoral questions the pamphlet by Laffon de Ladébat entitled *Observations sur la représentation du tiers état* in which the author championed the cause of universal manhood suffrage, the vote by head, and the numerical preponderance of the third estate in the National Assembly. At the same time twelve commoners, among them the Protestant Jean-Paul Nairac, were sent to Versailles with Laffon's *Observations* as their *titre d'instruction* to request of the king and the ministry "a number of representatives for the third estate proportionate to the immense number of individuals which make it up . . . , chosen by that estate and taken from among its own numbers."[75]

The activity of the Protestants spilled over into the ensuing electoral assemblies, where they played an active and sometimes leading role. On 28 October 1788 the principal members of the landed middle class and the bourgeois notables of Uzès were summoned to the city hall by the sound of trumpets. When assembled, their president, Chambon Latour, first consul, mayor and governor of the city, a Protestant, told them the purpose of the meeting: "You all know that the paternal benevolence of the king . . . has summoned to his person the Notables in order to consult with them on the formation of the Assembly of the States General. They are going to decide our destiny, for their deliberations will almost certainly determine the influence of the third estate in this important Assembly. The slightest misunderstanding in the choice and in the number of representatives from this class of citizens will forever overwhelm it. For if the third estate is not represented by a number equal to the representatives of the other two orders combined, it will not be able to avoid succumbing to the influence and authority of the others; or if it does not enjoy the free choice of its own deputies, its

[75] Marcel Marion, "Un épisode du mouvement de 1789 à Bordeaux," *Revue d'histoire moderne et contemporaine,* III (1901-1902), 739-753.

interests will be compromised or sacrificed. . . ."[76] In this and in subsequent assemblies at Uzès, the Protestant Chambon along with the lawyer Voulland, his coreligionist, were the leaders of the liberal bourgeoisie in the struggle for the recognition of the interests of their class. Both were subsequently chosen as deputies to the States General. At Nîmes, enjoying the prestige won by his essay on the interests of the third estate, Rabaut Saint-Etienne was everywhere recognized in his *sénéchaussée* as the leading spokesman for the *tiers*. It was he who was entrusted with the drafting of the cahier of the third estate. At Montpellier the Cambons (father and son), the Protestant lawyer Allut, and the pastors Rabaut-Pomier (younger brother of Rabaut Saint-Etienne), and Soulier played an active role in the deliberations of the general assembly and preparation of the cahier there, with Allut and Cambon subsequently being elected as alternate deputies to the States General.[77] At Montauban it was again the Protestants who spoke the loudest in the general assembly and who had the most suggestions to make in the preparation of the cahier of the third estate.[78] In Poitou the doctor Gallot actively campaigned for the return of confiscated Protestant property and not only succeeded in having a demand to this effect incorporated in the cahier of the *tiers* but was himself chosen a deputy to the States General.[79]

Vocal in the electoral assemblies, the Protestants soon became powerful in the local governments. As news of the fall of the Bastille and the municipal revolution in Paris spread throughout the southern provinces of France in mid-July of 1789, in most cities the former municipal authorities were forced to share the exercise of local government with new institutions which sprang up and in many places simply took over the administration. As a coup on the part of the bourgeoisie to safeguard the Revolution, this meant in several cases the subordination or extinction of administrations dominated by Catholics by those with a heavy weighting of Protestants. At Bordeaux, a *commission des XC électeurs* seized power from the municipality, and of its members at least ten were Protestants promi-

[76] Marcel Fabre, "Les Assemblées préparatoires aux élections des députés aux Etats-Généraux de 1789, tenues à Uzès," *Revue du Midi*, 1910, 525-539, 634-643, 667-677.

[77] For the role of the Cambons, see Félix Bornarel, *Cambon et la Révolution française* (Paris, 1905), chapter 1.

[78] L. Lévy-Schneider, *Le Conventionnel Jeanbon Saint-André*, I, 53-56.

[79] L. Merle, "L'Edit de 1787 dans le Bas-Poitou," BPF, LXXXI (1932), 132-158.

nent in the city's business and commercial activities.[80] At Montauban, a "patriotic committee" was elected by a popular assembly to aid the regular authorities in maintaining order. Its president and half of its members were Protestants. By the beginning of August it had all but displaced the municipal authorities and was actively engaged in the enrollment of three battalions of national guardsmen. As the Catholic-Conservative elements in the city chose to boycott the guard, Montauban found itself in the fall of 1789 with a nominal army of 2,400 men, the vast majority of whom were Protestants, at the command of a patriotic committee likewise dominated by non-Catholics.[81]

At Nîmes, the same story unfolded itself. On 19 July 1789 the citizens of the three orders of the *sénéchaussée* of Nîmes, fearful of the possible consequences of the new developments in Paris, met with the officers of the municipality to take steps toward the formation of a national guard for the city. The *légion nîmoise,* as it was called, numbered 1,349 men organized into twenty-four companies. As was the case in Montauban, it was the Protestants of the city who rushed to fill the ranks; comprising the largest part of the middle class in the city, they could meet the expenses of equipping themselves for service in the guard. Among the commanding officers of the legion, the colonel, lieutenant-colonel, and aide-major were all Protestants, and the major, although a Catholic, was married to a Protestant. The non-Catholics likewise dominated the lower commissioned posts. To direct the activities of the guard, the popular assembly appointed a "permanent committee" (*conseil permanent*), taking five members of the local administration and adding to them twenty-one new persons of their choice along with the officers of the legion itself. This, too, became the preserve of the liberal bourgeoisie, eight of them Protestants. Gradually it absorbed the functions of the old municipality, becoming the principal source of authority in the area.[82]

[80] Alfred Leroux, *Les religionnaires de Bordeaux de 1685 à 1802* (Bordeaux, 1920), p. 292.

[81] L. Lévy-Schneider, *Le Conventionnel Jeanbon Saint-André,* I, 57-62; and François Galabert, "Le Club jacobin de Montauban . . . ," *Revue d'histoire moderne et contemporaine,* I (1899-1900), 131-133.

[82] Chas. Pouthas, *Une famille de bourgeoisie française,* pp. 84-85; Albert Durand, *Histoire religieuse du Département du Gard,* pp. 36-41; and François Rouvière, *Histoire de la Révolution française dans le Département du Gard* (Nîmes, 1887-1889), I, 53ff.

The Catholics of the Midi had no cause to be alarmed at these developments, for, while their political power in the area was reduced somewhat, this in no way constituted a threat to the free practice of their religion. Nor did they at first seem overly alarmed. Late in July, the Protestants and Catholics of Vauvert (diocese of Nîmes) joined in celebrating the fall of the Bastille with a solemn *Te Deum* at the Catholic church and then repaired to the Protestants' place of worship to participate together in further ceremonies under the direction of the pastor Vincent.[83] Harmony still reigned between the two sects. Carried along by the ground swell of the Revolution, the people of the area formed, as one contemporary pamphlet put it, "une seule famille."

However, the fraternity between the sects and between social classes was transitory. The horizon soon darkened with the stirrings of the first counter-revolutionary movements in the Midi which all too easily aroused nascent jealousies between Catholic and Protestant. Events in the city of Montauban were the first to dispel the tranquillity which had characterized the first stages of the Revolution. The source of the approaching troubles is not hard to find, for the social stratification in the city was such that a conservative counterstroke against the first victories of the Revolution was almost inevitable.

The population of Montauban numbered about 25,000. Its Protestant church, one of the largest and most vigorous in France at this time, counted close to 6,000 members who, in their day-to-day lives, all but monopolized the commercial and industrial activities of the area.[84] The Catholics, in addition to comprising the largest part of the working population of the city, included within their ranks an inordinately large number of civil and ecclesiastical functionaries, for Montauban had been the seat of an Intendancy, a *cour des aides*, a bishopric surrounded by a galaxy of four convents, five monasteries, two religious chapters, a seminary and a college, an *élection*, a *bu-*

[83] F. Rouvière, *op.cit.*, I, 51.

[84] For descriptions of the economic and social characteristics of Montauban on the eve of the outbreaks against the patriots, see L. Lévy-Schneider, *Le Conventionnel Jeanbon Saint-André*, I, 49-52; François Galabert, "Le Club jacobin de Montauban; Son rôle politique pendant la Constituante," *Revue d'histoire moderne et contemporaine*, I (1899-1900), 126-131; and the report of the deputy Pierre-Jacques Vieillard to the National Assembly, 22 July 1790, in the *Archives parlementaires*, 1st series, XVII, 273ff.

reau des finances, a *sénéchal-présidial*, a *juridiction consulaire*, the *prévôté*, two *bureaux de direction*, and a *bureau principal de recette*. The personnel of these administrations welcomed, as an opportunity for recapturing control of the government which had been wrested from them by bourgeois parvenus, the decree of the National Assembly (4 December 1789) which called for municipal elections to replace the impromptu committees which had spontaneously overthrown the local governments earlier in the year. Their bid for power was facilitated by an economic depression which had pushed a large number of Catholic workers out of employment, making them prone to suggestions that the patriotic committee was responsible for their distress. Enjoying as they did a large numerical superiority over the middle-class Protestant patriots, the Catholic and aristocratic elements in the city had no difficulty in completely recapturing control of the municipal government. The elections of 1 February 1790 brought to power a municipality composed entirely of conservatives, with the exception of only two patriots, one of whom was a Protestant.

Having expelled the bourgeoisie from the actual government of the city, the new administration looked with suspicion and envy at the still unbroken monopoly of the middle class in the national guard. Profiting from a peasant *jacquerie* which ravaged the area later in the month of February, the administration brought into being a corps of volunteers entirely composed of Catholics to assist the national guard in the suppression of the peasant unrest. But once tranquillity had been restored, the administration, rather than disbanding its corps, saw an opportunity for breaking the power of the bourgeois guard by filling its understaffed ranks with members of its Catholic corps. The project backfired, however, for the members of the guard, sensitive of their position and still nursing the wounds left from their electoral defeat, protested to the National Assembly in Paris the attempted dilution of their ranks. They were supported by the president of the Assembly, who, in a letter to the guard, assured them that the attempted incorporation of new units was contrary to the decrees of the National Assembly. Failing in their attempt to infiltrate the national guard, the municipality tried to curtail its power first by compelling its commander to surrender the keys to the city's arsenals and then refusing to allow the guard to carry through its plans for a federation with the guard units of the surrounding area, the guard of Bordeaux, and the regiment of Languedoc. Both of these actions the guard carried to the attention of the National Assembly and thereby succeeded in winning permission from the municipality for the projected federations. But the latter showed its unrelenting hostility to the guard by refusing to attend the ceremonies at which the civic oath was administered to the guardsmen, nor would it relinquish the keys to the arsenals. Moreover, the municipality returned to the plan of bringing into force armed units more to its liking by calling for volunteers for a fourth battalion of eight companies which was to be added to the three battalions which already existed. Again the members of the legally constituted guard protested against the measure to the National Assembly, and again the Assembly returned a verdict in their favor. Notwithstanding the formal disapproval of the Assembly, the municipality, acting on the pretense that the decision in Paris did not apply to Montauban, continued with its plans for the enrollment of the additional battalion. By the end of April 1790, the administration ordered the general staff of the guard to recognize the newly formed units and to admit their officers into the staff of the guard as a whole.

Imperceptibly at first, but steadily increasing, an ugly undercurrent of religious hatred was added to the social animosities generated through the contest for the control of Montauban's national guard. In Paris the ministry, failing to find a satisfactory solution to the financial problems of the State, had by the fall of 1789 turned its eyes to the vast properties and wealth of the Catholic Church as a possible solution to its dilemma. On 24 September 1789 the National Assembly heard the motion of Dupont de Nemours that the ecclesiastical revenues of the Church be appropriated by the State. Two weeks later, a member of the clergy itself, Talleyrand, much to the horror of most of the other ecclesiasts sitting in the Assembly, proposed that the Church consign one-third of its revenues to the State to ease the financial crisis. The debates over the property of the Church became increasingly intense. With dismay, ecclesiasts and ardent Catholics heard the Protestant deputy from Grenoble, Barnave, assure the Assembly that the "clergy exists only by virtue of the nation, and the nation can thus destroy it; the obvious significance of this principle is that the nation can withdraw from the hands of the clergy the property which has been set apart and given to them only for the benefit of the nation."[85] Three weeks later (2 November 1789) a motion by Talleyrand, amended by Mirabeau, put the property of the Church "at the disposal of the nation." With the property in their hands, it was only another step for the ministers to seek the solution of the nation's financial difficulties by realizing its value through its sale on the open market. While the debates turned in this direction, the question of the religious orders was presented to the Assembly by its ecclesiastical committee. Again the Church went down in defeat. The law of 13 February 1790 declared that the State no longer recognized the legality of religious vows; in fact it forbade them in the future, and all members of the regular clergy were declared free to quit their monasteries and return to civil life. In effect, since the orders could no longer recruit members, and those that remained cloistered were subject to the vicissitudes of public support, the orders in France had been abolished. But as a noted historian of the Revolution has pointed out, "the Catholic Church was the oldest institution in French society. It was older than the three Orders, older than the feudal system, older than the crown. In any contest of national loyalties, it might well carry the day. Custom and emotion are stronger springs of action than reason and the hope of change."[86]

The Protestant Midi was the first area in France to feel the backlash of "custom and emotion," for repercussions to these actions were immediately felt in the provinces of the south. At Montauban, as elsewhere, the clergy began to organize resistance. Striking out blindly at the supporters of the Revolution, they espied the Protestants of the city as an easy target and found it to their advantage to rekindle the fanaticism which had been all but forgotten. Incendiary handbills and pamphlets were circulated in profusion to arouse the masses against the Protestants. "When hard times," read one, "oblige a commercial house to send away its workers, it is the Huguenots who are responsible and who seek to starve to death their Catholic employees."[87] With misguided Catholics attributing the attack upon their Church to the foul machinations of Protestants, the news of the election of Rabaut Saint-Etienne

[85] Session of 13 October 1789, in the *Archives parlementaires*, 1st series, IX, 423.
[86] J. M. Thompson, *The French Revolution* (London, 1944), 2nd edition, p. 140.
[87] L. Lévy-Schneider, *Le Conventionnel Jeanbon Saint-André*, I, 62-63.

to the presidency of the National Assembly (March 16) created consternation in the city. In April, in obvious sympathy at the humiliating defeat of the motion by Dom Gerle before the National Assembly that the Catholic religion be recognized as the religion of the State and the only cult enjoying the rights of public worship, the ecclesiasts of Montauban circulated an invitation to the Catholics of the area to attend a meeting on the 23rd at the Church of the Cordeliers to prepare a petition to the king and the National Assembly demanding the recognition of their religion as that of the State, the conservation at Montauban of the religious orders and other institutions of the Church, and the suspension in Montauban of the decree of the Assembly for the taking of inventories of church property—a meeting which the leaders of the national guard denounced as having been almost entirely devoted to declamations against the Protestants. The meetings in the churches continued through the month of April, the clergy whipping their parishioners into a frenzy against the Protestants, whom they accused of being responsible for all their misfortunes. They ordered prayers of forty hours. A cloud of hate spread over the city. The smallest incident was all that was needed to bring the storm.

May 10 was the first day of Rogations; as was customary, the Catholics of Montauban assembled to witness the religious processions. For three days bread had been scarce. Hunger, fear, and hatred were engraved on the faces of the assembled populace. Under the fulminations of the clergy, the social and religious tensions in the city had reached the breaking point.

By a twist of ill-fortune, May 10 was also the day which the municipality had designated for taking the inventories of the five religious establishments slated for suppression. At eleven o'clock the first officials arrived at the appointed buildings only to find their entrances blocked by an immense throng of excited women, who verbally assailed them for their intentions. The officials, failing to moderate their antagonists, were forced to withdraw.

Shortly thereafter, a mob appeared before the residence of the commander of the national guard and threatened to set the torch to it. They were dispersed by the timely arrival of the mayor. Somehow the rumor spread that members of the guard had assembled at the *hôtel de ville*. Thence the mass of citizens swarmed, seizing on their way weapons stored in the arsenals. By midafternoon the building was surrounded by the mob, which demanded the dispersal of the guardsmen. Threats, altercations. A shot. Treason! cried the mob, and in an irresistible wave crushed their way into the building and hurled themselves upon the hapless men inside. Within moments, three of the guardsmen were brutally murdered, two mortally wounded. It seemed that nothing could save their fellows. At the last minute, the constabulary and the regiment of Languedoc arrived, separated the surviving 55 members of the guard from their assailants and escorted them to the sanctuary of the city prison.

That evening and the following days, the Protestant inhabitants of the city emigrated en masse to avoid the wrath of a hysterical population. The populace jealously guarded the imprisoned guardsmen, and several of their more fanatical members offered prices for the heads of the leading patriots. The pastor Jeanbon Saint-André, who until this time had remained aloof from the political issues of the city, was branded as the arch enemy of the people by virtue of his position as the nominal leader of the Protestant community. The municipality seemed helpless in its attempts to quiet the armed throngs. Efforts at restoring public order were of little consequence. In the ensuing days, Montauban hung precariously on the verge of unconcealed civil war. The most extreme reactionaries hoped to profit from the disorders to strike the first concerted blow of the counter-revolution. "Our spirits were inflamed," one of them later wrote unabashedly, "and we thought that we were called upon to give impetus to a movement which might have had favorable results for the monarchy. For this it was essential that the commanding general for the king in the city and province, M. le comte d'Esparbès, profit from the favorable dispositions of the people and the troops placed under his command, and that he place himself at the head of the movement. . . . A number of volunteers presented themselves as auxiliaries, and the regiment of Languedoc . . . would have been proud to have been the nucleus of the army of liberation."[88] With the patriots routed, the municipality at last realized its ambitions; its Catholic corps was incorporated into the national guard and its general staff was purged of members "suspected because of their religious senti-

[88] *ibid.*, I, 70.

ments."[89] Only the firmness of the Comte d'Esparbès kept the situation from getting entirely out of hand.

For the terrorized patriots who remained in the city, help was on the way. Notified of the riots, the municipality of Bordeaux dispatched its guard of 1,500 men to the town of Moissac on the outskirts of Montauban, where they were halted to await orders from the National Assembly. The latter, on 17 May, ordered all citizens in the city to don the national cockade and declared the non-Catholics of the city under the protection of the law. The Protestant fugitives were received in the neighboring towns. Toulouse, along with twenty other towns and municipalities in the area, offered to mediate in the interests of restoring peace. Not until the end of May, with the arrival of a representative of the king, was any semblance of order restored. Only then did it become safe to release the imprisoned members of the guard.

10 May in Montauban—no more than a small riot. It might scarcely have been noticed in a France where riots were already becoming endemic, but its significance was out of all proportion to its size. News of the riot spread to all corners of the kingdom. The Bordelais in a letter to the National Assembly reported apprehensively that "the most alarming news has thrown despair into the hearts of all good Frenchmen; it is your decrees which are being attacked; it is the Constitution which they are trying to overthrow. Good citizens have been the victims of their patriotism. Several have been massacred, others have been clapped into irons where they still suffer. It is Montauban where these scenes of horror have transpired."[90]

To the people of the Midi, the riot was more than an attempt upon the Constitution, more than a flouting of the decrees of the National Assembly. Catholics had turned on their Protestant brethren. Memories of Saint Bartholomew's were revived. A shiver of apprehension coursed through the patriots of Nîmes, for their city, too, had divided itself into two armed camps, each awaiting a trial of strength.

Throughout France, the inhabitants of the Midi are known best for their excitable and at times frenetic temperaments. Easily pro-

[89] Report of Vieillard to the National Assembly, paraphrasing a letter of the municipality to the same body: *Archives parlementaires,* 1st series, XVII, 283.

[90] *Réimpression de l'Ancien Moniteur,* 20 May 1790.

voked, passionately opinionated, they are a people to be handled with care and circumspection, for once aroused their wrath is terrible. Toward the end of 1789 and on into the following year, enemies of the Revolution worked on their kaleidoscopic dispositions with invidiously inflammatory tracts:

"I am not afraid of affirming that granting freedom of religion and admission to civil and military offices and honors to the Protestants is an evil which contains no real advantage for you, and none to the State, but much worse it exposes both to the worst of disasters. . . . The heresy of Calvin ceased to be contagious only when its public cult was forbidden and abolished. This prohibition stamped it with the shameful character of universal disapprobation, and the horror which it has inspired since then has been the only force which has contained it.

"Completely prohibit to them all freedom of cult; bar them from all military and civil honors. Let a powerful tribunal be established in Nîmes to supervise day and night the exact observance of these articles, and you will soon see them abandon Protestantism; they are too proud to suffer a state of humility for any length of time. . . .

"They ask to participate with you in the advantages which you enjoy; you will no sooner have allowed them to associate with you in their enjoyment than they will think only of despoiling you of them and soon will have succeeded; while you suffer them to be Protestants, they will never pardon you for being Catholics. . . .

"These are the people you have preferred to your brothers in the deputation to the States General. . . . Let them reestablish the Edict of Nantes and soon you shall see the renewal of all the calamities to which it put an end. For to believe that the Protestants are not the same as they have always been is to totally misunderstand them. Repellent vipers who in the present numbness of their forces are unable to injure you, warmed again by your kindnesses they will return to life only to put you to death. THESE ARE YOUR BORN ENEMIES. . . . Your fathers miraculously escaped their bloody hands; have not your fathers related the horrible excesses which they exercised against your forefathers? It was not enough for them to have merely killed your forebears; but in taking their lives they could be content only in subjecting them to the most unheard of torments. Such were the Protestants, thus are they still."[91]

[91] *Pierre Romain aux catholiques de Nismes,* quoted in F. Rouvière, *op.cit.,* I, 77-79.

The purpose of these writings needs no explanation; that they were distributed principally in Nîmes was due to its peculiar position in France at this time. In 1790 Nîmes was the tenth largest city in the nation, its population variously estimated at from 43,000 to 54,000 persons. Travelers were most impressed with its Roman antiquities: the amphitheatre, the Maison Carrée, the Temple to Diana nestled in a lovely glade on the edge of town, the baths and the pavements. But the more perceptive visitor could scarcely overlook its economic activity, for, as Arthur Young noted, "this is one of the most considerable manufacturing places in France. They make a great variety of stuffs, in silk, cotton and thread, but the first [silk] is the great manufacture."[92] What made Nîmes singular was the number and position of its Protestants. The Calvinists constituted one-third of the city's population. They were wealthy, for in their hands was a large part of the city's commerce and almost all its manufacturing. Alquier, speaking before the National Assembly, estimated that the Calvinists' economic activities provided the livelihood for 30,000 workers scattered about in an infinite number of workshops, both in the city and in the surrounding countryside.[93] The vast majority of these workers were Catholics. Hence Nîmes in large part was a city of Protestant employers and Catholic workers. Add to this the economic situation at this particular juncture—the Revolution had brought depression, precarious markets, unemployment—and we can see that the fomentors of sectarian discord had chosen a promising field for their operations.

The Maison des Capucins at Nîmes had been transformed into a citadel of hate; from it the press of the counter-revolution inundated the surrounding towns with a steady stream of libelous tracts—"Paul Romain à Pierre Romain," "Pierre Romain aux catholiques de Nismes," "Charles Sincère à Pierre Romain," "Adresse aux Languedociens," "Le comité des finances dévoilé," "La feuille des erreurs et de la vérité," "Aux soldats, par un soldat," "Avis important à la véritable armée françoise," "Les républiques fédératives," "François, réveillez-vous!" The religious harmony of 1789 was lost in a labyrinth of lies and calumnies. "At Nîmes the Protestants have formed a conspiracy to bankrupt the commercial

[92] Arthur Young, *Travels in France,* ed. Constantia Maxwell (Cambridge, England, 1929), p. 304.

[93] *Archives parlementaires,* 1st series, XXII, 304.

houses of the Catholics." "The Protestants have so thoroughly dominated the *bureau de police* that Catholics are always condemned without examination." "Every winter, rather than distributing the work that has to be done to the silk workers of the city, the Protestant patrons give it instead to their coreligionists of the Vaunage." "The Catholics would indeed become the slaves of the Protestants if the government were to grant the freedom of cult to these fanatical republicans." "At the time of the naming of the deputies of Nîmes to the States General, there were no intrigues, no manoeuvres, no pecuniary sacrifices which the Protestants did not employ in order that all the deputies should be chosen from amongst themselves."[94]

In an atmosphere charged with anxiety, the citizens of the city prepared for the election of the municipality which was to replace the revolutionary government established in July 1789. As at Montauban, the Catholics saw in the elections an opportunity for breaking the power of the middle class as exercised through the permanent committee of the guard. The clergy itself took the lead in preparing the conservative counter-stroke. The abbé Clemenceau, at the head of a group of zealots, prepared lists of Catholic candidates, saw to their distribution among the Catholic workers of the area, and promised the latter remuneration for the time they lost in the process of voting. In meetings preparatory to the actual elections, the more moderate Catholics attempted to reach some sort of a compromise with the patriot group on the final list of candidates to be submitted to the electorate. The Catholics were willing to lend their support to a list giving the Calvinists one-third of the positions in the municipality, but the latter, conscious of their social and economic position in the city, demanded one-half the posts and tried to impose their candidate, a Catholic of liberal sympathies, as the mayoralty candidate. No middle ground could be found between the two positions, and the decision was referred to the choice of the people.

The elections brought the Protestant patriot party a crushing defeat; of seventeen municipal officers, only four were Protestants.[95] The Protestant candidate for mayor lost to the baron de Margue-

[94] *Charles Sincère à Pierre Romain* (Nîmes, 22 November 1789), 22 pp.

[95] Only three members of the former permanent committee were elected to positions in the administration. Cf. Chas. Pouthas, *Une famille de bourgeoisie française*, pp. 91-92.

rittes, hitherto a deputy of the nobility to the States General and first consul of the city, a man noted for his patriotism and probity despite the questionable motives of many of his supporters.

Repudiated at the polls, the members of the former government hastened to safeguard their position and that of the revolutionary cause by founding the Société des Amis de la Constitution, drawing their membership from the middle class of the city, the list of defeated candidates, and meeting under the presidency of their defeated candidate for the mayoralty. The composition of the club clearly reflected the way in which the lines were being drawn for the approaching contest for power. Of its 419 members, 355 were Protestants and one a Jew.[96] Following the same pattern as at Montauban, the issue between the municipality and the club was soon joined over the question of the national guard—the *légion nîmoise*.

The Protestant bourgeois control of the guard had already been weakened. In October of 1789, the Catholics, aroused by the religious debates in the National Assembly, had formed five new companies of their own and had obliged the permanent committee of the guard to admit them to the ranks. The new units, nominally under the direction of the permanent committee, actually looked for leadership to one François Froment, a zealous Catholic passionately devoted to the cause of the monarchy. Froment introduced a third element into the clash of political factions. He was violently opposed not only to the middle-class Protestants who had exercised control of the government since July 1789, but likewise totally unsympathetic to the endeavors of the new mayor, the baron de Marguerittes, to avoid a show of force in the city between the Catholic and Protestant camps.

Froment's antipathy for the liberal cause was both political and personal in nature. His father, a clerk in the *hôtel de ville* under the old regime, had been denounced to the *Cour des Aides* by Protestant merchants of the city for falsifying certain records. Writs of arrest had been issued, but Froment *père* had fled to Avignon, where he lived for five years, at the end of which time he had succeeded in clearing himself with the courts.[97] The matter might have ended

[96] The figures are given by A. Durand, *Histoire religieuse du Département du Gard*, p. 57.

[97] *ibid.*, 49-51.

there, but the son, François, continued to nurse a burning hatred of those who had sullied the name of his family. Thus his motives in creating an armed camp in the city were partly those of revenge against the Protestant community, but this in itself had by now become connected with a political cause. His ambitions, as he was to describe them years later under the Restoration, were as follows:

"Faithful to my religion and to my king, revolted by the seditious ideas which were being propagated from all sides, it is easy to see why I sought to spread the spirit with which I was animated. In the course of 1789 I published several writings [viz. those under the pseudonyms of 'Pierre Romain,' 'Charles Sincère,' etc.] in which I revealed the dangers with which the throne and the altar were menaced. My compatriots, struck with the justice of my observations, manifested the most ardent zeal for reestablishing the king in the exercise of his rights. Hoping to take advantage of these favorable dispositions, and judging it too dangerous to have recourse to the ministers of Louis XVI, watched as they were by the conspirators, I journeyed to Turin in January of 1790 to solicit the approval and support of the princes of France. In a council which was held upon my arrival, I demonstrated to them that, if they wished to arm partisans of the altar and the throne, and to advance at one and the same time the interests of [the Catholic] religion and those of royalty, it would be easy enough to save both the one and the other. . . . The real persuasion of the revolutionaries being force, I perceived that the real answer to them was force; for then, as now, I was convinced of this great truth, that one cannot stifle a strong passion except with a still stronger one, and that religious zeal alone could throttle the republican delirium. . . .The princes, assured of the truth of my report and of the reality of my means, promised me the arms and munitions necessary for containing the factious elements, and Monsieur the comte d'Artois gave me letters of recommendation to the leaders of the nobility of Haut-Languedoc so that I could concert my acts with theirs. . . . Returning to Languedoc (February 1790) I hastened to visit the principal cities of the province so as to confer with the correspondents of M. the comte d'Artois, the most influential royalists and several members of the estates and the parlement. Once having prepared a general plan of operations. . . , I returned to Nîmes where, awaiting the help promised me from Turin, I devoted myself to supporting and exciting the zeal of the inhabitants."[98]

How much of this tale of intrigue and conspiracy is worthy of credence is difficult to ascertain. However, Froment's authorship of the inflammatory pamphlets is generally accepted, and there is good reason to believe that he actually was in the employ of the comte d'Artois.[99] In any case, his actions in the ensuing events certainly gave weight to his claims.

The laws on the municipal reorganizations had stipulated that with the new elections the existing "permanent" committees in charge of the national guard should be dissolved and replaced. However, when the new administration in Nîmes took steps in this direction, the members of the permanent committee, with vigorous support from the patriotic club, protested the proposed action and refused to obey the directives of the administration until the National Assembly itself confirmed its actions. In the consequent confusion, the patriots and the followers of Froment entered into a contest for control of the regiment of Guyenne which was garrisoned in the city. With bribes and all manner of persuasions, they had within a few weeks totally undermined the discipline and reliability of the unit. The municipality was left stranded with no means of enforcing its decisions, and indeed no means of maintaining order—the troops of the Crown had been totally corrupted by one or the other of the extremist factions, the guard was insubordinate and looking to the club for direction, and the Catholic units, now increased to twelve companies, followed the lead of Froment.

[98] François Froment, *Recueil de divers écrits relatifs à la révolution* (Paris, 1815) quoted in P.-J. Lauze de Péret, *Eclaircissemens historiques en réponse aux calomnies dont les Protestans du Gard sont l'objet*; *et précis des agitations et des troubles de ce Département depuis 1790 jusqu'à nos jours* (Paris, 1818), II, 196-198.

[99] A. Durand accepts Froment's own word that he was an agent of the comte d'Artois and calls attention to the memoirs of one Général de Maleyssie, who, in referring to Froment in connection with a later mission, noted parenthetically that Froment had earlier been "employé par les princes dans les cours du Midi. . . ." Cf. Durand, *Histoire religieuse du Département du Gard*, p. 53, note 1. In reporting on the insurrection to the National Assembly, the deputy Alquier, while not specifically tying Froment to the conspiracy of the princes, called attention to the fact that "le sieur François Froment avait même fait . . . des dépenses très considérables, qui parurent disproportionnées à sa fortune; il acheta une très grand quantité de sabres, de baudriers et de fusils, et on fut frappé à Nîmes de l'affection qu'il mit à donner à ses volontaires des habits verts doublés de rouge, quoique le bleu et le blanc fussent les couleurs uniformes de la légion." *Archives parlementaires*, 1st series, XXIII, 311.

While the contest for control of the armed units in the area was being waged, the fears of the clergy and of devout Catholics for the safety of their religion were not allowed to subside. The legislation of the National Assembly, the first steps toward the confiscation of the property of the Church, the machinations of persons like Froment tended to convince a sizable part of the population that the altar was indeed under attack. On 20 April 1790 the Catholics of Nîmes met in the church of the Pénitents Blancs. After adopting a resolution that the patriotic club of the city be closed because of the fermentation which it created, they prepared a petition to the king and the Assembly protesting the impending confiscations. This much of the petition was largely the same as that at Montauban evoked by the failure of the motion of Dom Gerle. But the Nîmois went beyond a simple declaration of attachment to the Catholic Church and decried the restrictions put on the authority of the king. "Considering that . . . royal authority has been absolutely null since the sojourn of the king at Paris, and that this nullity has been the principal cause of all our troubles and of the anarchy which reigns in the kingdom . . . the Catholic citizens of Nîmes have unanimously decided to ask . . . that the National Assembly be supplicated to use all its authority to render to the king the executive power in all its scope, in conformity with its decree of 23 September last saying that the *supreme executive power shall reside exclusively in the hands of the king*."[100] The extremists of the right had succeeded in tying the attack upon the Church with a supposed subversion of the throne. Froment's plans for forwarding equally the interests of the altar and the throne were succeeding.

Joined to a letter bearing the signatures of well over 3,000 Catholics of Nîmes, the petition of 20 April was circularized throughout the south and then forwarded to the National Assembly. The latter, recognizing what the consequences of such a petition could be, declared (23 May) the signatories of the petition enemies of the public welfare and threatened them with the reproof of the king. The authors of the petition, Froment among others, chose to interpret the admonition as further proof of the king's enslavement and, meeting again, prepared another petition for circularization in which they readhered to the principles enunciated in their earlier address.[101]

[100] The full text of their petition is given in A. Durand, *op.cit.*, 65-67.
[101] *ibid.*, 89-90.

During this same period, the tension between the various armed groups in the city mounted. Froment's irregulars, dubbed *Cébets* (onion-eaters) by the patriots in derision of their lowly origins, had distinguished themselves from the patriots of the guard by wearing white cockades. Taking this as a sign of rebellion, the Club of Nîmes had petitioned the municipality in protest against the distinctive badges. But before the municipality took measures to suppress their use, disturbances broke out in the city which almost led to open armed conflict. On 1 May, hoping to exploit the disquietude of the Catholics over the presumed threat to their religion, the *Cébets* under the promptings of Froment commenced demonstrations before the city hall, filling the air with cries of "Vive le roi! Vive la croix! A bas la nation!" Their festivities continued on into the next day, when members of the regiment of Guyenne, most of whom had been won over to the patriots' cause, fell upon a group of the irregulars and forcibly separated them from their white cockades. Other members of the *Cébets* arrived and joined in the defense of their comrades. The mayor intervened in time to avoid a serious clash between the two groups. But the people, easily inflamed, continued for the next two days to vent their scorn on the regiment of Guyenne and upon occasional Protestants encountered in the streets. On 4 May the situation seemed out of hand. But with the declaration of martial law, the disturbances ceased as quickly as they had begun and turned into a demonstration of patriotic loyalty to the Revolution, with citizens and soldiers embracing one another, joining in the dancing of farandoles in the streets, and conducting mass celebrations lasting well into the night.

For the moment, peace was restored. But the concord between the antagonistic factions was at best superficial. The commander of the troops stationed in Languedoc, though mistaken as to the nature of the discord, was prophetic in his anticipation of what was to come. "This province is far from being tranquil," he wrote to the Minister of War. "Although there is an apparent calm, the cruelest sort of religious war can break out at any moment. All the cities and towns are divided into two camps according to religions. There have been meetings and assemblies on both sides. . . . Each courts the sympathy of the troops—that is of the non-commissioned officers and the soldiers. Another group of totally unscrupulous men who desire disorder, under the guise of patriotism, are trying to persuade the soldiers that they are free and seek to break down their discipline."[102]

The differences between the municipality and the patriots widened. Hoping to turn the demonstrations of 1-4 May to their own advantage, the members of the club denounced the baron de Marguerittes to the National Assembly, accusing him of negligence in office and of refusing to take measures which might have avoided the disturbances. The mayor was called before the bar of the Assembly to answer the accusations and successfully cleared himself of responsibility. But when he returned to Nîmes he found the patriots as adamant as ever in opposing attempts to replace the permanent committee with a newly elected staff for the *légion nîmoise*. Turning to the *Cébets*, the administration succeeded in forcing the abandonment of the white cockades. But the Catholics countered by adopting a uniform of green coats with red pompons, making themselves more conspicuously different than ever from the regular guard.

In the first week of June, activity on all sides quickened with the commencement of assemblies for the election of the administration of the Department. Two of the electors were insulted by *Cébets*, and to avoid further incidents of this sort the king's commissioners put the meetings under the protection of the regiment of Guyenne and the dragoons of the guard. Antagonized by the Protestant patrols, the Catholics made preparations for a derisory demonstration against them with patrols of *Cébets* mounted on she-asses. Warned of their intentions, the city officials succeeded in dissuading them only at the price of withdrawing the patrol of the guards. In the midst of the unrest, the electoral assembly continued with its deliberations. It became obvious that by virtue of the indirect elections the Protestants were winning control of the departmental administration. Not content with an electoral victory, members of the club attending the meetings demanded that the Catholic signatories of the declaration of 20 April be outlawed as traitors. Tensions mounted. The people became apprehensive.

On the evening of 13 June, a *Cébet* appeared at the bishop's palace where several legionnaires were stationed and demanded that the building be cleared. The porter refused entry to the emissary. Fifteen minutes later the *Cébet* reappeared at the palace with two companions

[102] Letter of M. de Boujols to the Minister of War, 10 May 1790, quoted in A. Durand, *op.cit.*, 81-82.

and delivered a note threatening the doorkeeper with death if he allowed any more legionnaires to enter the building. The *Cébet* was immediately arrested and taken inside. His companions spread the news. Shortly a throng of Catholic volunteers surrounded the building, hurled stones at the post of the legionnaires, and demanded the release of the prisoner. The crowd swelled; more and more stones were thrown at the besieged legionnaires. Unnerved by the demonstration, the legionnaires fired into the host of *Cébets,* killing and wounding several of their number. Falling back, the *Cébets* fled through the city streets, spreading the alarm to their comrades.

Efforts by members of the municipality to intercede were fruitless. Blood had been spilled and in the heat of battle neither side would listen to reason. There was no recourse but to declare martial law. But, as they carried the red flag through the streets at the head of a group of citizens, the officials were jostled by angry crowds of Catholics, fired upon by hidden snipers, and finally dispersed. Nightfall brought a temporary respite. Urgent messages from both sides were sent out into the countryside calling for reinforcements.

At dawn the following day reinforcements began to arrive. Perhaps no one whose ancestors have not endured the nightmares of religious war can envisage the fear and consternation the arrival of the Protestant peasantry brought to the Catholics of Nîmes. A faint reflection of the terror of the inhabitants at their descent from the mountains is in the description of the event written a century later. "It was four o'clock in the morning when the first battalions of these violent children of the Cévennes, steeped in Calvinistic fanaticism, aroused and envenomed with ancient resentments, arrived in Nîmes as if in a conquered city. Some wearing tricorns decorated with pompons, but most with wide-brimmed hats ornamented with tricolors which shaded their tanned skin and gaunt features from the sun, they were clad in cloth coats or linen tunics over which they had passed yellow baldrics holding regimental sabers and were armed with muskets, ancient pistols, scythes, and pitchforks. . . . Hundreds at their departure, they had recruited the companies of the towns through which they had passed. Appearing at Nîmes with the first rays of the sun, they were 12,000 strong. And their ranks grew larger still with loiterers and laggards. Among them were women pushing before them asses and mules saddled with 'banastos,' huge baskets to carry away the pillage of the day, for they had been promised the booty from the homes of the Catholics. This was the invasion of barbarians."[103]

Throughout the morning of the 14th these guardsmen of the environs arrived in ever-increasing numbers and took up positions within the city. Froment, on his part, sent an urgent message for help to the commander of the troops at Montpellier, but the missive was intercepted by the guard of Uchau. Cut off from outside help and with the larger part of his irregulars scattered through the city in confusion, he and three of his companies of *Cébets* hastily fortified themselves in a tower of the city walls.

Meanwhile a group of legionnaires, searching for caches of arms and hidden irregulars, entered the convent of the Capuchins. Finding nothing, they withdrew and took up stations outside the building. The morning passed without mishap. But shortly after noon a shot was fired, killing one of the legionnaires stationed outside the convent. The identity of the assassin will never be known. But the legionnaires saw no one in the vicinity and assumed that the shot could have been fired only from the Capuchin convent. Gathering their arms, they burst into the building to fetch out their hidden assailant. Inside, five Capuchins who had not succeeded in escaping were pitilessly massacred, along with three lay assistants. Aroused in a fury of revenge, the legionnaires sacked the building and poured forth to vent their rage on the *Cébets* besieged in the tower of the walls. Although hopelessly outnumbered, Froment saw that he could expect no mercy of the furious patriots. He refused entreaties to capitulate. Violent fighting ensued. The assault on the tower finally began late in the afternoon under a covering fire from six cannon which had been pulled into position. A breach in the walls opened the fortress to the army of legionnaires. The defenders, as many as could, fled across the rooftops into hiding. Their unfortunate comrades who were trapped inside were cut to pieces by the mob. Froment was among those to save himself, but his brother perished with a number of others in the tower. Spreading out in search of the *Cébets*, the legionnaires spilled into the adjacent Jacobin convent, destroying everything in sight. In the adjoining college, three fugitives were discovered and put to death on the spot. Throughout the night and into the morning of the 15th the *Cébets*

[103] Ernest Daudet, *Histoires des conspirations royalistes du Midi sous la Révolution* (Paris, 1881), pp. 19-20.

were hunted remorselessly through the city. By now the patriots were 15,000 strong and poured from one building to the next in search of their enemies, pillaging, burning, destroying. Toward evening the national guard of Montpellier arrived and set about calming the excited partisans. After three days of battle, their fury spent, the legionnaires were persuaded to give up their manhunts. The carnage subsided. The city had all the appearances of a town taken by storm. Three hundred persons had perished, almost all of them Catholics;[104] 120 houses had been destroyed. The Catholic irregulars had all been disarmed; their leaders had fled. Some 1,200 terrified Catholic families precipitously quit the city to avoid the general massacre they felt was imminent. The prisons of the city overflowed with Catholic prisoners.

Yet on the morrow of the riot, the passionate fury of the patriots of Nîmes gave way to a deep sense of remorse and contrition at the anarchy which had been unleashed. Above all else, the victors sought to remove any suggestion of religious animosities in the bloody demonstrations—to paint them instead as an incident where the real issue was totally independent of any sectarian hatreds, and as a struggle for power between enemies and defenders of the Revolution. This was the gist of a joint proclamation of 17 June issued by the electoral assembly and the municipal government. Within a week of the riots, the members of the Club of Nîmes attempted to demonstrate their religious impartiality by inviting the abbé Castan de la Courtade to speak before their assembly. The abbé, after roundly denouncing the perpetrators of the disturbances—"des furieux séduits par l'éclat de l'or et par les promesses des ennemis de la révolution"—rose to the occasion with an impassioned plea for fraternity: "Children of the same God, citizens of the same country, let us all have the same sentiments, since we all share the same interests. Let us reunite our wills and our hearts; let us love one another and live as brothers. Let friendship serve as a salutary balm to heal the wounds of the soul. If we were to try, we could live together so happily!—for while we were slaves, now we are free; where we were ruled by a despot, now we are governed

[104] According to the testimony of the baron de Marguerittes before the National Assembly (23 February 1791), the number of victims exceeded 300; only 21 were Protestants, "dont 7 ont été assassinés, hors des murs, par des étrangers cruellement égarés." *Archives parlementaires*, 1st series, XXIII, 484.

by a king."[105] In pamphlets the patriots retold the story of 13-15 June, minimizing the devastation, denouncing the conspiracies of the counter-revolutionaries.[106] The newly elected directory of the Department joined in the campaign in an address to its constituents, producing signed affidavits of Capuchin monks attesting to the proper conduct of the Protestant legionnaires, of ecclesiasts who vouchsafed that they had been given sanctuary and sustenance by a Protestant inhabitant of the city.[107]

In the following month, the anniversary of the fall of the Bastille provided the patriots with the opportunity of demonstrating that the religious elements of the disturbances were all but forgotten, of suggesting that they had even been of very little consequence. At Sommières the mayor's peroration was followed by a *Te Deum* sung first in the Catholic manner and then in the Protestant. At Saint-Jean-de-Gardonnenque the ceremonies in the public square were followed by a procession led by the Protestant pastor to the Catholic church to listen to a *Te Deum*, after which the celebrators trooped to the Protestant temple to listen to a service delivered by the pastor in the presence of the *curé* and his vicars. Similar demonstrations of intersectarian harmony were unfolded at Montauban, Vauvert, and Moussac. At Nîmes, the abbé Clemenceau, who had worked so assiduously earlier in the year to insure a Catholic victory in the municipal elections, urged the citizens to avoid any discussions of religious differences; in the city which had just emerged from the throes of civil war, the demonstrations of concord and devotion

105 *Discours prononcé le 20 juin 1790, devant la Société des amis de la Constitution, établie dans la ville des Nismes, par M. l'abbé Castan de la Courtade, Aumonier de la Légion de Béziers, Membre de l'Assemblée électorale au Département de l'Herault* . . . (s.l.n.d.), 16 pp.

106 See for instance the *Lettre d'un patriote volontaire dans la garde nationale de Nismes, sur les troubles de Nismes* (s.l.n.d.), 32 pp., where the author identified the source of the trouble as an aristocratic plot to disrupt the electoral assemblies meeting in the Department: "Vendus à l'aristocratie, ces hommes cherchoient chaque jour de nouveaux prétextes, pour ne faire envisager dans les bons citoyens que des non-Catholiques, et déchirer la Patrie avec le fer du fanatisme."

107 "Protestants et Jacobins. Adresse du Directoire du département du Gard, à ses commettants," BPF, XLV (1896), 544-549. Two of the Capuchins signed affidavits stating that the company of legionnaires which entered their convent "s'est comportée avec beaucoup de décence et d'honnêteté. J'atteste aussi, que quoique j'aie cru cette compagnie toute composée de protestans, je n'ai que des éloges à lui donner."

to the Revolution continued with scant interruption for three days and nights.[108] At the invitation of the municipality of Uzès, a Catholic town a few miles to the north of Nîmes, 246 delegates from all over the Department met on 25 July in the church of the Capuchins to join in an oath solemnly swearing to see in their fellow citizens nothing but friends and brothers regardless of individual differences in religious opinions.[109]

Sheer hypocrisy, many Catholic historians would observe. But such demonstrations of repentance were absolutely necessary in a Department where one in six of the inhabitants was Protestant. Only by such means and continuous vigilance on the part of the authorities could further violence be avoided. The enemies of the Revolution, although routed at Nîmes, did not waste a minute in continuing their subversive movements. Anonymous handbills told of Protestant plots to soak the countryside with the blood of Catholics.

In Paris the reports of the deputies Vieillard and Alquier to the National Assembly on the troubles at Montauban and Nîmes were designed to minimize the religious element in the disturbances and to stamp them instead as attempts upon the constitution by conspirators like Froment in league with intractable priests. Rabaut Saint-Etienne did the same both before the Assembly and in inspired articles in the *Moniteur*.[110] Such was the interpretation of the events at Nîmes by another Protestant deputy to the Assembly, Quatrefages de Laroquete. Prior to the actual outbreak, in a correspondence where privacy may have lent itself to candor, he warned the commander of the Legion of Vigan (who was both his friend and relative and a man of Protestant background) that enemies of the new regime were putting sectarian differences to scandalous use. "Such were the pretexts of the ambitious in the days of our fathers; such would

[108] Cf. F. Rouvière, *op.cit.*, I, 205-210.

[109] *ibid.*, I, 214-215.

[110] Session of 24 February 1791, in the *Archives parlementaires*, 1st series, XXIII, 503-504. Speaking of the invasion of guards from the surrounding countryside, Rabaut Saint-Etienne remarked: "Dans l'insurrection du 13 juin, dont l'objet était de dissiper le corps électoral et d'empêcher la formation des départements, les gardes nationales accoururent à Nîmes au secours de leurs électeurs, dont quelques-uns catholiques avaient été blessés ou menacés. Ces généreux citoyens étaient mixtes; des curés se mirent eux-mêmes à la tête des bandes courageuses, et les conduisirent eux-mêmes dans notre infortunée cité. Si des gardes nationales ont exercé des vengeances sur les ligueurs, ce sont des gardes nationales toujours mixtes, les patriotes du pays usant de répresailles contre les antipatriotes."

they be now with the malicious [even though] today people are too enlightened not to know that the two religions are the same, [especially in those particulars] which order one's behavior. . . ." In the interests of the Revolution and the preservation of local peace, he urged the commander to cooperate with the newly elected Catholic municipality of Nîmes.[111] In the following months, as the tension at Nîmes mounted and culminated in the rioting of June, he consistently held to the belief that the instigators of the rising had fanned religious differences only in order to bring about a restoration of the old political and social order. Anxious to give evidence of his own religious impartiality, and perhaps to set an example for both his Protestant and Catholic constituents, he refused to associate himself with the majority in the National Assembly when it voted to strip all signatories of the Catholic petition of April 1790 of their civic rights.[112]

There is more basis in fact to this interpretation of the discord than most historians have been willing to admit. In both Montauban and Nîmes it was the social and economic positions of the Protestants which made them the objects of abuse on the part of the populace. Religion—or, more accurately, the difference in religion between the middle class on the one hand and the aristocracy and working population on the other—was not the motive force of the riots. The insurrections were the first manifestations of the counter-revolution, led by implacable enemies of a government which would infringe upon the rights and privileges of the Church and the nobility. Had the bourgeoisie of the Midi been entirely Catholic, the attempted subversions of the revolutionary cause would almost certainly have been made against them all the same. Religious differences, not a prime cause, were no more than a force unscrupulously exploited by some of the clergy and the unbending defenders of the *ancien régime* to intensify and facilitate their attack upon the victories of 1789. It should not be forgotten that the Protestant fugitives of Montauban were hospitably received in a predominantly Catholic Toulouse, or that the Catholic émigrés of Nîmes were given succour in the Protestant towns of Gard; that

[111] François Rouvière, *Quatrefages de Laroquete, Constituant du Gard. Etude biographique pour servir à l'histoire de la Révolution française* (Paris, 1886), pp. 26-27.

[112] *ibid.*, pp. 28-31, 33-35.

among the guardsmen who perished at Montauban were Catholics, or that *curés* from the countryside were observed at the head of the "Protestant battalions" which descended the Cévennes to "butcher the Catholics" of Nîmes.[113] In other communities with mixed populations in the same area which were spared the intrigues of the conspirators, the month of June passed with no visible counterparts to the sectarian violence of Nîmes.[114] Moreover, not all Protestants were inextricably bound to the cause of the Revolution. We have only to cite the testimony of the marquis Henri-Philippe de Ségur, a Protestant who later emigrated to serve in the armies of the princes of France, to prove that in a province wracked with "religious war" there were Protestants who remained loyal to the Catholic-royalist cause and who were peculiarly indifferent to the sufferings of their coreligionists. "I was serving," wrote the marquis, "in a unit almost entirely composed of Protestants from the Cévennes and Languedoc, and the Jacobins never succeeded, despite all the means

[113] E. Daudet, *op.cit.*, pp. 19-20, says of course that they were forced to march at the head of the "Protestant" columns. The defenders of the Protestants insisted that they were there as voluntary participants in the pro-revolutionary movement. See, for instance, the *Discours prononcé devant la Société des amis de la Constitution par M. l'abbé Castan de la Courtade*, the address of Rabaut Saint-Etienne to the National Assembly cited earlier in footnote 110, and the "Adresse du Directoire du département du Gard," also cited earlier, where the administrators maintained that the legions which came to the rescue of the patriots were "indifférement composées de catholiques et de protestans" and led by *curés.*

[114] For example, the report of 24 June 1790 from Saint-Hippolyte-du-Gard in the *Réimpression de l'Ancien Moniteur.* "Tandis que des opinions religieuses divisent nos voisins, que des scènes sanglantes jettent l'alarme dans plusieurs villes, la nôtre donne l'exemple d'une modération et d'une confraternité qui entretient la paix, qui n'y a pas été troublée un instant depuis l'époque de la révolution. Les protestants forment la majorité des soldats de la garde nationale de Saint-Hippolyte. . . : ils on fait, à la procession de la Fête-Dieu, le service ordinaire des troupes réglées, et se sont conduits avec le respect que doit inspirer toute cérémonie religieuse; les catholiques ont voulu donner aux protestants les mêmes preuves de fraternité. La légion nationale a pris les armes le dimanche 6 juin, et, précédée de sa musique, elle s'est rendue, le drapeau déployé, à l'assemblée des protestants. Le ministre (M. Martin), dans un discours, a témoigné à son auditoire la satisfaction qu'il éprouvait de voir réunis des frères longtemps divisés par leurs opinions religieuses, qui savaient enfin se respecter et se chérir mutuellement. Tout le cortége militaire reçut la bénédiction du ministre, et se retira dans le plus grand ordre. Le soir, le même cortége accompagna la procession, et se rendit ensuit à l'église paroissiale, où le curé (M. Cavalier) développa dans la chaire les mêmes principes qui avaient dicté le discours de M. Martin." These demonstrations of fraternity transpired after the opening of the electoral assembly at Nîmes and a week to the day before the outbreak of the insurrection.

of seduction employed by them between 1789 and 1792, in breaking down their discipline. In accordance with our orders, our troops accepted the money which these monsters of iniquity, male and female, offered them in order to incite them to rebellion, and with it they drank to the health of the best of kings and his family. The upshot of it was that this corps, the gallant regiments of the Royal-Allemand, were the only ones the revolutionary scoundrels never succeeded in degrading. These three regiments were at least two-thirds Protestant."[115]

There is no indication that the patriots, in defending themselves at Montauban, in leading the attack against Froment at Nîmes, considered themselves the defenders of the Protestant religion against the machinations of their "born enemies." They were not fighting a "religious war." Rather, they were the militant arm of the patriotic and liberal bourgeoisie defending a political cause: the initial triumphs of the middle class in the first years of the Revolution. With the Catholics, on the other hand, the issue was not so clearcut. In attempting to disrupt the ecclesiastical legislation of the National Assembly, the defenders of the Church deliberately rekindled the old fears and animosities of the ignorant and impressionable peasantry of the Midi, and in so doing brought into existence a passion which the royalists easily and without hesitation turned to their advantage. Henceforth the higher clergy and their agents, in collusion with the aristocratic partisans of the Prince of Condé and the Comte d'Artois, incessantly fanned the flames of religious fanaticism in their efforts to destroy the work of the Revolution.[116] At monthly, and even at weekly intervals, the local administrations and patriotic clubs, in combatting their seditions, were called upon to scotch rumors that the Protestants were arming again with the

[115] E.-G. Léonard, "L'Institution du Mérite militaire," BPF, LXXXII (1933), 319.

[116] For instance, De Croy, the *curé* of Saint-Victor-de-Malcap, on Easter Sunday of 1791 preached resistance to the laws of the National Assembly and civil war against the Protestants, saying (as reported in the Departmental records) "qu'il n'y avoit pas un moment à perdre pour s'armer, pour détruire les protestans et venger la religion outragée, qu'il ne falloit pas s'armer de paroles, mais en actions, et que les huguenots détruits, les renégats disparaîtront devant eux." F. Rouvière, *op.cit.*, I, 338. Similarly, the *curé* of Saint-Ambroix was seized with letters in his possession advising all "bons catholiques, qu'il faut égorger les protestans et les mauvais catholiques, qu'il faut répandre toutes sortes de calomnies contres les prêtres constitutionnels, qu'il faut les insulter dans les rues, les huer, les fuir comme des monstres." *ibid.*, I, 340.

intention of slaughtering the Catholics.[117] Hence in the Midi, the reactionary party succeeded in stigmatizing the Revolution as a "complot protestant" in the minds of a large number of Catholics, creating a distorted picture of the nature of the movement which has lasted in a smaller degree to the present day. The counter-revolution in the Midi at times assumed all the characteristics of a Catholic crusade against the Calvinist heresy. As a consequence of this fanaticism, reaction developed earlier and was more difficult to suppress in the south than it was almost anywhere else in France.

Confronted with such violent opposition, the Protestant patriots of Montauban and Nîmes hastened to consolidate their positions. The frantic efforts of the Catholic administrators of Montauban to demonstrate their loyalty to the Revolution in ornate celebrations of 14 July did not succeed in salvaging their tarnished reputation. On 26 July the National Assembly, following the report by Vieillard, suspended the municipality. Late in August it was replaced with six commissioners, all patriots, appointed by the directory of the Department of Lot. Slowly the fugitive Protestants began to return to the city, and in September, in order better to further the interests of the Revolution, the patriot party drew together three political and literary societies in the city to found the Société des Amis de la Constitution de Montauban.[118] The Protestants, while not dominating the club, made up approximately one-third of its 1,500 members

[117] As an example, see the "Adresse du club des Amis de la Constitution et de la garde nationale de la ville de Calvisson en Vaunage, 19 décembre 1790," in F. Rouvière, *op.cit.*, I, 258-259. The address, bearing the adhesion of fifteen municipalities in the area, denied the existence of any such plots and went on to insist that "nous n'admettons parmi les françois de différence que celle des bons et des mauvais citoyens; et c'est aux catholiques de nos contrées que nous osons en appeler. Qu'ils parlent, qu'ils disent si, à l'époque fatale des malheurs de la ville de Nismes, quand le bruit se répandit qu'on égorgeoit dans les cantons catholiques des protestans qui les habitoient, un seul catholique de nos contrées fut inquiété dans ses propriétée? Si un seul fut insulté, si les jours d'un seul furent menacés. . . ? Qu'ils disent s'ils n'ont pas tous vécu parmi nous dans la plus parfaite sécurité et si nous ne les avons pas toujours traités en amis, en citoyens, en frères. . . ."

[118] The activities of the Jacobin club of Montauban are treated at length in L. Lévy-Schneider, *Le Conventionnel Jeanbon Saint-André*, already cited; and a series of articles by François Galabert entitled "Le Club jacobin de Montauban. Son rôle politique pendant la Constituante," in the *Revue d'histoire moderne et contemporaine*, I (1899-1900), 124-168, 235-258, 457-474; and "Le club de Montauban pendant la Constituante. Son organisation, son rôle dans l'administration locale," *Revue d'histoire moderne et contemporaine*, X (1908), 5-27, 273-317.

and constituted one of its most active groups. For all intents and purposes, the club served as the government of the city for the next few years. Purchasing the former building of the *Cour des Aides* for their headquarters across the street from the building in which the civil functionaries met, members of the club "charged with executing the deliberations of their assembly had only to cross the street to transmit the *orders* of the club to the functionaries of the municipality."[119]

The sectarian animosities aroused by the incident of 10 May continued to disrupt life in the city and constituted one of the chief problems with which the club had to deal. Convinced that the masses had been deceived and led astray by a few malicious leaders, the patriots adopted the tactics of persuasion and instruction to win them back to the Revolutionary cause. Through pamphlets and meetings in the club given over to public instruction, they actively propagandized their liberal principles and at the same time took all possible precautions to keep seditious literature from circulating. Recognizing the correlation between the continued economic depression and the restlessness of the Catholic working class, the patriots took the lead in demanding and organizing *ateliers de charité* in the city for their relief. In combatting fanaticism they were quick to see in the liberal ecclesiasts—those who accepted the Civil Constitution of the Clergy—their natural allies. These were always welcomed in the club, where their addresses were received, as the records often noted, "with transports of joy." Indeed, to minimize the sectarian jealousies, the patriots elected the Jacobin monk, P. Ginestet, as the second president of their society. The activities of the refractory clergy were curtailed in measure as the temper of the people would permit, and repeated attempts were made, although unsuccessfully, to induce the liberal Père Sermet, future constitutional bishop of Toulouse, to establish himself permanently at Montauban to aid in the campaign for religious and civil tranquillity.[120]

Early in 1791, the government of the city was restored to a formal basis with the election of a new municipality composed of leaders

[119] F. Galabert, "Le Club jacobin de Montauban," *Revue d'histoire moderne et contemporaine*, I (1899-1900), 140.

[120] See the collection of letters exchanged between the patriots of Montauban and Père Sermet published by F. Galabert, "Le Père Sermet à Montauban," in *La Révolution française*, XXXVI (1899), 396-405.

of the club with a liberal sprinkling of Protestants, among whom was the mayor himself. In the time which had elapsed before this, under the *de facto* rule of the patriotic club, the enemies of the Revolution never ceased their attempts to undermine the position of the liberal bourgeoisie. Every effort was made to sow discord between the troops garrisoned in the city; a new attempt was made to introduce a Catholic corps of volunteers, the "légion de Saint-Sébastien," into the National Guard. Indignantly the patriots complained that "the enemies of the Constitution have not ceased to brandish the torch of fanaticism, to nourish and even to intensify in the hearts of the Catholics a hatred of the non-Catholics—citizens who cherish their fellow citizens as Christians and brothers without regard to differences in cults and religious opinions."[121] On two occasions the city came perilously close to witnessing a reenactment of the riot of 10 May, but prompt action on the part of the club, the guard, and the city commissioners averted a crisis—an achievement which tended to corroborate the verdict of the National Assembly that the Catholic municipality of 1790 had been criminally negligent in its handling of the events of May.

At Nîmes, with the foundering of the Catholic-royalist party in the insurrection of June, the patriots were left in complete control of the administration. The general staff of the national guard was at last reorganized, and of its 24 companies, 22 were commanded by Protestant officers. The municipality of the baron de Marguerittes was put under the surveillance (17 June 1790) of a departmental committee of six notables, among whom were three Protestants and the first president of the patriotic society. Finally, in February 1791, at the recommendation of Alquier, who reported on the tumult at Nîmes, the National Assembly dismissed the municipality and ordered new elections for the summer of 1791 in which the former members of the municipality were declared ineligible.

Triumphant in Nîmes, the patriots were no less successful in capturing the administration of the Department and district. The electoral assembly, whose sessions had been the occasion for the insurrection, continued its deliberations minus the Catholic zealots who had implicated themselves in the violence. The most important posts in the directory of the Department (*président du directoire,*

[121] From the minutes of the club; quoted in Galabert, "Le Club jacobin de Montauban," *Revue d'histoire moderne et contemporaine,* I (1899-1900), 160.

procureur syndic, and *commissaire aux comptes*) went to three men who had served as provisional administrators since the provincial revolutions of 1789; all three were Protestants. Similarly, the 27 members of the general council (*conseil général*) were members of the landed middle class, lawyers, and merchants, at least eleven of whom were Protestants. Moreover the liberal bourgeoisie won complete control of the administration of the district of Nîmes and of the departmental judiciary as well.[122]

Thus the Society of the Friends of the Constitution of Nîmes, as the principal meeting place of the men who now dominated the administration of the Department, became the chief source of authority in the entire area. The problems it faced were staggering, for the passions of civil war had barely subsided. Some of the many demonstrations against the revolutionary cause with which it had to contend were of a comic opera genre, as when a Catholic who had served with the *Cébets* in June scandalized the authorities by decorating his herd of pigs with tricolor cockades and driving them through the city streets. More serious were the continual attempts at subverting the troops stationed in the area and of turning the people against one another. The tactics were generally the same. Referring to one such occasion, the *Moniteur* of Paris reported that "a new conspiracy has been discovered at Nîmes. While preparing their sedition in the city, the perpetrators at the same time announced all through the Vivarais that the Protestants of Nîmes were massacring the Catholics, that they were killing the priests and sacking the churches, in order to draw the inhabitants of the surrounding countryside into the city to put it to pillage. . . ."[123] At Jalès in the remote and mountainous western corner of the Department the counter-revolutionaries had established a camp where preparations were actively pushed for the formation of a clerico-royalist army which in the following year was to invade the Department and require the concerted efforts of the administrations of Gard and Ardèche for its suppression.[124]

With these and a host of related problems the club of Nîmes and the administration of the Department wrestled throughout the year. The obstacles to their attempts at consolidating the Revolution

[122] Chas. Pouthas, *Une famille de bourgeoisie française,* pp. 98-101.

[123] *Réimpression de l'Ancien Moniteur,* 17 October 1790.

[124] For the description of the formation of the camp of Jalès, see E. Daudet, *op.cit.,* pp. 27-112.

seemed without end. But it was a task to which they all devoted themselves religiously. For to the Protestants among them the gains of the first two years of the Revolution were impressive, even momentous. They had been elevated from the degrading station of second-class citizens to Frenchmen enjoying the rights of full citizenship. Members of their middle class had risen to the most important posts in the government, both local and national. Catholic and royalist attempts at dislodging them had proved abortive, had in fact only consolidated their positions. But in the face of fanatical opposition, seen so close at hand, the Protestants of the Midi realized full well how easily their gains could be erased. The year of fear, 1789, had given way to a year of fanaticism—a fanaticism which intended them as its victims. Some had already surrendered their lives in defense of the Revolution, making the Protestants of the south, in the words of Jeanbon Saint-André, "the first martyrs of French liberty." This is doubtless how they regarded themselves, making them in the coming year the most zealous defenders of the Revolution against its enemies, foreign and domestic.

CHAPTER IV

Protestants as Revolutionaries: "Conspirators" or "Patriots"? 1791-1795

"The ideologies of 1789," wrote André Siegfried in 1944, "were a perfect expression of Protestant aspirations at the end of the eighteenth century. Free inquiry, freedom of conscience, political liberty, civil liberty, respect of the individual and of his rights, these principles, essentially Protestant, were equally to be found in the demands of the Revolution. Hence the Protestants greeted the Revolution with enthusiasm. Protestantism since that day has remained firmly attached to the principles of the Revolution: everything that menaces these principles, menaces Protestantism equally. A Protestantism which would repudiate the Declaration of the Rights of Man and the Citizen would at the same time repudiate a most authentic part of the Protestant tradition."[1]

Of those Frenchmen who date the commencement of their liberty from the fall of the Bastille, not all would agree with Jeanbon Saint-André that the Protestants were "the first martyrs of French liberty." Nevertheless most have recognized, along with André Siegfried, that the Protestants of France were staunch supporters of the revolutionary cause. But is that all? A surprising number of people have gone beyond this to make more radical claims. Indeed, the Revolution had not yet begun before the king of France was being warned of the pernicious designs of his Protestant subjects. The abbé Bonnaud, the most outspoken enemy of the Edict of

[1] "Commémoration du Bicentaire de la naissance de Rabaut Saint-Etienne. Causerie de M. André Siegfried," BPF, 1944, 17-27. The publications of the Société de l'Histoire du Protestantisme français were suppressed in 1942. Nevertheless the Society was able to continue the circulation of brochures from time to time to members of its group. The volume for 1944, published immediately after the liberation of Paris, is one in which a number of distinguished French Protestants reassessed the traditional values of men of their faith and nationality. Siegfried chose to comment on the life of Rabaut Saint-Etienne because of the parallels it afforded between the struggle against the suppression of individual liberties under the Nazi occupation of France and that of the Protestants during the *ancien régime*. The affinity of Protestantism with the principles of the Revolution is a theme he develops more fully in his essay "Le groupe protestant cévenol sous la IIIe République," in *Protestantisme français*, eds. Marc Boegner and A. Siegfried (Paris, 1945), pp. 23-55.

Toleration (which was in preparation at the time of the writings of his *Discours*), went to great lengths to point out to his sovereign why he should deny civil rights to these subjects: "The head of the Protestants, Sire, is impregnated with republican ideas, and their general spirit, by the admission of Montesquieu, tends toward a popular government. Hence who can guarantee Your Majesty that the Protestants, once introduced into the provincial assemblies, and acquiring a marked predominance either by virtue of their numbers or by the ascendancy of their words, in the course of time will not disseminate their popular maxims, and that your Catholic subjects, by their connections and relations with these anti-monarchial colleagues, will not familiarize themselves little by little with these republican principles? Does not everyday experience demonstrate that the best elements in society allow themselves to be seduced and corrupted by the gangrenous members?" To the abbé Bonnaud, the Protestants were by nature, and had shown themselves in the past, to be republicans and inveterate enemies of the monarchy. Worse still, they were now seen to be in league with the Jansenists and the *philosophes* in a conspiracy to destroy the monarchy and the Catholic Church in France. Hence, in the estimation of the abbé, extending toleration to them at a time when the policies of Louis XIV had all but destroyed them would be the very epitome of folly.[2]

Such were the apprehensions of a self-styled Catholic patriot confronted with the possibility that the non-Catholics of France might be accorded a measure of liberty. He was not alone in his fears. At approximately the same time, the abbé Lenfant (a Jesuit), learning for the first time of the existence of the Protestant seminary at Lausanne, concluded that this institution was nothing less than a school for the training of subversives, subsidized by the anti-monarchial powers of Europe, whose pupils infiltrated into France for the purpose of destroying the nation; he warned Louis XVI of as much.[3] In 1793 no less a person than Pope Pius VI expressed the belief that the Revolution was the work of an alliance of Protestants with *philosophes* bent on destroying the Church and the

[2] The abbé J.-J. Bonnaud, *Discours à lire au conseil, en présence du Roi, par un ministre patriote, sur le projet d'accorder l'Etat civil aux Protestants* (s.l., 1787), pp. 211 *et seq.*

[3] Cited by Frédéric de Charrière, "Lausanne, centre protestant au XVIIIe siècle," *Revue suisse et chronique littéraire*, XIII (1850), 361-368.

monarchy in France.[4] Or again, Monseigneur de Royère, the refractory bishop of Castres, seized upon the Edict of Toleration as being one of the principal causes of the Revolution. In a circular letter of 1794 to the refugee French ecclesiasts in Spain, he described the Revolution and "its frightful consequences" as "a miracle of God's wrath," in which case the counter-revolution would be "a miracle of God's mercy." In order to hasten the manifestation of the latter, he instructed the ecclesiasts to offer the holy sacrifice of the mass "to ask that God inspire the king whom he will replace on the throne to tolerate no longer in his kingdom any other religion than the Catholic religion and to revoke and annul the gifts of tolerance to all manner of religions and errors, notably the Edict of 1787 in favor of the non-Catholics, an edict which . . . filled up the cup of God's just anger and must be regarded as the source of all the misfortunes which have fallen on the throne and on all the nation. . . ."[5]

The animus of these Catholics, on the one hand fearful for the future of their religion in a society on the brink of Revolution and on the other hand bitter and disillusioned at the cruel fate of their Church in the ensuing upheaval, very shortly found expression in the histories of the revolutionary period. One of the earlier manifestations of this malice was the history by Félix-Christophe-Galart de Montjoie, a lawyer from Aix-en-Provence, one of the founders of the journal *L'Ami du Roi,* whose ingenuous royalism forced him into hiding in 1793 and into exile in 1797. In writing his *Histoire de la Révolution de France* (1791), he was struck (as so many were to be later) with the similarities between the principles of the revolutionaries and those of the Calvinist sect. Adopting the theme of a *complot protestant* as one of the more plausible explanations of

[4] See Augustin Theiner, *Documents inédits relatifs aux affaires religieuses de la France, 1790 à 1800. Extraits des archives secrètes du Vatican* (Paris, 1857), I, Acta Sanctissimi Domini Nostri Pii Divina Providentia Papae Sexti in consistorio secreto, feria secunda die xvii Junii MDCCXCIII, Causa Necis Illatae Ludovico XVI, Galliarum regi Christianissimo, 182-185. An inquiry had been made as to whether the martyred king should be regarded as a martyr of the Christian faith. Pius VI, interpreting the Revolution as he did, concluded that Louis XVI should probably be so considered, but reserved final judgment because of the king's acquiescence to the handiwork of the Calvinist-*philosophe* conspiracy: the Civil Constitution of the Clergy.

[5] "Exhortation de Mgr. l'évêque de Castres aux prêtres français qui vont en Espagne pour faire des prières publiques et implorer la miséricorde de Dieu," in *La Révolution française,* XXXIV (1898), 455-460.

the distress in which France found itself, he proceeded to illustrate the influence of the Calvinists on the Revolution. The following excerpt shows the general line of his reasoning: "Calvinism from the moment of its birth has manifested the principles of license and rebellion. Repressed under the reigns of Francis I, Henry II, and Louis XIII, overthrown by Louis XIV, it has never lost the hope of rising again and of taking revenge for the humiliations which were the punishments for its arrogance and independence. It has been a hidden enemy which France has nourished at her breast, one which has profited from the new state of affairs to reopen all the wounds of the past."[6] After tracing in a summary fashion the history of Protestant insurrections in the past, both those of France and of England, Montjoie assured his readers that the Protestants fostered the Revolution with the sole purpose of overturning the throne and destroying it forever. Presenting his work to the king, Montjoie was cruelly disappointed when Louis XVI denied it his approbation. Nevertheless, out of loyalty and devotion to his sovereign ("[même] dans ces jours de délire où c'est presque un crime de rester fidèle à son prince"), he rushed his work into print to serve as a warning to all Frenchmen who shared his political convictions.

The theme of the Protestants as *faux frères* thirsting for the revenge of their former defeats was taken up and developed into a work of 624 pages by another lawyer and royal functionary who, like Montjoie, boldly defended the monarchy and the person of the king at the time of his trial. F. N. Sourdat, publishing his *Véritables auteurs de la Révolution de France* from exile in 1797, believing that the barbarity, cruelty, and ferocity of the Revolution were completely alien to the normal behavior of civilized Frenchmen, explained the revolutionary delirium as a consequence of Calvinist machinations: "Le CALVINISME est le ressort de la révolution." Apparently quiescent during the first half of the eighteenth century, the Protestants of France were in fact secretly preparing a black alliance with the Jansenists, the *philosophes,* and the Free Masons based on their

[6] F.-C.-G. de Montjoie, *L'Ami du Roi, des François, de l'Ordre et surtout de la Vérité; ou Histoire de la Révolution de France et de l'Assemblée nationale . . .* (Paris, 1791), chapter 2: "De l'influence qu'ont eu les calvinistes sur la révolution." These accusations were repeated in a later edition of his work: *Histoire de la Révolution de France* (Paris, 1797), I, 251-266.

common hatred of the Roman Church, their incredulity, their enmity of kings and government of any kind whatsoever. With the death of Louis XV, said Sourdat, the conspirators pushed their plans with increasing impatience. At Nîmes, Rabaut-Dupui amassed a tremendous treasury through solicitations made all over Europe by means of the masonic lodges. At Paris, Necker and Rabaut Saint-Etienne schemed and plotted, deliberately vitiated the financial position of the royal government to hasten the impending crisis and necessitate the calling of a States General. With the convocation of the latter, their treasury was opened to arm and equip the bourgeois militia and to purchase political positions for Protestants to the extent that three out of seven of the deputies to the States General were allegedly Calvinists. To undermine the position of the king and consolidate that of Necker, they turned their treasures (and even those of the government) to buying up the wheat of France, creating inflation and famine. When the monarchy had demonstrated its inability to remedy the dearth, they opened their secret granaries and flooded the market with food, accusing the king of having starved the people and covering Necker with benedictions for having procured manna from out of nowhere. Through these and similar maneuvers, by the time the States General had declared itself a Constituant Assembly, "public tranquility had already been destroyed, the obedience of the people repudiated, religion insulted, the dignity of the king called in question, his powers impaired."[7]

What sentiments induced Sourdat to write his jeremiad? Part of his behavior can be explained in terms of an ingrained hostility for Protestants and Protestantism; part as an unreasoning relief to a personal sense of humiliation and disillusionment at the collapse of the royalist cause; part, perhaps, as a means of expressing his resentment at the coalition of Protestant powers against his native France. But his approach to the work was meant to be disarming: "God forbid that I write this with the aim of exciting resentments and vengeance. Enough blood has been spilled, too long have disorders of every kind covered the kingdom with ruins and forfeits: it remains to us to give an example of moderation and forgiveness. Let us see in the Calvinists only men gone astray; let us extend to them a friendly hand; let us guide them with open and generous conduct

[7] F. N. Sourdat, *Les Véritables auteurs de la Révolution de France de 1789* (Neufchatel, 1797), p. 487.

to the point where they will regret their errors and their prejudices, and let us try to make even them detest their excesses and factiousness: let us disarm them with kindness, let us forget the past. Let all Frenchmen practice the maxim stated by a prince too little known: 'Who would dare to have his revenge, when the King himself has pardoned!' "[8] To Sourdat, the Calvinists of France are hapless men deluded and corrupted by the errors of Calvin to be made into the unwitting instruments of the forces of anarchy. Free inquiry, the insane belief that man can interpret the sources of authority—even of the highest, the word of God—inevitably leads him to an espousal of republicanism, which every good Christian sees for what it really is: pure and unadulterated chaos. Kings have made France great, have made her a mirror of civilization. Now, her honor sullied, her power destroyed, she can reassume her rightful position in the family of nations if the Calvinists can be led back to reason.

Such were the first attacks upon the revolutionary activities of the Protestants of France. They were followed by more. In 1798 Joseph de Maistre launched a bitter philippic against Protestantism, that "deadly ulcer which attaches itself to every sovereignty and gnaws at them relentlessly, that offspring of arrogance, that father of anarchy, the universal dissolvent," and painted Rabaut Saint-Etienne as a monster who preached devotion to the king and yet at the first sounding of the tocsin flew to Versailles to be among the most passionate enemies of the monarchy.[9] Time tempered the virulence of these attacks, but it did not stop them. Robinet, writing in 1896, adopted the theme expounded by Sourdat and assured his audience that the anti-monarchial, anti-ecclesiastic phases of the Revolution were the inevitable consequences of Calvinist beliefs put into action by Jansenists, *philosophes,* and Rabaut Saint-Etienne.[10]

[8] *ibid.,* p. v.

[9] "Reflexions sur le protestantisme dans ses rapports avec la souveraineté," *Oeuvres complètes de J. de Maistre* (Lyon, 1884), VIII, 64-93. De Maistre's main argument is that Protestantism is the enemy of all social order: "Le protestantisme naquit les armes à la main; il ne respecta la souveraineté civile qu'autant de temps qu'il lui en fallut pour acquérir des forces, et il fut rebelle des qu'il eut le pouvoir de l'être. De tout côté ses apôtres prêchèrent la resistance aux souverains; pour établir leurs dogmes, ils ébranlèrent les trônes, ils vomirent les injures les plus grossières contre tous les souverains qui leur resistèrent."

[10] Le docteur Jean-François-Eugène Robinet, *Le Mouvement religieux à Paris pendant la Révolution* (Paris, 1896), I, 52-59, 247-331.

A work by Ernest Renauld, *Le Péril protestant*, which the author began with amazing frankness by stating that "the purpose of this book is to unmask the enemy, the Protestant, allied with the Jew and the Free Mason against the Catholic, today's victim of this diabolic alliance," went through at least eleven editions, riding on the popularity given such works by the emotions engendered by the Dreyfus case.[11] In 1929, Pouget de Saint-André's *Auteurs cachés de la Révolution* treated the Revolution as the work of a "coalition Judéo-maçonnique-protestante."[12]

Such writings, weighted down with preposterous accusations and at the same time buoyant with the absence of documentation, would not be cited here if it were not for the degree to which they are taken seriously in France.[13] They have put French Protestants on the defensive. A glance at a list of Protestant publications is enough to show how often French Protestants feel called upon to demon-

[11] Ernest Renauld, *Le Péril protestant. Essai d'histoire contemporaine*, 11th edition (Paris, 1899). Like Sourdat, Renauld denies any desire of rekindling the flames of religious war: "Non, mille fois non, nous ne venons pas faire appel aux haines religieuses; nous venons réclamer une place au soleil de notre pays au nom des catholiques dépouillés par les protestants; nous venons demander tout simplement à être traités sur le même pied d'égalité qu'eux; nous venons faire valoir nos droits aux mêmes droits qu'eux." In a bid for popularity, Renauld devoted an entire chapter to demonstrating that the Protestants of France were in league with the Jews in a conspiracy to betray France to her Protestant enemies. A subsequent chapter, entitled "Protestant Favoritism," purported to demonstrate how Protestants, once in public office, discriminate against Catholics. By way of illustration, he cites (one case among many) how a particular charity office is dominated by Protestants: "Il y a des femmes en haillons qui vont au bureau de bienfaisance:

"—Donnez-moi un morceau de pain pour moi et mes petits.

"—Où mettez-vous vos filles!

"—A l'école des soeurs: la loi le permet.

"—C'est possible. Nous ne le permettons pas, nous. *Vous n'aurez pas de pain!*" (p. 558).

[12] Pouget de Saint-André, *Les Auteurs cachés de la Révolution française* (Paris, 1929). His chapter headings testify as to the nature of the study: "Les Francs-Maçons," "Les Israëlites," "Les Protestants," "Les Suisses," "L'invasion étrangère en 1789," "L'Autriche," "Les Agents anglais," "D'où vient l'argent," etc.

[13] Their popularity seems to lie mostly among the less critical reading public and few are the reputable historians who would use them with any seriousness. For instance, the canon Albert Durand, in writing his *Histoire religieuse du Département du Gard pendant la Révolution,* cited earlier, was definitely sympathetic with such writings, but he usually confined the elaboration of the theme of a *complot protestant* to his footnotes with nothing but leading suggestions in his text. Cf. chapter 1 especially.

strate through the press that, despite the many accusations to the contrary, they are loyal Frenchmen little different from their Catholic compatriots. Consequently these invectives have contributed to the making of the *esprit protestant,* that nebulous psychological phenomenon which differentiates the Protestant from the Catholic of France.

The Protestant reaction to the disrepute with which they are assailed is a curious one. On the one hand there are those who try to deflate the issue by minimizing the distinctiveness of Protestant behavior in the Revolution, while at the same time insisting that they nevertheless played an important role in its unfolding. The pastor Blachon, whose own role in the Revolution we shall have occasion to note in a subsequent chapter, expressed this stand as follows in a publication of 1804: "It would by no means be an injustice to attribute to the Protestants a distinguished part in the events of the Revolution. It was only natural for them to take it from the very beginning because of a particular interest relative to their position; but once freedom of worship had been declared, they had nothing more to desire than any other citizens. And, whatever the theory may be, it is certain that in actuality they could have been and were nothing more than a small weight in the balance. To convince those who are not aware of the true state of affairs, one has only to point out to them that the Protestants constituted only something in the vicinity of a twentieth part of the population of pre-revolutionary France. . . ; that in the Constituent Assembly there were only about fifteen [Protestants], among them one single pastor, Rabaut Saint-Etienne; . . . and that the Legislative Assembly and the National Convention together counted only about twenty Protestant members. . . ."[14] The upshot of his argument is that there were too few Protestants to be of any great importance to begin with, and these few acted "en bon français." Boissy d'Anglas expressed similar sentiments, although his approach was paradoxically different: "The Protestants formed too large a part of society for the opinions which divided the nation not to have been found among them as well. Whatever has been said with regard to their republican sentiments, they have been no more revolutionary than the majority

[14] J.-A. Blachon, *Recueil de discours ou fragmens de discours relatifs à diverses circonstances de l'Etat prononcés par J.-A. Blachon en sa qualité de pasteur de l'église réformée à Bordeaux, puis à Anduze* (Nîmes, 1804), pp. 93-94.

of other Frenchmen. Placed for the most part in the third estate, it was the opinions of the *tiers* which they professed most often. And since it can be ascertained that there were as many nuances among them as among other Frenchmen, one is justified in affirming that their religion has had no influence in determining their politics."[15] Two centuries later we find a Protestant like Pierre Chazel contending that in the eighteenth and nineteenth centuries French Protestantism was so busy defending itself against persecution, rationalism, romanticism, and modernism that it scarcely had any resources left to make any real contributions to its own or French life. This is but another variation on the theme of inconspicuousness, and Chazel did not mean to exclude the Revolution from this generalization. Yet, not too happy about its lack of distinction, Chazel consoled himself as follows: "To those who, in reckoning up French activities during this period, would ask with scorn of Protestantism: 'What have you achieved?', it would certainly be justified in responding, like Sieyès after the Revolution: 'I survived!' "[16]

In contrast to the modesty of Blachon, Boissy d'Anglas, and Chazel, the pluck of the pastor Charles Durand is both interesting and refreshing. Charles Durand is the only French Protestant to date who has attempted a general history of his coreligionists during the revolutionary period. This in itself is significant. Any number of pastors have written histories and monographs on the courageous resistance of the Church of the Desert. But all have balked at carrying their studies beyond the first one or two years of the Revolution. Durand alone has had the courage to attempt it. His approach to the problem of the political activities of the Protestants is part of the explanation of why he was able to bring himself to the task.

He admitted with candor and honesty that the faith of the Church was dead. What he meant by this we shall see in the following chapter. But in the realm of politics, he found a comforting consolation. "The faith is dead, but the passion for politics is born. Everything that is intelligent and consummate [*développé*] in Protestantism busies itself with the questions of the day. This is the only but the solid glory of Protestantism in this epoch" (p. 74). "The influence of Protestantism on the Revolution is far more vast

[15] Quoted by Pierre Chazel, "Génie français et protestantisme dans la France contemporaine," in *Protestantisme français*, cited earlier, pp. 81-82.

[16] *ibid.*, p. 78.

than the total of the achievements of the Calvinists in the last years of the eighteenth century. It is so great that one can say irrefutably that the Revolution, in everything in which it was excellent, is the daughter of Protestantism" (p. 76). Durand wisely refrained from developing this idea at any length. ("La thèse est trop vaste et trop connue—dans certains milieux au moins—pour que nous la développions en ce moment.") But for all his circumspection, he did not fear to face up to the accusations which had been levelled at his coreligionists, and even tried to turn them to their advantage.

Even if the Protestants had remained apart from public affairs, Durand argued, they would nonetheless have contributed to the preparing of the future. How? "Indirectly, because their organizing spirit inspired the *philosophes*, Rousseau in particular, and because everything of merit in the *Social Contract,* that catechism of the first phase of the Revolution, Protestantism can claim for its own. In this manner, its influence on the progress of ideas, on the formation of spirits, on the elaboration of the modern world is incalculable" (p. 76). Moreover, it must have had a direct influence, however unfathomable. For in a France with 26 million citizens only one million could read. (He documented this misleading statement from Taine's *Révolution.*) Now among them there were 600,000 to 700,000 Protestants, Bible in hand, the very great majority of whom certainly must have been able to read. Durand did not elaborate any further on this point, but the obvious inference is that the Protestants constituted one of the most enlightened segments of the French populace during the Revolution.[17] Their coreligionists, however few entered into political careers of the highest order, were in the first ranks of the "progressivists" so long as it was a question of acquiring the liberties indispensable to a modern society (p. 78). But the bravest admission of all, the

[17] In connection with this, it is very interesting to note that the Paris Jacobins were of the same mind. The population of the town of Aiguesvives was five-sixths Protestant, and the patriotic club of the community was almost entirely Protestant. The club was affiliated with the Paris Jacobins and in January 1792 they received the following letter from the mother club of the capital: "Les despotes veulent des sujets ignorants, les hommes libres doivent désirer des concitoyens éclairés: les protestans de Vaunage ne se conduisent si bien que parce qu'ils ont eu en général une éducation plus soignée que les catholiques. A l'avenir cette différence entre les cultes se remarquera moins, parce que l'instruction publique sera égale pour tous, et qu'il n'y sera pas question des dogmes des différentes sectes." Quoted in the *Mémoires de l'Académie de Nîmes,* 7th series, XLII (1924-1925), 66-67.

enormity of which they were accused most often in conjunction with their republican proclivities, was their complicity (not of Protestants, but of Protestantism and its heritage) in the drafting of the Civil Constitution of the Clergy. "This was the ruination of papal authority by means of episcopal independence; the ruination of episcopal independence by the enfranchisement of the *curé*; the ruination of the latter, as of the former, by their common subordination to civil power. Presbyterianism, the very basis of the Protestant Church, succeeded to Roman episcopalism. The pastors were able to accept the Revolution, not only because it brought them liberty, but without qualification, regarding it as their daughter in everything in which it was good—the greatest of the victories of the Reformation in Latin lands" (p. 85).

Since Durand neglected to illuminate the republican and "presbyterian" phases of the Revolution with a description of the political activities of any Protestants, he is only saying what other liberal (in this case anti-monarchial, anti-clerical) historians have said often enough before him: that the Reformation was a great force of social liberation, emancipating man's mind from the dominion of priests, and in a sense the first of a series of revolutions which ultimately culminated in the Revolution of 1789. But by confining himself to intellectual forces and the heritage of the Reformation, he evaded the real issue at question: how did the Protestants behave? Were they republicans? or any more so than other Frenchmen? Did they turn the Revolution into an attempt at raising their altar on the ruins of the Catholic Church? And what of this *complot protestant?*

Perhaps the most accurate answer to these questions is to be found in the statement of the pastor Blachon (cited above), modified with one or two corrections, and with the emphasis upon the "small weight in the balance." It should be noted at the outset that there were more Protestants sitting in the French legislative chambers than Blachon was aware of or willing to admit: approximately fifteen in the Constituent Assembly and again in the Legislative Assembly, and roughly twice that number in the National Convention (of whom five were Lutherans).[18] But of these, no more than a handful ever distinguished themselves in the nation's service. Fifteen to thirty men, sitting in a legislative body numbering from six to seven hundred, were not apt to carry much weight, or at least not enough

[18] See Appendix IV.

of and by themselves to overturn the throne and demolish the Church of the overwhelming majority of Frenchmen.

Were these fifteen to thirty men a compact group of conspirators, bound together and acting in unison by virtue of their religious beliefs? Ultimately they were scattered in a variety of political factions, but in the initial stages of the Revolution there was a conspiracy of sorts, one in alliance with the *philosophes*, as their enemies claimed, but not to destroy the Catholic Church, still less to republicanize France. The Protestants who went to Versailles in the late spring of 1789 shared in the common hope of finding in the impending reforms room for an amelioration of their religious position. Even before the elections, the consistory of Nîmes had taken the lead in forming a concert of all the churches of the kingdom with a center of correspondence in Paris to work for a revision of the Edict of Toleration—or more specifically to win permission for the right of collective worship, the legalization of Protestant schools, the admission of Protestants to the professions still closed to them, and, most important, the abrogation of the penal laws still in effect against them. Rabaut Saint-Etienne had been chosen to fulfill the delicate position of the Protestant negotiator in Paris, and for a time it was thought that he might journey to the capital by way of Geneva in order to consult with Necker as to their plan of action.[19] This "conspiracy" was abandoned as unnecessary, however, when their negotiator was elected a deputy to the States General, for it then became clear that the churches could carry their grievances into the very halls of the national legislature.

Once in Paris, the Protestant deputies from the Midi lost no time in consulting together and with their friends there to determine what steps should be taken to realize their objectives. The initial conversations were disappointing; although Malesherbes assured them that there would be no objections to moving their religious assemblies from the Desert into private homes, he advised that the moment was not yet ripe for speaking out openly in defense of their cause. Impatient to play a decisive role in the Protestant settlement, the deputy from Poitiers, Jean-Gabriel Gallot, turned his acquaintance with Madame Necker to advantage and managed to be received at the home of the Swiss banker several times during the month of

[19] Armand Lods, *Essai sur la vie de Rabaut Saint-Etienne* (Paris, 1893), p. 9; and "Les cinque dernières lettres de Paul Rabaut," BPF, XL (1891), 488-489.

May 1789. To the parlor of the Controller General he carried his plans for the solution to the Protestant question, only to find that the invitations had apparently been extended to him out of nothing more than social graciousness. By the end of the month, after several futile attempts at capturing an audience, the doctor from Poitiers was forced to admit that Necker, a Protestant from Geneva, was too occupied with other affairs to involve himself in the special problems of his French coreligionists.[20] The responsibility for the conquest of their rights fell to those who had patiently negotiated the Edict of 1787, chiefly Rabaut Saint-Etienne with the constant advice of Malesherbes.

In acquiring the rights they desired, the Protestants were not without friends. They had in fact become the darlings of the would-be reformers of the *ancien régime*, who saw in them model victims of royal absolutism and clerical intolerance, and hence joined their cause with sympathy and a certain amount of relish. It soon became apparent that such support was vital, for the instructions which the clerical delegates carried with them to the National Assembly were incompatible with an extension of Protestant liberties. In the first part of August, the Assembly received for consideration a number of proposed drafts of a Declaration of Rights which would have accorded the non-Catholics the religious liberty that was still denied them. But on 19 August the Assembly decided to use the draft of the *Bureau Six* as the basis for further discussions. This constituted a setback for the Protestants and the partisans of religious tolerance, for the articles concerned with religion, morality, and public worship dealt only in terms of those of the majority of Frenchmen: "(Art. xvi) Since private offenses are not within the realm of law, religion and morality must supplement the law. Hence it is essential to the tranquility of society that the one and the other be free. (Art. xvii) The maintenance of religion requires a public worship. Respect for public worship is consequently indispensable." As a concession to those Frenchmen who were not of the religion of the majority, the succeeding article stated that "No citizen should be disturbed who does not trouble the established worship."[21]

Discussion of the first articles of the proposed Declaration com-

[20] Excerpts from Gallot's diary and his letters to his wife are published in the BPF, LXXXI (1932), 154-158.

[21] *Archives parlementaires*, 1st series, VIII, 431.

menced on 20 August and proceeded quickly and calmly until the question of religious liberty came to the fore. The clerical members began by defending the proposed articles, but when their actions aroused heated protests from the more liberal members of the Assembly, notably the comte de Castellane and Mirabeau, they shifted their tactics and proposed that the matter be moved from the Declaration to the body of the Constitution itself. After acrimonious debates, the Assembly agreed that articles xvi and xvii properly belonged in the Constitution and the debate then turned on article xviii. Its original form was again attacked by Mirabeau and the comte de Castellane, the latter suggesting that it be revised to read: "No man may be disturbed for his religious opinions, or troubled in the performance of his worship." The clerical party rose in objection, their counter-proposal being the omission of a guarantee of public worship and the qualification of freedom of conscience by the clause: ". . . provided that their manifestation does not trouble public order."

Up to this point in the debates, the Protestants, hoping to minimize opposition to the proposals, had remained in the background and had allowed their allies to defend their cause. But when the tenor of the debates indicated that the Assembly would accept the crippling modifications of the clergy, Rabaut Saint-Etienne rose in a last effort to defend the interests of his coreligionists. His address, one of the longest and most impassioned on the provisional articles of religious toleration, illustrated more clearly than any other statement made hitherto the exact nature of Protestant demands in the first year of the Revolution. The pastor from Nîmes began by standing firmly on the instructions from his constituents, advising the Assembly that the citizens of his *sénéchaussée* had directed him to procure the complement to the Edict of Toleration. From the Assembly there was heard a cry from a throng of deputies that they, too, had been so instructed. To the hesitant and the unenlightened who were not familiar with the Protestant grievances, he turned to an indictment of the Edict of 1787. "The non-Catholics (some of you perhaps are not aware of it) received from the Edict of 1787 only what could no longer be denied to them. Yes, only what could no longer be denied to them; I do not repeat this without feeling a sense of shame; but this is not a gratuitous charge, it is the very wording of that Edict." This law, "more celebrated than just," has given them the enjoyment of civil rights—nothing more. "Hence it is, Gentlemen, that in France, in the eighteenth century, the maxim of barbarous times has been maintained; of dividing a nation into a favored caste and a disgraced caste. . . . The Protestants give their all for their fatherland, and their fatherland treats them with ingratitude; they serve their country as citizens, and they are treated as outlaws; they serve it as men whom you have rendered free, and they are treated as slaves. But there is still a French nation, and it is to her that I appeal on behalf of two million useful citizens, who demand today their rights as Frenchmen. . . . Gentlemen, it is not toleration that I claim, but liberty. Toleration! Sufferance! Pardon! Clemency!—ideas supremely unjust toward dissenters so long as it shall be true that religious differences, the differences of opinion, are not to be regarded as a crime. Toleration! I demand that 'toleration' in turn be proscribed. And it shall be—that unjust word which presents us only as citizens worthy of pity, as culprits to whom pardon is offered, men whom chance and education have led to think in a manner different from you. Error, Gentlemen, is not a crime: those who profess it, take it for the truth. For them it is the truth; they are bound to profess it. And no man, no society, has the right to forbid it to them. . . . I demand everything you demand for yourselves: that all non-Catholics be assimilated in every way and without reserve with all other citizens, because they are citizens, too. I demand that liberty and law, ever impartial, not distribute unequally the rigorous acts of their exact justice. . . . I ask for the non-Catholics what you demand for yourselves: the equality of rights, liberty; liberty of their religion, liberty of their worship, the freedom of celebrating their worship in houses consecrated to this purpose, the certitude of not being disturbed in their religion any more than you are in yours, and the perfect assurance of being protected as you are, as much as you are, in the same manner as you are, by a common law. . . . Europe, which aspires to liberty, looks to you for great lessons, and you are worthy of giving them to her. Let the code which you will form be the model for all others, and let it not be marred by a single blemish. If examples are to be cited, imitate the example of those generous Americans who have placed at the head of their civil code the sacred maxim of universal religious freedom; of those Pennsylvanians who have declared that all who adore one God, in whatever manner they adore Him, shall enjoy every right of citizenship; of those gentle and wise inhabitants of Philadelphia who see all forms of worship established in their city, with twenty different churches, and who perhaps owe to this profound acquaintance with liberty the liberty which they have won for themselves. . . . I conclude, Gentlemen, pending the time when you will abolish the laws concerning the Protestants and assimilate them completely with other Frenchmen, by asking that you insert this article in the Declaration of Rights: 'Every man is free in his opinions; every citizen has the right of freely professing his cult, and no one shall be disturbed because of his religion.' "[22]

While Rabaut Saint-Etienne laid the basis for becoming one of the better-known orators of the Constituent Assembly, he failed to move the clerical opposition. The bishops of Lydda and Langres, while admitting that they were willing to concede freedom of conscience to their "frères dans l'erreur," insisted that it was necessary to "draw a line of demarcation which would console our [Catholic] brethren and to avoid acts which would derogate from the rights of the dominant religion or be injurious to Catholic worship." They reverted back to the first clause of de Castellane's motion, amending it to read: "No one may be disturbed for his opinions, even in religion, provided that their manifestation does not trouble public order as established by law." The debates dragged on, the liberal faction bitterly opposing the new proposal. The president of the Assembly, M. Clermont-Tonnerre, despairing of a settlement, twice offered to resign. Finally, in the face of unrelenting clerical opposition, there seemed no solution to the problem but to put the Catholic proposal to a vote. Mirabeau demanded and was refused the floor. The motion carried, and article x of the Declaration of Rights, while it guaranteed the non-Catholics of France freedom of conscience, implicitly negated its logical corollary, the freedom of worship.[23]

This was a disappointment to the Protestants; not knowing that it was to be their last defeat before the legislative body of France, they felt that it denied them one of their most cherished ambitions. Momentarily, at least, it restricted the free development of their cult. Acting on verbal authorization in June of 1789, the Protestants of

[22] *ibid.*, 478-480.

[23] The debates on article X of the Declaration of Rights are treated in an essay by N. Weiss, "Les Séances des 22 et 23 août 1789 à l'Assemblée nationale," BPF, XXXVIII (1889), 561-575.

Paris had rented a room for their religious services on the rue de Mondétour. When it became apparent that this was insufficient to their needs, they looked for more spacious quarters and turned to Rabaut Saint-Etienne for advice. In a letter of 14 October 1789 to the pastor Marron (a few days before the Assembly was to follow the king to Paris) Rabaut Saint-Etienne counselled against the proposed move. "I think furthermore, that our friends of Paris must refrain from showing themselves as much as the others until such time as we obtain what we all desire. Any display would furnish the malevolent with the pretext for accusing the entire society of ambition and give them a means of carrying a bad impression of us before the National Assembly. . . . I beg of you, therefore, to see to it that this idea is deferred until another time, and that they await the great decisions which will be more favorably received in the heart of Paris than they were in the very holy and very strong council of 23 August, anniversary of the eve of Saint Bartholomew's."[24] It was to be another twenty months before the Protestants of the capital felt secure enough to move their semi-clandestine worship in rented rooms to a *bona fide* temple.[25]

Article x of the Declaration of Rights had aroused considerable opposition in the Assembly,[26] and the legislators wisely avoided trying to exact a more formal recognition of the religious liberties of the Protestants.[27] But with respect to their civil liberties, the As-

[24] *La Révolution française*, xxxv (1898), 160-161.

[25] Armand Lods, *L'Eglise réformée de Paris pendant la Révolution* (Paris, 1889), pp. 13-16.

[26] In a letter of 22 August 1789 to the pastor Marron, Rabaut Saint-Etienne described the first reading of the article as follows: "Cette motion ne prit pas fort bien, tandis que toutes les autres ont été vivement applaudies; il y eut un moment de silence, comme si chacun avait fait un profond examen, et il n'y eut l'instant d'après qu'une partie de la salle qui applaudit. Les Français n'ont pas encore secoué tous les préjugés." *La Révolution française*, xxv (1898), 159.

[27] On 21 December 1789 the comte de Custine interjected into the discussions on the Jewish question the demand that the non-Catholics be formally granted the freedom of public worship. The proposal was immediately attacked as unconstitutional by Thiebault, a *curé* of Metz, and its discussion was postponed. (Cf. *Archives parlementaires*, 1st series, x, 695, 705-714.) The Assembly continued to protect the rights of the Protestants to collective worship in the same oblique manner in which it had been guaranteed by the Declaration of Rights by rejecting, for instance, the proposals of the bishop of Nancy (13 February 1790) and later of Dom Gerle (12 April 1790) that the Catholic religion be recognized as the religion of the nation, alone in its enjoyment of public worship. On 24 August 1790, however, the Assembly formally recognized the right to public worship of

sembly did not stint in its generosity toward them. Articles IV and V of the Declaration of Rights, proposed by the chevalier de Lameth and inspired by Rabaut Saint-Etienne,[28] accorded all Frenchmen equal rights in the enjoyment of their liberties as citizens. More specifically, article VI went on to declare that "all citizens being equal in the eyes of the law, all are equally admissible to all public dignities, offices, and employments, . . . with no other distinction than that of their virtues and talents." Any doubts whether the Protestants were to be included in this guarantee were dispelled by the law of 24 December 1789, which decreed that non-Catholics (exclusive of Jews) could be elected to all degrees of the administration and could hold all civil and military offices without exception. In the following year the decrees of 10 July and 15 December awarded to the heirs of the émigrés of 1685 and to those subsequently condemned for religious crimes the properties which had been confiscated from them and which had hitherto been administered by the administration of taxes.[29] These acts coupled with a provision of the constitution recognizing as citizens any descendants of the

the Protestants of the two confessions of Augsburg and Switzerland in Alsace. (Cf. Robinet, *op.cit.*, I, 321-323.) Moreover, a decision of the directory of Paris (11 April 1791) made it possible for non-Catholics to rent former Catholic buildings for the celebration of their religious services. (See the *Réimpression de l'Ancien Moniteur*, 15 April 1791.) The Constitution of 1791 declared as a natural right of man "la liberté . . . d'exercer le culte religieux auquel il est attaché," but the word "public" was conspicuously absent. The Constitution of 1793, however, went further by declaring that "La constitution garantit à tous les Français . . . le libre exercice des cultes. . . ." (Cf. J. B. Duvergier, *Collection complète des lois, décrets, ordonnances . . . etc., 1788-1824* [Paris, 1825-1828], III, 241; V, 357.)

[28] Rabaut Saint-Etienne claimed authorship for these articles in the letter to the pastor Marron cited in footnote 26.

[29] In the three dioceses of Nîmes, Alais, and Uzès (the present Department of Gard), the annual rental of these properties amounted to 3,635 livres. 210 descendants of the Protestant émigrés submitted claims for the restitution of this property, and the properties of another 127 fugitives went unclaimed. See the study of this question by François Rouvière, *Les Religionnaires des diocèses de Nîmes, Alais et Uzès, et la Révolution française* (Paris, 1889), 211 pp. For illuminating material on the passage of these laws, see the article by Jacques Pannier, "La loi du 15 décembre 1790 sur la restitution des biens des religionnaires: son véritable promoteur, M. de Marsanne, descendant de réfugiés," BPF, XL (1891), 113-138, 188-200, 329-337; and the "Lettre de Beaumarchais à Barrère sur son rapport relatif à la restitution des biens aux religionnaires fugitifs," BPF, II (1854), 467-471—Beaumarchais' ancestors were Huguenots; his father abjured in 1721 in order to ply his trade as a watch maker: cf. E. and E. Haag, *La France protestante*, 2nd edition, III, 780-782.

religious émigrés who returned to live in France and who took the civic oath, fulfilled the Protestant demands of 1789 and, legally at least, won for them the integration into French society which they had all desired.

It should be noted that the Protestant Church profited from the emancipative legislation to organize their Church on a more formal basis. In Paris, with the support of Bailly, the Protestant congregation rented the church of Saint-Louis du Louvre in the interior of which, as an expression of their gratitude to the gifts of the Revolution, they prominently displayed a marble plaque upon which had been engraved the Declaration of the Rights of Man. It was here that they held their first public services in the capital since the reign of Louis XIV—services which, in the words of a member of the audience, were attended by "a large number of Calvinists and a still greater number of *philosophes*, curious at witnessing the first act of religious toleration."[30] The pastor Marron rose to the occasion by exclaiming from the pulpit: "What characterizes the French Revolution is that in every respect it is the work of reason. . . . It has not merely changed our master, it has rendered us free. . . . The Revolution is over, for now we live under the empire of the Constitution."[31] In Bordeaux the consistory, which had been trying in vain since 1790 to raise sufficient funds to build a church of its own, finally compromised in 1793 by renting the former chapel of the Carmelites.[32] At Nîmes the consistory leased the former church of the Dominicans (15 June 1791) and inaugurated Protestant services on 20 May 1792.[33] The records for the sale of the properties of the Catholic Church in Gard show that the Protestant Jean-Antoine Teissier purchased the church of the *Pénitents blancs* (14 December 1792) for 7,086 livres, "acting in the name of the non-Catholic citizens of Alais, vulgarly known under the denomination of Protestants, to exercise in the said church . . . their religious worship, in liberty, under the protection of the laws of the Republic."[34] Throughout France, those Protestant communities which possessed

[30] "Premier exercice public du culte réformé à Paris en 1791. Récit anonyme. . . ," BPF, XXXV (1886), 512.

[31] A. Lods, *Eglise de Paris pendant la Révolution*, p. 19.

[32] F. Leroux, *Les Réligionnaires de Bordeaux*, p. 306.

[33] A. Borrel, *Eglise réformée de Nîmes*, pp. 452-453.

[34] François Rouvière, *L'Aliénation des biens nationaux dans le Gard* (Nîmes, 1900), p. 369.

the resources availed themselves of the opportunity of moving their assemblies from the fields and barns where they had hitherto held them to more suitable surroundings. Since this usually meant the acquisition of property which had formerly belonged to the Catholic Church, it might easily have caused offense. But wherever possible, the Protestants tried not to offend Catholic sensibilities—Paul Rabaut, for instance, advised the elders of the Church of Lagorce to avoid choosing a locale where the sound of the singing of their psalms might interfere with Catholic worship[35]—and it does not appear that their actions occasioned any difficulties with their Catholic compatriots.

The "conspirators" who were responsible for the conquest of Protestant liberties undoubtedly profited from the advice of Protestant deputies, but the latter played a singularly small role in the debates for their acquisition. Rabaut Saint-Etienne alone of their number intervened in the discussion on article x of the Declaration of Rights, an intervention which had negative results. Barnave (deputy from the Dauphiné) spoke briefly in support of the measure admitting Protestants to all civil employments and offices (24 December 1789).[36] Otherwise the legislation which enfranchised the Protestants was carried through the Assembly by their friends and allies, the more liberal members of that chamber.

In fact a survey of the activities of the Protestant deputies in the Constituent Assembly as a whole would reveal that with the exceptions of Rabaut Saint-Etienne, Boissy d'Anglas, and Barnave, the non-Catholic representatives seldom called attention to themselves by addressing the chamber. Couderc (Lyons), Mestre (Libourne), Quatrefages de la Roquette (Nîmes), and Gallot (Poitou) seem not to have uttered anything of sufficient significance to be recorded in the *Archives parlementaires*. Chambon-Latour (Nîmes) and Soustelle (*idem.*) might have shared the anonymity of their coreligionists

[35] Paul Rabaut to the elders of the church of Lagorce, 3 July 1792: "Je me fais un vrai plaisir de répondre à votre obligeante lettre. Béni soit Dieu qui a brisé les chaînes de notre esclavage, et qui a dirigé les choses de manière que nous pourrons le servir sans crainte et sans empêchement! La route à suivre pour vous procurer une maison de prières n'est pas bien difficule. D'abord il faut jeter les yeux sur un endroit convenable, en observant qu'il ne soit pas trop proche de l'église, afin qu'on n'ait pas lieu de se plaindre que le chant des Psaumes trouble leur exercice religieux." BPF, XL (1891), 495-496.

[36] *Archives parlementaires,* 1st series, x, 781.

had they not each tried to claim for their respective home towns (Uzès and Alais) the seat of the bishopric in their Department.[87] The primary interests of Meynier de Salinelles (Nîmes) and Pierre-Paul Nairac (Bordeaux) seem to have been the economic questions which came before the Assembly with respect to foreign trade and colonies, although Nairac, much to the annoyance of his colleagues, insisted on taking the floor several times in connection with the riots at Montauban, in which the national guard of his city had played a part.[88] Garesché (Saintes) had occasion to appear before the Assembly in his capacity as a member of the committee of finances, Cussy (Caen) and Lamy (Caen) as members of the *bureau de monnaie*. But only Barnave, Boissy d'Anglas, and Rabaut Saint-Etienne were sufficiently involved in the questions of the day to become known outside the halls of the legislature.

Modest and retiring in the debates over civil and religious liberties, the Protestant deputies remained aloof from the negotiations concerned with the Civil Constitution of the Clergy. That is not to say that in their apparent detachment they did not show an interest in those tricks of fate whereby the nation, having rendered to the Protestants the liberties of which they had been deprived, turned upon the Catholic Church and commenced to strip it of many of its privileges. In view of the unrelenting hostility of the Catholic Church to the Protestants and the repeated efforts it made throughout the eighteenth century to stir the civil authorities into action against heretics, the Protestants must have followed the evolution of the Civil Constitution with considerable interest.

Indeed, sometime on the eve of the Revolution, Rabaut Saint-Etienne himself penned a *Projet* for the benefit of a hypothetical "homme d'Etat, désintéressé, exempt de préjugés, dont les vues soyent grandes et la main ferme."[89] The purpose of his *Projet* he described in an analogy to family life: "One can compare the authority which

[87] *ibid.*, XVI, 745.

[88] At the session of 3 July 1790 Nairac was hooted down by his colleagues when he tried to read a report on the Bordelais guard at Moissac. Cf. *Archives parlementaires*, 1st series, XVI, 689.

[89] Gustave Fabre, "Trois manuscrits de Rabaut Saint-Etienne," in the *Mémoires de l'Académie de Nîmes*, 7th series, XVI (1893), 193-240. The manuscript of his *Projet* is undated, but the mention of tithes and annates would place it at least as early as August of 1789, and it is quite possible that he wrote it prior to his election to the States General.

priests have usurped in society with the dominion which a haughty wife knows how to establish over a weak husband. In the home, the gentler virtues are properly the lot of the wife, and in society of the ministers of religion: both the one and the other should be submitted to a superior power, to the authority of force." In the family of society, a weak father (the State) has allowed the mother (the Catholic Church) to establish an unwarranted dominion over the household. This dominion, thought Rabaut Saint-Etienne, was injurious to society, for in turning the care of public morality over to the Church it enslaved society at the hands of the priests of superstition. Just as no family should be ruled by the wife, no society should be ruled by the Church. Rather, after having established law on the basis of sound morals, the State should direct morality in such a way as to encourage the observation of laws. In this we know that Rabaut Saint-Etienne did not exclude the Protestant Church (see Chapter V, page 251), but in his eyes it was the Catholic Church, reigning over 25,000,000 Frenchmen, which had to be restored to its proper role in society. Hence the state should "profit from the slumber of the Church, which at present jealously guards its dogmas to the neglect of its moral empire, to strip it little by little of this latter dominion." More specifically, Rabaut Saint-Etienne wanted to "humanize" the priests: diminish (always "imperceptibly") celibacy, religious brotherhoods, religious processions and holidays, vows of poverty, idleness, abstinence—in short, to "shut the priests up in their churches where they can do whatever they please." At the same time the State should take steps that would make them useful citizens. No celibate is a citizen; he is the enemy of society, so the marriage of priests should be encouraged. Domestic life would give them domestic virtues, "the mother of all others." Moreover it would isolate them from one another. They should be taxed as other citizens are. Annates should be abolished. "Restrict the Assemblies of the Clergy: have them presided over by a representative of the king." (Just, he might have added, as Louis XIV had mined the synods of the Protestant Church.) For the time being, the tithes should not be disturbed; the people will soon enough become tired of them. Increase the number of *curés*—"this is the desire of all France"—and when each diocese has but one bishop over a number of priests of equal station, the State will then be able to consider whether it has sufficient resources to salary them.

What of dogmas? Do not touch them, warned Rabaut Saint-Etienne. The philosophy of the century—"the daughter of the Renaissance and the younger sister of the Reformation"—made the mistake of trying to destroy superstition. Religion is necessary. "A simplified religion can be of the greatest utility; speaking only from a political point of view, it is the most magnificent instrument which legislation can use. Experience has proved that humanity needs religion. When Greek philosophy dethroned Jupiter, the world deified Jesus Christ. If European philosophy were to succeed in destroying the Christian religion, would anyone think that the world no longer would need a religion?"

The utopia which rose in the mists of his mind was one where people would be virtuous through the guidance of the State; where morality and ethics would be determined by laws rather than by priests. The father should reassert his dominion over the family; he should "seek the art of directing public opinion, . . . entertainments, Religion, philosophy, the sciences"; he should place himself "at the head of everything." "And the means of leading public opinion is always to desire and do good works." His advice to his "disinterested statesman, exempt of prejudices," was to "intrigue for the creation of a patriarchy." The reward was the promise that "the time will come when the Prince will be the chief of Religion."

Anti-Catholic? It cannot be denied that Rabaut Saint-Etienne's *Projet* revealed the scorn of a Protestant for the Roman Catholic conception of the role of the priest and of the Church in society. But at the same time, his *Projet* reflected his own experiences as a Protestant pastor who had dabbled in the philosophy of the century. As we shall see in the following chapter, he and a number of other pastors, dissatisfied with their own religion's function in society, had come to believe in a morality based on laws and the utility of a simplified religion "stripped of all accessories." They were just as scornful of the assemblies of the Protestant Church as Rabaut Saint-Etienne was of the General Assemblies of the Clergy, and while they longed for the establishment of an ecclesiastic hierarchy, the emphasis was upon the hierarchy, not its ecclesiastical nature. Had Rabaut Saint-Etienne survived the Revolution, he almost certainly would have joined with the pastors of the Church (among them his brother) in the scramble to have their sect included in the patriarchy established over French society and the Church by

Napoleon. From the religious point of view, the *Projet* was directed as much against the Protestant Church as against the Roman Catholic, even if the latter, by virtue of its privileges, had far more to lose.

Such were the religious reforms envisaged by the pastor from Nîmes, reforms which in some respects anticipated the Civil Constitution of the Clergy. But so far as is known, the "disinterested statesman" was never found, and the *Projet* was never submitted. The only known copy is the handwritten original, found more than a century later among an accumulation of private papers. Rabaut Saint-Etienne was not among those who broke the privileges of the Catholic Church. He took no part in the debates on the Civil Constitution; no Protestants were members of the Ecclesiastical Committee which prepared it. But the *Projet* does show that he must have been in sympathy with the work of the legislators, and it is not surprising that in November of 1789 he should have written to another pastor: "You surely know what the Assembly decreed on the 2nd with respect to the property of the clergy, and I congratulate the legislators for having carried the greatest victory yet of public interest over private interest. The clergy is no longer an order, it is no longer a corps, it is no longer a republic in an empire, it will no longer oppose itself *en masse* to the public welfare, it will no longer hold political assemblies, it will no longer decide the life of citizens, and, about to become citizens themselves, the priests will finally march in cadence with society. It only remains to marry them, and you can guess how far this idea has advanced. In a little time, the Assembly has made a great deal of progress."[40]

The one exception, the one Protestant who entered actively into the debates on the Civil Constitution, was Barnave. "Acting to satiate his Calvinist rancor or perhaps to neutralize the influence of Mirabeau whom he envied and despised," wrote the abbé Dedieu, "his role was preponderant." It was on his intervention that the Assembly was kept from modifying in a liberal fashion the text of the Civil Constitution initially submitted by the committee (1-9 June 1789); it was he who in the session of 27 November persuaded the Assembly to put the Constitution into immediate effect; it was he who watched over the Assembly to see that it did not relent in the

[40] Letter to Gal-Pomaret, pastor of Ganges, 4 November 1789, printed in *La Révolution française*, xxxv (1898), 161-162.

application of the measure.[41] But Barnave was only one man, and the majority of the Assembly voted with him. Dedieu does not claim that the Civil Constitution marked an attempt at Protestantizing France; no serious historian would. Nor in the eyes of the legislators was it a triumph of Protestant presbyterianism over Roman episcopalism, as Charles Durand was later to infer. If it had been, it is certain that few of the delegates would have approved it, and probable that some of the Protestants would have opposed it. To the men who drafted the Civil Constitution of the Clergy, it represented a return to the primitive church. It was an attempted synthesis of political and ecclesiastical Gallicanism. More than a product of the new regime, "it was simply a legacy of the past and belonged to the *ancien régime*."[42] It was not the work of Protestants who sought the destruction of the Catholic Church; it was the act of Catholics seeking to correct abuses in the old Church and pressed on by the financial necessities of the State.

There were Protestants of course who profited from the Civil Constitution and the accompanying ecclesiastical legislation. In the Department of Gard, the records for the sale of former church properties show that a number of Protestants did not hesitate to make heavy investments in such properties.[43] Its application occasioned

[41] J. Dedieu, *Histoire politique*, II, 343-345.

[42] Jean Leflon, *La Crise révolutionnaire, 1789-1846*, volume XX of the *Histoire de l'Eglise depuis les origines jusqu'à nos jours* by Augustin Fliche and Victor Martin (s.l., 1949), p. 59. Edmond de Pressensé (a Protestant) stated as much when he wrote: "Il est juste de reconnaître à la décharge de la Révolution que cette constitution n'a été qu'une rigoreuse application des maximes de l'ancienne monarchie." Cf. his *L'Eglise et la Révolution française. Histoire des relations de l'église et de l'état de 1789 à 1814*, 3rd edition (Paris, 1889), p. 134. Pierre de La Gorce, in his *Histoire religieuse de la Révolution française*, 11th edition (Paris, 1912), I, 256, was of a contrary mind: "Dans la Constitution civile, les jansénistes ont cherché une revanche contre Rome, les légistes la sujétion de l'Eglise, les âmes candides la réforme des abus; puis il y eut les voltairiens qui n'y voulurent mettre que ce qu'il fallait de religion pour le peuple, enfin les impies déclarés, qui n'y virent qu'une étape vers l'anéantissement de toute foi." But not even he singles out the Protestants for abuse, although he was sparing enough with his praise of the role of Barnave.

[43] In addition to the purchase made by Teissier cited above, the Protestant consistory of Nîmes purchased on 22 floréal an XII (12 May 1804) the former church of the Dominicans (item 959 in Rouvière, *Aliénation des biens nationaux*); Guizot père et fils, the chapel and part of the surrounding land of Coulorgues for 2,280 livres and the priory of Aubord for 2,150 livres, 14 Feb. and 18 Jan. 1791 respectively (items 1514-1515); Jean Allut and Guillaume Sabatier, the property of the Benedic-

embarrassing interludes. In a bishopric like that of Gard, the larger part of the Catholic population demonstrated their loyalty to the refractory bishop by refusing to participate in the elections for a Constitutional bishop to succeed him. His successor, the bishop Dumouchel, was recommended for the post by the Protestant patriotic clubs and owed his election in large part to the suffrages of Protestant electors—with the result that the bishop designate is reported to have been greeted by his future parishioners with cries of "Qui veut de la marchandise de Saint-Etienne! Aïci Moussu Paul Rabaut! Calvin! Calvin!"[44]

Potentially more troublesome than the real or imagined beliefs of the populace was the fact that in an area where sectarian rivalries had already been inflamed by the events of 1790, Protestant municipalities were charged with the thankless task of executing the Civil Constitution. Because of the religious differences and the widespread opposition to the measure, the civil authorities of Gard and the Protestant municipality of Montauban were extremely cautious in their actions and delayed the rigorous enforcement of the measure until as late as 1793.[45] To minimize any religious animosities, the authorities used the occasion of the administering of the oath to the

tines, 18 Nov. 1791, for 673,000 livres (items 34-35); Sabonadière, the chapelle de Robillard at Nîmes, 5 messidor an IV (23 June 1796), for 3,150 francs (item 2393); J.-A. Soustelle, properties of the Jacobins of Alais, 2 December 1791, for 7,000 livres acting on behalf of F.-M. Soustelle, ex-deputy to the Constituant, and in his own name properties at Alais worth 760 livres and 12,650 livres in April and October of 1792 (item 2508); Vincens-Planchut: at Alais, the chapter of Alais, 19 Dec. 1790, for 47,479 livres, a chapel at Aimargues and two fields, 2 March 1791, for 1,605 livres, *idem.*, the chapelle de Jean Audouin, 2 March 1791, and property for 866 livres, *idem.*, the almonry and adjacent land, 2 March 1791, for 1,625 livres, and at Saint-Laurent-d'Aigouze, the chapelle Saint-Lucie, 3 March 1791, and land for 198 livres (item 2672); Jean-Henri Voulland, deputy to the National Assembly, and d'Arnaud, part of the chapelle Saint-Jean at Saint-Quentin, 18 May 1791, for 6,200 livres (Voulland) and 8,200 livres (d'Arnaud) (items 2696-2697); etc. The religious identity of these persons can be established in Chas. Pouthas, *Une famille de bourgeoisie française*, cited earlier.

[44] Albert Durand, *Histoire religieuse du Département du Gard*, pp. 212-240.

[45] F. Rouvière, *Révolution dans le Gard*, II, 33 *et seq.*; L. Lévy-Schneider, *Le Conventionnel Jeanbon Saint-André*, p. 123. For an admirable survey of the religious aftermath to the disturbances at Montauban, see Daniel Ligou, "Protestants et sans-culottes. La bourgeoisie réformée de Montauban devant la Révolution," *Actes du Xe Congrès des Sociétés Savantes Pyrénées-Languedoc-Gascogne* (1954), 13 pp. According to M. Ligou, the Montalbanais Protestants abstained from elections of Catholic clergy to the local church offices. Although they were hostile to the refractory clergy, their animus was based on political rather than religious considera-

juring clergy for the celebration of inter-sectarian festivities similar to those which had seemed to promise religious concord at the commencement of the Revolution.[46] It was expedient for these officials to demonstrate a certain amount of sufferance for their Catholic compatriots. But should their tolerance be thought of only as an expediency? With the memories of their own religious trials so near at hand, would it be unwarranted to surmise that some of these Protestant administrators were more charitable of their Catholic compatriots out of compassion for their plight than Catholic administrators might otherwise have been? This was the observation of Gabriel Feydel, a commissioner of the Ministry of the Interior who was sent to the Department of Gard in the summer of 1793. In a report to his superiors in Paris (1 September 1793) Feydel observed that "in the past the Huguenot priests were persecuted by the papist flocks; today the Huguenot flocks, remembering their persecutions with a pious twinge, regard the law on the refractory priests only from a religious point of view, and evangelically return to them good for evil. They close their eyes to the conduct of those priests who, instead of submitting to the law, remain hidden in attics where they say mass to several of the elect among their partisans."[47]

Acts of compassion can similarly be found in the conduct of Protestants in Paris and elsewhere in France. In 1791 the pastor Koenig, a member of the *Société des amis de la Constitution d'Annonay*, preached to the members of that club concerning the honor which they owed to their constitutional priests and the love and respect which they owed as Christians to the non-juring priests.[48] When the Protestant Cambon proposed to the Legislative Assembly

tions. Rather than associate themselves with the persecution of these counter-revolutionaries, where their motives might have been misinterpreted, they preferred to leave the duty of taking measures against them to other authorities—the district, the Department, and the *comité de surveillance*, agencies which were largely Catholic in their personnel.

[46] A. Durand, *Histoire religieuse du Département du Gard*, pp. 185-186, 197-199.

[47] Pierre Caron, *Rapports des Agents du Ministère de l'Intérieur dans les Départements* (Paris, 1913-1951), I, 353-354.

[48] *Discours, prononcés à Annonay par J.J.H. Koenig, et imprimés par ordre de la Société des amis de la Constitution*, quoted in part by E. Arnaud, *Histoire des Protestants du Vivarais*, II, 323-324. Part of his address reads: "Frères et amis, si vous avez réformé vos ministres, gardez-vous bien d'avilir le ministère. Honorez vos pasteurs constitutionnels. Pénétrez-vous du respect que vous devez à ceux que vous avez choisis pour présider à votre culte. Comme chrétiens, aimez ceux qui ont refuté le serment prescrit par la loi et respectez leur conscience."

(23 August 1792) the deportation to French Guiana of refractory priests who otherwise would expatriate themselves "to swell the army of the émigrés or to disseminate in Spain, Italy, and Germany principles contrary to our liberty"—a proposal which elicited "vifs applaudissements" from the Assembly—the pastor Lasource, mindful of the fate of Protestants deported under Louis XIV, successfully attacked the measure. "Formerly I prescribed for myself the rule of never taking the floor when it was a question of religion and priests—being myself a priest of another religion—however I shall speak at this time and my opinion will not be suspect. Now I maintain that if you have the right to chase from the heart of society those individuals who disturb public order, from the moment you despoil them of all the advantages of the social contract, you are no longer permitted to say to them: you shall go here. Once separated from society, they are delivered to their own fate; and since they are no longer French citizens, they must no longer be submitted to French laws. They can go where they please. Can we sentence septuagenarians and octogenarians to forced labor? Under Louis XIV 12,000 Frenchmen were sent to Guiana and they perished there. . . . In the name of humanity, in the name of justice, I call for the previous question over Cambon's amendment."[49] In the Convention the following year, Lasource again placed himself in opposition to the proposal of penal measures against the bishop of Ardennes (25 March 1793). Jeanbon Saint-André defended in the Convention (26 June 1793) the maintenance of episcopal vicars when it was suggested that their number be reduced. The pastor Julien de Toulouse was responsible for the enactment of a measure protecting Catholic churches from public desecration (17 March 1793) and effected the release of two priests in the district of Orléans arrested for having insulted a representative on mission.[50] In the Franche-Comté, in Basse Champagne, in Alsace, and at Nîmes there were pastors who gave shelter to refractory priests at the risk of their own lives.[51] Or again, in 1794 and 1795 a Protestant merchant of Rochefort, Elie Thomas, whose family had previously suffered a number of in-

[49] *Archives parlementaires*, 1st series, XLVIII, 668; and BPF, XXXVIII (1889), 67-68.

[50] J. Dedieu, *Histoire politique*, II, 346-347. For further details on these and other acts of sectarian impartiality, consult chapter 3 of Léon Peyric, *Le Rôle religieux des pasteurs dans les assemblées politiques de la Révolution français* (Cahors, 1902).

[51] BPF, XLV (1896), 49-50; and Elisée Briet, *Le Protestantisme en Brie et Basse Champagne du XVIe siècle à nos jours* (Paris, 1885), p. 176.

justices at the hands of Catholic clergy, appealed repeatedly to the abbé Grégoire in the Convention on behalf of 600 unfortunate refractory priests who were imprisoned aboard ship at the Ile d'Aix.[52]

Not many legislators, burdened with the responsibilities of public office, were inclined to show much sympathy for the refractory priests who continually obstructed and preached against the Revolution. Those Protestants who joined in denunciations of these priests did so at the risk of being accused by posterity of giving vent to sectarian rancor, of seeking revenge for past humiliations—simply because they were Protestants. In like manner, a Protestant who exhibited republican leanings at any time during the Revolution was likely to be accused (or accredited, as the case may be) of being a republican as a consequence of being a Calvinist. "The head of the Protestants, Sire, is impregnated with republican ideas"—such was the warning addressed to Louis XVI by one of their enemies before the Revolution had even begun. But if republicanism was criminal then, it has since become fashionable. In the first decade of the twentieth century, when both the Republic and Protestantism came under attack again, we find the positivist Emile Faguet turning the republican stigma to the advantage of the Protestants. "If Protestantism blended in intimately with the history of France in general," he wrote in an essay entitled *Les Trois Anti*, "it did so especially with the history of republican France. The Protestants are the oldest of French republicans. The French monarchy, in defending itself against them, was quite aware of what it was doing, and if all the Saint Bartholomews' were crimes, they were by no means mistakes (i.e. from a monarchial point of view)."[53] Or again, a quarter of a century later, when the anti-republican storm had long since subsided, a historian writing a study on the petition of the revolutionary club of Montpellier in favor of a republic in June of 1791 called the attention of his readers to the religious composition of that club: "It should be noted that the club of Montpellier counted a large number of Protestants among their members; consequently the environment was much more favorable than others to republican ideas."[54]

[52] A. Lods, "Elie Thomas. Un Protestant défenseur de prêtres persécutés," BPF, XXXVIII (1889), 74-85.

[53] In the *Revue latine*, I (1902), 466.

[54] H. Chobaut, "La Pétition du club de Montpellier en faveur de la République," *Annales historiques de la Révolution française*, IV (1927), 547-563.

The Protestants have undeniably been republicans in the past. Whether or not this was a consequence of their religious beliefs is another matter which lies beyond the scope of this work.[55] What does concern us is the question of whether or not the Protestants were republicans in 1789, and if not whether they became republicans with any noticeable facility which distinguished them from their Catholic compatriots.

Perhaps the logical starting point in answering these questions would be the monumental work of Alphonse Aulard on the origins and development of democracy and the republic in the French Revolution. In his first chapter, on the idea of democracy and republicanism in France prior to 1789, Aulard concludes by saying: "In short, no one on the eve of the Revolution thought of establishing a republic in France: this form of government seemed impossible for a great state in the process of unification. It was through the king that men hoped to establish a free government. They wanted to put the monarchy in order, not to destroy it."[56] Was Aulard unaware of the existence of Calvinists in France? Quite the contrary. He went on in the course of his work to cite the royalism of several Protestants to prove his point—Barnave, Lasource, Rabaut Saint-Etienne, and the ferocious Marat—choosing them, it should be added, not because they should be suspected of republicanism because of their religion, but because they were sufficiently important persons to be cited along with a number of others.[57]

We have already had occasion to note the attitude of the Protestant Church toward the monarchy during the period of its trials in the Desert. It might be well to cite at this time a sermon preached in 1778 by the future regicide Jeanbon Saint-André merely as a confirmation of Aulard's contention. "Kings," declared Jeanbon, "are the mainstays of the state, the lieutenants of God on earth, His

[55] See the article by G. Bonet-Maury, "Le Protestantisme français et la République aux XVIe siècles," BPF, LIII (1904), 234-250, 364-384. Bonet-Maury, taking the statement of Emile Faguet that was cited above, attempts to show in these articles that the "republicanism" of the Protestants was not an outgrowth of their religious beliefs—"free inquiry" applied to social institutions—but solely a defensive measure against a monarchy which repeatedly violated its pledges to them.

[56] A. Aulard, *Histoire politique de la Révolution française. Origines et développement de la Démocratie et de la République, 1789-1804* (Paris, 1901), p. 28.

[57] *ibid.*, pp. 6-7 note, 51-53, 123, 181 note (although in this case Aulard thinks the statement in question may have been incorrectly attributed to Lasource).

delegates in the exercise of His justice, or in a word, our leaders and our masters. . . . What is a king? He is a father whom God has established over an immense family in order to watch after its security, provide for its needs, safeguard it against the attacks of its enemies. . . . In the worst of our tribulations, your pastors have unceasingly and forcefully exhorted you *to fear God and to honor the king.* This is the constant and invariable doctrine of our churches. . . ."[58] Always, of course, there was one limitation to the divine right of kings upon which the Protestants insisted. Daniel Armand, in a sermon of 1787 preached in the Bas-Dauphiné, expressed it this way: "Great Prince. . . . The totality of royal power rests in your hands. Over our civil existence you exercise a sovereign authority and an absolute power. Illustrious House of Bourbon, whom the ties of blood unite with our monarch, you also are our legitimate sovereigns; we recognize your authority over our persons and our obligation of obeying you." But, cautioned Armand, the monarch "must not be obeyed when he demands of his subjects unjust things in opposition to the sacred and inviolable duties which every true Christian must fulfill toward his God. The King of kings desires to reign alone over our hearts, and He alone has a right over our souls. The sovereign who seeks to order to his likings the sentiments of his subjects and to violate their consciences, obliges them to be rebels against him, and despite their filial obedience, he thereby compels them to infringe against those of his commands which they firmly believe would render them guilty in the eyes of God. But in disobeying, we must respect the hand which strikes us . . . , even to the point of suffering death without rebelling against him who condemns us."[59]

The French Protestants felt a sincere respect and even love for their sovereigns. By virtue of his graciousness to them, they had all the more reason to honor his person and respect his authority. "Thanks to God," Armand went on to say in connection with the Edict of 1787, "the restriction of passive resistance has become un-

[58] Quoted in L. Lévy-Schneider, *Le Conventionnel Jeanbon Saint-André*, p. 26 (italics Jeanbon's).

[59] BPF, LIV (1905), 131. N.B.: while André Mailhet attributes this sermon to Daniel Armand, Camille Rabaud attributes to Alba Lasource, the future *Conventionnel* who was to vote for Louis XVI's death and against a reprieve of the sentence. Cf. BPF, XXXVIII (1889), 32-33.

necessary; tortures have given way to tolerance, a furious fanaticism has fled before a sweet and Christian philosophy; the wisdom, the clemency, the kindness of our illustrious monarch seem to promise us religious peace and to have banished our fears. . . ." Grateful for the concessions made by Louis XVI in their favor, the Protestants awaited and soon received a fuller measure of recognition as loyal and devoted citizens of their country. These were the victories of the first years of the Revolution, victories carried by their benefactors in the capital. But if blessings came from the hands of legislators, the Protestants were no less grateful to their Bourbon king. "We are not forgetful," wrote the Protestant patriots of Montauban to the National Assembly in 1790, "that it is to our monarch, *the restorer of French liberty*, that we owe the first law which was rendered in the interest of reestablishing our liberty. Worthy of our love and respect, this citizen king shall always be infinitely dear to our hearts. Our fidelity to the laws will be equalled only by our attachment to his sacred person, and we shall strive to prove ever more by this means that this religion, our devotion to which was so long made a crime—that this religion, if it is favorable to liberty, is at the same time the declared enemy of insubordination and license."[60]

Rabaut Saint-Etienne had often and eloquently preached on the beneficence of this illustrious king; but at the first sound of the tocsin he flew to Paris to join the most passionate enemies of the monarchy—such was the charge of Joseph de Maistre, a preposterous charge unless the definition of monarchy is drawn to mean the absolute monarchy of Louis XIV. Rabaut Saint-Etienne began his *Considerations on the Interests of the Third Estate* by citing Louis XVI as "le meilleur des rois" and ended it with an appeal to the members of the third estate: "Fasten yourselves to the glory of your king. The king, he is the rallying-point of good Frenchmen: the king and the nation, there are two ideas which are inseparable, because together their interests are but one. . . .This interest is the happiness of the people, which constitutes the force and the glory of the king."[61] In a letter to a coreligionist describing

[60] François Galabert, "Les sentiments des Protestants au début de la Révolution; Adresse des non-catholiques de Montauban à l'Assemblée nationale (January 1790)," BPF, LI (1902), 151-157.

[61] *Oeuvres de Rabaut Saint-Etienne*, ed. Collin de Plancy, II, 322, 324.

the opening ceremonies of the States General, he told his correspondent of "the noble and touching address made by the king which was interrupted by repeated cries of 'Vive le Roi!' "[62] Later in 1789, when the debates in the Constituent Assembly turned to the matter of a constitution, the pastor from Nîmes had the opportunity of expressing his political views before the assembled nation. Relative to the royal sanction, Rabaut declared: "It is impossible to think that anyone in this Assembly would ever entertain the ridiculous thought of converting the kingdom into a republic. Everyone knows that the republican form of government is hardly suitable for even a small state, and experience has taught us that all republics end by succumbing to an aristocracy or to a despotism. Moreover, the French have always been devoted to the holy, to the venerable antiquity of the monarchy; they are attached to the august blood of their kings for whom they have lavishly shed their own. They revere this beneficent Prince whom they have proclaimed the restorer of French liberty. It is to the throne that people in affliction always turn their eyes for solace, and whatever the evils under which they groan, one word, one single word whose magic charm can only be understood by their love for it—the paternal name of the king—suffices to lead them back to hope. *Hence the French government is monarchial*, and once this principle has been pronounced in this chamber, all that I ask is that the word monarchy should be defined."[63]

Thus spoke one Protestant to the people of France. The sentiments of one of his coreligionists in the Assembly were notably similar. Quatrefages de Laroquete was a prominent bourgeois of Vigan who had actively participated in the political assemblies of his province in 1789 and later had been chosen as one of the representatives of his *sénéchaussée* to the States General. In a letter of 1790 he informed his correspondent of his fears at the move on the part of the Assembly to strip the king of his role in the direction of the nation's foreign policy. Had this succeeded, he wrote, "we should have had a government which would not have been monarchical, and this is the only kind which could suit us or any

[62] Letter of 9 May 1789, published in BPF, L (1901), 257.

[63] A. Lods, "Quelques notes sur les opinions politiques de Rabaut de Saint-Etienne," *La Révolution française*, XL (1901), 353-357 (Rabaut's italics).

great nation."[64] Nor was he any less immune than other Frenchmen to the adulation which surrounded the person of the king. On the eve of the first anniversary of the fall of the Bastille, he was deeply moved by the popular acclaim of Louis which he witnessed on the occasion of a public review. His friend was to know that the king "received the keenest, the fullest marks of the love which the people have for him; they all but worshipped him. Our good king, this king of men . . . received these testimonies from the whole of France with emotion. How splendid, how delightful it must be to be loved so much! He is the king of all our hearts, and he has an absolute empire over mine. The queen was the object of a like amount of affection. The Dauphin, that dear young child, the hope of his country, gave proof of the fulness of his heart: unable to express all the emotions he felt, he threw kisses to all those who were unable to gain his presence in order to kiss his hand. What a glorious day approaches! The nation and its leader reunited! The heavens will resound with cries of joy, cheer, and love. Tears of emotion will flow from the eyes of all. I wish that the entire universe could have witnessed a scene so worthy of the nation and the king."[65]

This king—what status would he enjoy under the constitution which all desired? Rabaut Saint-Etienne's definition of the word monarchy in these early years of the Revolution changed with time and with his political experiences at Versailles and Paris. Late in 1788 his political philosophy was similar to that of the party which was later to be known as the Anglophiles, Monarchicals, "Englishmen," or Anglomaniacs. He advocated, in his profound respect for the English constitution, a constitutional monarchy based on a bicameral legislature (100 clergy and 200 nobles in the upper house; 500 commoners in the lower) with an executive veto reserved for the king.[66] By early fall of 1789 he expressed surprise that anyone could consider applying such a system to France, a homogeneous society where privileges no longer existed, and he joined with the majority of the patriots under the Lameth brothers,

[64] François Rouvière, *Quatrefages de Laroquete*, pp. 32-33.

[65] *ibid.*, pp. 39-40.

[66] *A la Nation française; sur les vices de son gouvernement; sur la nécessité d'établir une Constitution; et sur la composition des Etats-Généraux* (s.l., November 1788), 91 pp.

du Port, and the Protestant Barnave as a partisan of the unicameral system with a suspensive veto for the king.[67] But in either case the polity of France was to be monarchical and constitutional, and in this Rabaut Saint-Etienne was in step with the overwhelming majority of the French.[68] As for his coreligionists in the Assembly, they, too, seem to have shared his beliefs. In the parliamentary crisis of mid-June 1789, all the Protestants except Chambon-Latour signed the Tennis Court Oath—"Whereas the National Assembly has been called to draft a constitution for the kingdom, effect the regeneration of public order and maintain the true principles of the monarchy . . . , all members of this Assembly shall at once take a solemn oath never to separate . . . until the constitution of the kingdom shall be laid and established on secure foundations . . . ," a pledge which only one member of the third estate refused to take.

But for Frenchmen who looked to the monarchy as the rallying-point of the Revolution, bitter disillusionments were in store. In June of 1791, Louis XVI, overwhelmed with remorse at having acquiesced to the Civil Constitution of the Clergy, hostile to the Constitution which his assembly had prepared for him, fled from Paris with the intention of placing himself at the head of the armies of the counter-revolution. Stupor, indignation, and fear in succession overwhelmed the partisans of a constitutional monarchy and a revolutionary France. The "Republic" was a word that began to be heard. Indeed, from 21 June to 14 September France functioned as a republic, for the royal power was provisionally suspended. The news of the betrayal reverberated throughout the provinces. In Montpellier, the impact of the news was especially violent. On 27 June a member of the city's patriotic club read an address expressing republican sympathies; the following day the club dispatched to Paris and to its affiliated societies an address denouncing the king as a "costly and superfluous ornament of the Constitution" and calling for the establishment of a republic.[69]

[67] See his "Principes de toute Constitution" and his address to the Constituent of 4 September 1789 in the *Archives parlementaires*, 1st series, VIII, 406-407, 567-572.

[68] The almost universal desire for a constitution in 1789 is a point which hardly need be elaborated upon here. But for an indication of the demands of the cahiers on this point, see Edme Champion, *La France d'après les Cahiers de 1889*, chapter 3.

[69] The text of the petition is given by A. Aulard, *Histoire politique de la Révolution française*, pp. 142-143.

"The club of Montpellier counted a large number of Protestants among its members; consequently the environment was much more favorable than others to republican ideas." However, the author of this statement himself admitted that the speaker of 27 June and the principal author of the republican declaration was not a Protestant, but a Catholic.[70] In Paris the declaration fell on deaf ears (its reading at the Jacobin club of the capital was interrupted and declared unconstitutional).[71] And what of the Protestant environment of the Midi? The patriotic club of Aiguesvives, almost totally Protestant, at first adhered to the republican manifesto. But a week later, on the intervention of the pastor Ribes, it decided that its adherence had been premature and stayed the dispatch of its earlier decision.[72] At Toulouse, the patriotic club meeting under the presidency of the pastor Jean Julien rejected the address and declared for the maintenance of the monarchy. At Nîmes, the Protestant club became the principal source of opposition to the proposal, and it was under its leadership that the clubs of Anduze, Saint-Hippolyte, and Annonay declared themselves for the monarchy.[73]

In Paris, the Protestant deputies of Gard (Rabaut Saint-Etienne, Voulland, Soustelle, Meynier, and Chambon-Latour) were dismayed at the talk of a republic. In a collective letter to the club of Nîmes, they warned the patriots at home that factionists were trying to turn the king's flight to their own personal advantage. "Foreigners have been seen, whose accents have betrayed them, pronouncing loudly that the throne is vacant, that Louis XVI must no longer be obeyed." These, they said, were supported by bad Frenchmen known for their evil morals and by some good Frenchmen who were given to making too much of everything in calling for who-knows-what kind of republic.[74] In the Constituent Assem-

[70] H. Chobaut, "La Pétition du club de Montpellier. . . ," *Annales historiques de la Révolution française*, IV (1927), 551.

[71] Aulard found no trace of the proposal's having been discussed in the Paris Jacobins; Chobaut thinks that it was read to the society in the session of 6 July and that the verbal proceedings incorrectly attributed it to the club of Perpignan. Cf. *ibid.*, 556.

[72] *ibid.*, 552; and the study of the popular society of Aiguesvives by Chobaut in the *Mémoires de l'Académie de Nîmes*, 7th series, XLII (1924-1925), 41.

[73] Chobaut, "Pétition du club de Montpellier. . . ," cited above, 552-554.

[74] Letter of 17 July 1791 published in *La Révolution française*, XXXV (1898), 265-268.

bly itself, it was Barnave who led in the attack upon the republicans. "Several men whose intentions I do not wish to accuse. . . , several men who perhaps seek to play at politics like Romans, because it is easier to work in this way than to contribute to the real and positive prosperity of their country, looking to other hemispheres for examples to give us, have seen in America . . . a republican government established over a vast territory. From this they have concluded that the same government might be suitable to us. These men . . . are the same ones who today contest the principle of the king's inviolability. Now, if it is true that an immense population is spread over our territory; if it is true that a multitude of men reside here exclusively occupied with those speculations of the mind which exert their imaginations, which carry them into ambition and the love of glory; if it is true that we are surrounded by powerful neighbors who oblige us to act in unison in order to resist them to advantage; if it is true that all these circumstances are real and are independent of us, then it is incontestable that the only remedy for them rests in a monarchical government."[75] According to Barnave, if the republican experiment in America was a happy one, it was only because America was a nation of farmers too busy hoeing their corn and planting their potatoes to discover for themselves the intrinsic weaknesses of a republican polity. France was a monarchy; if the Revolution were to stop, if it were to be kept from plunging forward and leading the country into anarchy, the monarchy would have to be maintained.

The enthusiasm with which the Assembly received Barnave's address undercut the plans of the republicans and for the time being saved the monarchy. But their king had undeniably tried to desert the Revolution; in so doing he shattered the prestige of the throne. Barnave, in defending the throne, did not appeal to tradition, to the love of the ruling family, to the emotional royalism of Frenchmen. His argument was reduced to one of sheer utility and necessity. Louis was no longer the national head of the Revolution, but an instrument, an expedient, for safeguarding what the Revolution had already achieved. For the moment Louis' inviolability was respected, but the Constitution was amended in such a way that if the king were ever again to place himself at the head of armies

[75] Session of 15 July 1791; *Archives parlementaires*, 1st series, XXVIII, 326-331.

hostile to the nation, or if he were ever to retract his oath to the Constitution once he had pledged it, he would be considered to have abdicated and to have devolved to the status of a common citizen, and as such would be held responsible to the nation for his conduct. The monarchy was saved, not so much in the interests of the monarchy as because of the bourgeois fear of a democratic republic, their fear of the *canaille* and their solicitude for their property. In 1788 Rabaut Saint-Etienne had called the king the rallying-point of the French people; in 1791, after the flight to Varennes, Barnave called the Constitution the rallying-point. On 16-17 July in Paris, the republican demonstrations of the mob they feared, the massacre of the Champ de Mars, showed how far the Bourbon star had fallen.

But the royalist victory was transitory. There followed a year of economic hardship which confirmed the Paris working class in their belief that somewhere the Revolution had gone awry. There came war and the development of a war hysteria; there grew an increasing belief that Louis XVI was associated with the enemies of France, that he was being used by bourgeois politicians as a bulwark against reforms in the interest of the people. On 10 August 1792 Paris erupted in revolt. The proletariat stormed the Tuileries and placed the king and his family in captivity. A revolutionary municipal government abrogated the Constitution and forced the calling of a National Convention. Universal suffrage was declared.

Meeting on 21 September, with slightly less than one half of its members in attendance, the new Convention unanimously voted the abolition of the monarchy. The next day, seemingly afraid to pronounce the word Republic, the members backed into a republican polity by pronouncing that 22 September 1792 should be dated as the first day of the Year One of the French Republic. What of the king? For three months he remained in prison. The presence of the armies of the coalition on French soil made the thought of putting him on trial too dangerous to entertain. But with subsequent republican victories in the field, with the discovery of papers incriminating Louis in treasonable activities, the trial could no longer be delayed. In December the proceedings began.

The Protestants in Paris were so much flotsam swept away in the revolutionary current of '92. Lasource, who had preached devotion to the monarchy in 1788, who as late as April of 1792 had declared that "no one is so ill advised as to desire a republican government, which is possible only in theory,"[76] this same Lasource on 10 August joined in the assault on the Tuileries, and was one of those who proposed that 22 September be dated the first day of the Republic.[77] Jeanbon Saint-André, entering national politics for the first time as a deputy to the National Convention, in his first message back to Montauban attacked the king "who has led us from crime to crime," and soon thereafter assured his constituents that "it was necessary for the happiness of France to overturn a throne soiled with all manner of crimes, to strike down an idol too long adored.[78] Rabaut Saint-Etienne, who had been so alarmed at the talk of a republic in 1791, exulted at the events of 10 August: "The French are back where they were at the time of the flight to Varennes, with this one advantage, that the treasons of the king have enlightened the most blind and separated him from his closest confidants. This king has delivered us from all kings. A year of his perfidies has done more than a century of reasoning to destroy the royalty which six thousand years of adulation had aged and sanctified."[79] Only one of the Protestants in Paris during the summer of 1792 appears to have remained loyal to the monarch. On 20 June, when the Paris mob invaded the royal palace and threatened Louis with his life, Laffon de Ladébat, a deputy from the Gironde to the Legislative Assembly, joined in the defense of the king and his family.[80]

So complete a change in the political complexion of these men is not easy to explain. Jeanbon Saint-André from the beginning of

[76] BPF, XXXVIII (1889), 64.

[77] *ibid.*, 67: regarding his conduct on 10 August, he later wrote to the patriotic club of Castres: "J'ai trahi ma patrie? Et quand? Quand j'ai bravé la mort, le 10 août, sous le canon du château et que j'ai fait chasser de la salle des représentants du peuple le tyran perfide, dont la présence compromettait le salut du Corps législatif!" In the session of 22 September, he insisted that "Il est ridicule de dater de l'an quatrième de la liberté; car, sous la constitution, le peuple n'avoit point de liberté véritable. . . . Non, messieurs, nous ne sommes libres que depuis que nous n'avons plus de roi. Je demande donc que l'on date de l'an premier de la République." See A. Aulard, *Histoire politique de la Révolution française*, p. 273.

[78] Letters of 23 September and 3 October 1792, published in *La Révolution française*, XXIX (1895), 64-65.

[79] Public letter to Garat, 25 August 1792, published in *La Révolution française*, XL (1901), 356.

[80] *Dictionnaire des Parlementaires français*, eds. Adolphe Robert, Edgar Bourloton, and Gaston Cougny (Paris, 1891), III, 522. Laffon de Ladébat was arrested the following December, accused of having received money from the king, but was subsequently released when the accusation proved unfounded.

his political career in the Jacobin club of Montauban had championed the cause of the populace against the wealthier interests in the city; perhaps it was only natural that 10 August should have found him among its partisans. But with Lasource, with Rabaut Saint-Etienne, who had expressed the fear in 1791 that if the constitution were changed Frenchmen would lose their liberty,[81] the change is harder to fathom. Undoubtedly they had been infected with the patriotism which came of war, unnerved by the equivocal position of the king. As Protestants who had gained more from the Revolution than almost any other Frenchmen, they may have felt they had more to lose should the Revolution have faltered, should the counter-revolution have triumphed.

Whatever the case, the trial of Louis XVI demonstrated how little respect they had left for the "restorer of French liberty." Late in December, Rabaut Saint-Etienne joined in the Girondin attempt to delay the trial by denying that the Convention had the right to try the king. "If the judges are at the same time legislators, if they decide the laws, the forms, the times, if they accuse and they condemn, if they have all the legislative, executive, and judiciary powers, then it is not in France, but in Constantinople, Lisbon, and Goa that one must look for liberty."[82] Only the people could decide on Louis' fate. But his appeal was less in the interests of his king than a political maneuver in the interests of his party, for the Girondins hoped that an appeal to the latent royalism of the provinces would strengthen their shaky position in the contest for power with the Paris Jacobins. The debates only postponed the decision, for the Girondin tactics failed. On 14 January 1793 the voting commenced on Louis' fate. The first question—Is Louis guilty?—was voted in the affirmative almost unanimously. The second vote—whether a plebiscite should be held to ratify the Convention's judgment of Louis—resulted in a substantial Jacobin victory: 425 deputies voting against the plebiscite, 286 for it. Of the twenty Protestant deputies present at the balloting, only five voted for the appeal to the people:

[81] See his letter of 27 August 1791 to the pastor Bruguier in *La Révolution française*, xxxv (1898), 269-270, part of which reads: "Depuis que la législature prochaine s'avance, tous les mécontents se réunissent pour la convertir en Assemblée constituant. . . . Sparte était une République, et elle avait deux rois. . . . Si nos successeurs maintiennent le Constitution, ils seront vos sauveurs; s'ils veulent en faire une autre, vous êtes perdus."

[82] Session of 28 December 1792: *Archives parlementaires*, 1st series LVI, 7-10.

Berthezène (Gard), Boissy d'Anglas (Annonay), Cussy (Calvados), Rabaut-Pomier (Gard), and Rabaut Saint-Etienne (now a deputy from Aube). On 16 January the vote on the penalty to be meted out to Louis began. One after another the deputies mounted the tribune to announce their decisions, often explaining them in a few words, sometimes with lengthy speeches. For twenty-four hours the poll went on. On the evening of the 17th, the final decision had been recorded: 361 had voted for the death penalty without qualifications. Of these, eleven were Protestants, and Lasource, absent on mission at the time of the voting, added the twelfth vote by letter. Two hundred and eighty-eight had decided on exile or imprisonment; only four of these were Protestants: Bernard-Saint-Affrique (Aveyron), Boissy d'Anglas, Cussy, and Rabaut Saint-Etienne. Louis Capet was condemned to death by a bare majority of one of all the members of the Convention, but of the twenty Protestants voting, seventeen had pronounced for the supreme penalty with or without modifications.[88] One more question still had to be decided: should Louis be granted a reprieve? On 19 January his fate was sealed: the reprieve was denied 380 to 310, nine Protestants casting their ballots for the reprieve, twelve against. On the 21st, Louis was led to the scaffold.

The Protestant vote at the king's trial revealed more than their attitude toward the monarchy. The trial had become a political issue in the contest between the Jacobins and the Girondins. All seven of those Protestants clearly identified with the party of the left (Moïse Bayle, Jean Jay, Jeanbon Saint-André, Julien de Toulouse, Marat, Voulland, and Eschassériaux aîné) had voted together on the questions of the penalty, plebiscite, and reprieve. Four were Girondins (Cussy and the pastors Lasource, Rabaut-Pomier, and Rabaut Saint-Etienne) and, as with the Girondin balloting as a whole, they split their votes. The remainder of the Protestants belonged to that amorphous "plain," the centrists who swung first one way and then the other, depending on which way the wind seemed to be blowing. Hence the Protestant camp in Paris was split along party lines, party affiliations being determined largely by the social and economic outlook of the deputies.

Similarly in the Midi the cohesiveness of the Protestant ranks

[88] See the chart of the Protestant vote in Appendix IV.

caused by the outbreaks of 1790 began to collapse as the Revolution drifted slowly but inexorably to the left. The first signs of a change came in the summer of 1791 over the crisis precipitated by the king's flight. Because of the way in which the Paris Jacobins had flirted with the anti-monarchical demonstrations which culminated in the massacre of the Champ de Mars, most of the deputies to the National Assembly who belonged to the Paris Jacobins withdrew from that club and established a rival and more moderate faction at the Feuillants. Among the secessionists were Barnave, Boissy d'Anglas, and the Protestant deputies from Gard. In Gard as early as June of 1791, the Protestant Griolet, the administrative head of the Department (*procureur général syndic*) and one of the dominant personalities in the bourgeois club of Nîmes, had been disquieted at the nature of the constitution being framed at Paris, which he interpreted as leaning too far toward a republic.[84] Hence when their deputies in Paris wrote to the club of Nîmes urging them to affiliate with the Feuillant faction, they did so immediately and announced their decision to the populace in an address denouncing the Jacobins and accusing them of trying to subvert the monarchy.[85] The members of the club at Nîmes, it should be pointed out, were members of the wealthier middle class in the city. The dues of their society, twenty-four livres, were sufficiently high to exclude the popular element. Hence their repudiation of the Jacobins and their displeasure at the trend of events in Paris were largely an expression of sympathy with the statement of Barnave in July 1791 that "one step more in the direction of liberty would be the destruction of the monarchy; one more in the direction of equality, the *destruction of property*." If they were loyal to the monarchy, it was largely because they were fearful for the safety of their property.

At Montauban, however, the social composition of the club was much less distinct. At its foundation, the club had established a

[84] Letter of 17 June 1791, quoted by Charles Pouthas, *Une famille de bourgeoisie française*, pp. 109-110 note: "La révision [de la Constitution] peut sauver la France et nous donner un ordre de choses stables, si nos représentants ont la sagesse de réformer plus que le courage de tout détruire. . . . Il nous faut un caractère plus monarchique, une pente moins rapide vers la république. . . ."

[85] The text of their address is given in F. Rouvière, *Révolution dans le Gard*, II, 65-68. It begins with the warning: "Vous le savez, l'évasion du Roi et de sa famille a fait concevoir à quelques spéculateurs hardis le projet chimérique de constituer la France en République. . . ."

scale of dues from six to twenty-four livres based on the ability of members to pay; for those of little means no fees at all were demanded. Thus at its foundation the membership was almost equally divided between well-to-do middle class and working men (including small merchants). Moreover, admissions to the club in the early part of 1791 were mostly from the lower middle class and the working population, although still largely Protestant.[86] Jeanbon Saint-André was the leader of the popular faction from the moment he joined the club. His sympathies as well as those of the majority of the club were expressed on the eve of the elections to the Legislative Assembly by his proposal that the club address the citizens of Montauban "to point out to them the futility of wealth and to invite them to consider it less than merit in the approaching elections."[87] A struggle for power in the club between the popular and conservative factions was being waged when the news of the flight to Varennes arrived. The reaction to the flight brought a conservative victory. A proposal that an address be sent to the Assembly demanding that the throne be declared vacant because of Louis' conduct was shelved and the club instead requested the punishment of those who were the authors and accomplices of the king's "abduction."[88] But this was the last of the conservative triumphs. When news came of the split in the Paris Jacobins and that Montauban's deputy, Poncet-Delpech, had joined the Feuillants, a motion for an adherence to the new club was defeated under the leadership of Jeanbon Saint-André. The club maintained its connections with the Jacobins and urged the secessionists to return to the mother club. With this, the attendance of the conservative element at the club began to wane and the Montauban patriots drifted steadily to the left.

[86] F. Galabert, "Le Club jacobin de Montauban. . . ," *Revue d'histoire moderne et contemporaine*, I, (1899-1900), 124-168, 235-258, 457-474; and L. Lévy-Schneider, *Le Conventionnel Jeanbon Saint-André*, pp. 95-100.

[87] Lévy-Schneider, *Le Conventionnel Jeanbon Saint-André*, p. 95

[88] F. Galabert, "Le Club jacobin de Montauban. . . ," cited above, p. 257. In a letter subsequently sent to the Feuillants, the club declared that "Nous sommes loin d'approuver les idées exagérées que la fuite et le retour du roi ont fait naître dans l'esprit de quelques citoyens qui se sont bien plus attachés à la rigueur des principes qu'à la nécessité souvent insurmontable de les faire plier aux circonstances. . . . Même avant que l'Assemblée nationale eût prononcé, nous avions exprimé par une adresse le voeu formel de la voir user de clémence et s'attacher bien plutôt à prévenir pour l'avenir les fautes des rois qu'à punir celle dont Louis XVI s'est rendu coupable."

The exclusiveness of the bourgeois club at Nîmes was resented by the lower classes. The latent social hostility was heightened by an economic crisis. Throughout France the value of money had steadily fallen. The olive groves in the area around Nîmes, killed by a heavy frost in 1789, had not yet begun to produce. In November 1791 torrential rains and floods ruined the winter wheat crop, making the economic prospects for the coming spring anything but auspicious. The local administration reopened its charity offices.

The economic crisis and the feeling that middle-class politicians were not taking all the measures they could to alleviate it had led to the formation of the Popular Society of the Friends of the Constitution of Nîmes on 13 November 1791. The leaders of the new society were two Protestants named Méyère and Leyris-Descombes (the latter a deputy to the Legislative Assembly) and the initial membership was drawn from the lower classes.[89] The new club adopted the statutes of what it regarded as the "club mère établi en cette ville," but in aiming its activities toward the popular classes set its dues at only six livres. Relations between the two societies were initially polite, but the bourgeois club realized that it had made an error in not broadening its social base. In hopes of avoiding rivalry between the groups, they invited the new society to amalgamate with their own. But it was too late. The workers rejected the invitation with the explanation that "the only difference which exists, brothers and friends, between your society and ours, is in the manner in which we express our thoughts; with you, the eloquence of a few imposes over the majority a respectful but dangerous silence; with us, on the other hand, everyone can be heard, because we all speak the same language. Otherwise the same spirit animates us, the same interests direct us. . . ."[90] The workers wanted to be heard and, while they accepted affiliation with the mother club, they steadfastly refused repeated efforts on the part of the latter to swallow them up.

The events of 1792 created political differences between the clubs to the point where neither could pretend any longer that they shared

[89] F. Rouvière, *Révolution dans le Gard*, II, 69 note: the thirty initial members were comprised of eleven stocking workers, seven taffeta workers, two merchants, two textile warpers, a shoemaker, a manufacturer of *eau de vie*, a landed proprietor, a bourgeois, and three unidentified persons.

[90] *ibid.*, II, 75.

the same interests. In March the popular club of Nîmes began corresponding with the Paris Jacobins. When Louis XVI dismissed his Girondin ministry in June, the bourgeois society of Nîmes petitioned for the reinstatement of the "patriot ministers" and asked its affiliated societies to adhere to its request. The popular club, however, while it complied by drawing up a similar petition, added to it the demand for the abolition of the royal veto. The Paris demonstration against the monarchy, 20 June 1792, consummated the rupture between them. The popular society sent its felicitations to the faubourg Saint-Antoine for the part it had played in the events, called for volunteers, armed and financed them, and sent them to Paris for the federation of 14 July—all measures in direct opposition to the express wishes of the bourgeois administrators of the Department. On 27 July, at the instigation of the Jacobins of Marseille, the popular club petitioned the Assembly for the suspension of the king.

The coolness with which the departmental administrators and the bourgeois club received the news of 10 August ended any sympathy the democrats of the area had left for them. Throughout the remainder of the summer and into the fall they repeatedly denounced the conservative group and tried in the elections of November to capture control of the local administrations. They succeeded in the ouster of Griolet, but the conservatism of the countryside allowed the wealthy interests to retain control of all but the district of Nîmes. Revitalized by their electoral victory and seeing clearly in the trial of the king the course which the Revolution was now taking in Paris, the bourgeois Protestants of Nîmes began to organize for the defense of their position. On 4 January 1793 they petitioned for the arrest and trial of Marat, and a week later, in answer to a subsequent petition from the conservative club, the *conseil* of the Department approved a plan for the creation of a departmental force "destined to repair to Paris at the first signal to place itself under the orders of the Convention"—a measure which Rabaut Saint-Etienne had urged from the tribune and which was designed to protect the deputies from the coercion of the Paris mob.

In Paris, the struggle for power between the Mountain and the Girondins increased in intensity after the trial of the king. The Jacobins, with the support of the Paris populace, tried to discredit and rid themselves of their opponents by attacking those who had voted for a plebiscite on the king's death (an act which the popular club of Nîmes had twice demanded) and accusing the Girondins of complicity in the treason of General Dumouriez. The Girondins countered by trying unsuccessfully to remove Marat from politics by bringing him to trial, by stirring up revolt in the provinces, and by proposing that the Convention be moved to Bourges to free it from intimidation by the Paris mob. The latter proposal was rejected, but they did succeed in establishing a Commission of Twelve to investigate the actions of the Paris commune. Its members were Girondins, among them Rabaut Saint-Etienne. Their attempts at breaking the power of the commune were thwarted. On 31 May 1793 the commune organized a band of democrats, invaded the Convention, and forced the arrest of the principal Girondins and the members of the Commission of Twelve. Rabaut Saint-Etienne and Lasource were among the proscribed; Rabaut-Pomier's arrest was subsequently ordered for his protest against the events of this day. Those who could fled into the provinces to raise the standard of revolt against the monster Paris. Hiding near Versailles, Rabaut Saint-Etienne appealed to the citizens of Gard: "If the Departments do not declare themselves with energy, liberty is done for. The good citizens of Paris await them and will bless them as liberators. It is France who must save France. . . . Long live the Republic, one and indivisible, but the Republic will survive only by a universal rising of all the republican Departments."[91]

The Protestants of Gard had closely followed events in Paris. As early as March, sections, or impromptu directive and vigilance committees, had been organized in Nîmes; in May the *conseil* of the Department called for the enrollment of 2,400 men, and shortly thereafter the sections of Nîmes warned Paris by petition that "too long we have counted on the virtuous republicans of Paris. . . . We want and we will have the Republic one and indivisible. We will obey neither a king, nor a dictator, nor triumvirs, nor a commune, but only laws conserving and protective of persons and property."[92] The administration of the Department approved the threat and several citizens, including Rabaut Dupui, were charged with presenting it to the Convention. News of the arrests of 31 May sparked open revolt. The bourgeois club and the sections declared the Paris commune in "open revolt against the entire nation." They closed

[91] Letter of 20 June 1793, printed in *La Révolution française,* XXXV (1898), 275-277.
[92] F. Rouvière, *Révolution dans le Gard,* III, 276-277.

the popular club, disarmed the democrats, and purged the administration of their sympathizers. Under the leadership of Griolet, they entered into correspondence with their counterparts in Grenoble to take steps for the calling of a convention and the establishment of a federal republic of the twenty-four Departments of the Midi. The Protestant bourgeoisie of the south plunged headlong into the ill-fated federalist revolt of 1793.

The rising of the bourgeoisie of Gard was directed against the democratic tyranny which they believed the Jacobins of Paris had unleashed in the capital. They were the revolutionaries of '89 turned against the revolutionaries of '93. Of their troops they demanded the oath to "maintain with all their power liberty and equality, the Republic one and indivisible, the security of persons and properties." Vague and undecided in their political goals, the center of their program was the preservation of their property. In their manifesto of 22 June 1793 they declared their aims to be "liberty without license, equality without anarchy, the Republic founded on inviolable laws, protective of properties and persons." Their enemy was that "murderous liberty which saps public order, ravages properties, and destroys industries." Their appeal: "You who desire peace and public order, to arms! You who have property, to arms, or soon it will be ravaged; you who wish to pass on to your children the fruit of your painful labors, the money you have earned by your services, to arms!"[98]

The manifesto of these federalists had been prepared by the representative assembly of the communes of Gard, meeting under the presidency of the Protestant Vigier-Sarrazin. Still without armed forces of any consequence, they called for a departmental force of 1,200 men "to march on the factious of Paris and liberate the Convention." To direct it, they created a Committee of Public Safety composed of the administrators of the Department and sixteen representatives of the districts (the majority of whom were bourgeois Protestants) under the direction of the Protestant Cardonnet. A military and political bureau were created, and a representative, Guizot-Gignoux, the father of the future premier of France, was sent to Hérault to spur resistance there.

The revolt was doomed. For all their committees and bureaus, for all their manifestos and elaborate plans for marching on Paris,

[98] Charles Pouthas, *Une famille de bourgeoisie française*, p. 131.

the rebels never succeeded in building muscle around their rising. Their cause was patently that of the rich. The masses were indifferent or even hostile. There were few volunteers; a *levée en masse* was ignored by the citizens. At the crucial test of strength, they had no more than 700 men to put in the field against the army of 4,000 which was sent against them. On 14 July 1793, the fourth anniversary of the Revolution which they felt had been betrayed, their pitiful legion surrendered without a fight. Their cause collapsed.

The following months were ones of revenge. On 20 July the popular club reopened; a few weeks later the bourgeois club was closed. Political power fell to the democrats; the leaders of the revolt went into hiding or fled from the scene. For the first time the laws against the refractory priests were enforced. Gard, which had tried to withstand the impetus of the Revolution, received its initiation to a revolutionary government. From December to February of 1794, the chiefs of the rising were tried and executed. The justice of revolutionary tribunals claimed the lives of ninety-five in Nîmes; forty-six of these were Protestants. Thirty-three of the victims had held public offices in the area, and of these twenty-four were Protestants, among them Guizot-Gignoux.[94]

A similar fate awaited Lasource and Rabaut Saint-Etienne in Paris. Lasource was discovered and arrested before the end of June. Tried and convicted of treason, he was executed on 31 October. At about the same time Rabaut Saint-Etienne and Rabaut-Pomier quit Versailles and returned to Paris, where they were taken in and sheltered by a Catholic family originally from Nîmes—an act of charity for which the latter were soon to lose their lives. There the two brothers were discovered in a hidden room on 5 December. Rabaut-Pomier was imprisoned but subsequently released after 9 thermidor. His brother, who had been outlawed, was taken before the revolutionary tribunal only long enough to be identified. This done, he was ordered put to death within twenty-four hours. His remains were buried in the cemetery of the Madeleine beside those of the king on whose behalf he had jeopardized his life. This was not the end of the tragedy for the Rabaut family. In Nîmes Rabaut Saint-Etienne's wife, on learning that her husband had been outlawed, committed suicide by throwing herself into an abandoned mine shaft. His father, Paul Rabaut, the apostle and heir to Antoine Court, covered

[94] Charles Pouthas, *Une famille de bourgeoisie française*, p. 168.

with suspicion because of the political activities of his three sons, was imprisoned during the summer of 1794. Released after the fall of Robespierre, he died within two weeks.

At the hands of posterity, the Protestants of France have been victimized by persons too eager to vilify them or by those too anxious to praise them. Their histories are either libels or encomiums. The former treat them as diseased (or at best incongruous) members of an otherwise Catholic society; the latter in overzealously trying to rectify such calumnies all too often give them a distinctiveness which is not really theirs. The Protestants are accused of turning the Revolution into a proscription of their purportedly ancient enemies, whereas in fact they acted no differently from their Catholic compatriots. There were Protestants in Paris who defended the Catholic Church. In the Department of Gard, where for four years the administration was dominated by bourgeois Calvinists, the rigorous enforcement of laws against the refractory priests waited till after power had fallen from the hands of these men, and then was executed by an administration that was more Catholic than it had been earlier.[95]

They are accused of subverting the throne, whereas in fact they merely sought what all other Frenchmen desired: a constitutional monarchy. Ostensibly the enemies of the Crown, their devotion to it cost some of them their lives. If Rabaut Saint-Etienne was proscribed, it was because he was a Girondin—but his vote at the trial of the king was never forgotten by his enemies. Barnave, who had defended the constitutional position of the king in 1791, subsequently endeavored in a voluminous correspondence with the royal family to preserve the monarchy by persuading the monarch to abide by the Constitution. The discovery of these letters after 10 August led to his imprisonment and subsequently to his death. An obscure pastor of Meaux, Jean-Baptiste Hervieux, accused of sympathy for priests and his king, was led to Paris and guillotined in June of 1794.[96]

Their partisans have made them disparate. "Almost all the Protestants," wrote Pierre Chazel, "had what Sainte-Beuve called the

[95] *ibid.*, p. 158.

[96] A. Lods, "Un ancien pasteur du Désert, mort sur l'échafaud," BPF, XXXIX (1890), 320-325.

Girondin temperament. Their provincial origins, their social position, their religious idealism, everything drew them toward what was less a political party solidly organized for battle than a great current of French thought and feeling. They were Girondins as a consequence of their optimism and enthusiasm for liberty. They had suffered too much from the oppression and the murderous conceptions of religious unity not to regard with horror the renaissance of that old idol of unity, the hypocritical shape of the tyranny of consciences: Jacobinism."[97] But were all Protestants Girondins? It was the Protestant Cambon who demanded the arrest of the Protestant Barnave.[98] During the period when the Girondins were proscribed in Paris, the Protestants Gasparin and Jeanbon Saint-André sat on the Committee of Public Safety; the Protestants Julien de Toulouse, Voulland, and Moïse Bayle on the Committee of General Security.[99] In Gard, the democratic administration which emerged from the ruins of the abortive Federalist revolt was led by the Protestant Cazalis and included the Protestants Elie Dumas, Maigron, Jean Rame, Bonicel, and Soustelle père; the Committee of Public Safety charged with cleansing the area of federalists counted among its members Méyère and Leyris-Descombes.[100] And in 1794 when the directory of the Department was again purged of those who had demonstrated "too much weakness for the revolutionary government," they were replaced by eight new zealots, two of whom had formerly been Protestant pastors.[101] In Castres, while the pastor Nazon was expelled from the revolutionary club as a Girondin, his former colleague Bonifas-Laroque was sufficiently Jacobin to survive the purging of the local revolutionary tribunal in 1794, where he served as judge until 1795.[102] And what of the federalist revolt? More than sixty departments and most of the large provincial cities

[97] Pierre Chazel, "Génie français et Protestantisme dans la France contemporaine," in *Protestantisme français*, eds. Marc Boegner and André Siegfried, p. 82. Or see Charles Durand, *op.cit.*, p. 78: "La ruine de parti girondin fut aussi la leur."

[98] Jean-Jacques Chevallier, *Barnave, ou deux faces de la Révolution* (Paris, 1936), p. 335.

[99] Jacques Godeshot, *Les Institutions de la France sous la Révolution et l'Empire* (Paris, 1951), pp. 274-275.

[100] Rouvière, *Révolution dans le Gard*, IV, 16.

[101] Charles Pouthas, *Une famille de bourgeoisie française*, p. 157. The former pastors were Elie Dumas and Jean Rame.

[102] Camille Rabaud, "Un ministre chrétien sous la Terreur, Bonifas-Laroque," BPF, XXXVIII (1889), 393-402.

of France rose in arms against Paris and the Convention in the summer of 1793. The Protestants who joined the revolt were "bien français."

Boissy d'Anglas contended that the Protestants formed too large a part of French society for the opinions which divided the nation not to be equally found among them; that as members of the third estate it was the opinions of the *tiers* which they most often espoused. If there were proportionately fewer Protestants in the armies of the princes (which was not necessarily so), it was because there were hardly any Protestant nobles left in France; because their ministers were lay ministries and not under the influence of a foreign and hostile Rome. And, in fact, it is by no means certain that there were proportionately fewer Protestants in the armies of the princes. The historian Emile-G. Léonard, as a consequence of more recent research in this field, maintains that "a substantial proportion of the Protestant nobility rallied to the royalist armies, either in France (where they had as leaders notably François Mallet in Haute-Normandie and in the Nord, and the Frottés in Basse-Normandie) or in the emigration, especially around the Prince of Condé, whose name is dear to the Protestants."[103] The first years of the Revolution brought their middle class to political power, propertied men who feared the democratic perils of a Republic; it saw a handful of their pastors elected to public office, men whose own experiences in the Protestant Church made them view presbyterianism and democratic government in the Church with grave suspicion. It is most unlikely that either the laity or the pastors should have been any more republican

[103] Emile-G. Léonard, *Le Protestant français* (Paris, 1953), p. 73n. See also p. 76, where he briefly mentions the royalist associations of other Protestants during the revolutionary period. A number of the Frottés had persevered in their religion after the Revocation and remained Protestant as late as the revolutionary period. Louis de Frotté, who among them figured most prominently in the Norman insurrections, would seem to have been a Catholic. He was baptized in the Catholic Church, and apparently his parents' marriage had been solemnized there (this, of course, was a common practice among eighteenth century Protestants). He was raised, however, by relatives on his father's side and by his stepmother, both of whom were Protestants, and received his first formal schooling in a Protestant school at Caen. In writing his memoirs from exile in England, he was later to cite his devotion to mass as evidence "for those who have tried to have it believed that [I] was a Protestant, as was my family, which did not fail to increase the obstacles which [I] had to surmount in [my] ventures in the service of the King." Cf. L. de la Sicotière, *Louis de Frotté et les Insurrections normandes, 1793-1832* (Paris, 1889), I, 1-11.

in these first years of the Revolution than other Frenchmen of the time. As for the charge that they sought to raise their altar on the ruins of the Catholic Church, we must now turn to a discussion of the impact of the Revolution upon their own Church, where it will be seen that from a religious point of view they suffered a crueler fate at the hands of the Revolution than the Church they supposedly attacked with the intent of supplanting.

CHAPTER V

The Crisis of Dechristianization: 1793-1794

Curiosity is an eternal element of man, the rational being. Change, the mystery of what lies before him, has always been an object of his curiosity. Now some French historians occasionally speak of the "souffle de la Révolution," metaphorically comparing the Revolution with a gust of wind which carried some persons along in its train, uprooted others to cast them into exile, and broke still others in the power of its blast. Whither this "souffle" of the Revolution? The experiences of Rabaut Saint-Etienne, Père Sermet, and Madame Hummel of Nantes were straws tossed into that current of air, revealing its course, suggesting its end.

The eldest son of the pastor Paul Rabaut was known everywhere in France as Rabaut Saint-Etienne. Such was the name of the man who served the Protestant Church so nobly in the struggle for the Edict of Toleration; such was the name of the deputy who boldly spoke out on behalf of full liberty for the non-Catholics of France in the Constituent Assembly. Rabaut Saint-Etienne was the most distinguished of the Protestants in the period of the Revolution. The giant of his people, it is he who is remembered today most fondly by his coreligionists when their thoughts turn to the last decade of the eighteenth century. Protestants in the Revolution? Inevitably, Rabaut Saint-Etienne is the first name called to mind.

This, however, was not his name. Baptized Jean-Paul Rabaut, he was given the sobriquet Saint-Etienne by his father when he entered the ministry of the proscribed church. Saint-Etienne became his *nom de guerre*, the cloak behind which he ostensibly concealed his true identity from the agents of the crown. Indeed, almost all the pastors of the Desert had their pseudonyms. In the early stages of the reorganization of the Church, scarcely any dared pass by their true names. But Rabaut Saint-Etienne did not enter the ministry until 1764 when the State had all but abandoned its proscription of the pastors of the heretic Church. Nor was this particular pseudonym sufficiently mysterious or undecipherable to conceal the identy of its bearer, especially in the Midi, where the Rabaut family was well known to almost all officials. Saint-Etienne was something else. It was a symbol of the Desert, a reminder of the persecution which the Protestants had sustained, a manifestation of the tradition and spirit of a "Church on the Cross."

That Rabaut Saint-Etienne continued to use this name after leaving the active ministry and devoting himself to politics probably indicates that he was ever conscious of this heritage. Throughout the year 1789, his letters to coreligionists and to members of the administration were always signed "Rabaut de Saint-Etienne." As president of the National Assembly, he continued to use this alias of the Desert. But in the summer of 1790 we notice a change. In a letter of 18 August 1790 to the president of the Assembly's Committee on Reports, the distinctive signature is unaccountably absent. In its place we find the simple appellative "Monsieur Rabaut." From that time on his correspondence bears the signature Jean-Paul Rabaut.[1] In the whirl of political activities in Paris, the symbol of the Desert was put aside. The leading spokesman of the Protestants, although still an ordained minister, had laicized his name.

By the decrees of 5 October and 24 October 1793, the National Convention of France replaced the Gregorian calendar with a new "Republican Calendar." Henceforth all official documents were to be dated, not from the birth of Christ the Savior, but from what the revolutionaries fondly expected to be the beginning of the social, political, and moral regeneration of all mankind. Each of the months was given a poetic name denoting its especial natural characteristics, the spring months, for instance, becoming *germinal, floréal*, and *prairial*. The years were counted from the first year of the new Republic. Hence a date like 5 April 1794 became "16 germinal de l'an IIe de la République française." The people were not compelled to adopt the new system at first, but all public documents were to be dated by it. It was hoped that with the spread of reason and the waning of "religious superstition" its use would become universal.

Antoine-Pascal-Hyacinthe Sermet, better known as Père Sermet, was a Carmelite monk. From the very beginning of the Revolution he was noted for his fervent patriotism. In 1791 he was elected the metropolitan bishop of the diocese (or Department) of the Haute-Garonne. He devoted himself to organizing the constitutional Church

[1] Cf. Armand Lods, "Rabaut de Saint-Etienne. Sa Correspondance pendant la Révolution," in *La Révolution française*, xxxv (1898), 78-89, 157-177, 259-277.

and appeasing the religious difficulties created by the refractory clergy. On 5 brumaire an II (27 October 1793) he was arrested and imprisoned for his reported opposition to the marriages of priests and divorcees. He was still in detention eleven months later when Mallarmé, a representative of the people, arrived in Toulouse to institute the measures of dechristianization. Père Sermet wrote to Mallarmé protesting his innocence and imploring his release. In the course of his plea, he repeatedly referred back to his patriotic acts as a constitutional bishop. In doing so, he inadvertently, or perhaps deliberately, dated his earlier activities according to the Gregorian calendar, making a number of citations such as "le dimanche 20 octobre 1793, vieux style." Under any other circumstances, this would not have been unusual, for it is more than likely that the republican calendar had not as yet come into common use at Toulouse at the time of the incidents he was recounting. But Père Sermet was in an unusual position. As a member of the clergy he was highly suspect for lack of sympathy with the revolutionary cause. He was accused of obstructing the religious legislation of the National Assembly. Moreover he was pleading his case before the administrator who had come to Toulouse to dechristianize and safeguard the revolutionary movement from the activities of the clergy. A person of less temerity than Sermet might have taken the pains to convert these dates to the republican chronology in an attempt to remove the least suspicion of any hostility on his part toward the legislation of the State with respect to the Catholic Church. But Père Sermet, a Catholic, at the mercy of what he certainly considered "les impies révolutionnaires," did not choose to do so. A Christian above all else, he cast his actions in a Christian terminology.[2]

In March of 1793, a municipal officer of the city of Nantes celebrated the marriage of one Citizen Hummel, a cloth merchant, and Citizeness Louise Schweighauser. From the first day of her marriage, Madame Hummel began in a methodical fashion to keep a close record of the expenditures of her household. From these records, we can easily enough see how readily the Hummels, both Protestants, followed the drift of the Revolution. They purchased a national cockade, entertained soldiers stationed in the city, contributed to the equipping of a cavalryman, subscribed to the com-

[2] E. Lamouzèle, "Une lettre inédite de Sermet, évêque constitutionnel de la Haute-Garonne,' in *La Révolution française*, XLIII (1902), 470-475.

pulsory loan of brumaire an III. They bought the lists of ceiling prices (*affiche du maximum*) at the time of their appearance and the table of the newly devised metric system. The term "Monsieur" disappeared from the notes the very moment its use was forbidden and was properly replaced by the republican epithet "Citoyen." Especially noteworthy is Mme Hummel's reaction to the republican calendar. In order not to confuse her records, she continued to make her entries under the dating of the Christian era until the end of the year 1793. But the entry for 1 January 1794 was made under the heading of 12 nivôse, and thenceforth she continued to make her notations of the family expenses under the republican nomenclature.[8] Madame Hummel, in the privacy of a notebook which no one was calculated to see but her husband and herself, did what only the most intoxicated of the revolutionaries could have hoped she would do: she voluntarily adopted a republican device especially designed to make her and others like her forget what they, the revolutionaries, would call the absurd superstitions of all supernatural religions.

Straws in the wind, carried along by the "souffle de la Révolution." What did they portend? A Church deserted by its pastors, a religion forgotten by the faithful. How well could such a Church withstand the anti-religious drift of the Revolution?

The close alliance of the monarchical and clerical causes had been trying for the Protestants of the Midi in the summer of 1790. That same alliance proved disastrous for the Gallican Church in the following years. The popularity of the monarchy ebbed and waned. Its cause finally collapsed in utter disgrace during the summer of 1792. Soon thereafter the Church, tainted with its monarchical sympathies, followed it in defeat.

The Civil Constitution of the Clergy, voted by the Constituent Assembly, had been the first step toward the destruction of the French Church, even though it was never meant to have had this result. It divided the ecclesiasts of the kingdom into two increasingly hostile camps, the juring clergy who accepted the Constitution and the refractory or non-juring clergy who rejected it. The latter could

[8] Gaston-Martin, "La vie bourgeoise à Nantes sous la Convention, d'après le livre de comptes de Mme Hummel," in *La Révolution française*, LXXXVI (1933), 236-258.

expect little sympathy from the statesmen of France who met in the new Legislative Assembly. The new deputies belonged to the social milieu of the *petite bourgeoisie*; they had been raised under the influence of the cult of antiquity and the philosophy of the eighteenth century. They were areligious; some were declared deists and atheists. With Voltaire before them and Napoleon after, who saw in religion an instrument for avoiding the moral disintegration of society, many of them would not have agreed. Almost all of them had been local administrators during the Constituent. As such they had been plagued by the difficulties occasioned by the application of the Civil Constitution. Thoroughly secular, they readily confused the religious problem engendered by the Civil Constitution with the larger issue of loyalty or disloyalty to the Revolution. Their debates in the fall of 1791 showed that they increasingly thought of the refractory clergy as counter-revolutionaries, persons who should be deprived of their cures and stipends, treated as suspects, and when necessary imprisoned or deported. Such was the nature of their decree of 29 November 1791. The king refused to sanction the measure; at the same time he refused to approve punitive legislation passed against the émigrés, with the result that the two groups, refractory clergy and political émigrés, were associated as being of the same political party.

The position of the non-jurors was further compromised by the declaration of war, the maneuvering of the Pope with the enemies of France, the initial military reverses which gave rise to cries of treason on the home front. The non-jurors were singled out as potential fifth columnists; a law of 26 May 1792 provided for the deportation of those denounced by twenty active citizens of the district. The fall of Louis XVI (10 August 1792) removed the strongest bulwark defending the interests of the Church. The path was clear for a whole succession of measures against the non-jurors: suppression of secular congregations (18 August), deportation of non-jurors denounced by any six active citizens of a Department (14 August), prohibitions on the wearing of ecclesiastical costumes except by constitutional clerics in their own dioceses (18 August), deportation to Guiana of those who had refused the oath of 1791 and who had not as yet emigrated. The September massacres were the final blow. Seeing the futility of their position in France, the non-jurors emigrated by the tens of thousands.

The constitutional Church, which had remained somewhat isolated from these controversies, soon faced a crisis of its own which led to its embroilment in the religious struggle. The dissolution of the monarchy necessitated a new oath of loyalty on the part of all functionaries, including ecclesiasts, repeating the conflict of loyalties which had divided the Church in 1791. The last religious measure of the Legislative, secularizing the registration of births, deaths, and marriages, created added difficulties. To the State alone belonged the right of determining restrictions on the marriages of citizens, and as the State no longer recognized the validity of clerical oaths and vows, the marriage of priests, nuns, monks, and divorced persons became legitimate in civil law. This was regarded by many constitutional clerics as an unjust encroachment on the spiritual domain of their affairs, especially when the Convention subsequently went beyond this by deciding that married priests who were forced to leave their parishes would continue to be financially supported by their parishioners wherever they went. Most of the constitutional bishops openly opposed the measure, among them the patriotic Père Sermet of Toulouse. There were new denunciations and new deportations. The juring clergy fell under a suspicion which at first had been the lot of the non-jurors alone.

The inability of the constitutional clergy to keep apace with the increasingly secular drift of the Revolution was only one aspect of the growing hostility to the Church and religion itself. The Church was faced with competition from a rival religion, the cult of revolutionary patriotism. Far more than the love of one's country and the willingness to defend it at all costs, revolutionary patriotism encompassed the firm belief that the Constitution and its laws, the sovereignty of the people, liberty and equality, were inestimable blessings which would work the rebirth of all mankind. Its holidays were the anniversaries of the Revolution, which prior to 1793 had often been celebrated in ornate ceremonies led by both local officials and ecclesiasts, ceremonies whose religious aspects were fulfilled with the singing of a *Te Deum* in the local church and whose civil or secular side was the administering of the civic oath to national guards and in fact to entire populations. But war kindled the patriotic fervor of the people to new heights, while at the same time the coolness of the clergy to the legislation of the State cost them favor with public authorities. Hence the cult of the nation tended to be disassociated from that of the altar. In Paris the festivities of 10 August 1793 commemorating the fall of the monarchy were the first to be completely secular. In the fall, the adoption of the republican calendar marked the attempt at dechristianizing the day-to-day lives of the people by abolishing Saints Days, holidays, the Sabbath, and by substituting "the realities of reason for the visions of ignorance, the truths of nature for sacerdotal illusions."[4] The insurrection of the Vendée, the complicity of constitutional ecclesiasts in the Federalist revolt tended to confirm the accusation made by Marat that the "constitutional priests are our mortal enemies. They seek to raise their sacerdotal throne on the ruins of liberty. They are aristocrats and royalists, for no one but kings would favor priests."[5] With the nation threatened from abroad by the coalition and attacked from within by civil strife, patriotism and devotion to the Church seemed incompatible to many zealots. The time was not distant when Frenchmen could no longer avoid choosing between the one or the other. A report to the Convention on 5 November by the imaginative Marie-Joseph Chénier was the first step in supplying such citizens with a new liturgy, new saints, a new altar at which to worship. "You [the legislators of France] must sow the year with noble memories, compose, with the ensemble of our civic festivals, an annual and commemorative history of the French Revolution.... In the future you must consecrate both the immortal epochs when various tyrannies crumbled before the 'souffle' of the nation and the majestic progress of Reason which passes over Europe and will reach to the ends of the earth. Finally, free of prejudices and worthy of representing the French nation, you will be able to found on the debris of dethroned superstition the only universal religion which brings peace rather than the sword, which makes citizens instead of kings and subjects, which has neither sects nor mysteries, whose only dogma is an equality oracled by the laws, whose pontiffs are the magistrates, and for which one burns the incense of the great family of mankind nowhere but before the altar of *la patrie*, the common mother and divinity."[6]

In spite of the progress of incredulity, the Catholic Church had

[4] *Réimpression de l'Ancien Moniteur,* 18 December 1793, quoting the report of Fabre d'Eglantine to the National Convention on 24 October 1793.

[5] Jean Leflon, *La Crise révolutionnaire,* 1789-1846 (s.l., 1949), p. 115.

[6] *Archives parlementaires,* 1st series, LXXVIII, 375.

not as yet suffered legal restrictions on the exercise of its rites. The attack upon it fell, not in Paris, but in the provinces. The apostle of dechristianization was the ex-Oratorian Fouché. On 22 September 1793 he celebrated in the cathedral of Nevers a festival in honor of Brutus given over to denunciations of the sophisms of religion. That same day he ordered the ecclesiasts of Nevers to marry, or to adopt a child, or nourish an indigent elder. Soon thereafter he falsely claimed that he had been authorized by the Convention "to substitute the religion of the Republic and natural morality for the superstitious and hypocritical cults to which the people are still so unfortunately devoted."[7] This was followed by a carnival of antireligious demonstrations, an auto-da-fé of relics and religious images, all of which was brought to a close by the constitutional bishop Laurent, who unfrocked himself "avec éclat." Finally on 9 October Fouché prohibited all public worship in the area and the wearing of the ecclesiastical costume in public. All funerals and cemeteries were laicized; the dead of all sects were interred in a common graveyard which had been stripped of all religious emblems. On the gates to the burial grounds was inscribed the message "Death is eternal sleep." Rühl at Reims, Dumont at Amiens, Laplanche at Bourges were taking similar measures. From the provinces the movement was carried to Paris by Chaumette, Fouché's alter ego. The Commune fell in with the designs of the dechristianizers. Abetted by the Convention, which recognized the right of a commune to renounce the Catholic cult, they succeeded in forcing Gobel, the bishop of Paris, and his vicars to renounce their functions and deposit the emblems of their office at the bar of the National Convention (17 November). Encouraged by their success, the enemies of religion seized the cathedral of Notre-Dame and converted it to a "temple of Reason." Before the choir they raised, with the aid of pillars, scaffolding, and drapes, a mountain topped with a temple dedicated to philosophy. Somewhat lower they attached a torch representing the lamp of truth, and at the base of their mountain they arranged busts of their saints: Voltaire, Rousseau, and Franklin. For the central attraction of their religious travesty they availed themselves of an actress, "a masterpiece of nature," and decked her out in flowing robes to personify the Goddess of Reason or the

[7] A. Aulard, *Christianity and the French Revolution*, translated by Lady Frazer (Boston, 1927), p. 102.

Deity Liberty, which of the two no one seemed to be quite sure. There, on 10 November, with members of the Convention in attendance, they celebrated their "fête de la Raison." Elsewhere in the capital, section after section closed or converted their temples, held anti-religious demonstrations, surrendered the plate of the churches to the national treasury, forced their priests to renounce their callings. On 24 November the Commune ordered the closing of all churches and chapels of every religion and sect in Paris and the arrest of anyone who cast suspicion upon himself by demanding their reopening.

The sponsors of the cult of Reason drew no distinction between Catholic and Protestant. A cleric was a cleric; all were agents of superstition and hypocrisy. All must be reduced to the common level of lay citizens. The altars of all churches were to be overturned. Exported from Paris to the provinces through the medium of patriotic clubs and representatives on mission, the dechristianization movement and the cult of Reason fell upon Catholic and Protestant alike.[8] France succumbed to an orgy of irreligion.

In uprooting the Church, these zealots of Reason adopted the same line of attack as had Louis XIV: a Church without pastors and public ceremonies cannot long survive. Hence the artillery of irreligion was levelled at the clergy.

[8] Aulard completely underestimated the impact of the movement on the Protestant churches. See his *Etudes et leçons sur la Révolution français*, 2nd series, 3rd edition (Paris, 1906), pp. 155-156: "Pendant la période du culte de la Raison et du culte de l'Etre suprême, les protestants n'avaient pas été complètement à l'abri des violences exercées, malgré la loi et malgré le Comité de salut public, contre le Christianisme. On avait fermé des temples, emprisonné quelques pasteurs non abdicaires, affecté de traiter les protestants de la même façon que les catholiques. Les quelques sociétés jacobines et les quelques représentants en mission qui agirent ainsi obéirent moins à un esprit de haine qu'à un esprit de logique, si je puis dire, anti-chrétienne. On voyait dans les protestants d'intéressantes victimes de l'ancien régime, et aussi les initiateurs de la démocratie et du système parlementaire, dont ils avaient offert d'avance l'image en leurs assemblées élues. Aussi ne ferma-t-on que peu de temples, et il semble bien que la grande majorité des protestants des deux communions continuèrent à exercer leur culte pendant toute la Terreur." While it is true that the Protestants were sometimes highly regarded as the initiators of democracy and the parliamentary system—see the speech of Boulay de la Meurthe quoted in Aulard, *Histoire politique de la Révolution française* (Paris, 1901), p. 649, note 4, where they are described as "les principaux auteurs de la résurrection et de l'établissement de la liberté morale, politique et civile dans tous les états où elle est plus ou moins réalizées"—this did not shield them from the assault of irreligion.

The Protestant church of Paris, whose ceremonies had once attracted the disciples of that philosophy whose new manifestation was the cult of Reason, was among the first to be closed. The pastor Marron had been arrested as early as 21 September 1793 for expressing what the *comité de surveillance* of his district interpreted as dangerously conservative opinions. He was released a few days later, but in the succeeding months he lived under the constant fear that he might be rearrested at any moment. His subsequent actions were designed to keep his church abreast of the mood of the Commune and Convention, whatever the cost. On 21 October the council of the church resolved that its religious services should be held on the *décadis* (the tenth and last day of the week in the republican calendar). For a time "exercices de piété" continued to be held on the Sabbath, but in November Marron dispensed with even these. On 15 November he proposed in his consistory that the communion plate be surrendered to the State. He himself made the presentation, pledging to the members of the Commune "to extend the reign of Reason with a zeal jealous of remaining inferior to yours, to establish the august empire of Liberty, Equality, and Fraternity upon resolute laws. Hate to all those displays of errors and puerilities which ignorance and dishonesty have decorated with the pompous title of Theology! Homage to good sense, to virtue, to the immortal and eternal principles of truth and morality! Long live the Republic!"[9] His panegyric to the revolutionary cause did not save him from further molestation. On 28 May 1794 he was arrested again, accused of being a Feuillant and Hébertist—an incongruous charge which probably meant that he had not cultivated a Jacobin mien with sufficient zeal. He remained in prison until the end of the Terror.

At Bordeaux the dissolution of the church had begun in the spring of 1793. A Protestant member of the Society of the Friends of Liberty and Equality, whose sensibilities had been unwittingly offended by the sermons of Silva Blachon, denounced his pastor to the club for lack of "civisme." Other denunciations followed. Fearful for his safety, Blachon fled to Nantes, where he continued to preach until the total suppression of the cults.[10] In his place Olivier

[9] The full text of his declaration is given in BPF, XXXVIII (1889), 364.

[10] The denunciation by his coreligionist is worth noting. In a letter to the consistory of the church, Blachon's enemy accused him "d'avoir tenu des propos plus

Desmons continued to serve the Protestant community. In November the consistory, some of whose members had implicated themselves in the Federalist revolt and hence were anxious to appease the city's republicans, authorized Desmons to present the church's plate to the government. In doing so "citizen Olivier-Desmons delivered a discourse fraught with civicism which closed with his solemn declaration to live and die a republican and to propagate the principles of liberty and equality with all the powers at his command."[11] In return the mayor bestowed the fraternal kiss on each member of the deputation. But the following month, the consistory, noting that several Catholic churches in the city had been closed, voted unanimously that it would be prudent to suspend their own religious services. Bordeaux was cleansed of "idolatry." Early in January 1794 Tallien, a representative of the Committee of Public Safety on mission to the Gironde, reported back to Paris that "liberty and reason have annihilated fanaticism and superstition. All the churches are closed; it is the people themselves who have demanded this. The Popular Society (Jacobin Club), the temple of Reason, and the meetings of the constituted authorities, these are the only churches they now attend. . . ."[12]

---

qu'inconsidérés contre l'heureuse Révolution qui régénère la France, d'avoir manifesté des principes inciviques, d'avoir surtout répondu que—semblables à nos lâches ennemis . . .—les Protestant sont les auteurs des troubles de Nismes, de Montauban, et contribuent à toutes les scènes d'horreurs pareilles qui affligent malheureusement encore le royaume." Cf. Alfred Leroux, *op.cit.*, pp. 316-318. He was subsequently denounced for having given a cool reception to a delegate from the club who appeared at the temple with the intention of reading an act of the Convention to the congregation. Blachon's own explanation of his embarrassment is different. In a sermon he preached on the "patience of David," "on crut y voir la passion de Louis XVI. Bientôt après je quittai cette ville pour épargner à mes ennemies des deux communions le scandale dont ils menaçaient, de m'arracher ouvertement de la chaire, et peut-être celui d'un meurtre pareil à celui qui avait été commis en la personne d'un abbé Langoyran, dont on me mettait l'exemple sous les yeux." See J.-A. Blachon, *Recueil de discours ou fragmens de discours relatifs à diverses circonstances de l'Etat prononcés par J.-A. Blachon en sa qualité de pasteur de l'église réformée à Bordeaux, puis à Anduze* (Nîmes, 1804).

[11] Alfred Leroux, *op.cit.*, p. 307 quoting the records of the municipality.

[12] Report of 20 nivôse an II (9 January 1794) printed in Aulard, *Recueil des actes du Comité de salut public* (Paris, 1889-1933), x, 146. Desmons remained in Bordeaux through the summer of 1794. In August the consistory accepted his resignation and at the same time terminated the charitable activities which it had maintained despite the cessation of religious services. In September 1794 Desmons appeared before the Jacobin Club and spoke on "justice and virtue as the bases of

Throughout the Protestant strongholds of France, the same story was repeated. Describing the collapse of the church of Montpellier after patiently recounting the heroic trials of its Church of the Desert, Corbière, the historian of that city's Protestant community, says simply: "Here we touch on the saddest epoch of the French Revolution. Like a vessel in the midst of a frightful tempest, the Protestant church of Montpellier disappeared for several years in the middle of the tumult of the Terror."[13] That is all! On 30 January 1794 the consistory of the church of Uzès rendered its two chalices and its silver basin to the state. In April the Catholic cathedral was converted to a temple of Reason, the Protestant temple to a factory for the manufacture of army uniforms. Priest and pastor abjured their functions and disappeared.[14] At Rouen, the church which the Protestants had only recently rented for the recommencement of their services was repossessed by the municipality and turned into a saltpeter factory.[15] At Montauban, the Protestant consistory complied without demur with the anti-religious recommendations of the representatives Taillefer and Paganel. On 24 November 1793 they obligingly donated two black robes and two silver chalices to the coffers of the Republic; they voiced no misgivings at the introduction of the republican calendar and commenced holding their religious services on the *décadis,* as instructed. The parishioners attended the cult of Reason in addition to their own religious ceremonies, regarding the atheistic cult perhaps as civic devotions in no way contrary to their own religious beliefs. In fact a Protestant former noblewoman, Mlle. de Preissac, personified the goddess of Reason in the celebrations of 10 frimaire an II (30 November 1793), and the Protestant Périès-Labarthe sometimes honored these assemblies in the capacity of presiding officer. On 16 ventôse an II (6 March 1794)

---

the Republic." His address struck a false note among his auditors. In a letter to a member of the consistory just prior to going into hiding, his discouragement and fear for his own safety prompted him to say that "when things come to the point where they have with respect to pastors and especially myself, there only remains to withdraw into one's home or to those places where Providence has prepared an asylum." See A. Leroux, *op.cit.*, p. 314.

[13] Philippe Corbière, *Histoire de l'église de Montpellier*, p. 492.

[14] Marcel Fabre, "La réaction thermodorienne et la liquidation de la Terreur à Uzès," *Mémoires de l'Académie de Nîmes*, 7th series, XLI (1922-1923), 84.

[15] N. Weiss, "L'Eglise réformée de Rouen de l'Edit de tolérance à la réorganisation officielle des cultes," BPF, LII (1903), 313-339.

the arrival of the representative Bô brought new intensity to the irreligious movement, and that same evening the municipality decreed that "all edifices of the commune which up until now have been used for the exercise of any cult whatsoever shall be closed." The consistory terminated its activities on 21 ventôse and the last public sermon was delivered one week later.[16]

But the richest prize for the shock troops of the army of irreligion was the cluster of churches in the Department of Gard. The assault began under the direction of the representative Boisset:

"Frenchmen, virtuous patriots, inhabitants of Gard:

"Each individual, after his own way of thinking, recognizes a God; he prays to him in the manner of his beliefs and feelings; public worship is unobstructed. Republican inhabitants of Gard, cast your eyes over all parts of the Republic and you will see the people themselves, enlightened people, starting from the sleep of superstition; see how at Paris the people convert the churches into temples dedicated to Reason, creating philosophic festivals every *décadi*. The history of ancient republics offers nothing more majestic. See your neighbors, your friends, the inhabitants of Hérault, marching with great strides to the summit of philosophy. See how Hérault is becoming the emulator of Paris. Patriots of Gard, make your Department the rival of Hérault, contest its progress on the road into the light. Every part of free France is awakening. Do not be the last. Let this country, hitherto the easiest prey of fanaticism, be worthy at last of enjoying the rights of nature, liberty, equality, and fraternity."[17]

On 10 December 1793, the Catholics and Protestants of Nîmes presented their silver to the civil authorities.

When the representative Borie arrived in the city toward the end of February 1794, the dechristianization movement was already well under way. The communes, the priests, the ministers on all sides "spontaneously" abdicated all public worship. Town after town, village after village, 233 in all, Catholic and Protestant, turned their

[16] Daniel Ligou, "Protestants et sans-culottes. La bourgeoisie réformée de Montauban devant la Révolution," *Actes du Xe Congrès des Sociétés Savantes Pryénées-Languedoc-Gascogne* (1954), 13 pp. Nor did the Protestants show any apparent aversion to the cult of the Supreme Being, inaugurated at Montauban somewhat later: "Dans son organisation des protestants sincères, comme Preissac et Bergis-Portal, jouent un rôle de premier plan."

[17] F. Rouvière, *Révolution dans le Gard*, IV, 103-104.

churches and temples into temples of Reason. Almost immediately this was followed by the abdication of the ministers. In a Church which lived by the memories of its heroism through a century of persecution, some of the abdications were astounding. Hear Jean Rame, the pastor of Vauvert:

"As a minister of the Protestant religion . . . , totally convinced that under the present circumstances the celebration of all public and exterior cults can only serve to feed the flames of fanaticism, create discord within the body politic, and in a word impede the progress of the revolutionary cause which every good republican should accelerate with all his powers, I have come to you today to renounce with all the sincerity of which I am capable, all functions of a Protestant pastor, and to assure you that henceforth my ambition will be limited to repairing to the temple of Reason with my brothers, our dear fellow citizens, to take upon myself the duties of a citizen and a man, to sing hymns to Liberty and Equality, and to learn to die if need be in their defense. Let my example be imitated by many! May I hope soon to see extinguished the fires of that horrible fanaticism which so often have ravaged this Department. . . . Such is my wish, and I shall die content."[18]

His example was followed. The number of abdications in the area exceeded 320. Fifty-one pastors, of a church which possessed few more than a hundred, renounced their ecclesiastical functions and returned to civil life.[19]

Resistance? There was none. The Church collapsed like a house of cards. While one representative passing through the Departments of Ardèche and Gard commented on the grumbling of several pastors at the abdications,[20] the reports of Borie suggest that the Protestants, lay and ecclesiasts, accepted the new state of affairs more

[18] F. Rouvière, *Révolution dans le Gard*, IV, 397.

[19] Consult the "Liste des ministres des différent cultes qui ont abdiqué leurs fonctions et renoncé à leur état pour ne connaître que le culte de la Raison," in F. Rouvière, *Révolution dans le Gard*, IV, 382-400.

[20] Report of the representative Châteauneuf-Randon to the Committee of Public Safety, 9 pluviôse an II (28 January 1794), printed in F.-A. Aulard, *Recueil des actes du Comité de salut public*, x, 501: "C'est un nouvel hommage fait à la raison, et un triomphe de plus pour les principes et la tranquillité publique; car, si j'ai entendu parler de quelques votants [sic] sérieux contre les heureuses abdications de tout culte public, qui assurent sans violences la liberté de tous, ce n'est que dans [sic] quelques ministres protestants."

readily than the Catholic population.[21] The Catholic population vexed the authorities by demanding the reopening of their churches and hawking little wooden crucifixes on street corners.[22] For a short time the consistory of Bordeaux continued its charitable activities, as did several elders of the church of Nîmes. But when the funds of the latter church were exhausted (an indication that no more were to be raised), the activities ceased. The invalids who had been cared for in their private infirmary were transferred to the hospital of the city. In the hope of celebrating their cult in the Desert, the elders of the church made a feeble attempt at moving the furnishings of their church out into the countryside. But before it was done, the municipality requisitioned their property for public use and the plan had to be abandoned. The elders do not even seem to have protested the seizures.[23]

Where was the spirit of the Desert? Where the heroic resoluteness which had breathed new life into a Church proscribed and hounded for almost a century? A plaintive cry was heard from the Wilderness. "I see with grief," wrote Daniel Encontre, "that we live absolutely without worship. You speak of obstacles; then let us go into the countryside and place ourselves in the shadow of the oak or the shelter of a wall; this is what our fathers did. Should we blush at the thought of imitating them? Someone has proposed our going to the cemetery; as a matter of fact I should prefer it if we could reassemble in a spot already consecrated to the sad and precious remains which have been committed to it. In treading on the ashes of the dead, we would feel invited to meditation and silence; our ceremonies would be more solemn, more majestic, and would bring forth more good."[24] The cry could scarcely have come from a more unlikely source. The son of a pastor of the Desert, Encontre was directed, perhaps pushed, into the calling of the Church by his father. His bent was for science. While a *proposant* he established a certain reputation for himself by delivering a scientific dissertation to a

[21] *ibid.*, XI, 347, the report of Borie, 4 ventôse an II (22 February 1794): ". . . Me voici arrivé au point où, par la persuasion seule, les ministres protestants *et quelques prêtres* abjurent leur état" (author's italics).

[22] *ibid.*, X, 531, 714; XI, 684.

[23] Abraham Borrel, *Histoire de l'église réformée de Nîmes depuis son origine en 1533 jusqu'à la loi organique du 18 germinal an X*, 2nd edition (Toulouse, 1856), pp. 456-457.

[24] Charles Durand, *Histoire du Protestantisme français pendant la Révolution et l'Empire* (Paris, 1902), pp. 32-33.

group of savants at the *Obsérvatoire* in Paris. Subsequently consecrated a pastor of the Church (1790), his ministry lasted but a year before his thirst for the comforting sureties of nature and numbers led him to resign. No child of the Desert, Encontre was a mathematician.[25]

Nor does it appear that his counsel was adopted. During the Terror, the Desert remained singularly uninhabited. Writing in 1807, Rabaut-Dupui (or le Jeune), the youngest son of Paul Rabaut, methodically traced the history of the churches of every Department in France. In place after place he cited the same funereal fact: during the disastrous period of the revolutionary government, the churches were closed, the pastors dispersed. In all of his researches, he could cite but one consoling exception: "While the rest of France was without temples and pastors, while the revolutionary storm burst over all parts of the country, neither in Sainte-Foi nor its environs was worship interrupted."[26] It has been held that the Protestants, "habituated as they were to muting the manifestations of their religious sentiments," weathered the epoch of dechristianization more successfully than the Catholics.[27] All evidence points to the contrary, as we shall see in tracing the reorganization of the Church under the Directory. But in passing, to cite one example of the lamentable collapse of all religious practices,

[25] Léon Maury, *Le réveil religieux dans l'église réformée à Genève et en France,* (Paris, 1892), I, 279-297.

[26] Rabaut le Jeune, *Annuaire, ou Répertoire ecclésiastique à l'usage des églises réformées et protestantes de l'Empire français* (Paris, 1807), p. 113. Two other exceptions were at Besançon, where the government had settled a group of Swiss watchmakers who continued to celebrate their cult publicly without interference (noted by Charles Durand, *op.cit.*, p. 34), and the little church of Réalmont, which for reasons unknown escaped the revolutionary violence: *ibid.*, 73.

[27] Pierre Guérin, "Histoire d'une commune rurale de 1780 à 1800 (Milhaud)," *Mémoires de l'Académie de Nîmes,* 7th series, XXXIII (1910), 190: "La proclamation du culte de la Raison et la déchristianisation de la France devaient cependant atteindre le piétisme protestant autant que la bigoterie catholique. Mais le premier souffrit assez peu des rigueurs du pouvoir. La grande raison en est que depuis fort longtemps les religionnaires étaient habitués à mettre une sourdine à la manifestation de leurs sentiments religieux. Leur culte essentiellement individuel ou familial se passait volontiers de pompe et d'éclat. Un cadre restreint, humble, y suffisait, et l'epoque de la terreur put paraître à beaucoup une époque de trêve et de tolérance à côté des persécutions traditionnelles et séculaires de l'Eglise." Even if this were so, it is doubtful that a cult restricted to the family level, if it persisted for any length of time, would have mitigated the devastation of the Terror. See the conclusions of Emile-G. Léonard on the *culte familial* cited in chapter 2, note 46.

the story told by the consistorial records of the church of Saint-Maixent may well be the norm for all of France: "Soon after [the period of open toleration], the disorders which fell on all religious institutions occasioned the closing of all the temples, and the vertigo was propagated to such an extent that scarcely any families performed their devotional exercises in the privacy of their homes."[28]

The Church, for all its apparent vitality on the eve of the great upheaval, collapsed before the "souffle de la Révolution." It was a church deserted by its pastors and forgotten by the faithful.

In the short span of a few months the high priests of Baal succeeded where the intendants of the French monarchy had failed in the course of one hundred years. The Protestant Church had been demolished. There were no rebellions; there was no emigration. We might well ask why dechristianization had proved so much more effective than the plethora of laws and enactments which Louis XIV showered down upon the Protestant population.

Part of the explanation lies in the nature of the Revolution itself. War, both foreign and civil, had created a psychosis of patriotic fervor which made dissent even more dangerous than it had been before. The Republic, as its sponsors so often exclaimed, was one and indivisible. To survive the stresses and strains which worked at its fabric, it demanded of its citizens a singleness of purpose, a uniformity of action, hitherto unknown to European societies. True, Louis XIV had tried to achieve something of the same sort of social homogeneity, especially in the realm of religious thought. But few accepted their master's resolve, and few worked with any zeal for its realization. During the Revolution, there were tens of thousands of French citizens who worked with a religious frenzy for the realization of what have been called "the paper Utopias of eighteenth century thought." To them the Revolution was a calling, a crusade which given sufficient impulsion would surely work the regeneration of all mankind. Under such circumstances nonconformity was infinitely more difficult and dangerous at the local level than it had been under the reign of the Sun King.

Moreover dechristianization coincided with the suppression of the Federalist revolt. The agents of the dechristianization move-

[28] "Registre des délibérations du Consistoire de l'Eglise protestante de Saint-Maixent, département des Deux-Sèvres," BPF, LIV (1905), 410-412.

ment came into the Protestant Midi not only to overturn altars, but to institute the *gouvernement révolutionnaire*—the Terror. Anyone who had not been sedulous in his devotion to the Republican cause they regarded with deep suspicion. The Catholic Church had demonstrated to their satisfaction its hostility to the republican experiment. Religion and patriotism were incompatible. The altar was subversive. Unfortunately for the Protestants the logic of intolerance made their cult appear just as seditious as that of Rome. In a sense, the Protestant Church was pulled down by the weight of its sinking partner.

Thus the Protestants were suspect because they had a cult other than that of *la patrie*. They found it difficult, almost impossible, to continue their religious activities. Sensing that their synods, colloquies, consistories, and even their religious services would attract attention, and worse still the suspicion of agents who were looking for victims to offer up to the new deity, they simply dispensed with all exterior manifestations of their religion.

The abbé Dedieu, after tracing the eighteenth-century political history of the Protestants, concluded that the prime weakness of the Protestant Church in the face of the surge of irreligion was its lack of martyrs. "It was the martyrs who saved the Catholic religion," he wrote. "The faithful nourished their courage at this sanguinary source. Protestantism lacked confessors of the faith."[29] There is much to be said for this point. The martyrdom of pastors at the hands of Bourbon hangmen created a reservoir of spiritual strength for the laity during the eighteenth century. Protestant historians have tried to find their counterparts for the period of the Terror. In desperation Charles Durand tried to elevate the pastors Ribes and Soulier to this lofty station, but their crime was not devotion to their Church, but rather the political offense of Federalism.[30] Henry M. Baird suggested by inference that Rabaut Saint-Etienne should be so regarded. Both he and Durand cite with pride the subterfuges by which Oberlin continued a modicum of religious activities at Ban de la Roche.[31] But Oberlin was a Lutheran. The abbé Dedieu was right;

[29] J. Dedieu, *Histoire politique*, II, 369.

[30] C. Durand, *op. cit.*, p. 71. Cf. D. Benoît, "Les pasteurs et l'échafaud révolutionnaire. Pierre Soulier de Sauve," BPF, XLIII (1894), 561-594; and A. Lods, "Encore un pasteur mort sur l'échafaud, Pierre Ribes," BPF, XL (1891), 91-104.

[31] C. Durand, *op.cit.*, pp. 69-70; and H. M. Baird, *The Huguenots*, II, 563-566.

the Protestants simply had no martyrs. The closest they came is the case of the sexagenarian Alègre of La Salle (Gard), cited proudly by Rabaut-Dupui. Alègre, a laborer, who had been imprisoned for the republican crime of resting on the Sabbath, had the courage to face the *comité de surveillance* and insist that he could not and would not work on the seventh day—an act which in Rabaut-Dupui's words constituted "un exemple qui mérite d'être conservé." But, alas, Alègre did not claim immunity under the Fourth Commandment ("Remember the sabbath day, to keep it holy. Six days you shall labor, and do all your work; but the seventh day is a sabbath to the Lord your God. . ."), but only insisted that old as he was his powers were spent by the seventh day, rendering him useless to his employer. His auditors, "stunned" at this claim, released him—and cheated the Church of a martyr.[32]

For that matter, the pastorate of the Church had not resisted in 1685. The martyrs appeared only later (and of course earlier). More serious to the Church was the degree to which its spiritual leaders were attracted to political careers. "In the political assemblies and in the administration of the Revolution the pastors of the Church found a fertile field for their oratorical gifts and administrative abilities."[33] The political opportunities which opened up before them, combined with patriotism, drew many of them away from their pastoral duties. In the Vivarais, the pastor Koenig and the *proposants* Rattier and Rattier-Léorat abandoned their religious functions for military careers in 1793. Koenig died a captain of the cavalry, and it does not appear that either of the *proposants* returned to the ministry.[34]

The church of Castres was especially hard hit by such desertions. The pastor Crébessac became secretary of the *comité révolutionnaire* of Castres in 1790. Both he and the pastor Bonifas-Laroque were elected to the *conseil général* of their commune in 1791. The third and only other pastor of the community, Nazon, joined them there somewhat later. Once in politics, Bonifas-Laroque slowly drifted away from his pastoral functions. In October 1793 he was appointed

[32] Rabaut le Jeune, *op.cit.*, p. 100.

[33] E.-G. Léonard, *Problèmes et expériences du Protestantisme français. L'Urbanisation, l'embourgeoisement, les déviations ecclésiastiques, l'attrait catholique* (Paris, 1940), p. 34.

[34] E. Arnaud, *Histoire des Protestants du Vivarais et du Velay*, II, 327, 342.

secretary of the *comité révolutionnaire* and three months later became the judge of the tribunal of the district. He formally abdicated his ministry in November 1793, and the following summer we find him organizing the festival to the Supreme Being. In the meantime, the registry of the Protestant church in Castres stopped at the date 23 March 1793—eight months before the beginning of dechristianization.[85]

Later than the others, Lasource, pastor of Castres, did not involve himself in politics until his election to the Legislative Assembly (28 August 1791). Reelected to the Convention by the Department of Tarn, he became embroiled in the political faction within the Paris Jacobin Club. In the general proscription of the Girondins, he was among the first to be denounced by the Mountain and perished on the scaffold in October 1793.[86]

Bernard-Saint-Affrique of Ariège accepted the mandate of his Department to the National Convention and continued as a legislator in the Council of the Five Hundred. He retired to private life in 1798 and died within a year.[87]

Less worthy of his people was Jean Julien (dit Julien de Toulouse), pastor of Cette and then of Toulouse. Julien took leave of his church in May of 1789 in order to pursue a career in politics. Subsequently he became a member of the administration of the Haute-Garonne and represented that Department in the Convention. When the Archbishop of Paris abandoned the priesthood before the Convention in November of 1793, Julien followed his example, declaring: "I have never had any ambition other than seeing the reign of Reason and Philosophy established on this earth. Minister of a cult long proscribed by the barbarity of our laws, I openly preached the maxims of universal tolerance. As such I worked for the advancement of the torch of Reason which one day was to enlighten my fatherland, and I am pleased at having seen the day when beneficent Philosophy, mother of all social virtues, has made of all Frenchmen a nation of brothers." Suspended from the Convention for his financial speculations, he remained in Paris during the Directory

[85] Camille Rabaud, "*Un ministre chrétien sous la Terreur, Bonifas-Laroque,*" BPF, XXXVIII (1889), 337-357, 393-402, 449-464.

[86] Camille Rabaud, "Lasource, député à la Législative et à la Convention," BPF, XXXVIII (1889), 18-34, 57-69, 113-130.

[87] A. Kuscinski, *Dictionnaire des Conventionnels* (Paris, 1916-1919), pp. 51-52.

and became a devotee to the cult of Theophilanthropy. While holding minor administrative offices, he was denounced in 1798 for reasons unknown and ordered deported. He fled to Turin.[38]

Jean Jay, relative of the American John Jay and pastor of Sainte-Foix, became an administrator of the Department of the Gironde and represented that Department in the Legislative and the Convention. Like Julien, he served as a member of the Committee of General Security. A Jacobin, and for a short time alternately secretary and president of the Paris Jacobin Club, he managed to keep himself in the background during the Thermidorian Reaction and at the end of the Convention retired from public life to resume his pastorate.[39]

At Orléans, the pastor Lombard-Lachaux became a member of the directory of the Department of Loiret and subsequently mayor of his city. A deputy from Loiret to the Convention, he, like Julien, abdicated from the pastorate in November 1793. Under the Directory he held a number of posts in the administration and returned to the ministry during the Consulate.[40]

Perhaps the best example of the way in which the Revolution cut short, and in many cases permanently ended, the pastoral functions of ministers of the Church is that offered by the career of Jeanbon Saint-André. The career was a notable one, and Charles Durand cites it with considerable justification as being worthy of the Protestants of France. No other French Protestant rose to such political heights, and none in his capacity survived the vicissitudes

[38] Léon Peyric, *Le Rôle religieux des pasteurs dans les assemblées politiques de la Révolution française* (Cahors, 1902), p. 23; and A. Kuscinski, *Dictionnaire des Conventionnels*, pp. 352-354.

[39] *ibid.*, pp. 345-346. It is amusing to note that the editors of the *Biographie moderne* (cited earlier in chapter 1, note 13) confused Jay with his American cousin. After tracing his career in the Gironde, the Legislative, and the Convention, the recital suddenly shifts with a painfully audible clashing of gears to "En déc. 1794, il conclut et signa avec lord Grenville, alors min. des affaires étrangères, le traité de commerce et de navigation entre l'Angleterre et les Etats-Unis d'Amérique. Le parti français fit brûler son effigie à Philadelphie, et exhala sa haine contre ce négociateur qui s'etoit montré si favorable aux intérêts de l'Angleterre" (volume II, 473).

[40] Kuscinski, *op.cit.*, p. 414. He accompanied his renunciation of pastoral functions with the declaration: "J'ai été ministre protestant lorsque je fus nommé député à la Convention; j'ai renoncé alors à la prêtrise, aujourd'hui je renouvelle ma déclaration d'une manière plus solonnelle. Je n'ai jamais prêché que l'amour de la liberté, de l'égalité et de mes semblables; mon unique désir est de continuer à concourir au bien des sans-culottes."

of the Revolution more honorably or more successfully than he. In the words of Charles Durand, ". . . he was elected to the Convention 26 August 1792. First he was connected with the Girondins, then with the Mountain. He was the first member elected to the Committee of Public Safety, and there he succeeded in saving a good number of heads [from the guillotine]. In the midst of the most unrestrained anti-religious excesses, he did not fear to set himself against the suppression of public worship."[41] This last sentence is worthy of attention—". . . he did not fear to set himself against the suppression of public worship." The picture of a Protestant pastor, raised by fate to a position of political import, risking his reputation at the most critical juncture of the Revolution to shield the City of God from those who would destroy it, is indeed an inspiring one. Unfortunately, the oils are smeared; the true picture is somewhat different.

Jeanbon Saint-André's particular occupation at this time was the development of the French Republic's fleet, an extremely important mission in view of the existing hostilities with Great Britain. On 3 December 1793 the Committee of Public Safety ordered him to Cherbourg to supervise the transfer of troops stationed in the area to another Department and to calm any unrest their departure might create.[42] Jeanbon arrived in the city a few days later and perceived at once that the greatest cause of unrest in the area was the religious turbulence generated by the war in the Vendée. It was the steps he took to calm the population that Charles Durand referred to in the passage cited above. "Under the circumstances," wrote Jeanbon, "I saw the necessity of speaking the language of reason to my fellow citizens and of bringing them back by the force of principles to their patriotic duties."[43] His words of reason, which merit being quoted at length, were a patriotic address to the inhabitants of Cherbourg delivered 11 December.

Jeanbon began by reassuring the flagging spirits of the patriots and by warning them of the nature of the forces they combatted: "The honorable sentiments of the Republicans among you, ever ready to second the views of the National Convention and to concur

[41] C. Durand, *op.cit.*, p. 79.

[42] Aulard, *Recueil des actes du Comité de salut public*, IX, 121-123.

[43] Dispatch to the Committee of Public Safety dated 22 frimaire an II (12 December 1793), printed in Aulard, *Recueil des actes du Comité de salut public*, IX, 358.

with it in the destruction of the homicidal coalition of the kings and their satellites, this noble élan for the cause of liberty would have filled me with a lively joy if it had not been mingled with the sorrow of finding citizens . . . ready to divide against themselves on the basis of religious opinions. This is the evil which superstition would work: that of disuniting patriots! And this would be a new crime with which we would reproach it! No citizens, this shall not be. Firm, invariable in our principles, we shall listen to the holy voice of our country, and all the errors, all the prejudices of superstition will disappear before the conquering thunder of truth.

"The reign of reason progresses with rapid strides; the people, tired of the vulgar deceptions by which their enemies have all too long abused their credulity, want no despot other than the law, no guide other than morality, no priesthood other than the magistrates. Elevated by the sublimity of philosophical conceptions . . . to the point of grandeur which restores man to his primitive dignity, they blush at having been enveloped for centuries on end in the trammels of superstition, and they break with scorn these disgraceful shackles which stood in the way of the free exercise of their faculties. Man, freed at last, has become a rational being."

Jeanbon then castigated those who had exploited their superstitions to foment war against the Revolution. The frightful horrors of the Vendée had been the result. Pointing out how they had been misled, he turned to reassure them as to their religious rights: "And you, timorous souls, set your minds at ease. The National Convention has no desire of robbing you of the objects of your veneration. It knows full well the extent to which long habit and a theological education can establish their empire over the soul of man. It realizes that a weak and tender heart has need of a support; you believe you find it still in the old prejudices breathed into you by your fathers, it has no desire of breaking this support in your hands. It hopes undoubtedly for the development of those great maxims which bind all citizens to their duties with the holy and burning love of their country, but it does not seek to interfere with your opinions, it does not intend to sound your consciences, and the first of the laws which it has rendered in the name of the people of whom it is the organ contains the formal recognition of the liberty of all forms of worship.[44] Follow, then, without fear the practices

[44] In effect, Robespierre had already denounced the dechristianizers as "cowardly

which you believe to be good. Serve the author of nature after your own manner. Jews, Christians, Mohammedans, disciples of Confucius, or votaries of the Grand Lama, you are all equal in the eyes of a free people."

But he cautioned them: "You owe it to one another to be faithful to the Republic, to cherish it, to do battle and conquer for it; and, in the ranks of the defenders of our country (for this we all are), the individual nuances should disappear and one will count among you nothing but citizens. It follows from the absolute liberty of worship that there can be no one dominant religion, that each religious aggregation is only a special association, free in the exercise of its rites, but subject to the laws of the civil administration, without whose observance order is not possible in civilized societies. Henceforth each sect should withdraw itself into those places set aside for its assemblies; without, nothing must draw the attention of citizens but the worship of our country and the cherished symbols of liberty.

"Citizens, such are the incontestable principles which wisdom dictates on a matter too long confused by interminable discussions and by the arrogant pretensions of a religion which, in order to reign over us, demands as its first sacrifice of us the abandonment of our reason. Pontiffs of all religions, if you have not renounced all sense of decency, you will be sensible to the justice of what I say; you will do more, you will profit from the ascendancy which you still conserve over the people to spread and propagate these principles. Venture to join us as the founders of mankind, the terror of vice, the scourge of prejudices. Glory awaits you in the career of fighting at our sides. . . .

"Citizens, let peace reign, let public order be respected, let the law be venerated, let our country be adored, and soon these trifling differences of opinion, purified in the flames of a burning patriotism, will disappear to give way to the fond embraces of a common brotherhood!"[45]

---

emissaries of foreign tyrants" who sought to destroy France with civil war and discredit her abroad as a nation of atheists. On 18 frimaire (8 December) the Convention had solemnly reaffirmed the liberty of worship. For the religious policies of the Committee of Public Safety itself at this time, see F.-A. Aulard, "La politique religieuse du Comité de salut public," in *La Révolution française*, XXX (1896), 97-103.

[45] "Adresse du représentant du peuple dans les départements maritimes aux

Strange words for a Protestant pastor! The religion of Christ equated with "trammels of superstition." "No priesthood but that of the magistrates." A religion which robs man of nature-given reason. Citizens of France, strike off the irons with which Christ has shackled you!

". . . He did not fear to set himself against the suppression of public worship." Jeanbon's oration was terminated with the following decree. Henceforth the liberty of cults was to be safeguarded against all outrages. But (article 2) "the ministers of the cults to celebrate their rites must withdraw into the interior of those places set aside for their assemblies, and they shall appear in public only in the customary dress of citizens." The public magistrates (article 3) would devote themselves to the devising of a civil form of burial; in the meantime citizens attached to a particular sect were free to celebrate for their dead any ceremonies which they judged appropriate—"but only in the interior of their temple."

To the Catholics of Cherbourg, Jeanbon Saint-André conceded only what he himself in a humility born of persecution had asked the monarchy to render to the Protestants: a church, as he had written prior to the Edict of Toleration, "with no exterior pomp which would call attention to its existence," one which "in its obscurity must even be subject to a regulation which would keep it from overstepping the limits assigned to it."

In the meantime, the new priesthood of magistrates, tolerating the superstitions of their less enlightened brethren, would work for their regeneration. (Article 4) "Good citizens, the administrative corps, the municipalities, and the Popular Societies are exhorted to develop the principles of social morality on every possible occasion so as to prepare the triumph which that morality deserves; but they are especially invited to employ no arms but those of reason, and to evince to their brothers that fond condescension which will ensure their success. . . ."

The City of God was to be no more than an instrument for achieving the republican paradise. How strange are the tricks of time, that from the mouth of a child of the Desert should be heard an echo of the barbarous code of Louis XIV! One hundred and eight years earlier, Louis XIV had closed his Edict of Revocation

citoyens de la ville et du district de Cherbourg, 21 frimaire an II," printed in Aulard, *Recueil des actes du Comité de salut public*, IX, 358-361.

with the promise that "while waiting until it shall please God to enlighten them as He has the others, [the Protestants] shall be permitted to live in the towns and countryside of our kingdom, both to pursue their commerce and to enjoy their property, without being molested or hindered under pretext [of their religion]." True, Louis XIV forbade the assemblies which Jeanbon protected by the law. But the underlying motive was strikingly similar. The unenlightened, the victims of false dogma, would be permitted to live in peace, while their superiors worked for their salvation with kindness and persuasion. But the cult which now awaited their conversion was no longer that of Rome, but the new cult, the cult of revolutionary patriotism and of reason.

It was to this cult that Jeanbon Saint-André devoted the remainder of his life. To the Church he was lost forever. No longer a pastor, he died a "pontiff of the Republic" in 1813, serving his fatherland to the very end.

Paris claimed a number of the pastors of the Church. But not all pastors went to the mecca of the Revolution. In the area around the Department of Gard alone, there were fifty-one who remained in the provinces to renounce their pastorates before the representative Borie. What of these? How can their behavior be explained? It has been suggested that in the dechristianization movement, as in the Revolution as a whole, the representatives on mission were more efficient and quicker in their actions than the intendants had been under the Bourbon monarchy. "Arrest, judgment, execution followed each other within twenty-four hours. A century earlier, the intendants were more tactful about it. People had time to collect their wits, to pray to God for the strength to endure martyrdom."[46] But this hypothesis supposes that the pastors resisted in 1685. We have already seen that they did not. With few exceptions, the pastors of the Church either converted to Catholicism or fled into exile.

Taken in a broader light, the supposition nevertheless suggests another explanation for the behavior of the ministry in the critical years of 1793 and 1794. The Revolution succeeded where the monarchy failed because its policies were implemented by an army of devoted adherents who worked with incredible zeal. This is just as true of the dechristianization movement in the Midi as it

[46] Charles Durand, *op.cit.*, p. 48.

was of any other phase of the Revolution. The reports of the representative Borie give us a clue as to the identity of these adherents in the provinces. In a dispatch of 4 ventôse an II (22 February 1794) to the Committee of Public Safety, Borie reported that "the Popular Societies and the communes are sedulous in asking me to permit them to convert the churches into temples of Reason. I am giving in to their eagerness and employing no other means of executing their demands than printing the discourses which are addressed to me by them from all sides."[47] In like manner Tallien at Bordeaux had claimed that "it is the people themselves" who requested the closing of the churches. These Societies and these communes were in many cases composed largely of Protestants. Hence it appears that the laity, either through fear or acting in accordance with their own desires, were just as instrumental as the representatives on mission in the conversion of their churches.[48] This and their subsequent behavior is in sharp contrast with the suppression of 1685. At that time, although the pastors fled and the laity converted to a quasi-Catholicism, the latter resisted in the Desert of France. Their pathetic appeals to the pastors of the Refuge were sufficiently moving to inspire some of the former ministers to return to the beleaguered Church and run the risk of martyrdom. In 1793 many pastors undoubtedly abdicated their functions because they saw the handwriting on the wall: their churches were disintegrating around them. Under such circumstances it is easier to understand why none of them were tempted to resist.

The laity, then, share responsibility with the pastorate for the utter disintegration of the Church during the Terror. Their behavior is symptomatic of certain fundamental weaknesses in the Church

[47] Aulard, *Recueil des actes du Comité de salut public*, XI, 347. Hence the authorization for the closing of the churches of Nîmes reads: "Vu la délibération de la Société populaire de Nismes et le voeu unanime de la municipalité de la même commune, exprimé par ses commissaires députés, à l'effet de convertir la ci-devant cathédrale en un temple dédié à la Raison; . . . ." Cf. F. Rouvière, *Révolution dans le Gard*, IV, 106.

[48] A case in point is the misfortune of Guillaume Bruguier, pastor of Ners, who was incarcerated in the prisons of Uzès-la-Montagne (the revolutionary name of Uzès) by order of the administration of the district "pour avoir donné un acte de renonciation à son état de Ministre du culte protestant qui n'a pu été régardé que comme suspension," (quoted from the local records) even though his inquisitors noted at the time that his political record up until that time had been exemplary. He was released 12 fructidor an II (29 August 1794). Cf. BPF, XXXIV (1885), 217.

of the Desert, the origins of which lie in the eighteenth century. Even before the Revolution, forces were at work which presaged the catastrophe of the years 1793-1794. It is to the "Wilderness of France" that we must turn for the underlying causes of the Protestant collapse.

In retrospect, it seems undeniable, despite the heroic labors of Antoine Court and his disciples, that the Edict of Revocation had been far more effective, had come closer to achieving its desired end, than Protestant historians have been willing to admit. Indeed it had been far more successful than Frenchmen themselves believed in 1789. For if there is strength in numbers, the Protestant Church in France labored under a tremendous disadvantage in its prospects of weathering the storms of the Revolution. Numerically, the Protestant community in France had been permanently maimed by the rigorous measures of Louis XIV. Even today, with the total population of France roughly twice that of the mid-seventeenth century, the Protestant community is less than half of what it was reputed to be in the middle of the seventeenth century.[49] The claims of the *philosophes* and the partisans of the Protestants to the contrary, there were no three million Protestants in France in 1789, but rather considerably less than one million lost in a sea of Catholics. Furthermore, in those areas (especially in the north) where the restoration of public cult was delayed until the end of the eighteenth century, the diminution in Protestant strength continued, for without the spiritual guidance of pastors the temptations of conversion were far greater than the forces of tradition.[50]

[49] For the seventeenth century estimates, see Appendix I, note 12. The Protestant population of France today is not thought to exceed one million individuals of all denominations out of a total population of 41 million. See *The Statesman's Yearbook. Statistical and Historical Annual of the States of the World for the Year 1952*, ed. S. H. Steinberg (Macmillan, London, 1952), p. 957. This figure, of course, is merely a rough approximation. But in 1872, the last date at which the French government included religious inquiries in its national census, there were a reported 468,000 Calvinists in a France of 36 million individuals—this following an impressive Protestant revival in the middle of the nineteenth century. See E. Levasseur, *op.cit.*, I, 338-339.

[50] Cf. Emile-G. Léonard, "Le problème du culte public et de l'église dans le protestantisme français du XVIIIe siècle," in *Foi et Vie*, 1937, pp. 431-457. Léonard demonstrates this argument with the following census figures for the city of Caen in Normandy; in 1660 the Protestant community numbered approximately 4,000 individuals; by 1698, after thirty-five years of repressive measures, the figure had fallen to 1,350; in 1789, after a century of nothing but a "culte familial" there were scarcely 500 Protestants remaining in the city.

Equally significant were the intellectual consequences of the Revocation. The spiritual élite of the Church were scattered abroad. The seminaries of the Church were closed. The pastors of the Desert were, in the words of Charles Durand, nothing more than "peasants up-rooted from their farms, scarcely rough-hewn by their two years at the Academy of Lausanne, and flung into an adventurous life which allowed them no further development."[51] These children of the Cévennes filled the need of the Church in its early revival. Their audiences were nothing but peasants themselves, clinging to the traditional religion of their ancestors, for whom the reading of psalms, the reciting of memorized sermons, and the administering of communion sufficed to keep them from drifting into the Catholic Church. But in the latter part of the century, as the middle class found it possible once again to return to the Church of their fathers and interjected into the ranks of the faithful a more critical audience, the lay ministers of Languedoc were no longer able to satisfy the needs of their parishioners. Especially was this true when the Enlightenment brought into being a new group of priests, *philosophes* against whom most of the ministers of the Church were incapable of holding their own in the contest for men's minds. It is no accident that our traveler to Montpellier should have noticed that religious questions were no longer at issue in the city, that their place had been taken by the discussion of philosophic works, or that the elders of the church of Bordeaux should have complained in 1778 that "les pasteurs d'un vrai mérite sont malheureusement rares en France."[52]

Under such circumstances, the tempered persecution of the eighteenth century actually became one of the chief sources of strength for the Protestant Church. After a quarter century of *de facto* toleration, this became apparent to one of the more perceptive pastors of the Church. Writing in 1783, Olivier Desmons, the pastor of Bordeaux, cautioned a friend in England that "it would be true to say that the recent calm has been more baleful for us than the persecution of old. . . . In fact, the more favors the Church has received from the government, the less piety there has been within it. . . . Persecution purifies the faith of the congregation, and the blood of martyrs has always been the seed of the Church. . . ."[53]

[51] C. Durand, *op.cit.*, 54-55.

[52] BPF, XXXV (1886), 520.

[53] Olivier Desmons, *Mémoire sur la situation actuelle des protestants de France*

In 1789, with the granting of the Edict of Toleration two years earlier, the effects of toleration on the Church became all the more real to Desmons, and again he wrote, this time more emphatically, that "persecution is less deadly, *a thousand times*, than a treacherous tolerance which would furnish our enemies with the means of secretly *mining* our forces and of lulling us to sleep in a fatal secularity."[54] In effect the persecution of the eighteenth century, so long as it was mitigated by the condescension and indifference of the Court, created among the Protestant communities of the Midi a spirit of resistance, a sense of solidarity and cohesiveness, which they would otherwise have lacked. The entire energies of the pastorate and the elders in the Church were absorbed in keeping the Church alive, and as long as the persecution lasted the Church was vigorous and unified. But with the relaxation in this persecution came anarchy and dissension, introduced into the community of the faithful through the medium of the middle class.

The middle class has traditionally been an unstable element in the ranks of the Protestant population. At no time was this more true than in the eighteenth century. Living in cities and communities where their personal habits were easily observed, excluded from the professions they pursued unless they could give proof of their Catholicity, they were more reluctant to frequent the Church of the Desert than the peasant who enjoyed the anonymity of the countryside.[55] Hence in the early part of the reorganization of the Church in the Desert, it was largely among the peasants that Antoine Court found a following. But, by the middle of the century, the crypto-Protestants of the middle class had found it possible to return to their former religious practices without jeopardizing their

. . . (Bordeaux, 1783), reprinted in Emile Doumergue, *La Veille de la loi de l'an X*, pp. 109-131.

[54] *ibid.*, pp. 26-27, from Desmons' *Mémoire à communiquer aux provinces sur la nécessité de convoquer des synodes nationaux* . . . written in the course of 1788 and 1789. (Desmons' italics.)

[55] In the 1730's the vicar of Alais, speaking of the marriages in the Desert, remarked that "il n'y a guerre que la canaille qui s'en tienne à ses sortes de mariage, quoiqu'ils soient regardés comme bons par tous les religionnaires, mais les personnes d'une certain façon s'adressent à l'église pour éviter les peines portées contre les concubinaires et pour assurer l'état de leurs enfans." Cf. *Mémoire au sujet des religionnaires du Bas Languedoc et des Cévennes présenté à la cour par l'abbé de Saint-Maximin, . . . vicaire d'Alais* in E. Hugues, *Antoine Court*, II, 423-439.

material well-being. Hence in 1744 Antoine Court could write that "le gentilhomme, l'avocat, le medecin, le bon bourgeois, le riche marchand a le même empressement [pour nos assemblées] que le laboureur et l'artisan."[56] But these new communicants were not of the same mettle as the commoners. At the least sign of the recommencement of persecution, they were the first to quit the ranks of the faithful and the compromising company of the pastors.[57]

In these periods of alarms, the Church of course continued its activities quite well without them. But their presence interpolated a note of skepticism born of their urban quasi-Catholicism which almost certainly contributed to the diminution of faith among the flock as a whole. To the blind, unquestioning faith of the stubborn Huguenots they added a Protestantism of the "Moriscos."[58] Lacking the faith of the peasants, and as the century wore on increasingly contaminated with the teachings of the Enlightenment, they looked upon the religious assemblies as a means of social diversion rather than of spiritual enlightenment—a tendency still true all too often today. Such was the observation of Jeannette-Philippine Leclerc, the daughter of an émigré of 1685 who returned from Germany to Montauban in 1773 to visit the home of her husband. In letters back to her friends in Germany she could not conceal her scorn (admittedly that of a cosmopolitan for the rubes of a provincial city) for the lack of devotion exhibited by the Protestants of the city in their religious meetings. "I was scandalized by the lack of decency which reigned in this assembly; the people spoke out loud; in spite of the censures of two or three elders, it was impossible to quiet these people, the worst chatterboxes there are in the world.

[56] *ibid.*, II, 158.

[57] In spite of his elation at the progress of the revival as measured by the return of these elements to the fold, Antoine Court was forced to admit on several occasions that the middle class had none of the constancy of the peasants and artisans. "L'Eglise n'a eu dans ses grandes épreuves de fidèles constamment attachés que ceux qui n'étaient ni des sages, ni des nobles, ni des puissants selon le monde." Quoted by Lévy-Schneider, "Les Protestants et la Révolution dans le Sud-Ouest," in *La Révolution française*, XXXIX (1900), 16. In letters of 1744 to 1749 he admitted that "la moindre bourrasque jette l'alarme dans les coeurs et rend mes soins presque inutiles. Il n'y a que la petit peuple qui tient ferme et qui ne se déconcerte point, quelque violente que soit la tempête." Quoted by Charles-H. Pouthas, "Guizot et la tradition du Désert. La vie des protestants du Languedoc au XVIIIe siècle," *Revue historique*, CLXIX (1932), 52.

[58] Emile-G. Léonard, *Problèmes et expériences du Protestantisme français*. . . , p. 18.

Old people got up to greet others who arrived, and in doing so tramped on the feet of the unfortunate who found themselves in their way." The service began with the reading of a chapter of Scripture followed by a reprimanding by the dean of the elders who gave "a very strong censure on the paucity of devotion and the negligence in participating in Holy Communion. . . . These people [speaking of the audience] are simply incapable of keeping still: chatterboxes they were born, chatterboxes they are, chatterboxes they will die."[59] The records of the synods of the churches confirm Mme Leclerc's observations. The instructions to the churches drawn up in these assemblies, hitherto distinguished by the frequency of their requests for days of prayer and fasting to express the submission of Protestants to the temporal authorities and for the deliverance of the Church from persecution, become after 1760 monotonous in their complaints of the "extreme corruption which is creeping into the Church." Apropos of Mme Leclerc, the Synod of Béarn (10 March 1763) remarked that "it has been noticed that a great deal of irreverence and lack of devotion have manifested themselves in our assemblies during the reading of Holy Scriptures, the singing of psalms, and the recital of catechisms. The Assembly, deeply concerned at these abuses, exhorts and beseeches the faithful to mend their ways. . . ."[60] Similarly the Synod of Saintonge (17-18 July 1771), noting "with great sadness the corruption which reigns among Christians and the indifference toward our religion which is finding expression in our churches and which seems to increase in proportion to the toleration with which Heaven favors us," called upon the congregations to observe solemn and general fasting on an appointed day, "the surest means of inflaming zeal, exciting repentance, and drawing to us more and more the benedictions of God."[61] Dancing, gambling, loose morality, drunkenness, blaspheming; the wearing of hats in religious meetings, the introduction of arm chairs for the wealthy in the fore of the assemblies; the "dissoluteness of spirit and heart," "the tepidity of piety"—these and any number of other sores, in many cases nothing but manifestations of urban levity, harassed the church.[62]

[59] "Montauban en 1773-1774. Trois lettres de Jeannette-Philippine Leclerc," BPF, LII (1903), 59-72.

[60] E. Hugues, *Synodes du Désert*, II, 288.

[61] *ibid.*, III, 19-20.

[62] *ibid.*, II, 328, 356, 362, 367, 378, 386, 391, 394, 412, 421-423, 430, 436, 458; III, 5, 13, 19-20, 47, 66-67, 73, 78, 109, 115, 155, 177 note, etc.

More serious to the Church than the problem of moral turpitude was the social and administrative anarchy created within the Protestant community by the return of the middle class to the fold. Socially aloof, the bourgeois Protestants were reluctant to participate in the assemblies and ecclesiastical affairs of the Church at the same level with the rabble of the countryside. Wherever they could, they remained apart from the meetings of these stalwart peasants who alone had kept the Church alive throughout the first half of the century. Yet in the historic Church it was considered important, indeed essential, that there be a maximum amount of religious intercourse among the faithful. Calvin's position on this point is well summarized by Professor John T. McNeill: "Calvin notes that the phrase 'communion of saints' admirably expresses the reality of the Church, since in it the members mutually communicate all the benefits God confers upon them. This thought of communion and communication is strongly emphasized. Calvin has no tolerance for any solitary piety that detaches itself from this active interchange of spiritual values. The Church is an indispensable agent in the divine plan of salvation. . . . She is Mother to all to whom God is Father; and she remains the nurse of the Christian life in her children 'since there is no way of entrance into life unless she conceive us in her womb, give us birth, unless, moreover, she keep us under her protection and guidance. . . . For our weakness is such that we may not leave her school until we have spent the course of our life as her pupils.' (*Institutes*, IV, i, 4) Writing on Ephesians 4:13, Calvin makes this crisp statement: 'The Church is the common mother of all the godly, which hears, nourishes and brings up children to God, kings and peasants alike; and this is done by the ministry.' [Therefore] it is a grave sin to depart from the fellowship of a true visible Church. . . ."[68]

To these theological considerations must be added still others springing from local factors and problems peculiar to France, especially the shortage of pastors and the need for unity during a period of persecution. Under these circumstances the Church could not afford to be sympathetic toward any tendencies in the direction of atomization along social lines. The Discipline did make an exception for those who were too old or ill to make sorties into the Desert

[68] John T. McNeill, *The History and Character of Calvinism* (New York, 1954), pp. 214-215.

for the purpose of worship by allowing them to hold small meetings of their own in their homes and to receive spiritual guidance from their pastors there. Presumably such meetings were to be authorized by the local colloquy. But from the very outset of the revival the bourgeoisie were only too willing to stretch this concession to their own convenience. As early as the 1720's, meetings were being held at Nîmes and St.-Hippolyte for the benefit of "demoiselles . . . whose feet are too delicate to traverse the roads" and for "distinguished" men of Uzès who were reluctant to grope through the night of the Desert in order to attend the customary assemblies.[64] At Nîmes the pastor Paul Rabaut contributed to this tendency by founding a Masonic Lodge where such persons could meet to discuss the affairs of their church "entre messieurs" (and these "messieurs" carried swords and used the title "gentilhomme").[65] Mme Leclerc noticed and commented upon the same phenomenon at Montauban: "Well-bred people, Protestants—and there are a goodly number of them—have for the most part abandoned the exterior acts of divine worship to the lower classes; they think it would be degrading to communicate in public. . . . A number of them invite the minister to their homes and there, after assembling fifteen or twenty of their friends and having supped together, the minister, while they relax and let their meals settle, preaches to them and gives them communion. You must confess that this is most edifying!"[66]

In this manner the wealthier bourgeoisie tended to remain apart from the assemblies of the Desert in favor of small exclusive "societies" composed of their own relatives, friends, and persons of their class. By such means people of distinction avoided mingling with the common herd. They also spared themselves the risks involved in attending the larger meetings in the countryside, and in fact the government authorities encouraged them to avoid such tumultuous affairs. This development was especially marked in the southwest and north of France, where exclusive societies emerged in such towns as Bordeaux, Paris, and La Rochelle. In these areas they went so far as to disassociate themselves from the consistories and colloquies of the Church and formed what they called "comités" for the administration of their religious affairs—committees which

[64] Emile-G. Léonard, *Histoire ecclésiastique des Réformés français au XVIIIe siècle* (Paris, 1940), pp. 17-18.

[65] Emile-G. Léonard, *Problèmes et expériences du Protestantisme français*, p. 29.

[66] BPF, LII (1903), 59-72.

excluded (in the case of La Rochelle) "any person exercising a mechanical art."[67]

Even from the purely religious point of view, this social trend within the Protestant community led to serious disadvantages. It accentuated the class differences within the fold of the faithful and weakened the fraternal bonds which were such an important element in the successful resistance of the Protestants against their foes. Pastors were in such short supply that it was not possible to provide competent spiritual direction to the growing number of religious groups. In some cases this meant that the societies went without their administrations and thereby escaped their surveillance, making such groups more prone to doctrinal and philosophical deviations than would otherwise have been the case. There are also examples where societies and committees which did enjoy the ministrations of pastors went to extremes to monopolize their attentions at the expense of the less distinguished members of the sect. The committee of La Rochelle attached to the person of their parson "comitants alternatifs" whose function it was to accompany him wherever he went, seeing to it that no one approached him without proper introductions. Ostensibly this was to protect the pastor from physical harm at the hands of his enemies, but these enemies were apparently not the local governmental authorities since the committee itself occasionally met in the presence of the local intendant or his representative.[68] Almost certainly their function was to keep the pastor under surveillance, making sure that he distributed his attentions in the best interests of the local society. Similarly, the Protestants of the Isle de Ré divided into two communities according to wealth and remained separate for more than a decade with the richer of the two groups refusing to permit the local pastor to give his services to the other.[69]

As a concomitant to the social fissures within the Church there developed a growing conflict within the Church's administration between an aristocratic and authoritarian group on the one hand

[67] E. Hugues, *Synodes du Désert*, II, 242-251. The committee of La Rochelle numbered fourteen members, of whom six were permanent and the remaining eight were appointed for terms of two years. No debtors were admitted. On the death of a member, his successor was appointed by cooption. The proceedings of the committee were secret.

[68] Emile-G. Léonard, *Histoire ecclésiastique des Réformés français*, pp. 70-74.

[69] *ibid.*, pp. 93-94.

and a decentralized, lay, and democratic group on the other. To the bourgeoisie the organization of the Church left much to be desired. Its government was characterized by a democratic decentralization which conferred almost complete autonomy to the local communities. According to the Ecclesiastical Discipline of the Church, "the ministers shall not be permitted to assert a primacy over any of their fellow ministers, and they shall not be allowed to undertake anything on their own authority which might be of any interest to their colleagues or the churches; . . . no church shall be able to lay claim to a primacy or any form of domination over any other church, nor any province over another province."[70] Moreover, the representative councils of the Church (the colloquies, provincial synods, and the national synod) were not meant to be directive or legislative in their activities so much as to serve the churches as courts of appeal. Hence most power rested with the local consistories. And since the consistories and synods possessed considerable disciplinary powers over the ministers, the description of this organization by the eminent historian Emil-G. Léonard is especially apt: "a synodal federation of congregationalist, egalitarian communities under presbyterian direction."[71]

Now to men of "bon ton"—Protestants of the middle class who were proud of their wealth, education, culture, and social position—there were two major drawbacks to this system. First, administrative decentralization combined with the preponderant role of the peasantry in the reorganization of the Church meant that the Church, both in its composition and its direction, was primarily peasant. As we have just seen, the *bon bourgeois* of the eighteenth century was not especially anxious to mingle socially with the peasant, and he was decidedly opposed to subordinating himself to the peasant when it came to administering the affairs of the Church. Second, the interests of these two groups were divergent. The prime objective of the rural Protestants of the Midi was the reestablishment of their Church along its traditional, democratic lines of organization, and in Paris they pressed the monarchy and the ministry for reforms which ultimately would have recognized the total freedom of their cult. The notables or wealthier members of the Church cared little enough for the rights of public worship and concerned themselves

[70] E. Hugues, *Synodes du Désert*, I, 359, 368.

[71] Emile-G. Léonard, *Histoire ecclésiastique des Réformés français*, p. 4.

instead with their own particular interests. To them, the recognition of their civil status and the removal of civil disabilities were the most important issues at stake. In matters of church government, they were primarily interested in whatever polity would best lend itself to harmonious and efficient relations with the government authorities; they desired an organization which could take maximum advantage of the different attitudes of the constantly changing government personnel at the local level and one that could at the same time deal expeditiously and compatibly with the government in Paris and Versailles. They were well aware that this government feared and distrusted their Church for its democratic nature.

These two factions clashed in Paris, where the local *comité*, by virtue of the importance of its members and its seniority over the committees in the provinces, claimed to represent the interests of the Protestants as a whole in their relations with the state. In their pursuit of civil recognition to the exclusion of religious toleration, they did not hesitate to obstruct the efforts by the general deputy of the Church of the Desert in Paris, Court de Gébelin, to purchase toleration for the Protestants, even to the extent of denouncing him and his projects to the enemies of their faith.[72] They were also sympathetic with the ambitions of another enemy of the democratic church, Jacques-François Armand, chaplain of the Dutch embassy in Paris. Like so many Protestants from the Refuge, Armand nurtured a bourgeois disdain for the assemblies of the Desert. He also aspired to power in a Protestant Church which, in his opinion, should make whatever sacrifices the government demanded in return for a minimum of freedom. Therefore in northern France, where there were strong tendencies toward the *culte familiale*, or at best worship in restricted societies, he proposed to restrict the membership of such societies to fifteen or twenty members. To avoid attracting attention, their services should be kept as discreet as possible, which would preclude the singing of psalms. In the Midi, where the revival was well advanced, he planned to make Protestantism more palatable to the authorities by reducing the number of pastors by one-half and subordinating those who remained to

[72] Eugene Arnaud, "Court de Gébelin. Ses tribulations comme agent général des églises réformées," BPF, XXXII (1883), 269-280, 311-322; and A. Lods, "Court de Gébelin et la représentation des églises réformées auprès du gouvernement de Louis XV," BPF, XLVIII (1899), 244-275.

the authority of a bishop and a superintendant. Armand, of course, would become the superintendant. Such a scheme could be expected to have certain attractions to a government which had become increasingly resigned to the revival of Protestantism. By subordinating the Protestants to Armand, and Armand in turn to the government, the State could hope for far more control over the activities of the Protestants than normally would have been possible so long as the Church retained its traditional democratic government. Consequently in June of 1779 Armand, with the sympathy of the Parisian "messieurs" and probably with the approval of the controller-general Necker (a Swiss Protestant), toured northern France, where he announced that the court had charged him with the expulsion of the pastors from the area. Encountering resistance on the part of the rural Protestants of the Bocage, he went so far as to have two of their ministers arrested and imprisoned by the authorities.[73]

In his bid for what would have been a fundamental reorganization of the Church along episcopalian lines, Armand came into direct conflict with the leading spokesmen of the Church of the Desert. What support he did find within the pastorate seems to have been due less to acceptance of his schemes than to personal antipathies for his chief opponents: the Rabauts, father and son, Court de Gébelin, Olivier Desmons, and Blachon. As a consequence of his failure to enlist widespread support for his plans, Armand was ordered by the Dutch ambassador to cease interfering in the affairs of the Church and the government withdrew its support from his plans.[74] But if Armand failed to find an adequate following within the Church, there nevertheless were influential groups in the provinces equally hostile to the existing ecclesiastical organization. The province of Normandy, where the aristocratic movement was strong, refused to send a representative of their churches to the fifth, seventh, and eighth (the last) national synods, giving reasons which, in the words of the members of the synod, "ont été trouvées insuffisantes."[75] The church of Bordeaux, another province with tendencies in this direction, was attacked by the delegates to the seventh national synod for its "esprit de parti et d'indépendance."[76]

[73] Emile-G. Léonard, *Histoire ecclésiastique des Réformés français*, pp. 172-174.

[74] *ibid.*, pp. 176-179.

[75] E. Hugues, *Synodes du Désert*, I, 267n.; II, 158, 305.

[76] *ibid.*, II, 163.

And finally, it was the *comitants* of La Rochelle who led the opposition to the calling of a ninth national synod in the year 1766—a synod which was never to meet, to the great disadvantage of the Church.[77]

The defenders of the presbyterian tradition had more important enemies with whom to contend than Armand of the Dutch embassy and the bourgeois *comitants* of the west. During the second half of the century a number of the more prominent members of the pastorate itself became increasingly critical of the Church's democratic government, a development which in many cases was indicative of a gradual change in the social composition of the ministry. Peasant pastors were amenable to consistories composed of persons of humble origins. Bourgeois pastors were not. Paul Rabaut, as we have seen, became the leading spokesman of the Church in France following Antoine Court's departure for Switzerland, and Paul Rabaut was a bourgeois in origins and even more so in temperament. The son of a cloth manufacturer, he had married into a well-to-do family of Nîmes and lived in the better part of the city. That he chose to appear in public wearing a wig, and even so attired his young sons, clearly indicates that he did not want to be mistaken for a man of common means.[78] He had opposed Armand's attack on the Church, but this did not keep him from railing against the government of the Church in a way that showed that he had authoritarian inclinations of his own. "I shall not try to conceal from you," he wrote to another pastor of the Desert, "that our presbyterian government displeases me greatly. The smallest elder carries on like a person of importance, and the most insignificant pastor preens himself as if he were among the most distinguished. This leads to an anarchy which often has fatal results. If any sort of reform were possible, as I hope that it will be, we should doubtless conserve the episcopate, which entails far fewer

[77] *ibid.*, II, 395-396.

[78] See A.-B. Vienney, "L'Etat de fortune de la famille de Paul Rabaut en 1794," BPF, LXXX (1931), 430-434; or Emile-G. Léonard, *Histoire ecclésiastique des Réformés français*, pp. 45-46n. Quoting the latter, "la déclaration de fortune faite en 1794 par Rabaut-Pomier prouve que la famille jouissait à la fin de l'Ancien Régime d'une certaine aisance: le mobilier de Paul Rabaut (y compris, il est vrai, livres, linge et argenterie) était évalué à 10,000 livres, 'valeur métallique,' celui de Saint-Etienne à 15,000, même valeur. Ils avaient des vignes et des olivettes, ainsi que deux maisons sises dans le meilleur quartier de Nîmes."

inconveniences."[79] Since no episcopacy existed in the Church outside Paul Rabaut's imagination or personal pretensions, what he was asking was that the Church be centralized, that an ecclesiastical hierarchy be established similar to that which existed in the Catholic Church. In like manner, Jeanbon Saint-André (the son of a well-to-do merchant) wrote on the necessity of authorizing "les personnes d'un certain rang [et d']une bonne education à se mettre à la tête de nos affaires."[80] The pastor Gal-Pomaret abused the synods as "assemblies of confusion," and Rabaut Saint-Etienne wrote that the Church "must profit from the occasion of a reform in its discipline to remove the yoke with which the pastors are harnessed by the elders," and that in their functions and salaries they should be freed from the "caprice" of the elders and the "multitude." In his opinion, the existing Discipline and the synodal organization of the Church were conducive to divisions, factions, and an anarchy which not only weakened the Church from within but also brought discredit and suspicion upon it from without. The Court would never tolerate such tumultuous synods and perhaps justifiably feared that they might again become political assemblies. "Of what value have they been to us? Were they a blessing to our fathers? Are they to us? What do we stand to gain by keeping them? Mark my words, this anarchy [which they produce] has always hurt our churches and never helped them."[81]

Such grumblings of discontent were echoes from a long, sustained, and futile attempt on the part of their authors to introduce basic reforms into the Discipline of the Church. Throughout the century the elders of the Church remained faithful for the most part to its democratic form of government, but quite early in the period some pastors had become increasingly critical of its limitations in the management of their affairs during a period of persecution. Struggling to preserve a Church threatened with extinction by the State, they saw a need for coordination, positive leadership, and effective authority which the synods seemed incapable of giving. Further-

[79] Emile-G. Léonard, *Problèmes et expériences du Protestantisme français*, p. 52. Similarly the pastor Gal-Pomaret, in a letter to Olivier-Desmons (17 February 1772), observed that "tous ceux qui pensent reconnaissent aujourd'hui qu'il faut dans l'Eglise une hierarchie, et Calvin ne vouloit qu'il y eut entre les ecclésiastiques aucune primauté." BPF, XVIII (1869), 336.

[80] *ibid.*, p. 54.

[81] Emile-G. Léonard, *Histoire ecclésiastique des Réformés français*, p. 166.

more, with the advance of time, they came to realize, along with their coreligionists of the west and north, and even with Armand in Paris, that modifications or the elimination of the democratic aspects of the Church might make it more acceptable to the Crown and thereby hasten the acquisition of toleration. Attempts to bring about reforms to this end can be traced back as far as 1726, when Antoine Court proposed the creation of a "conseil extraordinaire" composed of designated elders which could assemble more speedily than a synod whenever the occasion demanded.[82] Such a council was established, but it was immediately attacked by members of the Church and subsequently its authority was so completely circumscribed that it soon ceased to meet.

Under the direction of Paul Rabaut the effort was renewed. The organs which he tried to introduce into the government of the Church varied in name—inter-provincial deputations, secret councils, correspondence committees, permanent committees, general commissions, a national committee—but their purpose was always the same: to create a board which would, as he put it, "manage the general affairs [of the Church] and would be, as it were, a national synod in permanent session."[83] By careful parliamentary maneuvering Rabaut succeeded in having such councils and committees created by the synods on a number of occasions, but in every case, once his real intentions were known, they were promptly attacked and either debilitated or eliminated by the champions of the presbyterian regime. His opponents in the provincial synods argued (and correctly) that no such body could speak in the name of the Church as a whole unless it were authorized by a national synod. Consequently he turned to this body and tried to win its approval of his plans. But in this, he was similarly defeated. The committees which Paul Rabaut desired were to have been dominated by a handful of the more enlightened and prominent pastors of the Desert. In this regard they differed fundamentally from the local committees which had sprung up in the west and north, for in these the laity or elders were supreme and maintained a close supervision over the ministers. The *comitants* of these areas had no intention of allowing the pastorate of the Desert to gain additional authority within the Church, especially when they sought this authority in order to further projects for toleration to which they

[82] *ibid.*, p. 42.

[83] *ibid.*, p. 105.

were indifferent or hostile. And it was precisely for these reasons that they prevented the calling of the ninth national synod (1766) in which Paul Rabaut had hoped to achieve his reform. In an issue such as this, they had the support of the voting majorities in the principal provincial synods of the Desert itself. Failing here, Rabaut tried to impress upon his opponents the need for such reforms and the absurdity of their democratic organization by enforcing the Discipline of the Church beyond its letter and spirit. The synod of Bas-Languedoc in 1772 was persuaded to pass a measure which enjoined the consistories and colloquies to terminate as many of their problems at the local level as possible and to refer as few as possible to the provincial level. This measure appeared inoffensive on the surface, but it was Paul Rabaut's intention that by it the authority and influence of the synods would be weakened and that of the leading pastors correspondingly increased. Again his efforts were unavailing. The local organs ignored the measure; the synods remained active. Having failed at every turn, Paul Rabaut ceased attending provincial synods in 1777. He excused his absence by calling attention to his advancing age and increasing difficulty in hearing. But since he did not retire from the ministry itself until 1785, it is more likely that he simply took this means of showing his disfavor for the synodal organization.[84]

During his semi-retirement, however, men of like mind continued the attack. Writing on the eve of the Edict of Toleration, Olivier Desmons appealed for the convocation of a national synod in the hope that it would in turn establish a "sovereign consistory" which could better handle the relations of the Church with the State and turn the Edict of Toleration to further advantages.[85] His associate in the ministry, Jeanbon Saint-André, went further and spoke of measures which scarcely differed from those sponsored earlier by Armand: "The institution [of bishops] in itself is not contrary to the ideas of the Protestants, for the Anglican Church has its bishops and the Church of Sweden has superintendants which, in spiritual affairs, have the same authority and fulfill the same functions. It cannot be doubted that if similar superintendants were established in the Reformed Churches of France, the discipline would become infinitely more simple as a consequence. The government itself, in according a legal status to the Protestants, would have a less com-

[84] *ibid.*, pp. 131-132.

[85] *ibid.*, pp. 192-193.

plicated machine to direct, since several individuals dispersed in different districts would in a certain degree be responsible to it for the other Protestants." Jeanbon, however, was not sanguine, for he concluded this remark with the observation that "there is little hope that the Protestants might adopt this reform."[86]

The churches themselves, on the other hand, while they were perhaps ignorant of the causes of this new spirit of independence on the part of their pastors, refused to assume any responsibility for the increasing divisions.[87] The discontent of the pastors and the unbending attitude of the elders when it came to the suggestions of reform of their discipline led to a steady collapse of discipline within the Church, reaching the point on the eve of the Revolution where local consistories and colloquies were refusing to send deputies to the provincial assemblies and where consistories met to discuss measures of importance to the Church without inviting their pastors to attend.[88] Whatever reforms were needed to mend these divisions could be effected only in a national synod. But the churches of the west and north continued to obstruct the various steps taken toward the convocation of such a body. The pastor Desmons, charged with preparing a memoir on the need for such a synod, warned the churches that the faction had reached the point where "the churches may diverge imperceptibly from the faith of our fathers, the pastors can surrender themselves to the passion of new ideas and of a philosophy opposed to the sacred principles of our theology, the art of preaching can [be reduced] to favoring the introduction of anti-Evangelical errors and dogmas [into our midst]. It is entirely possible that one day our churches will find themselves

[86] *ibid.*, p. 194.

[87] For instance the colloquy of the Agenais, 15 August 1765, maintained "que la discorde qui règne dans les églises de ces contrées ne vient ni de la part du peuple, ni de celle des anciens, mais uniquement de celle de MM. les pasteurs. . . ." E. Hugues, *Synodes du Désert*, II, 370, note. The perspicacious Olivier Desmons of Bordeaux expressed the same sentiments in trying to place the responsibility for the divisions and the lack of piety in the Church. Threatening to resign from the church of Bordeaux, he advised the elders in choosing his successor not to "rechercher les ministres qui brillent par l'esprit et l'agrément," but rather those "qui joignent la science au zèle et la piété. Votre église ne peut se soutenir et conserver l'amour de la religion qu' autant qu'elle aura à sa tête des hommes pieux et fidèles serviteurs de Jésus-Christ. Hélas! combien d'églises se sont relâchées par la faute des pasteurs." *ibid.*, III, 588 note.

[88] *ibid.*, III, 243, 488-489, 576-577, 607, 635-636, 637.

infinitely remote from the principles upon which our blessed Reformation was founded."[89] His warning, as prophetic as his other observations, went unheeded. Even he was forced to admit that with the coming of the Revolution the assembly of a synod would have to be delayed.

In short, the organization of the Protestant Church was crumbling from within long before the representatives Borie, Boisset, Tallien and their like dealt it the fatal blow. The relaxation of discipline following on the waning of persecution and the social pretensions of the middle class, which soon led to provincial faction within the Church, "mined its strength" and convinced both pastors and laity that their Church left much to be desired.

Even so, the Church might still have survived the revolutionary upheaval if it had possessed the cement of faith to bind together its members before the assault of revolutionary patriotism and the cults of the Republic. But of faith it had all too little. The early pastors of the Desert were unlearned, some of them even illiterate. Even with the establishment of the Seminary of Lausanne, the course of studies was too brief to impart to the students from France much in the way of "theological baggage." There was no opportunity for them, in the rigors of the life in the Desert, to further their learning once they had returned to France. The devotional books of the seventeenth century had been lost or burnt. For resources, the pastors had but a few Bibles imported from abroad, a few Psalters, the catechisms of Dreilincourt or Osterwald, all of which were in short supply and tended to gravitate into the hands of the rich. Thoughts of establishing a printing press in France to remedy the situation came to nothing. Neither Antoine Court nor Paul Rabaut, the two deans of the Church in the first and second halves of the century respectively, could read Latin or Greek. It is most doubtful that any of the pastors of the Desert in the first half of the century had really plumbed the depths of their faith, really knew in any manner of precision the doctrinal differences between their religion and that of the Roman Catholic Church. Dogma did not interest them.[90] Paul Rabaut had been preaching as an ordained minister

[89] *Mémoire à communiquer aux provinces sur la nécessité de convoquer des synodes nationaux. . .* , cited above, pp. 16-17.

[90] Only once in the century did the churches seem to indicate a concern for this void. In the fifth national synod (1748) it was resolved that "les controverses

in the church of Nîmes, the most important Protestant congregation in all France, for twelve years before reading Calvin's *Institutes.*

As the Church of the Desert matured and the dearth of pastors became less acute, it was possible for the synods to allow their candidates for the ministry three years' time at the Seminary of Lausanne. But the additional schooling did not necessarily remedy the doctrinal weaknesses of the Church, for it was almost certainly abroad, under the tutoring of Swiss theologians, that the pastors of the Desert became acquainted with the theological trends of eighteenth-century Europe—trends which weakened the spiritual vitality of the Church.

In the previous century, there had been a marked tendency within the Calvinist Churches of Europe to modify, or "soften," the more rigid and uncompromising strictures of Calvin's theological system. One of the leading figures in this movement was a theologian at the University of Leiden, James Arminius (1560-1609). Caught up in the intracredal disputations which raged around him in Holland, Arminius addressed himself to those very particulars of Calvin's system which even today puzzle more thoughtful persons in their first exposure to the theology of the Reformed religion. Calvin, in his consideration of the relationships between God and man, had maintained that with the Fall Adam and all his descendants had been plunged into a state of total and unconditional depravity, involving bondage of the will and the inability to do any spiritual good. Out of His own mercy, however, God had elected or predestined some men for salvation through the Atonement of Christ. "For [men]," wrote Calvin, "are not all created with a similar destiny; but eternal life is foreordained for some, and eternal damnation for others. Every man, therefore, being created for one or the other of these ends, we say he is predestined either to life or to death" (*Institutes,* III, xxi, 5). Since only the elect would be saved, Christ's Atonement was strictly limited to their benefit and was

qui nous séparent de l'Eglise romaine étant une partie de la théologie sur laquelle les ministres ont besoin d'être bien instruits, principalement dans le pays et dans les circonstances où nous nous rencontrons, l'on priera par une lettre ceux qui dirigent les études de nos proposants de leur faire bien connaître ces matières." E. Hugues, *Synodes du Désert,* I, 254. However, a study by Albert Monod of the 233 extant sermons preached by Paul Rabaut indicates that only three were devoted to the doctrinal differences which separated the Calvinist from the Catholic. Cf. Albert Monod, *Les Sermons de Paul Rabaut, Pasteur du Désert* (s.l.n.d.), pp. 70-72.

of no relevancy to the reprobate. Salvation thus accorded was thought to be quite independent of individual merit, for all men by the Fall were equally sinful, the elect and reprobate alike. From this position there emerged a number of considerations which in the eyes of more humanistic theologians threw a questionable light on the equity and justice of God. A group of Calvin's followers, among them Theodore Beza, had come to hold that God, in decreeing the process of salvation, must also have preordained the Fall of Man and his consequent depravity. Such a belief implied that God was Himself the author of evil; furthermore, Calvin's interpretation of original sin meant that God was condemning Adam's descendants for a sin in which they had had no part. Clearly this was incompatible with man's sense of justice and hence repugnant to those theologians who thought of God as just.

Arminius' approach to the doctrines of the Fall, original sin, predestination, and Atonement were founded on anthropological and rational considerations. An omniscient God foreknew the Fall of Man, he argued, but did not foreordain it; rather, Adam sinned of his own volition. Nor did the Fall bind Adam's descendants in sin; it merely created within man a bias toward sin. Christ had died for all men, not just for the elect, and all men were thereby given an equal opportunity to avail themselves of the redemptive processes which God had made available through his sacrifice. Since man was gifted by God with reason and free will, he was enabled by the former to believe in God through Christ, and by the latter to choose either the path of righteousness or that of sin. With the Arminians, predestination thus ceased to be an eternal decree to salvation or damnation, but was limited to God's foreknowledge of those who would choose to believe and be saved, and those who would not. Furthermore, with election redefined and depending upon a rational faith and freedom of choice, it ceased to be regarded as indefectible; such a belief had disturbed Arminius, for it led to an ethically dangerous and false sense of security on the part of those who considered themselves among the saints. Election became a state conditioned upon continued faith and obedience to God's will.

In reacting against Calvin's absolutist interpretation of predestination, the Arminians set out on a path which easily led many of their sympathizers to still further modifications of Calvinist theology. Their rational approach to dogma made them tolerant of theological differences, and some progressed to a latitudinarian or to a completely rationalist position; the heightened importance which they gave to man's free will led others perilously close to Socinianism and Pelagianism. The Socinians, in emphasizing the omnipotence of God, rejected predestination and original sin altogether, regarding them as inconsistent with God's complete sovereignty and freedom of action. For similar reasons they were anti-Trinitarians. Christ they regarded as a high-priest who intercedes with God on our behalf, salvation being accorded those who trust in God through His son and who surrender themselves to His will. But, more important, Christ is a prophet who in his life and teachings revealed to man the hidden will of God and the nature of the obedience which He desires of men. From this there followed a reinterpretation of the fundamental nature of Holy Scripture, and especially of the New Testament. The latter was not to be interpreted dogmatically, but rationally; it was viewed as a textbook of information about doctrines and moral precepts.

Socinianism was a seventeenth-century movement which made inroads in both the Catholic and Protestant camps; Pelagianism, which had developed within the Christian community contemporaneously with Augustinianism, was akin to the Socinianism in rejecting both original sin and predestination. Each man at birth from a moral point of view was thought to be a second Adam before the Fall. By nature man is good, for God would not create him otherwise. Even the desires of the flesh were not thought of as sinful, because they are God-given; rather they become sinful only when indulged to excess. Man's free will is absolute and indefectible. Consequently, the mediatory role of Christ was all but forgotten, and instead of turning to him, man should face God, before whom he is responsible for his sins. Endowed with reason and free will, man is free to sin or not as he chooses, but he is assisted in this choice by the Grace of a merciful God—i.e. by the revelation of His law and through the example set by Christ of what he should do. Since Grace was also thought to be accorded to men according to their individual merits, the emphasis in Pelagianism fell upon man's freedom and upon the performance of good works. In effect the Pelagians preached the message that God helps those who help themselves.

Although condemned by the synods of the Church in the

seventeenth century, these beliefs survived the persecution which was directed against them and increasingly permeated Calvinist theology. The content of their theology was more in harmony with an Age of Reason than orthodox Calvinism. Socinianism and Pelagianism were both anti-Trinitarian. All three were alike in being, to varying degrees, rational in their approach to Holy Scripture and in their condemnation of dogmatic interpretation of the literal word. All three stressed the ethical aspects of Christianity, and in breaking with Calvin's concept of man's total depravity gave renewed significance to man's reason and free will.

The extant sermons from the period of the Desert are so few in number that it is difficult to pass judgment on their general theological content with any degree of absolute certainty, but it does seem clear that the spiritual leaders of the eighteenth-century Protestants had been noticeably infected with these beliefs. To a man like Paul Rabaut, the essence of the Reformation was "the right of each individual to explain the Holy Scriptures to his own tastes, that is to say, to fashion a religion for himself after his own understanding (suivant ses lumières)." What, then, was the utility of Holy Scriptures? In the historic Church they were received as the Word of God, the testimony of the Lord superior to all reason, the source of a progressive revelation with a divine power to enlighten; they were the medium through which the God of Nature and the God of Grace is revealed to man and a meeting place where the Lord and His creation stand spirit in touch with spirit. But to Paul Rabaut they appeared as something less, as little more than a text on ethical values. "We read the Holy Scriptures," he wrote, "for no other purpose than to enlighten the faithful and to make them honest men. . . . We deliver discourses not on points of religious controversy, but upon the important points of morality, and notably on the good-will that men owe to one another, and on the respect, submission, and obedience which inferior persons owe to their superiors. . . . The people (le peuple), who in general have little education, little free time, and little intelligence, have no other means of self-instruction than what these religious exercises offer them."[91]

Morality was Rabaut's chief concern, and in this he was not alone

[91] Emile-G. Léonard, *Problèmes et expériences du Protestantisme français*, pp. 76-77.

in the pastorate. In their role as moralists, the ministry tended to become what Joseph de Maistre was later to define as epitomizing the Protestant pastor: "un homme en habit noir qui dit des choses honnêtes."[92] Stressing the ethical side of religion, they sometimes muted many of the principal articles of Christian faith. This tendency varied, of course, from one pastor to another. Preaching in 1770, Paul Rabaut warned his congregation that salvation was not to be had by the mechanical performance of almsgiving and other good works, that works of this kind were quite unavailing. "So long as you are not intimately united with Jesus Christ by an intense faith you are spiritually dead. . . . Consequently you must begin by recognizing your state of destitution, helplessness, and condemnation, and in a deep awareness of your worthlessness approach Christ with complete confidence that he will receive us even as we are—as miserable creatures who have nothing, who are capable of nothing, and who place all our hopes in his mercy and his help." He wanted his listeners to understand that good works must necessarily be a consequence of love and faith in Christ and he called their attention to Christ's admonition that "as the branch cannot bear fruit by itself, unless it abides in the vine, neither can you, unless you abide in me."[93] With Paul Rabaut, it is through Christ that man is saved, yet his supreme confidence that Christ will receive us apart from any predestined state is worthy of note. But his son, Rabaut Saint-Etienne, drifted further from the teachings of Calvin and seems to have moved to an anti-Trinitarian position; when questioned on the *Theses* of Vernet, where Christ's divinity was formally denied, he answered only that "il n'y a pas là de quoi faire tant de bruit."[94]

Pastors who deemphasized the redeeming work of Christ, who rarely concerned themselves with atonement and justification by faith, placed themselves in a position where they were easily lured by a Roman Catholic and even a Pelagian belief in the efficacy of good works. Strangely enough, to judge from the printed sermons which are still extant, it appears that Olivier Desmons, notwithstanding his concern at the diminution of piety among the faithful,

[92] Daniel Benoît, *Du Caractère huguenot et des transformations de la Piété protestante* (Paris, 1892), p. 47.

[93] Albert Monod, *Les Sermons de Paul Rabaut*, pp. 189-191.

[94] Emile-G. Léonard, *Problèmes et expériences du Protestantisme français*, p. 77. Translated loosely, it reads: "There is nothing here to warrant getting so excited."

was the worst offender in this matter. *Pardon des injures, la Providence, la Restitution, la Nécessité des aumônes, les Merveilles de la Création et de la Providence, la Force des mauvaises habitudes*: such were the subjects of his sermons.[95] In one of them we read: "Sin separates man from God, charity draws him closer: hence it follows be charitable. Have you fallen into the sin of avarice? Perform good works, be liberal toward the poor, redeem your sin with alms. Have you been deaf to the voices of the unfortunate? Has your heart been insensible to their misfortunes? Multiply your works, redeem your sin with alms. Has envy penetrated into your heart? Try to stifle it, redeem your sin with alms. Have you sullied the reputation of your neighbor with slander or calumnies? Be repentant; do not forget to be charitable and to share your possessions with others, for you know that God is pleased with such sacrifices; redeem your sin with alms. Time separates man from God during life, charity draws him closer to Him for an eternity; hence be charitable. Christians, if there is a state of retribution after this life, if virtue is not a fanciful being, if, finally, religion is not a chimera, for whom are reserved the rewards which religion promises us, if the charitable man does not have the right of laying claim to them? If pure religion consists in visiting the widows and orphans, to whom does religion promise the blessings of another life, if he who exercises hospitality and who renders services to others is not justified in awaiting the celestial city of which God Himself is the architect and founder?"[96]

The departure from a strict Calvinist orthodoxy was an experience common to the greater part of the Protestant world during the eighteenth century. But at the same time the experience of the French Church was somewhat distinctive, for the State's persecution of the Church during the first half of the century made the Protestant community as a whole peculiarly receptive to theological deviations of this kind. It has already been noted that persecution

[95] P. de Félice, *Sermons protestants prêchés en France*. . . , pp. 32-33. For sermons of a similar nature preached by other pastors, see pp. 31, item xv; 34-35, items xx and xxi; 38, item xxviii; 39, item xxx; 44, item xl (in this case Olivier Desmons again); 45, item xlii.

[96] Quoted in Daniel Benoît, *Les Frères Gibert*. . . , pp. 287-288. Desmons delivered this sermon first at Anduze, then as one of his first sermons at Bordeaux, where the Protestants had reacted so strongly against pietist sermons dealing with man's total depravity.

made it extremely difficult to establish the means for thoroughly educating either the pastors or the laity in the early period of the Desert. This would explain in part why sermons were rarely devoted to dogma, for it was easier for half-educated preachers to devote their sermons to moral problems than to more complicated theological questions. Furthermore, persecution led to an increasing emphasis upon the Old Testament, in which the sufferings of the Hebrews seemed in the eyes of French Protestants closely to parallel their own plight under the Bourbon State. They were inclined to attribute all events, the felicitous and the cruel, to the will of God, thinking of persecution and misfortune as His punishments, toleration and periods of prosperity as His rewards. They became more acutely aware of the Covenant and of the workings of celestial wrath against those who violated His law. This in turn deflected their concern in religion from questions of Grace to those dealing with good works, or morality.[97] Consequently when candidates for the ministry were introduced to a more careful consideration of theological points at the Seminary of Lausanne in the second half of the century, a propensity for the ethical emphases of the doctrine of the period had already been established. Had their spiritual rector at the seminary chosen to keep close watch on their theological development, he might of course have protected them from contamination with the theological spirit of the times. In fact there were a few Frenchmen who were conscious of the threat to orthodoxy and who suggested that the seminary be moved to France, where their students might be kept in a spiritual quarantine; at the very least they insisted that the students be required to sign a Confession of the Church. No one denied the desirability of having a seminary in France, but this was altogether impossible so long as the State continued its persecution. As to insisting upon the signing of confessions of faith, such an idea was alien to Antoine Court, who detested compulsion in matters of doctrine. "I do not believe they should be obliged to sign the confession unless they do so voluntarily," he wrote. "It is enough to ask that they refrain from teaching anything which might be contrary to it or might disturb the common peace. . . . Those who have forced people to sign confessions have

[97] Albert Monod, *Les Sermons de Paul Rabaut*, pp. 23-24.

narrowly missed doing great harm to religion."[98] Such tolerance permitted the students a fair degree of latitude in their theological development.

Now there were pastors who, given the opportunity, could appreciate the theology of the historic Church. When after more than twenty years in the ministry Paul Rabaut obtained a copy of the *Institutes of the Christian Religion*, he confessed that he read them "with very great pleasure" and that in his opinion the "old-time theologians were superior to the modern."[99] Moreover, when the first stirrings of the eighteenth-century Protestant revival reached France through the activities of Moravian Brethren—pietists who stressed the doctrines of the total depravity of human nature, of reconciliation unto God and justification through the sacrifice on the Cross, who urged that man through faith and devotion to Christ could experience a spiritual rebirth whereby he could live in a personal and intimate union with Him—Paul Rabaut, as well as many of the Protestants of the Desert, were both interested in and sympathetic with their teachings. Antoine Court, however, when he learned that the Moravians had established missions in the Desert, feared that their activities might weaken and divide the Protestant community. In something of the same sort of fear and intolerance that a Communist today feels for a Socialist, he repeatedly warned Paul Rabaut against the pernicious influence of these "fanatics."[100] This would appear on the surface to be inconsistent with Court's latitudinarian leanings, but it was the unity of the Protestants more than their faith that concerned him. Time proved him right in his fear that the Moravians might further

[98] G.-Edouard Guiraud, *Le Séminaire de Lausanne et le Pastorat en France pendant la période du Désert, 1715-1787* (Geneva, 1913), p. 46.

[99] In a letter to the pastor Pradel (1755) Rabaut wrote: "Mille et mille remerciements pour *l'Institution* de Calvin. Je lis cet excellent ouvrage avec un très grand plaisir. Nos anciens théologiens sont, à mon avis, préférables aux modernes." C.-H. Pouthas, "Guizot et la tradition du Désert," *Revue historique*, CLXIX (1932), 64n. The remark can, of course, be taken as a revealing testimony to his religious superficiality (Pouthas prefaces it with "Et quel commentaire!"), and if indeed this was the full extent of his impressions, it would seem that however pleasant he found his contact with the teachings of Calvin, he cannot have taken them very much to heart.

[100] See D. Benoît, *Les Frères Gibert*, pp. 249-259; E. Hugues, *Antoine Court*, II, 18-21, 79; and A. Salomon, "P.-C. Fries, Emissaire morave en France, 1760-1761," BPF, LXXI (1932), 29-34.

aggravate the discord within the Church. When the pastor Gibert of Bordeaux, after coming into contact with Moravian missionaries, commenced preaching on the depravity of man and the need for a personal reconciliation with God through Christ, the middle class *Bordelais* found such thoughts either distasteful or disconcerting and began proceedings against their pastor. The matter was fought out in the local consistory and provincial synod during 1769 and 1770. The consistory, after failing to quiet their spiritual leader by forbidding him to preach on matters of salvation and the impotence of man, relieved Gibert of his functions and called Desmons to their church.[101] Similarly the pastor Monod of Lyon was removed from his functions for preaching on matters of dogma rather than treading the safer grounds of morality.[102]

Whether it be in terms of dogma or ethics, the pastor is expected to preach the message of Christ to his parishioners. He is their spiritual instructor. "By the faith of the gospel Christ becomes ours, and we become partakers of the salvation procured by him, and of eternal happiness. . . ," wrote Calvin in the *Institutes*. "But as our ignorance and slothfulness, and, I may add, the vanity of our minds, require external aids, . . . God has provided such aids in compassion to our infirmity; and that the preaching of the gospel might be maintained, he has deposited this treasure with the Church. He has appointed pastors and teachers, that his people might be taught by their lips; he has invested them with authority, in short, he has omitted nothing that could contribute to a holy unity of faith, and to the establishment of good order." Ill-trained, unresolved in their doctrines, the pastors of the Church of the Desert were poorly equipped to bear the responsibilities of their office. Worse still, perhaps, were the limitations in the calibre of men who entered the pastorate. Too many ministers had no calling for their positions. In the estimation of an indignant pastor of the Vivarais, writing in 1791, large numbers of persons flocked to the

101 E. Hugues, *Synodes du Désert*, II, 497-499. See Gibert's defense in BPF, XIX-XX (1870-1871), 70-73; XXI (1872), 398-402. In his words, "on m'a fait un grief, d'avoir dit que l'homme ne peut rien de bien, avant d'avoir la foi; et que la philosophie est inutile dans la Religion. J'ai prouvé que ce que j'ai enseigné là dessus est conforme à notre confession de foi. . . . On s'est récrié sur ma manière de prêcher; parce, m'a-t-on dit, que j'en revenois toujours au même but; c'est-à-dire, à Jésus-Christ. . . ." Gibert fled to England, where he was ordained in the Anglican Church in 1771.

102 D. Benoît, *Les Frères Gibert*, p. 273.

ministry without having either the necessary talents or virtues to acquit themselves of it worthily; too many fathers and mothers had destined their sons to the ministry with no view other than that of procuring honorable places for them. He was alarmed at the number of men who engaged in the career uniquely for mundane purposes and who prepared themselves for it by spending their youths in libertinism or consuming their time in learning things which they should not teach. Most appalling were the number of those who were submerged in a crass ignorance of their religion.[103] The ministry began to pall on such pastors. "You are fortunate, my dear brother," wrote Barre (pastor of Anduze) to Olivier Desmons in 1773, "in being able to dispense with making sermons and to employ your time in more useful occupations. I am writing as few as possible, but these few are too many for me. In the long run, such work bores one and prevents one from acquiring the aptitudes necessary for the writing of good compositions."[104] In like manner, Gal-Pomaret (pastor of Ganges) confessed to Desmons during the same period that "Je ne fais, Monsieur, presque plus de sermons. Eh! pourquoi tant de sermons?"[105] What was it that occupied such pastors to the extent that they felt justified in neglecting their functions? Gal-Pomaret supplies the answer in an earlier letter: "I want to know what people are writing and what is going on in the world; consequently I have renewed my subscription to the *Journal Encyclopédique* and I hope to receive it any day. I should not make this expense if I did not find myself in a city where there are, so to speak, no men of letters."[106]

The eighteenth century was a dangerous century for pastors with idle minds. Restless at the ennui of life in the Desert, fancying themselves to be littérateurs and men of enlightened views, fascinated with the world around them, they dabbled in the philosophy of the century and in the end only succeeded in denaturing their religion. The brilliance of the Enlightenment blinded them to the dangers it posed to their faith. They welcomed the advances of the *philosophes*, not realizing that the latter befriended them, not as Protestants, still less as Evangelical Christians, but as a cat's-

[103] Pierre Astier, *La vocation et les devoirs des pasteurs* (Valence, 1791), partly reprinted in BPF, XXXV (1886), 520.

[104] BPF, XIX-XX (1870-1871), 34.

[105] BPF, XVIII (1869), 340.

[106] *ibid.*, 336.

paw in the baiting of royal despotism and clerical intolerance. The alliance with the forces of Reason overpowered them. Gal-Pomaret is a case in point. In 1772 he feared that the philosophy of the century would undermine the faith. "Already our flocks are swarming with unbelievers."[107] A year later he wondered if Voltaire would not succeed in converting the world to deism.[108] But when he was informed that the sage of Ferney had taken their church under his protection, he hesitantly surmised "that if this is so, then he is a Christian."[109] In 1776 he had been reduced to the point of assuring Voltaire that at Ganges, "there is a man who loves you, honors you, and respects you with all his heart."[110] And finally he could contain himself no longer: "Bless God for having given you life. . . . You shall see Jesus Christ in all His glory and you shall share His blessings!"[111]

Rather than winning defenders to their faith, such pastors were increasingly beguiled into the attempt to reconcile their religion with the philosophy of the century. Thus Paul Rabaut could write in 1768: "In this century, more than in any other, it is necessary to simplify religion, to cast aside all accessories. This done, it will be to the tastes of the *philosophes* and within the reach of the

[107] Letter to Olivier Desmons, 17 February 1772, BPF, XVIII (1869), 335-337: "Nous sommes dans un siècle philosophe, mais pensés vous que la philosophie qui est tant en vogue, tourne à l'avantage du christianisme? Je crois le contraire. Dejà nos troupeaux même fourmillent de mécréants. Que fera-t-on quand on aura beaucoup philosophé? Il est fort à craindre qu'on ne retourne au fanatisme; au moins voit-on souvent la fièvre ardente suivre de près la fièvre frilleuse."

[108] *ibid.*, 337-339, letter to O. Desmons dated 11 January 1773: "Si j'étois plus jeune et plus habile que je ne le suis, je me formerois de justes idées du système de M. de Voltaire, et je chercherois ensuite à y répandre le même ridicule qu'il a cherché à répandre sur le nôtre: ne pourriés vous pas vous charger de ce travail là? Ce grand homme traite le christianisme sans aucun ménagement dans ses nouveaux mélanges philosophiques. Je crains qu'il ne rende tout le monde déiste."

[109] *ibid.*, 339-341, letter to the same dated 2 May 1773: "Un homme qui a passé plusieurs semaines chés le philosophe de Ferney, et qui m'a fait présent de son portrait, m'assuré qu'il fesoit grand cas de ma Religion. Si cela est, il est donc chrétien."

[110] "Lettre inédite de Gal-Pomaret à Voltaire (8 March 1776)," BPF, VII (1859), 484-485: ". . . Pour voir approcher la mort sans crainte et la recevoir sans émotions, il faut être, selon moi, dans la croyance des vérités évangéliques; je ne doute pas que vous n'y soyez. Il est vrai que vous avez formé contre elles plusieurs difficultés, mais on peut en faire sans être incrédule, et plus encore sans être impie. . . . Daignez croire qu'il est à Ganges un homme qui vous aime, qui vous honore et qui vous respecte de tout son coeur."

[111] D. Benoît, *Du Caractère huguenot. . .*, p. 50.

people, who are not at all capable of comprehending, and still less of discussing, that multitude of articles of which religion is composed, and to which most are foreign."[112]

Turning to the sermons of his son, Rabaut Saint-Etienne, we find that his faith, too, revealed the temper of the times. In a sermon on the "Superiority of Christianity," he maintained that "the Christian religion is nothing more than natural religion revealed to mortals and confirmed by Jesus Christ."[113] As with Locke and later Condillac, the Christian doctrine of total depravity, the belief in innate ideas, was immersed in the ablutions of the comforting belief that man's mind at birth is a *tabula rasa*, imprinted through life by the experiences of the world around him. In the words of Rabaut Saint-Etienne, "Our conscience is neither the secret voice of God which makes itself heard in our souls, nor a judge placed within us to whom our being should be submitted; it is nothing other than the judgment which our soul or our reason places on our actions, in such a manner that when one says that a man consults his conscience, it is as if he were saying he consults his reason; when one says he acts in spite of the voice of his conscience, he is saying that he acts against the counsels of his reason; when one says he experiences remorse, it is the same as saying that he is reproached by his reason. Once again, then, our conscience is our reason."[114] What is the fuel upon which our reason feeds? Whence the origin of man's passions and sins? Again it is the determinism of the Enlightenment to which Rabaut Saint-Etienne turns for an answer—a belief in a materialistic universe where good blends and becomes indistinct with evil, for phenomena, whether physical or moral, are the products of the world in which we live, and hence are necessary. "All our thoughts originate in the senses, that is to say our soul has no thought, no reflection, no sentiment which is not given to it from the body." "Our passions, criminal in their excess, are innocent in their principle [because] our passions are nothing more than our needs, and since these needs are given us by our creator, they are inseparable from our nature."[115] Man, gifted with reason, can infallibly arrive at a better world if he will

[112] E.-G. Léonard, *Problèmes et expériences du Protestantisme français*, p. 77.

[113] Chas.-H. Pouthas, "Guizot et la tradition du Désert," *Revue historique*, CLXIX (1932), 74.

[114] *ibid.*, 74.

[115] *ibid.*, 74-75.

only use his reason. Rabaut Saint-Etienne believed in progress and felt, as did many Protestants, that dogmatic quarrels could only delay it. One must not hold to the Bible as the sole source of authority: "The people who have only one book, like the Jews and the Moslems, never change their minds; they would go to the end of time without truth making the slightest progress with them; their doctors are always right, because they are never contradicted. But with people who read and study, there are men who extricate themselves by degrees from ignorance and error in such a way as to arrive infallibly at the truth, for there is absolutely no limit to the perfectibility of our reason."[116] "Oh divine Reason, precious gift of God bestowed on man as the counterpoise to his weakness, you, whom the throng of mortals abandon and who dictates your peaceful lessons to the dutiful Christian who listens to you, come preside in this assembly of Christians! Let your voice be heard in our midst, and let our hearts rally in throngs beneath your standards!"[117]

The dangers of reducing their religious services to moral discourses embellished with philosophical banalities were twofold.

First, the laity did not have to seek such mundane expositions in the temples of their pastors. Since there were distinct material inconveniences to being Protestant, and few spiritual compensations, a Frenchman could well ask himself why indeed he was a Protestant. Some apparently did just that, and failing to find a satisfactory answer drifted away from the Church to literary salons, to the patriotic clubs of the Revolution, to the growing ranks of the unbelievers, and even to the Catholic Church. By the 1780's the Protestant Church in France had passed beyond the zenith of its spiritual and numerical strength. New churches were still being founded, but church attendance seems to have begun to diminish. The general consistory of the church of Nîmes reported in 1782 that "our religious assemblies have greatly diminished in the last few years; they are no longer frequented by persons of high standing at all, who at the most attend only on the days of solem-

[116] Quoted by Pierre Chazel, "Génie français et protestantisme dans la France contemporaine," in *Protestantisme français*, eds. Marc Boegner and André Siegfried, p. 80.

[117] Chas.-H. Pouthas, "Guizot et la tradition du Désert, *Revue historique*, CLXIX (1932), 74.

nities. . . ."[118] Olivier Desmons observed the same trend at Bordeaux. "The Protestants are neither persecuted nor free. It would seem that this state would preserve them from falling off. But ambition loses some: they seek [public] honors and they feign being Catholics. Lack of zeal takes the others, and they are Protestants without making an open profession of their faith; at least they do not attend public worship, and they do not communicate."[119] Although the State was increasingly tolerant of Protestant marriages in the Desert, although their wills and testaments were now generally recognized in the courts, although they found it increasingly easy to enter public offices and the forbidden professions, nonetheless the Protestants continued (and perhaps with increasing frequency) to celebrate their marriages and the baptisms of their children in the Catholic Church.[120] More than before seemed to be marrying Roman Catholics.[121] Tradition held the majority to the religion of their fathers, but there were many others who were being lost.

Secondly, the consequences were equally grave for the pastorate. Beguiled by the lessons of the Enlightenment, a number of them began to feel it was quite possible that through the forces of reason a paradise could be realized on this earth, and that it was up to them

[118] "Articles relatifs à rétablir l'ordre et la discipline de l'Eglise présentés au consistoire général de Nîmes, le 12 septembre 1782," in Emile Doumergue, *La Veille de la loi de l'an X*, pp. 79-83.

[119] O. Desmons, *Mémoire sur la situation actuelle des protestants de France*, in E. Doumergue, *La Veille de la loi de l'an X*, pp. 125-126.

[120] In a letter to the *comité* (of correspondence) of Bas-Languedoc, dated 1764, the pastor Cavalier of Bordeaux spoke of the toleration which the Protestants enjoyed, and then complained: "Une chose qui continue à nous faire une extrême peine, à mon collègue et à moi, c'est l'article des baptêmes. Il ne nous est pas possible de faire entendre raison là-dessus à la plupart des membres de notre troupeau. Ils continuent toujours, malgré nos représentations, surtout les plus riches, à faire administrer cet auguste sacrement à leurs enfants dans l'Eglise romaine." Cf. E. Hugues, *Synodes du Désert*, II, 341 note. The Synod of Haut-Languedoc, 1 May 1788 resolved that "tout protestant qui ferait à l'avenir bénir son mariage ou baptiser un de ses enfants à l'Eglise romaine, se trouvant entièrement sans excuse, serait traité selon la rigueur de la discipline." *ibid.*, III, 558. For protests in the synods against such marriages and baptisms after 1770, see *ibid.*, III, 22 note, 74-81, 114, 207, 345 note, 350, 595, 604. E. Doumergue, *La Veille de la loi de l'an X*, pp. 76-77, cites a number of cases from the records of the consistory of Uzès for the decade of the 1770's indicating the frequency of the violations.

[121] The question of mixed marriages appears hardly at all in the records of the synods before 1760, but thereafter with increasing frequency. Cf. E. Hugues, *Synodes du Désert*, II, 246, 352, 461, 497 note, 501; III, 7, 48, 345-346 note, 349, 373 note, 376, 503, 558, 596, 640.

to help in the work of its realization. Such pastors were easy prey to the élan and optimism of the Revolution. Note Rabaut Saint-Etienne writing to another pastor in 1791: "I am convinced that our fellow pastors could do nothing better than to preach from time to time on the Constitution, and by so doing to explain it. For the Constitution serves as the code of morality for the State, and there is only one such code. Before the Revolution, I gave considerable thought to a plan of education for the Protestants, and in large part these plans have found expression in what the Revolution has just achieved. [Hence these sermons] would be worthy of the nation and an infallible means . . . for giving to the people just and healthy ideas of natural law, of the political law of France, and of the Constitution. The decrees of the nation could serve as the text, and the Gospel could also furnish abundant material. Your flocks, drawn to you by this double bond, would experience the utility of a class of men moulded by both political and religious virtue, which are the same."[122] To Rabaut Saint-Etienne, religious worship should be extended to something more than a reverence of God, instruction in His word, and an encouragement to the faithful to aspire to immortality. He already stood on the slope which led precipitously down to that of the position of Jeanbon Saint-André in addressing the Catholics of Cherbourg in 1793. Nor did Rabaut Saint-Etienne mark the extreme in which pastors took up the cause of the Revolution. Another pastor, Jacques Molines, left the ministry in 1790 to become the president of the revolutionary club of Ganges. That same year he offered the local patriots a work of his own composition, "The Prayer of a Free Man to the God of Nature and Liberty," which illustrates how far men of the cloth could fall: ". . . The cult of Thought and of the Heart are at last succeeding to bizarre and repulsive forms; *Holy Fraternity* appears in the place of sanguinary factional hatreds; the morality of man and the citizen, as luminous as truth, as pure as virtue, replaces those sinister dogmas which brutalized reason after having degraded it and hardened the heart after having depraved it. Without temples, without altars, without *priests*, and WITHOUT KINGS, we raise toward you the prayer of free men who desire no temple but the vault of the sky, no altar but a pure soul, no

[122] Armand Lods, "Rabaut de Saint-Etienne. Sa correspondance pendant la Révolution," in *La Révolution française*, xxxv (1898), 176.

offerings other than *social virtues*, no priesthood other than Reason, no masters other than the Law, no God but you, Grand Being, and la PATRIE!"[128]

We have already seen that in 1794 the pastors of the Church abdicated their functions. Undoubtedly they were frightened men who trembled before the swift hand of revolutionary justice. Yet enough of them went beyond a simple declaration of abdication to elaborate on what it was that prompted them to abandon their life's calling to make one suspect that something more than fear alone accounts for their action. They claimed that they wanted to forward the march of Reason, of Liberty and Equality; they declared that they found their religion inimical to the development of social fraternity; they maintained that they had no ambition but to forward the prosperity of the Revolution and their fatherland, no desire but to sing hymns to liberty and to serve their fellow man. It is just possible, notwithstanding their fear of the priests of Reason, that there was an element of sincerity in what they said. Their Church, the Church of the Desert, weakened from within by social faction, enervated by the subsidence of persecution, stunted by the lack of capable spiritual leaders, corrupted by the philosophy of the Enlightenment, had begun to founder years before it felt the souffle of the Revolution. It was a Church deserted by its pastors, a religion forgotten by the faithful. To some of these pastors how puny an instrument it must have seemed beside a Republic which promised the regeneration of all mankind, not in an afterlife, but here, on this earth.

[128] BPF, XLVIII (1899), 242-244 (Molines' caps and italics).

CHAPTER VI

Exhaustion—and Recognition: 1795-1815

Paris, 1795. Robespierre has fallen. The Mountain is chained. The specter of social revolution has been annihilated. France is on the threshold of that precarious bourgeois limbo between Republic and Empire known as the Directory. Its leaders are sampling the constitutions of the past to see what can safely be salvaged of a discredited Revolution. It is February. In the National Convention, a man takes the rostrum, a man who despite his stutter commands the attention of his audience out of respect for his dexterity at surviving the vicissitudes of the Revolution. He is a Protestant. Listen to what he says:

"Ah! If man must have a religion, if he can find the basis of moral obligations nowhere but in supernatural beliefs, if religious fantasies have rendered any advantage to humanity, it is impossible for me, in looking back over the long course of past centuries, not to be grievously moved at the sight of the frightful evils for which religion has been the source and the pretext. Religion has sold itself dearly to men who seek to find in it consolation. . . . [Yet] man desires illusions and chimeras. Under an oppressive government which never ceases to plague his thoughts, his only recourse is to look beyond himself for those consolations which he cannot find in his own life; he must look to a supreme authority, one superior to that which injures him. He would be the most miserable of creatures if, when oppressed in this life, he could not hope to find an avenger in heaven; and this hope is the creator of all religious errors. . . . The secret of governing in matters concerned with religion lies perhaps in these words: *If you seek to destroy fanaticism and superstition, offer man knowledge; if you desire to dispose him to receive knowledge, know how to render him happy and free.*

"Why, Legislators of France, should you not follow with respect to the cults, of whatever kind, this simple and easy tack: a liberty supervised by the civil authorities, a tolerance subordinated to public instruction? . . . The empire of opinions is sufficiently vast that everyone can inhabit it in peace, and the heart of man is a sacred asylum where the eye of the government must no longer try to penetrate. Experience has shown that the attraction of religious practices to frail souls increases in measure as you try to prohibit them. . . . All those sentiments whose source is in the heart have need of sacrifices in order to increase; religion thrives on martyrs just as love prospers by obstacles.

"You, the Legislators of France, are continually preparing the reign of philosophy and morality alone. Soon one will gain an understanding of the absurd dogmas of religion only in order to be contemptuous of them, these offsprings of error and fear, whose influence on the human race has constantly been injurious; soon mankind will be guided by nothing but the attractions of virtue. Man will be good because he will be happy, happy because he is free. Soon the religion of Socrates, Marcus Aurelius, and Cicero will be the religion of the entire world, and you shall have the glory of having had the wisdom to initiate this. Your national celebrations, your republican institutions will be able to embellish and activate the sacred precepts of that morality which you hope to engrave on the hearts of men. But the more this political religion should be beneficent and sweet, the more you must avoid tainting it in advance by persecutions and injustices. Listen to the voice of reason: it will tell you that you must leave it to time, to the increase of knowledge, to the progress of the human mind alone, to annihilate all errors so that you can complete your sublime work and lead man to that perfectibility prepared by the institutions of your making."[1]

This could have been the Jacobin Jeanbon Saint-André addressing the Catholics of Cherbourg. But in 1795 Jeanbon was in prison. Instead it was the royalist Boissy d'Anglas, member of the Committee of Public Safety charged with the provisioning of the capital during the winter of 1794-1795 where his abilities (or lack of them) won for him the sobriquet Boissy-Famine. It was Boissy d'Anglas, shortly to become a prominent member of the Committee of Eleven charged with the preparation of the Constitution of the Year III under which he was to be elected to the *Corps législatif* by no less than seventy-two Departments of France—an honor which caused him to remark: "Ils me nomment plus qu'un roi!" On behalf of the "superstitious," Boissy d'Anglas proposed, and the Convention accepted, a measure which effected the complete separation of

[1] Boissy d'Anglas, *Rapport sur la Liberté des cultes, fait au nom des Comités de Salut public, de Sûreté générale et de Législation, réunis, dans la séance du 3 ventôse An IIIe de la République française* . . . (Versailles, 1795), 18 pp.

Church and State. Freedom of worship was decreed. The Republic would no longer salary nor provide churches for any sects. The concessions which Jeanbon Saint-André had sought for the Protestant prior to the Revolution and had conceded to the Catholics of Cherbourg in 1793 were now given to all religions. Religious ceremonies were confined to the interior of churches devoid of all exterior signs. No ministers could appear in public wearing the cloth. Religious services were under the surveillance of the police.[2]

For the first time in the revolutionary period the State recognized the absolute equality of the Protestant and Catholic Churches, but it had little sympathy for either. The members of the Convention who enacted the liberties of 3 ventôse an III hoped that both religions would soon give way to a lay morality and a universal virtuousness conceived and nurtured by the magistrates of the Republic. Again there was that echo from 1685: ". . . while waiting until it shall please God to enlighten them as He has the others. . . ." But whatever the motives of the law, it restored a measure of peace and toleration to all the churches of France.

Catholic worship resumed almost immediately. In a number of places in Paris mass was celebrated on the very Sunday following the enactment of the law. Easter services of 1795 were marked by their liveliness and enthusiasm. There were complications, notably over the continued rivalry between juring and non-juring ecclesiasts, but this did not prevent large masses of Frenchmen from returning to their devotional duties.[3]

With the Protestants, on the other hand, the revival was slower, more difficult, in fact almost painful. The collapse of the Church had been more complete. The Catholics had continued to worship in hiding, but Protestant religious activity had been all but throttled by the Terror. There were few enough pastors in 1793; there were scarcely any in 1795. Throughout the Midi, many of those persons who had formerly been elders of the Church had incriminated themselves in the Federalist revolt. They were reluctant to enter upon activities which were now tolerated but nonetheless frowned

[2] See J. B. Duvergier, *Collection complète des Lois, décrets, ordonnances, réglemens . . .* etc., VIII, 25-26, 240-241: the law of 3 ventôse an III (February 21, 1795) and article 354 of the Constitution of the Year III.

[3] P. de La Gorce, *op.cit.*, IV, 49-53.

upon. A religious torpor had fallen over the Church. Of faith there was very little.

In the Protestant stronghold of the south, the town of Castres was probably the first to feel the stirrings of a revival. The former pastors Nazon and Bonifas-Laroque continued for a while to devote all their time to political functions. But under the direction of Crébessac, the Protestant community succeeded in acquiring the former church of the Capuchins, which they dedicated on 23 August 1795. The religious life of the community might soon have returned to normal had Bonifas-Laroque not decided in 1796 to return to his pastoral functions. His desire to be reappointed to the ministry met with considerable opposition. It was pointed out to him that he had stated in his abdication that he had no intention of resuming his pastorate. It was also remembered that he had preached on the *décadis* at a time when no compulsion was being applied to make this excusable, and that he had repeated his abdication in the interests of furthering his political career. As a former judge of the revolutionary tribunal, he had enough supporters to gain his ends, but his reentry into the community's religious life precipitated a "schism" which lasted for several years and must have dampened the enthusiasm of the laity for the reorganization of their church.[4]

The Protestants of Nîmes held their first services after the Terror on 13 August 1795, but only a few persons attended and the church was without a pastor until February of 1796. Any services held in the intervening period were apparently led by the laity. Of the normal consistory of twenty-four men, only thirteen were present at the meeting of 26 February 1796 when David Roux was elected pastor, and these were careful to make a declaration of their political beliefs, showing that the chastisements of the representative Borie had not been forgotten: "The principles of our cult are known. They have never in themselves given umbrage to the government because they are the same as those which directed our founder, Jesus Christ, who under no circumstances interfered in political affairs and who always demanded respect for the superior powers."[5] The pastor Roux accepted the calling in the first part of April 1796. Thereafter the religious life of the inhabitants returned slowly to normalcy.

[4] BPF, XXXVIII (1889), 393-402, 449-464.

[5] A. Borrel, *Histoire de l'Eglise de Nîmes*, p. 460.

The first post-thermidorian entry in the registers of the church of Montpellier was 9 January 1797, at which time the Protestants met to elect one Louis Buisson as their spiritual leader. But the revival of their church was delayed until the arrival of their pastor designate the following November. Even then religious activities were intermittent. Buisson was so weak in health that he was obliged to retire in May of 1798. His successor, Honoré Michel, had had little prior experience in the ministry and it was another half year before the church enjoyed regular services.[6] Smaller towns in the area, with little to attract the few pastors available, were generally slower in resuming their religious activities.[7]

In the west, the reorganization was slower than that of the Midi. At Bordeaux the Protestant community resumed its services under Olivier Desmons in October 1796, thirty-eight months after they had terminated their activities on the eve of the Terror. The Catholics of the city, on the other hand, had recommenced worship twenty months earlier. The beginnings of the revival were modest and uninspiring. Five members of the consistory were unavailable for service and had to be replaced. The Protestant community, estimated at 6,000 persons in 1789, had fallen to 3,700 in 1796. The remainder presumably had been scattered, abandoned all religious attachments, or converted to Catholicism.[8] Those who remained faithful to the church were too few in number and too impoverished by the economic crises of the Revolution (most of the Protestant wealth in the area was derived from the colonial trade) to lend sufficient financial assistance to the church to reopen their hospital and school until after 1800. The church at Nantes resumed its

[6] Georges Michel, "Le pasteur Honoré Michel et la reconstitution de l'Eglise réformée de Montpellier après la crise révolutionnaire," BPF, 1949, 1-23.

[7] Milhaud opened its services at the home of one of the members of the congregation in January 1796, and soon thereafter they received the services of the former pastor of Nîmes, Jean Gachon. The town of Bernis followed suit in December. Uchaud and Langlade were delayed until February of 1798, their services being conducted in a private abode and a paddock respectively. Cf. Pierre Guérin, "Histoire d'une commune rurale de 1780 à 1800," *Mémoires de l'Académie de Nîmes*, 7th series, XXXIII (1910), 298.

[8] The figures are those of Alfred Leroux, *Les Religionnaires de Bordeaux*, pp. 99, 345. Faced with severe financial difficulties, the consistory of the city took a census of the members of the congregation who might be counted upon to contribute to the expenses of the church. The results showed 370 bourgeois families, or roughly 1,850 individuals. To account for the poorer families who were not solicited, Leroux doubled this figure to arrive at 3,700.

services in 1797, but most of the other areas in the west probably did not reorganize their cult until sometime in 1803.[9]

In view of the frailty of the revival, it is not surprising that the government of the Church languished. The last of the provincial synods had met in June of 1793. Thereafter, with the foundering of the churches during the Terror, all religious activities on a provincial scale ceased. Toward the end of 1796 the pastor Crébessac of Castres, hoping to revitalize the reorganization, succeeded in bringing together a synod for the province of Haut-Languedoc (now in the Department of Tarn). It was to be the last of the provincial synods in the eighteenth century, and it did not present a very imposing sight. Only four pastors were present to sign its proceedings, and one of these was ordained at the meeting itself.

There were several causes for this languor. The synod of 1796 complained of the "dearth of pastors."[10] They were in short supply indeed. Eventually half of those who abdicated from the ministry in the Department of Gard returned to the pastorate, but most of these waited until the reorganization of the churches under Napoleon to do so.[11] In the interim, the Church resorted to the expedient employed during the Desert of sharing those pastors they had with other communities. And as there were few candidates for the ministry in France, appeals for ministers were made to Switzerland, but few answered the call.

Another obstacle was the lack of suitable buildings for their use. Only the wealthier communities had been able to acquire temples in the period from 1790 to 1793, and most of these were rentals. By 1796 scarcely any communities still had their churches. Under the Directory, there were a number of cases where the civil authorities in towns with mixed populations had authorized but one building for the celebration of religious services. Since the Catholics had resumed their worship earlier, they had come into possession or occupancy of the designated buildings. This left the

[9] B. Vaurigaud, *Essai sur l'histoire des Eglises réformées de Bretagne* (Paris, 1870), III, 302; G. Pilastre, "Les Eglises de Vendée; réorganisation du culte protestant au début du XIXe siècle," BPF, LXXXII (1933), 60-78.

[10] The proceedings of the synod are given in E. Hugues, *Synodes du Désert,* III, 669-675.

[11] Compare the list of abdicated pastors given by F. Rouvière, *Révolution dans le Gard,* IV, 382-400 with Rabaut Dupui's *Répertoire ecclésiastique . . . des Eglises réformées* of 1807 where the personnel of the Church is listed.

Protestants with three alternatives: conducting their ceremonies in the same building with Catholics, going out into the Desert, or not holding them at all. The ministry, for fear of antagonizing the Catholics, discouraged the first possibility.[12] The second was forbidden by the laws of 3 ventôse an III and 7 vendémiaire an IV.[13] It was possible to meet in the homes of private individuals only if the number of persons in attendance did not exceed ten. Unless the Protestants were willing to contravene the law, those who met with these obstacles were obliged to enter into long negotiations with the authorities for locales of their own.[14]

Enthusiasm is contagious. A little of the fervor which had characterized the renaissance of the Church under Antoine Court might have stimulated the reorganization under the Directory. But the record of the Church during the Terror was anything but inspiring. Nor was that of most of the pastors who now urged the faithful to return to their churches. The weaknesses of the Church which had contributed to its collapse had not been corrected. Incredulity gained where faith and piety waned. In a word, the laity did not distinguish themselves by their enthusiasm for contributing to the reorganization. At Nîmes the middle class and the incredulous who were still willing to have their marriages and baptisms administered at the hands of pastors balked at entering the church for the performance of these ceremonies. Efforts to correct the abuse were ineffectual, and the pastors, to avoid even greater abuses, condescended to perform the sacraments in the homes of the recusants.[15] The same problem was encountered at the church of Bordeaux.

[12] E. Hugues, *Synodes du Désert,* III, 673: article 19 of the proceedings of the synod of 1796: "Le synode applaudit aux ménagements et à la prudence que les diverses églises ont fait paraître, en ne se prévalant pas de la faculté qui leur était donnée de célébrer leur culte dans le même locale que nos concitoyens les catholiques, réserve qui a pu prévenir de fâcheux résultats."

[13] See J. B. Duvergier, *Collection complète des lois, décrets, ordonnances . . . etc.,* VIII, 293-296, the Décret de 7 vendémiaire an IV sur l'exercice et la police extérieure des cultes, article sixteen of which reads "Les cérémonies de tous cultes sont interdites hors l'enceinte de l'édifice choisi pour leur exercice. Cette prohibition ne s'applique pas aux cérémonies qui ont lieu dans l'enceinte des maisons particulières, pourvu qu'outre les individus qui ont le même domicile, il n'y ait pas, à l'occasion des mêmes cérémonies, un rassemblement excédant dix personnes."

[14] The officials were not disposed to be overly sympathetic with them. See "La Réorganisation de l'église réformée de Mazamet," BPF, LV (1906), 533-542; and "La Séparation des églises et de l'état à Aulas," *ibid.,* 226-234.

[15] A. Borrel, *Histoire de l'Eglise de Nîmes,* p. 461.

Moreover, after straining their resources to resuscitate their school, they met with a most discouraging apathy. The cantor was entrusted with the instruction of the children of the poorer families. But no children appeared—even when the cantor sought to encourage matriculation by offering free music lessons.[16] There was still one force, however—the same which had nourished the obstinacy of the Protestants during the desperate period from 1685 to 1715—which kept the Protestant Church alive: the aversion to Catholicism and the fear of being submerged in a Catholic society. Such sentiments undoubtedly explain why the laity rarely availed themselves of the opportunity of sharing churches with the Catholics. But even this force showed signs of diminishing. Confronted with the apathy of his parishioners and the outright irreligion to be found almost anywhere in France at this time, the pastor Blachon was led to declare in a sermon of 1797: "I shall not repeat here the reproaches which are made at the expense of the communion of Rome; but I will say that its system, such as it is professed in France today, is infinitely preferable to the spiritual void into which so-called freethinkers who know only how to destroy would cast their fellow man."[17]

If Protestant services were generally uninviting, Paris was the exception to the rule. Within a few days of the execution of Robespierre and the release of the pastor Marron, the word of God was again being preached at the church of Saint-Louis du Louvre. Worship continued there with such success that a second church was rented in the fall of 1800.[18] Among the auditors of these services were two men named Chemin-Dupontès and La Révellière-Lépeaux, the latter of whom was subsequently to admit that he, his wife, and his two daughters were so impressed with the majesty and simplicity of the services that they were moved to tears.

Chemin-Dupontès was the founder of Theophilanthropy, one of the last of the revolutionary cults. Pure deists, the theophilanthropists held as the central articles of their cult the belief in God, the immortality of the soul, and the virtue of man. Blessed with the favor of the government, which saw any weakening of Catholicism a weakening in political royalism, they acquired ten churches in Paris.

[16] A. Leroux, *Les Religionnaires de Bordeaux*, pp. 350-352.
[17] J.-A. Blachon, *Recueil de discours. . .*, p. 89.
[18] A. Lods, *Eglise de Paris pendant la Révolution*, pp. 29-30.

These they decorated simply: the walls were ornamented with a few moral maxims, the altar was a plain table covered with fruit or flowers. The ministering officer was anyone in the congregation who felt disposed to speak. Sermons varied from descriptions of the beauties of nature to morality lessons drawn from the lives of Socrates, Vincent de Paul, Rousseau, and Washington. These were interspersed with songs and moments of silence devoted to meditation. Baptism was reduced to the mere presentation and naming of the child; marriage to the announcement of a civil marriage performed earlier accompanied with felicitations and admonitions. The member of any sect was encouraged to belong so long as he believed in the central articles: God, immortality, and virtue.

Whence the origins of Theophilanthropy? "Several times," wrote Chemin-Dupontès, "I attended the worship of the Protestants in Paris, and there I saw the essential forms of Theophilanthropy."[19] The founder of the cult thought of Theophilanthropy as a revolt against the rites and dogmas with which the Roman clergy had befouled Christianity. In Protestantism he thought he had found a kin: both rejected saints, the visible head of the church, bishops, priests, pilgrimages, auricular confession, mass, benedictions; both used the vulgar tongue; one sang the hymns of David translated by Marot, the other odes of Jean-Baptiste Rousseau. "Hence," Chemin went on to say, "the principles and the forms of the two cults are very similar. The slight nuances which distinguish them can be traced only to the differences of character of the centuries in which each one took birth."

It seemed only logical to the Theophilanthropists that the Protestants should be among the first converts to their cult. La Révellière-Lépeaux, a member of the Directory who took the new cult under his protection and sponsored its spread, tried to encourage conversions by publicly stressing the similarities between the religions and by flattering Protestant vanities. In a speech of 1797, the same one in which he told how he had been moved to tears by a Protestant worship at Saint-Louis du Louvre, he went on to say: "Look at a Catholic and a Protestant country and compare them.... In Calvinist lands you will find happier homes, women more chaste and economical, tenderer and more industrious husbands, children more cherished

[19] Albert Mathiez, "Protestants et théophilanthropes," *La Révolution française*, XLIV (1903), 385-401.

and more respectful, a healthier reasoning, a people more active, more industrious, more charitable, better and more content, much more public spirit and a more genuine love of their country."[20]

Given the debility of the Protestant Church at the time, the common opposition to Catholicism, and the real similarities between the cults as a consequence of the decline in Protestant theology, the efforts of the Theophilanthropists to spread their cult in the Protestant areas of France might have posed a serious threat to the struggling Church. Yet the reaction of the pastors was the same as it had been to the efforts of the Moravian Brethren to evangelize in the Desert earlier in the century: in alliance with the Catholics, they opposed the cult. If the laity were attracted to the teachings of the Moravians in certain areas of the Midi, they do not appear to have been tempted by Theophilanthropy. A missionary sent into the south to plant the cult in the area around Nîmes reported his failure in a letter of 1797: "I have made several attempts at establishing Theophilanthropy and the preaching of republican morality in this area, but what would seem unbelievable is that I met with fewer difficulties on the part of Catholics than with Protestants who, however, profess a worship much less absurd than the Roman and who hold freedom of thought as a principal article of their beliefs. I have been led to believe that after the elections, providing they reflect a marked republican victory, it will be easier to win over the less fanatical persons to the cult of reason and laws."[21]

The elections in the following month resulted in a resounding victory for the royalists; only about ten Departments in France remained loyal to the Republic. Even so, it is doubtful that many responsible Protestants would have been seriously tempted by the Theophilanthropist's advances. The new cult was rightly regarded as more political than religious in its aims. As such it was to be avoided, for the Protestants had no desire of associating themselves with a movement that at any moment might become politically dangerous with an unsuspected change in the drift of the Revolution. After the collapse of their Church and the failure of the Girondin and Federalist movements, the universal desire was for security rather than for further political adventures. Inconspicuousness had become a definite asset.[22]

[20] *ibid.*, 387. [21] *ibid.*, 388.

[22] So complete was the revulsion for politics that in the reorganization of the

Yet if the Directory brought a degree of liberty to the Protestant Church, it did not bring them security. The way the State first flirted with the idea of making Theophilanthropy the official cult of the Republic and then began to advance by legislation the *culte décadaire* was disconcerting to the Protestants. In Paris, an unsympathetic administration of the Department considered depriving the Protestants of the church of Saint-Louis du Louvre. Two years later, in 1799, a deputy from Moselle (J.-P. Couturier) proposed the nationalization and sale of the properties of the Protestant Church and succeeded in having the measure approved in the lower house of the legislature. The churches themselves were in financial straits. When it first became known that the First Consul had entered into negotiations for a religious settlement with the Vatican, there were added causes for alarm. It was only to be expected that as a price for a settlement and a recognition of the Revolution, the Church of Rome would demand that its cult be recognized as dominant in the State.[23] Bonaparte refused to go this far, but he did comply with the papal demand that the revolutionary cults be abolished,[24] and there was the danger that similar measures might be taken against the non-Catholics. But the whole purpose of the arrangements with the Vatican was to put an end to confessional struggles in France. The Protestants could not be ignored, especially since Geneva had been annexed (1798) and France was soon to push her frontiers to the left bank of the Rhine, further augmenting her Protestant population.

Departmental administration of Gard during the Thermidorian reaction the representative Perrin had to threaten Protestants with the law of the suspects in order to persuade them to accept public posts. Even then four members of the new Directory resigned after their appointments. Cf. Charles Pouthas, *Une famille de bourgeoisie française*, p. 174. In time this aversion for public service disappeared, but it is illustrative of the impact of the Terror on Protestants who had greeted the civil legislation of the Revolution in their favor with marked enthusiasm.

[23] See A. Lods, "Bonaparte et les églises protestants de France," BPF, XLVI (1897), 393-417. At the commencement of the negotiations, the Holy See requested that "On devrait donc commencer par établir que la religion catholique, apostolique et romaine sera en France la *dominante*; l'établissement de cet article doit être la principale base de tous les autres, comme cet article seul peut fournir à Sa Sainteté des raisons de condescendre et de relâcher, en faveur de la nation française, la rigueur de la discipline eccl**é**siastique."

[24] A decree of 4 October 1801 forbade the use of nationally owned buildings by the Theophilanthropists, which in effect suppressed their worship.

In 1800 the First Consul charged his foreign minister Talleyrand and the latter's assistant Blanc d'Hauterive with preparing plans for the reorganization of all the cults in France. The initial draft would have allowed the Protestants to exercise their worship freely upon petitioning the commission for the surveillance of cults, and the State was to assume responsibility for subsidizing the pastors. This was amended in subsequent drafts, the financial support being dropped and the appointment of pastors being made subject to the approval of the State.[25] The overall plan was not very liberal, for the State would have controlled the activities of the Church without the compensation of financial support. Upon the signing of the Concordat with Rome (which recognized Catholicism as "the religion of the great majority of Frenchmen"), the plans were dropped. But the Ministry of the Interior was now charged with resuming the work, and in doing so it was instructed to seek the advice and cooperation of the Protestants themselves. News of this brought joy to the Protestant population, for the official charged with the negotiations was the lawyer Portalis, whose sympathetic disposition to the Protestants was everywhere recognized by virtue of a memoir he had written in their favor in 1770. The former pastor Rabaut-Pomier (now the sub-prefect of Vigan) hastened to take advantage of this favorable development by offering the minister the assistance of the Protestant committee of Paris and venturing to suggest that there were two million Protestants in France whose services would demand something under one thousand pastors at the expense to the State of one million francs per year.[26]

In the subsequent steps toward the elaboration of the Protestant settlement Portalis relied heavily for information and advice on the committee of Paris, composed of Rabaut-Dupui (who had just been elected to the *Corps législatif* by the Department of Gard), the pastors Marron, Frossard, and Lombard-Lachaux, and several notables of the Paris church—in short on those *comitants* who had been opposed to the democratic organization of the Church throughout the second half of the eighteenth century. A memoir submitted to Portalis by the Protestants of the Midi defending the traditional discipline and organization of the Church was waived as the basis

[25] A. Lods, *Traité de l'administration des Cultes protestants*, pp. 4-11 gives the texts of these plans.

[26] *ibid.*, pp. 13-14: letter of 28 October 1801.

for further discussions in favor of the proposed draft of the Paris *comitants*.[27] Moreover, in personal interviews with the First Consul, Rabaut-Dupui was captivated by such blandishments as the assurance from Bonaparte that he wished that the entire world were Protestant.[28] At the crucial moment of the reorganization, the democratic church of Antoine Court was without defenders. Bonaparte would not have accepted it anyway, and even the modest demands of the *comitants* were considerably modified. The final project worked out between Portalis and the *comitants* was submitted to the *Conseil d'Etat* on 12 germinal an X (2 April 1802). Further modified it was accepted by the *Tribunat* on 7 April and reported to the *Corps législatif* on 18 germinal by the Protestant deputy Jaucourt. Passed as a law of the State, it was to regulate the Protestant Church in France for the next hundred years until the separation of Church and State in 1905.

The law of 18 germinal was incorporated into the body of the settlement with the Catholic Church as the "Organic Articles of the Protestant Cults." Under its provisions,[29] the French Calvinists were divided into consistorial churches of 6,000 souls. At the head of each of these churches was a consistory composed of the pastor (or pastors) of the church and from six to twelve elders, the latter chosen from among the highest tax-payers from the rolls of direct contributions. Meeting under the presidency of the pastor, the consistories watched over the maintenance of discipline, the administration of the property of the Church, and accounted for the financial receipts of the Church. In effect, the consistories became the preserve of a wealthy aristocracy within the Church. Half of its members were renewed every two years, the new elders being elected by the remaining members and an equal number of Protes-

[27] The memoir of the Protestants of the Midi is given in E. Doumergue, *La Veille de la loi de l'an X*, pp. 98 et seq. A. Lods, *Traité de l'administration des cultes protestants*, pp. 20-23, gives the text of the project of the Paris committee.

[28] In a letter to Olivier Desmons, 23 November 1801, Rabaut-Dupui described Bonaparte as saying: "Quant à moi, je voudrais qu'il y eût vingt religions en France. On a manqué l'occasion d'établir en France la religion protestante, ce n'est pas ma faute." And again in a letter of 3 December 1801: "Nous savons, m'a-t-il dit, que nous sommes au XIXe siècle, et nous ne ferons pas rétrograder les Français jusqu'au IVe ou au Ve. Nous voudrions que tout le monde fût protestant." See Armand Lods, *Traité de l'administration des cultes protestants*, pp. 16-20.

[29] See J. B. Duvergier, *Collection complète des lois, décrets, ordonnances . . . etc.*, XIII, 101-103.

tant citizens who were "heads of families chosen from among the highest rate-payers on the rolls of direct taxes of the commune where the church was situated." Hence what some pastors earlier in the eighteenth century had called "assemblies of confusion" were abolished; the direction of the Church fell to the propertied middle class.

The only ecclesiastical institution above the consistories was the synod of the arrondissement made up of five consistorial churches. Each of the churches was to delegate its pastor and one of its elders to the synod. Those pastors in exercise of their functions were provisionally confirmed in their offices. Where a pastor died or retired from the ministry, his successor was to be elected by a plurality vote of the consistory of the church. No foreigners were allowed to exercise the pastorate. To train future ministers, three seminaries were to be established: two in the east of France for the Lutherans, one in Geneva (now part of France) for the Calvinists. No pastor could henceforth be received into the ministry unless he had studied and received a certificate from one of these seminaries.

The most salient feature of the law was the degree to which the Church was subordinated to the State. Every provision was made to insure its submission. Neither the churches nor the pastors were permitted to have relations with any foreign power or authority. In their capacity as ministers, the pastors were to preach in behalf of the well-being of the Republic (soon to be the Empire) and the consuls. No doctrinal decisions, no confessions, no changes in the discipline could be made without the formal authorization of the State. The First Consul appointed all faculty members to the seminaries, and all matters of internal nature within the seminaries were under the jurisdiction of the government. Persons elected to the pastorate by consistories could not answer their callings until their elections had been confirmed by the First Consul and until they had taken the prescribed oath of allegiance to the State.[30] Nor could pastors be dismissed from their offices without the approval of the government. In everything but name, the ministers were civil

[30] "Je jure et promets à Dieu, sur les saints Evangiles, de garder obéissance et fidélité au Gouvernement établi par la constitution de la République française. Je promets aussi de n'avoir aucune intelligence, de n'assister à aucun conseil, de n'entretenir aucune ligue, soit au dedans, soit au dehors, qui soit contraire à la tranquillité publique; et si, dans mon diocèse ou ailleurs, j'apprends qu'il se trame quelque chose au préjudice de l'Etat, je le ferai savoir au Gouvernment."

servants. As for the synods, they became absolutely null. They were to be held in the presence of the prefect or sub-prefect; their decisions were to be submitted to the government for approval; their sessions could not exceed six days duration. Moreover, they could not meet without the prior approval of the government—and the government never authorized their convocation. They never met.

Even so, the Protestants, especially those of Paris and of the larger cities, had reason to be grateful for the law of 18 germinal. They had now found in the State something akin to the hierarchy which they had desired during the eighteenth century. The pastors enjoyed a considerable amount of independence from the lay organizations of the Church, and their financial security was assured by the provision that they were to be salaried by the State. The scale of these salaries was not set until April of 1804, but they were considerably larger than those accorded to the celibate ministers of the Catholic Church.[81] The Protestant Church had received the recognition, support, and protection of the French State. This in itself was a major triumph.

In its original form, the Organic Articles had a number of disadvantages against which even the Protestants of Paris were quick to protest. During its formulation, they had asked for and been denied the official recognition of a general or national synod. In a memoir presented to Portalis shortly after the ratification of the Articles, they asked that a "central commission" composed of a pastor and elder from each synod be set up to serve as the highest authority within the Church organization in matters of ecclesiastical discipline. They felt that one seminary would be insufficient to their needs and inquired whether a second might not be established at Nîmes for students of the Reformed Church. Moreover, nothing was said in the Organic Articles about churches for the Protestants, and they requested that steps be taken to ensure them the proper edifices in which to worship. But in their eyes the most important defect in the law was the manner in which the consistorial church in France had been defined. According to the law, no church could extend from one Department into another. Now, out of forty-five Depart-

[81] The pastors of the Church were divided into three classes according to the population of the seat of the consistorial church. Those of the first class received 2,200 francs per annum; those of the second 2,000; and those of the third 1,800. *Curés* of the first class received 1,500 and those of the second 1,000.

ments in pre-revolutionary France inhabited by Protestants, only eighteen had a Protestant population which reached the figure necessary for the establishment of a consistorial church. Hence in those areas where the Protestant population was scattered, there were no provisions for providing the Protestants with religious services. The Protestant petitioners asked that the "local church" be substituted for the consistorial church.

Portalis and the First Consul received these complaints with sympathy. They had no intention of allowing the Protestants to have a national synod or commission of their own. This was amply demonstrated by their refusal to convene even the provincial synods during the Consulate or the Empire. Not even the Catholic Church was permitted its national councils, although Napoleon subsequently summoned one in 1811 for reasons of his own. But as a concession in favor of the demand for local churches, a law of 1 November 1805 permitted the establishment of oratories in those areas where the Protestant population did not reach 6,000 souls. Moreover, between 1804 and 1811 forty churches confiscated during the Revolution were conceded gratuitously to the Protestants for their use and others were built at their own expense. A decree of 17 September 1808 provided for the establishment of a Protestant seminary at Montauban, which commenced its teachings in a modest way in 1810.

The churches of France were enthusiastic enough in their praise of the measure and its author. "You have rendered peace to the State and to the Church," declared the pastor Marron in the name of the consistory of Paris. "The former is the conquest of heros, the latter of wisdom. Enjoy the fruit of your labors, the admiration of Europe, the benedictions of your fellow citizens. . . . Through you and through those who share so honorably with you the cares of a paternal government, the happiness of the Republic . . . will be as secure as its glory, and posterity, which never flatters, will call the nineteenth century of the Christian era the century of Bonaparte." "You have restored our sanctuaries," wrote the Protestants of Anduze. "You have consecrated the great principles of religion which people have too long forgotten. We shall implore the Supreme Being with ardor for the conservation of your person! Our children, witnesses to our rapture, will join with our children's children and will repeat by common consent: Long live Bonaparte!" The Protestants of Bordeaux were almost without words: "The military admire you, the philosophers praise you, the politicians respect you, the people bless you, Christians venerate you, Frenchmen adore you, and the Protestants are unable to express the sentiments which you inspire in them."[32]

But the Church of Antoine Court, both in form and in spirit, was dead. The pastors were civil functionaries. The local consistories no longer existed; the colloquies were replaced by subservient consistories dominated by the wealthy. The provincial synods had been nullified. The Protestants were not to be permitted a general synod until 1872. The Church was a self-governing body only to the extent that it pleased the temporal sovereign. To the plaudits of the Protestants themselves, Napoleon had peacefully won more control over their Church than the kings of France had ever been able to exercise.

The period of the Empire was spiritually barren for the Protestant Church of France.[33] The sermons were of the same variety as those which had bored their audiences in the last decade of the eighteenth century, only now they were intermixed with panegyrics to "our new Cyrus," "the second Moses," "the modern Joshua." The seminary of Montauban did not lack for students, but as one of the professors complained: "They came to Montauban not in search of knowledge, but security. The *Faculté* was not a school, but a shelter, a shelter all the more secure the more sacred it appeared."[34] It was here that the first stirrings of the nineteenth-century revival were to be felt in France, but this was a phenomenon which was scarcely perceptible during the period of the Empire. The religious torpor continued. The ministers preached dutifully on the glories of their emperor. The people listened. The consistories met and worship preserved its traditional forms. But it was all formality. Few seemed

[32] A. Lods, "Bonaparte et les églises protestants de France," BPF, XLVI (1897), 414-415. Similar addresses of the churches of Sommières, Saussines, Durfort, Saint-Nazaire, Logrian, Saint-Jean du Gard and Tonneins are reprinted in the *Moniteur* for 5 prairial an X; Montpellier, Colmar, and Geneva on 23 floréal; Sainte-Foy, Castillon-sur-Dordogne, and Aigues-Vives for 30 prairial; Montauban for 19 floréal. Also see Félix Kuhn, "L'Accueil fait à la loi de germinal," BPF, XLIX (1900), 320-326, 375-387.

[33] See Charles Durand, *op.cit.*, chapter 7: "La mort spirituelle"; and the article by Félix Kuhn, "La vie intérieure du protestantisme sous la premier Empire," BPF, LI (1902), 57-73.

[34] Léon Maury, *Le réveil religieux*, I, 274.

to care about the cataleptic state of spiritual life. The pastors themselves were affected by the spiritual paralysis. "Because of the state of languor, decay, the total consumption from which our Church suffers," declared Daniel Encontre in opening the scholastic year of 1816 at the seminary of Montauban, "our soul is seized with a sadness nigh unto death. Alas, God, we have fallen so far that even several of those whom you have called to say and prove from the pulpit that the love of this world is inimical to your teachings do not blush at appearing in places specially dedicated to frivolity, dissipation, luxury, and the false pleasures of the world. . . . The tenderest exhortations will not turn them from it; only laws, threats, and penalties have effect. One must appeal to their self-interest and vanity to obtain what piety and Christian charity would otherwise solicit in vain."[35] The same doctrinal uncertainties and doubts which had weakened the spiritual fiber of the pastors before the Revolution were still as strong as they had been then. "Are you orthodox in your faith?" wrote the pastor Joux to Rabaut-Dupui in 1806. "I am, and the Protestants of France desire that one should be. Are you a Socinian like . . . like. . . , my God! Who is not? I lament it, but one must hide his offenses and not reveal them. . . . Most of the Calvinists, and perhaps the pastors of our Church as well, lean toward Socinianism, or at least are Arians; I am aware of infinitely few orthodox persons. I have preached and sincerely believe in orthodoxy; but I am tolerant, an enemy of theological disputes, and one need not place the divinity of Jesus Christ on the level with Calvinist dogma, or the Trinity either, in order to raise protests from most of the ministers who do not believe in it, although they do not care to acknowledge it."[36]

From a religious point of view, the Protestant population of the nation was listless. A census of the churches taken in 1806 by Portalis showed that there were seventy-eight consistorial churches and twenty-one oratories served by 210 pastors within the limits of pre-revolutionary France. But the Calvinist population was 479,312—perhaps as much as one-third smaller than what it had been in 1789.[37]

[35] *ibid.*, I, 274-275.

[36] F. Kuhn, "La vie intérieure de protestantisme sous le premier Empire," BPF, LI (1902), 63.

[37] A. Lods, *Traité de l'administration des cultes protestants*, p. 35. The figure for pastors includes Mulhouse (annexed in 1798) and Alsace, with roughly 30 pastors serving in the latter. These figures were graciously supplied by M. Daniel Robert, whose doctorate deals with French Protestantism of the period 1800 to 1830.

Habit and tradition more than anything else held these to the Church. A nineteenth-century writer from the Dauphiné was later to recall how in his youth "there used to be discussions between Catholics and Protestants in the social evenings of the winter. It was difficult to establish any agreement between them. The Catholics remained Catholics; the Protestants, Protestants. Basically the differences were less deep than they appeared. The behavior, the tastes, the habits, the customs were the same, or very nearly. Some went to mass, the others to their assembly. At the conclusion of each, they indulged in the same pastimes. Inner light was unknown to them; salvation through grace, through faith, through the redeeming work of Jesus, these were things that no one discussed. Religion was pure formalism: it was confined to exterior acts, more or less simple, more or less complicated, depending upon whether it was Reformed or Roman worship."[38] Such a church was incapable of expansion. It lacked the zeal necessary to win converts. At Toulouse, where the Protestant church had been refounded in 1789 after a century of quiescence, religious services languished. The pastor complained of assemblies where fifteen, twenty, or at best thirty persons attended, and these preferred to hear "la philosophie" rather than the word of God.[39] At the time of the Napoleonic reorganization, Rabaut-Dupui tried to arouse the enthusiasm of the wasted Protestant population of the Vendée; he encouraged them to show their heads and demand recognition of the government. After three years of efforts, he noted "with considerable sadness the silence of our brethren of the Vendée and their apparent coolness for Religion. I have often asked at the offices of M. Portalis if he has received demands from your part of the country; and the answer has always been no."[40]

Disinterested in their dogmas, conscious of their weakness, the spokesmen of the Church toyed with the idea of a union of the Protestant churches—"a memorable reconciliation which would operate reconciliations more memorable still."[41] The latter was nothing less than the reunion of all Christian faiths. Who would effect it? "It is to the great NAPOLEON that this new triumph is

[38] L. Maury, *Le réveil religieux*, I, 240-241.

[39] Letter of the pastor Chabrand to Olivier Desmons, 6 January 1808, published in BPF, XL (1891), 494-495 note.

[40] BPF, LXXXII (1933), 66.

[41] E.-G. Léonard, *Problèmes et expériences du Protestantisme français*, p. 79, quoting Rabaut-Dupui.

reserved. Already he has rendered great and important services to the Church; the most precious of all, the reunion of all the Christian communities, shall be due to his powerful intervention."[42] Indeed the only important obstacle these men saw to such a reconciliation was the interpretation of Holy Communion. "We are convinced," wrote the pastors Rabaut-Pomier and Mestrezat to the archbishop of Besançon, "that no reunion of the Reformed with the Gallican or Roman Church can succeed if the liberty is not left to the faithful to believe that in the Holy Communion they partake of the bread and wine figuratively or in reality."[43]

We have already had occasion to note how a century earlier, as a consequence of persecution, radical aberrations developed within a Church which had been deprived of its intellectual leaders and spiritual conductors. Prophets appeared who roamed the desolate hills of the Cévennes preaching all manner of wild auguries. The spiritual twilight of Protestantism following on the Revolution brought curious reminders of these earlier deviations. The last synod of the Church meeting in 1796 appointed a committee to inspect a work written by the pastor Fosse (dit Richard) entitled "The Verity of the Oracles of the Apocalypse, or the French Revolution Predicted by Saint John eighteen centuries ago." The question before the commissioners was whether or not the publication of such a work would be to the advantage of their Church when it was known that its author was a pastor of their faith. Their decision was negative, not because they disapproved of the careless application of Scripture to mundane experience, but because the author had announced the imminent ruination of Rome and its pontiff—a prophecy which they feared would be injurious to their community.[44] Again, some fifteen years later Rabaut-Pomier preached on the accord of the Biblical prophecies with the advent of the emperor. When he later published this sermon, he added to it several pages of "succinct details on the prophecies which announced the reign of Napoleon," and announced that he intended to write a work entirely devoted to this subject.[45]

[42] Quoted by Charles Durand, *op.cit.*, p. 172 from the work of Rabaut-Dupui entitled *Détails historiques et recueil de pièces sur les divers projets de réunion de toutes les communions chrétiennes* (Paris, 1806).

[43] *ibid.*, p. 167.

[44] E. Hugues, *Synodes du Désert*, III, 675-676.

[45] Charles Durand, *op.cit.*, pp. 135-136.

To be sure, these were not ignorant peasants of the Cévennes seized with religious ecstasies born of their personal sufferings. They were not attempting to prophesy the future so much as to correlate Scripture with events of historical occurrence. They were intelligent men grappling with the momentous events of a revolutionary epoch. But their turning of Scriptures to profane uses, either to bolster their sagging convictions or as an inane diversion for idle minds, did not speak well for their spiritual state. The seriousness with which men among them considered a reconciliation with the Catholic Church highlighted the decline of their religious convictions. A complete disintegration of their doctrinal beliefs and religious identity, of which these events were perhaps the harbingers, was avoided, thanks to the relative religious peace and freedom which Napoleon had brought to France. For in their seminaries the Protestants had the means, given time and sufficient provocation, to shake themselves from their spiritual sleep and to train men with sufficient ability and purpose to defend them from the corrosive forces of the modern world.

The fate of the Protestant Church during the revolutionary tempest has been a source of embarrassment to Protestant historians of subsequent generations. Beside the century-long resistance of the Church of the Desert and the heroic work of Antoine Court, the total collapse of the Church Visible, the decay of spiritual life among the Protestant population, the slow recovery from the trials of the period of the Terror are all disconcerting. François Puaux, for instance, in his classic study of the French Reform from its origins to the Empire, admitted with obvious sadness that "the Roman Church reconstituted itself and was able to salary with its own revenues more than thirty thousand priests and support the expenses of its own worship. The Protestants, we confess to their shame, did not show the same salt and experienced much more difficulty in reorganizing their cult."[46] He himself offered several explanations for this lamentable failing: the Church lacked pastors, the principal members of the laity had fallen into incredulity, religious questions were completely dominated by the momentous political and social events of the Revolution. It might be added that in all probability the very nature of the Church

[46] F. Puaux, *Histoire de la Réformation Française* (Paris, 1868-1869), VII, 353.

organization contributed to its collapse. The partisans of the democratic and decentralized polity of the Church—historians like Doumergue, Durand, Léonard, Vincent, and Félice—attribute the strength and vitality of the Protestants during the eighteenth century to the old discipline of the Church. They attack those who spoke in terms of the need of a hierarchy; they criticize the nature of the Napoleonic reorganization by stressing the way in which it denatured the traditional forms of the Church. Yet in justice to the malcontents of the eighteenth century, it must be said in their favor that one advantage which the Catholic Church enjoyed over the Protestant during the critical phase of the Revolution was its leadership. In the face of the dechristianization movement, the pastor was alone, by himself. Assuming that he was devoted to his faith, assuming that he might have been willing to lay down his life in its defense, the decision to resist was left to his own discretion. There was no authority above him but God and his conscience to help him meet his dilemma, to issue the order "resist"; he had no courage-giving assurance that there would be others like himself who would enter the ranks of those fighting the high priests of irreligion. There were no émigré bishops, no Pope in Rome, no exiled princes of France to help him in his moment of indecision. Moreover, the thought of resistance was a more challenging decision for him than it was for the Catholic priest. To those who carelessly cite examples of Catholic martyrdom in contrast to Protestant pusillanimity, it should be pointed out that martyrdom may have been a more difficult consideration for a Protestant pastor with a family than it was for a celibate Catholic priest wedded to the Catholic Church.

But in the final analysis these are hypothetical considerations. In actual fact, the ship of the Protestant faith had suffered terrible damage at the hands of Bourbon monarchy. Antoine Court, for all his apparent successes, never succeeded in mending it sufficiently to weather the storm of the Revolution. The real challenge to his work did not come at the hands of the intendants, military governors, and bailiffs; it came after the mid-point of the century from within the community of the faithful when it ceased to be a docile conglomeration of devoted and stubborn peasants—that is when the middle class returned to the fold and contested the peasant control of the Church—and when the full impact of the philosophy of the

Enlightenment was felt in their midst. The Church failed to meet either challenge. The middle class was sufficiently strong to keep the Church from completing its reorganization. They gained control of some of the nerve centers of the Church, the churches of the larger cities. Their opposition to the institutions of the Church had vitiated the organization as it existed, but at the same time they had not had sufficient time to consolidate their own position to the point where they were able to reorganize the Church after their own tastes in such a way as to have restored to it a certain vital degree of efficiency. Hence the advent of the Revolution found the Church disorganized within, divided along class and geographical lines, without the institutions which might have given it leadership. Moreover, the lay pastors had been incapable of dealing with the forces of the Enlightenment. Some of the pastors had fallen victim to the alluring promises of the eighteenth-century philosophy, making them dissatisfied with their own religious functions. The dissatisfaction spread to the laity. To all too many Protestants, the Revolution seemed a far nobler enterprise than the activities of their Church. They deserted their temples for the political clubs of the Revolution. Under such circumstances there was little to encourage resistance on the part of either laity or ministers.

But if the renaissance of the Protestant Church under Antoine Court was defective and incomplete from a spiritual or religious point of view, his lasting achievement and perhaps his greatest contribution to French Protestantism was in the civil field. He and his apostles, the pastors of the Desert, succeeded both in keeping Protestantism alive where it otherwise would certainly have foundered and in making it respectable to a sizable number of Frenchmen. They presented the legislators of revolutionary France with a large and important community of loyal Frenchmen (who could no longer be accused of being an oppressive and disloyal group within society) who demanded civil, political, and religious liberty. By their very existence they provoked the measures rendered in their favor which thereafter made it possible for Frenchmen to be Protestant without incurring personal disgrace and humiliation and for succeeding generations of Protestants to enjoy a liberty and freedom which otherwise might not have been theirs. In the final analysis, they emancipated their Church, put it on an equal footing with the Catholic Church in the eyes of the State, and laid the foundations for the future enrichment of their spiritual life in a free environment.

This was the legacy of Antoine Court to future generations of French Protestants. He also bequeathed something to the French nation as a whole. In 1808 Napoleon answered a panegyric delivered to him by the president of the consistory of Bordeaux with the following statement: "From all parts of France I have received the most flattering marks of affection from the Protestants. I value them as my best subjects. They serve me zealously and with distinction. It is not I who gives them freedom; it is the century. The conscience of man is not subordinate to men; it is above the laws. The Revocation of the Edict of Nantes injured France greatly: it drove industries and arts into foreign lands. I have seen a horde of French refugees in Prussia and as far as the northern reaches of Poland. That is the fruit of persecutions."[47] The emancipative legislation of the French Revolution opened up to France a new reservoir of talent which the barbarous code of Louis XIV had denied to her. More than a half million energetic, industrious, and capable people were freed and allowed to play their role in the affairs of the French nation. They entered the service of the nation immediately. In a number of cities and towns of the Midi, the Protestants were heavily represented in the men of the middle class who seized control of the municipalities in the summer of 1789. Thereafter cities like Nîmes, Montauban, Montpellier, Bordeaux, and La Rochelle often had Protestant mayors. Protestant representation in the national assemblies was sometimes disproportionate to their numbers. Although they comprised only a little more than two per cent of the total population, five per cent of the National Convention were Protestants. As a member of the committee on the Constitution in the Constituent Assembly, Rabaut Saint-Etienne helped construct the first constitution of the revolutionary period. Cambon, as the dominant figure in the committee of finances in the Legislative Assembly and the Convention, was in effect the minister of finances for France during these periods. Jeanbon Saint-André was one of the more capable members of the Committee of Public Safety and an able prefect of Mont-Tonnerre from

[47] F. Kuhn, "L'Accueil fait à la loi de germinal," BPF, XLIX (1900), 326.

1801 to 1813. The armies of the Republic and the Empire counted among their generals the Protestants Ménard, Mathieu de Saint-Maurice, Jaucourt, Soulier, and Laserre. Under the Consulate a petition to the government by the notables of the church of Nîmes bore the signatures of Henri Lacoste and Vincens Saint-Laurent, *conseillers de préfecture*; Barthélemy Meynier, *conseillers du département*; Vincent Valz, Gaujoux, and Bordarier, *juges au tribunal de première instance*; Pagezy, *juge criminel*; Casimir Fornier, mayor of Nîmes; and Trélis, *bibliothécaire de l'école centrale et membre de l'académie.*[48] Or again, in the city of La Rochelle in 1807 the mayor was a Protestant, twelve out of twenty-four members of the *conseil municipal* were Protestants, as were six out of nine members of the *chambre de commerce*, and three out of five members of the *tribunal de commerce.*[49] In the commercial and industrial reorganization of France during the Empire, a number of Protestant bankers and industrialists were among Napoleon's ablest coadjutors. In reward for their services to the State either in the administration or the military forces, the emperor raised the Protestants Boissy d'Anglas, Jaucourt, Mathieu, Pelet de la Lozère, and Sers to Counts of the Empire; Eschasseriaux aîné, Jeanbon Saint-André, Lascours, and Pieyre to the baronage.

Once emancipated, the Protestants continued on into the nineteenth century to play distinguished roles in their nation's activities. François Guizot, Waddington, and Charles de Freycinet served as premiers of France. The cabinet formed by Waddington in 1879 is said to have included a majority of Protestants. Indeed, under the Third Republic, they held an embarrassingly large number of positions in the administration. A work written by one of their enemies at the turning of the century included a chapter of eighty pages (entitled "La Conquête protestante") which was little more than a listing of administrative offices held by Protestants in the various Departments of France.[50] In the military field, Admiral Jauréguiberry served his nation with distinction in the Crimean, Indo-Chinese, and Chinese wars of the nineteenth century. Both he and the General de Chabaud-Latour played creditable roles in the Franco-Prussian War. The *Lion de Belfort* stands as a perpetual

[48] Borrel, *Histoire de l'Eglise de Nîmes*, p. 463.

[49] Rabaut-Dupui, *Annuaire. . .*, p. 45.

[50] E. Renauld, *Le Péril protestant*, pp. 427-507.

memorial to the valiant defense of that city against the Prussians in 1870-1871 by its military commander, the Protestant Colonel Denfert-Rochereau. All of these are positions which they would not have had were it not for the fruits of the first years of the Revolution. This does not take into account their contribution to the field of French thought in the same century: the historians Quinet, Taine, Renouvier, de Pressensé, Guizot, and Gabriel Monod; the literary critics Vinet and Edmond Schérer; the theologians Reuss and Sabatier; the sculptors Bartholomé and Bartholdi; the scientists Pierre Curie, Cuvier, Quatrefages de Bréau, and Friedel; the journalist Prévost-Paradol; the administrator Haussmann; writers from Madame de Staël and Benjamin Constant in the first part of the century to André Gide at the end of the century—many of whom held positions in the French academic world which would have been closed to them under the *ancien régime.*

These men were Protestants. They and their ancestors of the eighteenth century were a credit to France. Above all, they were Frenchmen. Once they had been a seditious minority within the nation. Painful experience, the conversion of their nobility, the ministrations of their pastors had changed all this. By the end of the eighteenth century they yearned for nothing more than to be accepted for what they were: Frenchmen. In temperament, in political philosophy, there was little to distinguish them from their Catholic neighbors. As a group they had reason to be more hostile to the Catholic Church than the majority of other Frenchmen. But they knew full well that any actions taken on their part against the Church would almost certainly have redounded to their disadvantage. Discretion and self-interest demanded that they remain apart from the legislation enacted against the mother Church of France. If Cambon and Barnave violated this rule, were they any less French than a Talleyrand or a Fouché? If they distrusted the Catholic Church, they respected their king. He was the father of their family; he won their love by restoring them to their liberties. They were not the born republicans that they are sometimes accused of being. Still less were they partisans of social anarchy. Even assuming that Calvinist theology leaned heavily toward republican ideas—or did, once kings turned to proscribing their faith—their theology had degenerated to the point where one wonders whether many of them were barely conscious of its teachings on civil government. Those from their midst who rose to political positions in the French Revolution had long since tuned their ears to the teachings of Rousseau, Voltaire, and Montesquieu. Calvin was almost a forgotten man. Their nobles rebelled against the constitutional monarchy and joined the armies of the princes. Their middle class rebelled against the popular democracy which many of their plebeians espoused and joined in the Girondin and Federalist revolts. The opinions of the century and of the Revolution divided them as they did their fellow Frenchmen. The violence of the Revolution exhausted them as much as any others. Their religion suffered more than did that of their presumed enemies. Ultimately they rallied to the cause of Napoleon with its promise of social peace and stability: in this, they were true Frenchmen of their day.

APPENDIXES

APPENDIX I

The Protestant Population of France in the Eighteenth Century

Rippert de Monclar, the *procureur général* of the Parlement of Provence estimated in 1755 that there were more than 3,000,000 Protestants in the kingdom.[1] His *Mémoire théologique et politique au sujet des mariages clandestins des protestants de France* in which this estimate was made elicited a series of refutations and counter-refutations which ended only with the Edict of Toleration in 1787. The first of these appeared in 1756. In it the abbé Caveyrac, taking issue with Rippert de Monclar, insisted that there were no more than 400,000 Calvinists remaining in France.[2] These two estimates—3,000,000 and 400,000—constitute the two extremes. Some writers leaned toward the higher figure. Condorcet, writing in 1778, asserted that the Protestants constituted about "a twentieth part of the population of the kingdom"[3] (or somewhat more than 1,000,000 individuals), but six years later in a work done in conjunction with Rabaut Saint-Etienne he repeatedly referred to the "two millions" of Protestants in France.[4] By 1790 he had pushed the figure to the upper limit and went on record as believing that there were 3,000,000.[5] The figure 2,000,000 was also cited by Rabaut Saint-Etienne, the son of the most distinguished Protestant pastor in France in the 1780's, in his writings and speeches in defense of the Protestant cause both prior to and during the Revolution.[6]

[1] Cf. E. Hugues, *Antoine Court*, II, 291. The most convenient summary of the varying estimates made during the eighteenth century can be found in Armand Lods, *Traité de l'administration des cultes protestants* (Paris, 1896), pp. 549-555.

[2] Armand Lods, *Traité de l'administration*, pp. 550-551.

[3] "Réflexions d'un citoyen catholique, sur les lois de France, rélatives aux protestants," in *Oeuvres de Condorcet*, ed. A. Condorcet O'Connor and F. Arago (Paris, 1847), V, 447.

[4] *Le roi doit modifier les loix portées contre les Protestans* (London, 1784), pp. 14, 31, 68, 92, 100.

[5] *La Bibliothèque de l'homme public*, a joint work by Condorcet, Peyssonnel and Le Chapelier cited by Arthur Young in his *Travels in France*, ed. Constantia Maxwell (Great Britain, 1929), p. 276.

[6] See, for instance, his speech in support of the Protestant cause during the debates on the Declaration of the Rights of Man and the Citizen in the National Assembly, where he claimed he represented the interests of 2,000,000 of his coreligionists. *Archives parlementaires de 1787 à 1860. Recueil complet des débats législatifs et politiques des chambres françaises*, eds. J. Mavidal, E. Laurent and E. Clavel (Paris, 1867-1913), 1st series, VIII, 479. At the time of the Edict of Toleration, both Rabaut Saint-Etienne and his brother Rabaut-Pomier, used the figure 3,000,000 when they found it convenient to do so: cf. "Instructions de Rabaut Saint-Etienne aux pasteurs du Languedoc au sujet de l'édit de tolérance," *Société de l'histoire du Protestantisme français.* BPF, XXXVI (1887), 548-551; and "Discours de Rabaut Po-

Most estimates were lower, however. Malesherbes,[7] the baron de Breteuil,[8] Rulhière,[9] and the pastor Olivier Desmons[10] made evaluations varying from 1,000,000 to 1,500,000. On the eve of the convocation of the Estates-General, the Protestants of Lyon petitioned the king in a memoir, asking that 600,000 of his most faithful and adoring subjects (i.e. the Protestants) not be disenfranchised in the elections about to take place.[11]

The estimate of 3,000,000 made by Rippert de Monclar in 1755 was unquestionably greatly exaggerated. A census taken by the government six years before the Revocation of the Edict of Nantes showed that there were scarcely more than 2,000,000 Protestants in the kingdom.[12] A sizable number of these (variously estimated at from 250,000 to 1,000,000) emigrated from France in the period 1680-1720, and a large proportion of those who remained were forced to return to the fold of the Catholic Church.[13] During the course of the eighteenth century, the Protestants succeeded in reorganizing their Church in the southern provinces of France, and while we can assume that they may very well have built up their numerical strength there to what it had been before the Revocation,[14]

---

mier, pasteur à Montpellier, fait à l'occasion de l'édit," BPF, XXXVI (1887), 596-604. In a letter of 26 April 1766 to Court de Gebelin, Rabaut Saint-Etienne spoke of 3,000,000 Protestants; cf. BPF, XLVIII (1899), 265.

[7] *Mémoire sur le mariage des protestans* (s.l., 1785), p. 14.

[8] *Mémoire ou Rapport général sur la situation des Calvinistes en France* in Claude-Carloman de Rulhière, *Eclaircissemens historiques sur les causes de la Révocation de l'Edit de Nantes et sur l'état des protestans en France* (Geneva, 1788), II, 20.

[9] Claude-Carloman de Rulhière, *Eclaircissemens historiques. . . ,* II, 6.

[10] *Mémoire sur la situation actuelle des protestants de France en réponse aux questions qui m'ont été faites par M. Gibert, pasteur réfugié à Londres* (Bordeaux, 1783) in Emile Doumergue, *La Veille de la loi de l'an X. Etude sur l'église réformée à la fin du XVIIIe siècle* (Paris, 1879), p. 112.

[11] *La Révolution française*, XXXIII (1897), 133.

[12] Cf. BPF, XXXVII (1888), 28-31. In a letter dated 6 August 1680, N. de La Mare revealed that the *procureur général* of the Parlement of Paris had told him in an interview that "l'année dernière, il s'est faict un dénombrement dans le Roiaume, de tous ceux de cette religion en aage de participer à la Ceine, qui c'est trouvé monter à dix-sept cens mil. . . ." The editors of the BPF, taking this figure and adding to it the presumed number of children too young to take Communion, arrived at the figure 2,000,000 for the approximate number of Protestants in France.

[13] See the BPF, LVII (1908), 82. The editors of the BPF report finding in the Archives of Hérault a document entitled "Estat des nouveaux convertis du Roy-aume par Generalitez" which was apparently drawn up *c.* 1698. Of the Protestants remaining in France at that time, 597,829 had returned to the Catholic Church. This figure undoubtedly increased up until the end of Louis XIV's reign.

[14] The baron de Breteuil, in his *Mémoire sur la situation des Calvinistes,* expressed the belief that there were as many Protestants in France as before the Revocation of the Edict of Nantes (underestimating their numbers in the earlier

many of the Protestants in the center and north of France were lost to them. Moreover, since the seventeenth century the Protestant Church in France has had little success in proselytizing among Catholics, and in the period after the death of Louis XIV the efforts at rebuilding the Church were directed almost entirely toward those families and individuals with Protestant backgrounds. This being the case, Rippert de Monclar's estimate can only be considered fantastic.

At first sight, the abbé Caveyrac's figure of 400,000 would seem to be no more enlightening that Rippert de Monclar's with respect to the probable numerical strength of the Protestants on the eve of the Revolution. It was made at a time when the government still engaged in intermittent persecution of Protestants, and hence at a time when most Protestants did whatever was necessary to conceal their religious beliefs. Moreover, it does not reflect the growth of the Protestant Church in the southern and southwestern provinces in the second half of the century, nor does it take into account the substantial increase in the French population as a whole in the quarter century after 1762.[15] Another adversary of the Protestants, the abbé Bonnaud, who shared Caveyrac's interest in keeping his estimate as low as possible, was willing to concede in 1787 that there might be as many as 1,000,000 Protestants in France.[16]

Few of these figures have any basis in fact. One suspects that the higher estimates were deliberate distortions made in the interest of attracting attention to the Protestant cause in France. Those in the vicinity of 1,000,000 were mere impressions occasionally supported by reference to fragmentary records of Protestant births, marriages, and deaths in the latter part of the eighteenth century. Indeed, looking at the two sets of relatively accurate statistics which are still available, we find that the abbé Caveyrac and the Protestants of Lyon, despite their lack of external evidence, came surprisingly close to the truth. The first of these statistics are presented by the editors of the leading Protestant historical journal

---

period), and probably did so by making his estimate on the basis of the situation in the Midi. The vicar of Alais complained in 1737 that whatever gains the Catholic Church had made as a consequence of the Revocation had since been lost, and that the Protestants of Languedoc were as numerous as before the Revocation. Cf. the "Mémoire au sujet des religionnaires du Bas Languedoc et des Cévennes. . . ," in E. Hugues, *Antoine Court*, II, 423, 428.

[15] See Emile Levasseur, *La population française* (Paris, 1889-1892), I, 221-223. The population of France in 1762 was approximately 22,000,000; by 1789 it may have risen to 26,000,000—a possible increase of more than 18 per cent.

[16] The abbé Jacques-Julien Bonnaud, *Discours à lire au conseil, en présence du Roi, par un ministre patriote, sur le projet d'accorder l'Etat Civil aux Protestants* (s.l., 1787), pp. 170-171.

in France, the *Bulletin de la Société de l'histoire du Protestantisme.* Sifting through and weighing the testimonies of eighteenth-century pastors and church records which had survived into the nineteenth century, they appraised the Protestant population in France for 1760 at 593,307 individuals.[17] If the Protestant population increased at the same rate that the population as a whole apparently did in the following twenty-five years (and there seems to be no reason for assuming otherwise),[18] there may have been approximately 700,000 Protestants in France on the eve of the Revolution.

The second set of available statistics were compiled during the Consulate. In preparation for the general religious settlement being effected at that time, the minister of the interior ordered on 3 thermidor an X (22 July 1802) that a general census of French Protestants be taken. The results showed that in *ancienne France* (i.e., within the 1789 frontiers of France) there were 479,312 Protestants exclusive of Lutherans.[19] And while this count was being made, the Protestants of Paris, apparently fearful that the government census takers might do them an injustice, decided to take a census of their own. The figure at which they arrived was considerably higher, namely 615,000.[20] While the Protestant census may well have been slightly padded, the official government figure is probably somewhat low as an indication of the possible number of Protestants in France in 1789. Two factors might account for this: first, modern Protestant historians are inclined to believe that the government censuses are careless in counting the dispersed Protestant population,[21] and, second, it is more than likely that the Protestant Church in France was numerically weaker in 1802 as a consequence of the Revolutionary experience than it had been in 1789.

[17] BPF, XXXV (1886), 471-473.

[18] See E. Levasseur, *op.cit.*, I, 338-339. The French censuses of 1861 and 1866 indicated that the Protestant population was increasing at roughly the same rate as the Catholic population, or if anything, somewhat more rapidly. In Bavaria, the proportion of Protestants to Catholics remained essentially the same in the period 1840-1880. There is no reason for assuming that the same would not also be true of eighteenth-century France.

[19] BPF, XXXIX (1890), 159-161. Also see BPF, XXXVIII (1889), 109-110. Armand Lods reports having found a note by Portalis dated brumaire an XII (i.e., before the results of the census were known) in which the Minister of Religion estimated the Protestant population to be in the vicinity of 454,000, and certainly no more than 500,000.

[20] Armand Lods, "La population protestante en France au lendemain du Concordat," in the BPF, XXXVIII (1889), 47-52.

[21] For instance, consult the *Encyclopédie des sciences religieuses*, ed. F. Lichtenberger (Paris, 1878), V, 109.

APPENDIX II

Protestant and Catholic Population of Languedoc in 1698

DIOCESES	NOBILITY		OTHER INHABITANTS	
	Catholics	*Convertis*	*Catholics*	*Convertis*
Toulouse	753		134,140	497
Montauban	62		34,396	1,240
Alby	214	18	84,187	1,008
Lavaur	126	79	44,462	5,320
Castres	142	72	55,469	12,567
S. Papoul	95		23,010	
Mirepoix	76		56,791	1,065
Rieux	117	3	26,948	4,165
Commenges	9		7,311	
Aleth	124		33,178	
Carcassone	113		56,691	
Narbonne	160	1	55,592	
S. Pons	91		30,443	1,024
Lodève	52		26,203	336
Béziers	197		63,087	2,505
Agde	101		30,528	1,514
Montpellier	395	29	20,674	10,348
Nîmes	212	59	40,720	39,664
Alais	117	96	30,390	41,766
Uzès	226	44	78,502	23,112
Vivarais contenant Vienne et Valence	339	25	198,336	33,199
Le Puy	213		83,127	974
Mendes	162	14	128,302	18,189
TOTAL	4,096	440	1,342,487	198,493

[Cite from de Boulainvilliers, *Etat de la France. . . , Extrait des Mémoires dressés par les Intendans du Royaume, par ordre du Roi Louis XIV à la sollicitation de Monseigneur le Duc de Bourgogne, père de Louis XV à présent regnant* (London, 1752), VIII, 322: "Extrait du mémoire de la généralité du Languedoc . . . par Monsieur de Lamoignon de Basville, Intendant des deux Généralités de Toulouse et de Montpellier."]

APPENDIX III

Population (in families) of Catholics and New Converts in the Communities of the Vivarais, *c.* 1740

ARRONDISSEMENTS *Communautés*	*Anc. Cath.*	*Nouv. conv.*
ANNONAY		
SAINT-PÉRAY		
Annonay	895	90
Saint-Péray	150	50
Toulaud	95	48
Ste-Eulalie ou Guiherand	25	15
Soyons	38	47
Saint-Georges	11	48
St-Marcel-de-Crussol	10	30
	1,224	328
BEAUCHASTEL		
Beauchastel	50	72
Charmes	50	70
Pierregourde, le Pape et St-André-de-Bruzac	21	100
	121	242
BOFFRES		
Boffres	35	120
St-Sylvestre et Champis	102	118
Saint-Didier	52	98
St-Romain-de-Lerps	55	3
	244	339
VERNOUX		
Vernoux	195	168
Châteauneuf-de-Vernoux	17	68
St-Julien-le-Roux	8	52
Saint-Fortunat	44	211
	264	499

	Anc. Cath.	*Nouv. conv.*
CHALENCON		
Chalencon	92	45
St-Apollinaire-de-Rias	22	46
St-Michel-de-Chabrillanoux	22	100
Silhac	60	128
St-Maurice-en-Chalencon	13	56
	209	375
ST-PRIX-EN-CHALENCON		
Saint-Prix	60	25
Mounens et Cluac	16	22
St-Jean-Chambre	30	100
St-Julien-Labrousse	80	48
	186	195
EMPURANY		
Empurany	264	20
Le Crestet	65	1
Monteil	54	10
Boucieu-le-Roi et Colombier-le-Jeune	125	3
St-Barthélemy-le-Pin	25	19
	678	128
DESAIGNES		
Desaignes	175	205
Lamastre	105	40
Macheville et Retourtour	120	25
Saint-Bazile	60	58
	460	328

APPENDIX III

SAINT-AGRÈVE	*Anc. Cath.*	*Nouv. conv.*
Saint-Agrève	165	125
St-Romain-le-Désert	42	59
Les Vastres	103	72
Devesset	30	35
Le Pouzat	15	1
Chaudeyrolles et Mezenc	90	0
	580	292

ROCHEPAULE	*Anc. Cath.*	*Nouv. conv.*
Rochepaule	90	9
St-André-des-Effengeas	73	29
La Coste-la-Fare	64	0
	167	38

LE CHEYLARD	*Anc. Cath.*	*Nouv. conv.*
Le Cheylard	174	84
Arric	77	15
St-Barthélemy-le-Meil	30	80
St-Michel-le-Rance	40	28
	321	207

MÉZILHAC	*Anc. Cath.*	*Nouv. conv.*
St-Giles-de-Mézilhac	119	9
St-Julien-du-Gua	21	57
Issamoulenc	20	55
St-Genest-Lachamp	15	104
Ajoux	12	38
	187	263

SAINT-PIERREVILLE	*Anc. Cath.*	*Nouv. conv.*
Saint-Pierreville	115	74
Gluiras	60	236
Saint-Christol	16	78
St-Julien-D'Orcival ou Marcols	15	135
Pranles	25	151
St-Etienne-de-Serres	24	70
	261	744

PRIVAS	*Anc. Cath.*	*Nouv. conv.*
Privas	178	277
Tournon et Lyas	18	86
Lubillac et Coux	12	99
Veyras	6	37
Saint-Priest	46	24
	260	523

ST-VINCENT-DE-DURFORT	*Anc. Cath.*	*Nouv. conv.*
St-Vincent-de-Durfort	10	85
St-Sauveur-de-Montagut	0	57
St-Cierge-la-Serre	7	62
Pourchères	17	22
St-André-de-Creysseilles	1	62
Gourdon	55	0
	90	288

CHOMÉRAC	*Anc. Cath.*	*Nouv. conv.*
Chomérac	85	153
St-Symphorien	10	52
Alissas	12	70
Rochessauve (a)	34	65
Bressac et St-Lager	12	48
St-Vincent-de-Barrès	6	110
St-Bauzile-en-Barrès	6	29
	165	527

LA VOULTE	*Anc. Cath.*	*Nouv. conv.*
La Voulte	146	72
Royas	11	11
Rompon	10	68
	167	151

LE POUZIN	*Anc. Cath.*	*Nouv. conv.*
Le Pouzin	10	144
Baix	9	130
Flaviac	6	78
Creissac	1	39
St-Julien-en-St-Alban	6	24
	32	415

APPENDIX III

	Anc. Cath.	Nouv. conv.
VILLENEUVE-DE-BERG		
Villeneuve-de-Berg	430	50
St-Jean-le-Centenier	87	0
St-Maurice-d'Ibie	48	12
St-Genest-en-Coiron et Montbrun	45	0
	610	62
VALLON		
Vallon	67	195
Lagorce	25	120
	92	315

	Anc. Cath.	Nouv. conv.
SALAVAS		
Salavas	52	41
Vagnas	72	8
La Bastide-de-Virac	17	18
Bessas		.....
	141	67
VALS		
St-Martin-de-Vals	20	290
LES SALELLES		
Les Salelles	47	48

GRAND TOTAL

Catholic families	7,626
Families of new converts	6,664

[Cited from E. Arnaud, *Histoire des Protestants du Vivarais et du Velay, Pays de Languedoc, de la Réforme à la Révolution* (Paris, 1888), II, 419-423.]

APPENDIX IV

Protestants in the National Assemblies

In consulting this list of the Protestants who sat in the National Assemblies of France from 1789 to 1795, the reader should understand that the list does not pretend to be complete. Few of the Protestants participating in public office during this period advertised their religious beliefs. Like Barnave, Cambon, and Jeanbon Saint-André, many of them (and perhaps even most of them) were baptized in the Roman Catholic Church, making their religious identity all the more difficult to establish.

The sources for identifying the religious attachments of such men are varied. The works of the enemies of the Protestants usually list a number of them, but they cannot be trusted. For, in trying to stigmatize the Protestants, such persons will also cite as Protestants those who were not: for instance, Ernest Renauld, *Le Péril Protestant,* cites Alquier, Anacharsis Cloots, Billaud-Varenne, and Collot d'Herbois. Various French biographical dictionaries, especially those of A. Robert and A. Robinet, will often mention the Protestant extraction of a person. Since most of the Protestant deputies to the various National Assemblies originated from the Midi of France, the studies of the Revolution in this area are of great assistance, especially the works of François Rouvière and Charles-H. Pouthas.

The States General and the Constituent Assembly

1. Barnave, Antoine-Pierre-Joseph-Marie (Dauphiné)
2. Boissy d'Anglas, François-Antoine (Annonay)
3. Chambon-Latour, Jean-Michel (Nîmes)
4. Couderc, Guillaume-Benoit (Lyons)
5. Cussy, Gabriel de (Caen)
6. Gallot, Jean-Gabriel (Poitou)
7. Gareschè, Pierre-Isaac (Saintes)
8. Lamy, Michel-Louis (Caen)
9. Mestre, Mathias (Libourne)
10. Meynier de Salinelles, Etienne-David (Nîmes)
11. Nairac, Pierre-Paul (Bordeaux)
12. Quatrefages de La Roquette, Henri (Nîmes)
13. Rabaut Saint-Etienne, Jean-Paul, pastor (Nîmes)
14. Soustelle, Jean-François-Mathieu (Nîmes)
15. Voulland, Jean-Henri (Nîmes)

APPENDIX IV

The Legislative Assembly

1. Allut, Antoine (Gard)
2. Cambon, Pierre-Joseph (Hérault)
3. Eschasseriaux aînè, Joseph (Charente-Inférieure)
4. Garrau, Pierre-Anselme (Gironde)
5. Gasparin, Thomas-Augustin de (Bouches-du-Rhône)
6. Haussmann, Nicolas [Lutheran] (Seine-et-Oise)
7. Jaucourt, Arnail-François marquis de (Seine-et-Oise)
8. Jay, Jean, pastor (Gironde)
9. Laffon de Ladébat, André-Daniel (Gironde)
10. Lasource, Marie-David-Albin, pastor (Hérault)
11. Leyris-Descombes, Augustin-Jacques (Gard)
12. Ménard, Jean-François-Xavier (Gard)
13. Pieyre, Jean (Gard)
14. Sers, Jean-Pierre (Gironde)
15. Vincens-Planchut, Jean-César (Gard)

The National Convention

1. Bayle, Moïse-Antoine-Pierre-Jean (Bouches-du-Rhône)
2. Bernard-Saint-Affrique, Louis, pastor (Aveyron)
3. Berthezène, Jean-Etienne-Antoine (Gard)
4. Boissy d'Anglas, François-Antoine (Annonay)
5. Cambon, Pierre-Joseph (Hérault)
6. Chambon-Latour, Jean-Michel (Gard)
7. Cussy, Gabriel de (Calvados)
8. Dentzel, Georges-Frédéric [Lutheran pastor] (Bas-Rhin)
9. Dupuch, Elie-Louis (Guadeloupe)
10. Ehrmann, Jean-François [Lutheran] (Bas-Rhin)
11. Eschasseriaux aîné, Joseph (Charente-Inférieure)
12. Eschasseriaux, René [brother of the above] (Charente-Inférieure)
13. Garrau, Pierre-Anselme (Gironde)
14. Gasparin, Thomas-Augustin de (Bouches-du-Rhône)
15. Grimmer, Jean-Gotthard [Lutheran pastor] (Bas-Rhin)
16. Haussmann, Nicolas [Lutheran] (Seine-et-Oise)
17. Jay, Jean, pastor (Gironde)
18. Jeanbon Saint-André, pastor (Lot)
19. Johannot, Jean (Haut-Rhin)
20. Julien de Toulouse, Jean, pastor (Haute-Garonne)
21. Lasource, Marie-David-Albin, pastor (Hérault)
22. Leyris-Descombes, Augustin-Jacques (Gard)
23. Lombard-Lachaux, Pierre, pastor (Loiret)
24. Marat, Jean-Paul (Paris)

25. Pelet de la Lozère, Jean (Lozère)
26. Rabaut-Pomier, Jacques-Antoine (Gard)
27. Rabaut Saint-Etienne, Jean-Paul (Aube)
28. Servière, Laurent (Lozère)
29. Voulland, Henri (Gard)

The Protestant Vote at Louis XVI's Trial

	Death	*Reprieve*	*Plebiscite*
Moïse Bayle	for	against	against
Bernard-Saint-Affrique	against[1]	for	against
Berthezène	for	for	for
Boissy d'Anglas	against[1]	for	for
Cambon	for	against	against
Chambon-Latour	—not a member until April 1793—		
Cussy	against[1]	for	for
Dupuch	—not a member until Sept. 1793—		
Eschasseriaux aîné	for	against	against
Eschasseriaux, R.	—not a member until August 1793—		
Garrau	for	against	against
Gasparin	for	against	against
Jay	for	against	against
Jeanbon Saint-André	for	against	against
Johannot	for[2]	for	against
Julien de Toulouse	for	against	against
Lasource	for	against	(absent)
Leyris-Descombes	for	against	against
Lombard-Lachaux	for	for	against
Marat	for	against	against
Pelet de la Lozère		—absent—	
Rabaut-Pomier	for	for	for
Rabaut Saint-Etienne	against	for	for
Servière	for[2]	(absent)	against
Voulland, Jean-Henri	for	against	against

[1] Detention and exile at the conclusion of the war.

[2] Death with Maihe's amendment, qualifying the vote with the demand for a reprieve.

[A. Kuscinski, *Dictionnaire des Conventionnels* (Paris, 1916-1919).]

APPENDIX V

Letters of Abdication from the Ministry

Abdication of the Pastor Elie Dumas, 20 prairial an II (8 June 1794)

J'ai exercé pendant quelques années les fonctions de ministre protestant dans différentes communes du Gard et de l'Aveyron. J'ai prêché aux hommes la vertu et la morale universelle, puisée, non dans les ouvrages mensongers des soi-disant docteurs, mais dans le livre de la nature qui ne nous trompe jamais, et je n'ai été attaché au culte public que par le bien que je pouvais faire. Dès le commencement de la révolution, j'ai fait l'abandon de cet état et des fonctions qui y sont attachées, parce que je les ai regardées comme contraires aux progrès des vertus civiques, à la profession d'un franc républicain, et diamétralement opposées aux principes de la raison et au bonheur des hommes. Patriote avant que nous eussions une patrie, républicain avant l'établissement de la république, dévoré par le saint amour de l'égalité et de la liberté, je me suis livré tout entier à la révolution, et j'ai la douce satisfaction d'avoir contribué à former l'esprit public dans des montagnes où le feu de fantisme n'étoit pas encore entiérement éteint.

Dans une lettre qui a été lue à la Société populaire de Brion-du-Gard, lieu de ma naissance, j'ai manifesté les sentimens que je développe ici, et les motifs qui m'ont porté à renoncer de bonne heure à un culte qui ne doit plus exister. J'ai cru devoir rendre cet hommage à la raison, à la patrie et aux principes de philanthropie que j'ai professés dans tous les tems; j'ai cru que ne pouvant plus être considéré comme ministre protestant toute autre abdication de ma part étroit inutile. Cependant, soumis à ce respect aux loys de la République, aux oracles salutaires de nos sages représentans, je viens vous déclarer, conformément à l'arrêté du représentant du peuple Borie, dont les principes et les travaux révolutionnaires ont puissamment contribué à la régénération des peuples du Gard, que j'ai renoncé et que je renonce de plus fort à l'état et aux fonctions de ministre protestant; que je ne reconnois d'autre culte public ou privé, que celui de l'être suprême, de la raison et de la patrie. Je déclare encore qu'imperturbablement attaché au nouvel ordre des choses, je consacrerai tout ce que la nature m'a accordé de talens et de vertus à l'affermissement de la République une et indivisible, à propagation des principes populaires, et à la consolidation du bonheur de mes concitoyens.

[Quoted in F. Rouvière, *Révolution dans le Gard,* IV, 387-388 note.]

APPENDIX V

Public Abdication of the Pastors Jean Gachon and Adrien Vincent, 4 ventôse an II (22 February 1794)

Citoyens,

Une obéissance passive à la loy a toujours été dans nos plus rigoureux principes. Quand la loy nous a permis l'exercice de notre culte, nous avons profité de la liberté qu'elle nous donnoit, pour exhorter les hommes à la vertu, et surtout au patriotisme qui est la première vertu.

Aujourd'hui nous voyons que la tranquillité publique demande la suppression de ce même culte; nous faisons à ce grand objet le sacrifice de notre état; nous rentrons dans la classe commune des citoyens; et sous ce rapport, nous ne cesserons jamais de concourir de tout notre pouvoir à la prospérité de notre patrie.

Citoyen représentant, nous nous félicitons d'avoir pu faire cette déclaration devant toi; elle est franche et loyale. Notre conduite y répondra et, dans tous les tems, le voeu le plus cher à nos coeurs sera celui de tous bons françois: vive la République une et indivisible.

[*ibid.*, 390 note.]

Abdication of the Pastor Paul Gautier, 27 ventôse an II (17 March 1794)

Citoyens,

Ennemi du fanatisme comme de l'impiété, en montrant toujours les dangers de ces deux extrêmes, je tâchai d'imprimer chez tous l'amour de l'ordre et de la vertu. J'aimois d'autant plus mon état, qu'il me donnoit un heureux ascendant pour amener les hommes à la pratique de toutes les vertus, comme à l'éloignement de tout vice, et je puis dire que, quoique je n'eusse d'autre ressource que celle que me donnoit mon état, l'horreur que j'ai pour le mensonge et pour tout dissimulation est telle, que si je n'avois été bien persuadé moi-même des vérités que j'annonçois aux autres, je n'aurois pas attendu jusqu'à ce tems pour y renoncer. Mais comme tout doit céder au bien de la paix et de la tranquillité publique, et que les circonstances présentent l'exigent, je viens cejourd'hui vous déclarer l'abdication de mes fonctions, de laquelle déclaration je demande acte; déclarant, au surplus, qu'en qualité de ministre protestant, je n'ai jamais eu de lettre de prêtrise.

[*ibid.*, 391 note.]

Abdication of the Pastor Jean Rame, 13 pluviôse an II (1 February 1794)

Ministre du culte protestant, nos discours, j'ose le dire, n'ont respiré que la saine morale, n'ont eu pour but que de former l'homme et le citoyen; néanmoins, parfaitement convaincu que la célébration de tout culte extérieur et public, dans les circonstances actuelles pourrait alimenter le fanatisme, irriter la malveillance et par cela même, entraver la marche du mouvement révolutionnaire que tout bon républicain doit accélérer de tout son pouvoir, je viens, en conséquence, vous déclarer avec toute la sincérité dont je suis capable, que je renonce, dès à présent, aux fonctions de prédicateur, et que mon ambition se bornera désormais à me rendre dans le temple de la Raison avec nos frères, nos chers concitoyens, pour m'entretenir avec eux des devoirs de l'homme et du citoyen, chanter des hymnes à la Liberté et à l'Egalité et apprendre à mourir, s'il le faut, pour les défendre. Puisse mon exemple avoir beaucoup d'imitateurs! Puissé-je bientôt voir les torches de l'horrible fanatisme entièrement éteintes dans ce département qui en a été si souvent incendié! . . . Tel est mon voeu, et je mourrai content!

[*ibid.*, 397 note.]

Abdication of the Pastor Pierre Encontre, 28 ventôse an II (18 March 1794)

Le 28 ventôse l'an second de la République une et indivisible en étant requis une infinité de témoins atteste tenir que pendant plus de cinquante années j'ai prêché la pure vérité, la saine morale, l'obéissance aux loix, la juste horreur que mérite l'imbécile superstition et le cruel fanatisme. C'est à cette cause si légitime que l'on me vit sacrifier durant si longtemps, ma fortune, mes parens, ma vie même en affrontant mille et mille morts. Animé de ces sentiments après avoir prévu notre heureuse Révolution je témoigné de tout mon pouvoir avant même qu'elle commença, et vous savés combien je l'ay soutenue dans le temps le plus contraire et par mes discours et par mes actions, et par mes sacrifices bien audessus de mes facultés. Mais vous ignorés ce que j'aurais toujours tenu sous le voile de serment s'il n'était devenu urgent de le publier, que tandis qu'il me venoit de toute part des avis, au cas je ne renonçasse pas à mon état, vous ignoré dis-je qu'alors je portais mon zéle à servir la patrie au point de déposer sur son autel le prêt d'environ la moitié de ma petite fortune.

Dire que par de tels principes et ne pouvant me dissimuler que les sociétés populaires aussy bien que mon troupeau réclament que je cesse mes fonctions publiques, par ce qu'on assure qu'elles ne pourraient qu'être funestes dans les circonstances.

[BPF, XLVII (1898), 658-659.]

APPENDIX V

Abdication of the Pastor Jean Mirial, 21 ventôse an II (9 February 1794)

Renoncer à un état qui était mon unique ressource, c'est plonger ma famille dans la misère, mais l'intérêt public fut et sera toujours mon unique mobile, et je lui fais volontiers ce nouveau sacrifice.

J'étais ministre protestant et j'en ai rempli les fonctions en honnête homme, en véritable ami de la Patrie, tant qu'elles m'ont paru devoir être remplies; j'ai constamment prêché la fraternité, l'amour de la liberté et de l'égalité; le dévouement à la République, l'obéissance aux lois, et la pratique de toutes les vertus, unique source du bonheur.

Malheureusement plusieurs sectes religieuses divisaient les hommes entre eux, et les différens cultes n'ont que trop servi de prétexte aux malveillans de toubler l'ordre et la paix publiques; plusieurs événements funestes ont fait sentir la nécessité de renoncer à toutes ces sectes, pour ne plus former entre nous qu'une seule et même famille. Depuis quelque temps je suis pénétré de cette nécessité, et vous savez qu'en conséquence j'avais renoncé par le fait à mon état; il ne manquait que d'en faire la déclaration authentique. Je préparais les esprits de mon mieux et j'attendais un moment favorable pour m'acquiter de ce devoir; ce moment se présenta hier dans le temple de la Raison, j'y fis publiquement mon abdication en présence de tous les citoyens et du digne représentant du peuple Borie, et je viens aujourd'hui déclarer devant vous, en conséquence, que je ne suis plus ministre d'un culte religieux; qu'ayant renoncé franchement à cet état et à toutes les fonctions qui y étaient attachées, le seul titre dont je veux être décoré est celui de citoyen français et de patriote incorruptible, étant toujours prêt à me sacrifier pour la prospérité de la République une et indivisible. Je ne saurais vous remettre des lettres de prêtrise, la plupart des ministres protestants n'en eurent jamais et je suis de ce nombre. Je vous demande acte de la présent abdication. . . .

[BPF, XLV (1896), 549-552.]

Abdication of the Divinity Student François Astruc, 20 ventôse an II (9 February 1794)

Cejourd'hui 20e ventôse an II (1794), de la République une et indivisible, je certifie, en présence de la Loi et du représentant du peuple, que j'abdique toute fonction de ministre protestant, que je renonce à toute célébration du culte public, au titre de proposant, et je déclare, en outre, consacrer mon temps, mes talens et ma vie pour la défense de ma Patrie.

[*ibid.*, 552.]

BIBLIOGRAPHY

BIBLIOGRAPHY

Primary Sources, Printed Source Material, and Contemporary Works

Almanach des Réformés et Protestans de l'Empire français pour l'an bissextile 1808, (Paris, 1808).

L'Ancien Moniteur, Réimpression de.

Archives de la ville de Montpellier, volume IV, ed. Joseph Berthelé (Montpellier, 1920).

Archives parlementaires de 1787 à 1860. Recueil complet des débats législatifs et politiques des chambres françaises, eds. J. Mavidal, E. Laurent and E. Clavel (Paris, 1867-1913).

Aulard, A., *Recueil des actes du Comité de salut public* (Paris, 1889-1933).

Blachon, J.-A., *Recueil de discours ou fragmens de discours relatifs à diverses circonstances de l'Etat prononcés par J.-A. Blachon en sa qualité de pasteur de l'église réformée à Bordeaux, puis à Anduze* (Nîmes, 1804).

Bligny-Bondurand, E., *Cahiers de doléances de la sénéchaussée de Nîmes pour les Etats Généraux de 1789* (Nîmes, 1908-1909), 2 vols.

Boissy d'Anglas, *Discours et opinions de Rabaut Saint-Etienne suivis de ses deux derniers écrits et précédés d'une notice sur sa vie* (Paris, 1827).

Boissy d'Anglas, *Rapport sur la Liberté des cultes, fait au nom des Comités de Salut public, de Sûreté générale et de Législation. . . , dans la séance du 3 ventôse An IIIe de la République française* (Versailles, 1795).

Bonnaud, l'abbé Jacques-Julien, *Discours à lire au conseil, en présence du Roi, par un ministre patriote, sur le projet d'accorder l'Etat Civil aux Protestants* (s.l., 1787).

Boulainvilliers, Henri comte de, *Etat de la France. . . ; Extrait des mémoires dressés par les Intendans du Royaume*, volume VIII (London, 1752).

BPF. See *Société de l'histoire du Protestantisme français* cited under "Periodicals."

Caron, Pierre, *Rapports des Agents du Ministère de l'Intérieur dans les Départements* (Paris, 1913-1951), 3 vols.

Charles Sincère à Pierre Romain (Nîmes, 22 November 1789).

Collection des procès-verbaux des Assemblées-Générales du Clergé de France.

Condorcet, *Le roi doit modifier les loix contre les protestans* (s.l., 1784).

Condorcet, Oeuvres de, eds. A. Condorcet O'Connor and F. Arago (Paris, 1847), volume v.

Discours prononcé le 20 juin 1790, devant la Société des Amis de la Constitution, ètablie dans la ville de Nismes, par M. l'abbé Castan de la Courtade, aumônier de la Légion de Béziers. . . (s.l.n.d.).

Duvergier, J. B., *Collection complète des lois, décrets, ordonnances . . . etc., 1788-1824* (Paris, 1825-1828).

Fabre, Gustave, "Trois manuscrits de Rabaut Saint-Etienne," *Mémoires de l'Académie de Nîmes*, VIIe series, XVI (1893), 193-240.

Falconetti, Jean, "Adresse des Jacobins de Montpellier à Louis XVI [April 1791]," *La Révolution française*, LXV (1913), 55-57.

Félice, Paul de, *Sermons protestants prêchés en France de 1685 à 1795 et imprimés alors et depuis en France ou à l'étranger. Essai bibliographique* (Paris, 1885).

Flammermont, Jules, *Remonstrances du Parlement de Paris au XVIIIe siècle*, volume III (Paris, 1888-1898).

Galabert, François, "Le Père Sermet à Montauban," *La Révolution française*, XXXVI (1899), 396-405.

Gottschalk, Louis, ed., *The Letters of Lafayette to Washington, 1777-1799* (New York, 1944).

Hugues, Edmond, *Les synodes du Désert. Actes et règlements des synodes nationaux et provinciaux tenus au Désert de France de l'an 1715 à l'an 1793* (Paris, 1885-1886), 3 vols.

Isambert, François-André, ed., *Recueil général des anciennes lois françaises . . . jusqu'à la Révolution de 1789* (Paris, 1822-1833).

Journal du Marquis Dangeau, volume XVIII, ed. F. de Conches (Paris, 1854-1882).

Lamouzèle, E., "Une lettre inédite de Sermet, évêque constitutionnel de la Haute-Garonne," *La Révolution française*, XLIII (1902), 470-475.

Lettre d'un patriote volontaire dans la garde nationale de Nismes, sur les troubles de Nismes (s.l.n.d.).

Lévy-Schneider, Léon, "Documents inédits. Lettres de Jeanbon Saint-André et de Cavaignac à la municipalité de Montauban," *La Révolution française*, XXIX (1895), 63-86; XXX (1896), 461-466.

Ligou, Daniel, *Documents sur le Protestantisme montalbanais au XVIIIe siècle* (Toulouse, s.d.)

Lods, Armand, "Documents inédits. Correspondance de Jeanbon Saint-André avec Lasource," *La Révolution française*, XXI (1891), 338-373.

Lods, Armand, *La législation des cultes protestants. Recueil complet des lois, ordonnances, décrets . . . relatifs aux églises protestantes* (Paris, 1887).

Lods, Armand, "Quelques notes sur les opinions politiques de Rabaut de Saint-Etienne," *La Révolution française*, XL (1901), 353-357.

Lods, Armand, "Rabaut de Saint-Etienne. Sa correspondance pendant la Révolution," *La Révolution française*, XXXV (1898), 78-89, 157-177, 259-277.

de Maistre, Joseph, "Réflexions sur le protestantisme dans ses rapports avec la souveraineté," *Oeuvres complètes de J. de Maistre*, 2nd edition (Lyon, 1884), VIII, 64-93.

Malesherbes, *Mémoire sur le mariage des protestans* (s.l., 1785).

Malesherbes, *Second mémoire sur le mariage des protestans* (s.l., 1786).

Montjoie, F.-C.-G. de, *L'Ami du Roi, des François, de l'Ordre et sur-tout de la Vérité; ou Histoire de la Révolution de France et de l'Assemblée nationale* (Paris, 1791).

Rabaut le Jeune, *Annuaire ou répertoire ecclésiastique à l'usage des églises réformées et protestantes de l'Empire français* (Paris, 1807).

Rabaut Saint-Etienne, Jean-Paul, *A la Nation française; sur les vices de son gouvernement; sur la nécessité d'établir une Constitution; et sur la composition des Etats-Généraux* (s.l., November 1788).

Rabaut Saint-Etienne, *Idées sur les bases de toute constitution* (s.l.n.d.).

Rabaut Saint-Etienne, *Projet du préliminaire de la Constitution* (Versailles, 1789)

Rabaut Saint-Etienne, *Le vieux Cévenol* (London, 1784).

Rabaut Saint-Etienne, Oeuvres de, ed., Collin de Plancy (Paris, 1826), 2 vols.

Royère, Mgr de (refractory bishop of Castres), "Exhortation de Mgr l'évêque de Castres aux prêtres français qui vont en Espagne pour faire des prières publiques et implorer la miséricorde de Dieu," *La Révolution française*, XXXIV (1898), 455-460.

Rulhière, Claude-Carloman de, *Eclaircissemens historiques sur les causes de la Révocation de l'Edit de Nantes et sur l'état des protestans en France* (Geneva, 1788), 2 vols.

Saint-Simon, Mémoires de, ed. A. de Boislisle (Paris, 1879-1930).

Theiner, Augustin, ed., *Documents inédits relatifs aux affaires religieuses de la France, 1790 à 1800. Extraits des archives secrètes du Vatican*, volume I (Paris, 1857).

Turgot, "Mémoire au Roi sur la tolérance," in *Oeuvres de Turgot*, ed. Eugène Daire (Paris, 1844), II, 492-502.

Secondary Sources

Adolphe, Lydie, *Portalis et son temps* (Paris, 1936).

Aigan, Etienne, *De l'état de Protestans en France depuis le XVIe siècle jusqu'à nos jours*, 2nd edition (Paris, 1818).

Arnaud, Ernest, *Histoire des Protestants du Dauphiné aux XVIe et XVIIIe siècles* (Paris, 1876), 3 vols.

Arnaud, Ernest, *Histoire des Protestants de Provence et du Comtat Venaissin* (Paris, 1884), 2 vols.

Arnaud, Ernest, *Histoire des Protestants du Vivarais et du Velay* (Paris, 1888), 2 vols.

Aulard, A., *Christianity and the French Revolution*, translated by Lady Frazer (Boston, 1927).

Aulard, A., *Etudes et leçons sur la Révolution française*, 2nd series, 3rd edition (Paris, 1906).

Aulard, A., *Histoire politique de la Révolution française. Origines et développement de la Démocratie et de la République, 1789-1804* (Paris, 1901).

Aulard, A., *Les Orateurs de la Révolution, la Législative et la Convention* (Paris, 1906-1907), 2 vols.

Baird, Henry M., *The Huguenots and the Revocation of the Edict of Nantes* (New York, 1895), 2 vols.

Benoit, Daniel, *Desubas, son ministère, son martyre, 1720-1746* (Toulouse, 1901).

Benoit, Daniel, *Du caractère huguenot et des transformations de la piété huguenot* (Paris, 1892).

Benoit, Daniel, *L'Eglise sous la croix* (Toulouse, 1896).

Benoit, Daniel, *François Roux, compagnon d'oeuvre d'Antoine Court* (Toulouse, 1892).

Benoit, Daniel, *Les frères Gibert. Deux pasteurs du Désert et du Refuge, 1722-1817* (Toulouse, 1889)

Benoit, Daniel, *Marie Durand, prisonnière à la tour de Constance* (Toulouse, 1894).

Biographie moderne, ou Dictionnaire biographique de tous les hommes morts et vivans. . . (Breslau, 1806).

Boegner, Marc and Siegfried, André, eds., *Protestantisme français* (Paris, 1945).

Bonnefon, Daniel, *Benjamin du Plan, Deputy-General of the Reformed Churches of France from 1725 to 1763* (London, 1878).

Bornarel, Félix, *Cambon et la Révolution française* (Paris, 1905).

Borrel, Abraham, *Histoire de l'église réformée de Nîmes depuis son origine en 1533 jusqu'à la loi organique du 18 germinal an X*, 2nd edition (Toulouse, 1856).

Bost, Charles, *Prédicants protestants des Cévennes et du Bas-Languedoc, 1684-1700* (Paris, 1912), 2 vols.

BPF. See *Société de l'histoire du Protestantisme français* cited under "Periodicals."

Briet, Elisée, *Le Protestantisme en Brie et Basse Champagne du XVIe siècle à nos jours* (Paris, 1885).

Champion, Edme, *La France d'après les Cahiers de 1789*, 4th edition (Paris, 1911)

Charrière, Frédéric de, "Lausanne, centre protestant au XVIIIe siècle," *Revue suisse et chronique littéraire*, XIII (1850), 361-368.

Chassaigne, Marc, *L'Affaire Calas* (Paris, 1929).

Chassin, Charles-L., *Le génie de la Révolution* (Paris, 1865), 2 vols.

Chevallier, Jean-Jacques, *Barnave, ou deux faces de la Révolution* (Paris, 1936)

Chobaut, H., "La pétition du club de Montpellier en faveur de la République," *Annales historiques de la Révolution française*, IV (1927), 547-563.

Chobaut, H., "La Société populaire d'Aiguevives, 1790-1794," *Mémoires de l'Académie de Nîmes*, VIIe series, XLII (1925), 35-67.

Coquerel, Athanase fils, *Les forçats pour la foi* (Paris, 1866).

Coquerel, Charles, *Histoire des églises du Désert depuis la fin de règne du Louis XIV jusqu'à la Révolution française* (Paris, 1841), 2 vols.

Corbière, Philippe, *Histoire de l'église réformée de Montpellier depuis son origine jusqu'à nos jours* (Montpellier and Paris, 1861).

Crottet, Alex., *Histoire des églises réformées de Pons, Gemozac et Mortagne en Saintonge* (Bordeaux, 1841).

Dartigue, J.-Albert, *Rabaut de Saint-Etienne à l'Assemblée Constituante de 1789. Thèse présentée à la Faculté de Théologie protestante de Montauban* (s.l., 1903).

Daudet, Ernest, *Histoire des conspirations royalistes du Midi sous la Révolution, 1790-1793* (Paris, 1881).

Dedieu, l'abbé Joseph, *Le rôle politique des Protestants français, 1685-1715* (Paris, 1920).

Dedieu, l'abbé Joseph, *Histoire politique des Protestants français, 1715-1794* (Paris, 1925), 2 vols.

Denys-Buirette, A., *Les questions religieuses dans les Cahiers de 1789* (Paris, 1919).

Douen, O., *Les premiers pasteurs du Désert, 1685-1700* (Paris, 1879), 2 vols.

Doumergue, Emile, *La Veille de la loi de l'an X. Etude sur l'église réformée à la fin du XVIIIe siècle* (Paris, 1879).

Dumas, Mathieu, *Memoirs of His Own Time; Including the Revolution, the Empire, and the Restoration* (Philadelphia, 1839), 2 vols.

Dupont, André, *Rabaut Saint-Etienne, 1743-1793* (Strasbourg, 1946).

Durand, le chanoine Albert, *Histoire religieuse du Département du Gard pendant la Révolution française* (Nîmes, 1918)

Durand, Charles, *Histoire du Protestantisme français pendant la Révolution et l'Empire* (Paris, 1902).

Fabre, Marcel, "Les assemblées préparatoires aux élections des députés aux Etats Généraux . . . tenus à Uzès," *Revue du Midi* (1910), 525-539, 634-643, 667-677.

Fabre, Marcel, "La réaction thermidorienne et la liquidation de la Terreur à Uzès," *Mémoires de l'Académie de Nîmes*, VIIe series, XLI (1922-1923), 64-85.

Febvre, Lucien, "Un village du Languedoc sous Louis XV," *Annales d'histoire sociale*, III (1941), 68-71.

Félice, G. de., *Histoire des synodes nationaux des églises réformées de France* (Paris, 1864).

Félice, G. de., and F. Bonifas, *Histoire des Protestants de France*, 7th edition (Toulouse, 1880).

Galabert, François, "Le club jacobin de Montauban. Son rôle politique pendant la Constituante," *Revue d'histoire moderne et contemporaine*, I (1899-1900), 124-168, 235-258, 457-474.

Galabert, François, "Le club de Montauban pendant la Constituante. Son organisation, son rôle dans l'administration locale," *Revue d'histoire moderne et contemporaine*, X (1908), 5-27, 273-317.

Garrett, Mitchell B., *The Estates General of 1789* (New York, 1935).

Gaston-Martin, "La fuite à Varennes et l'impression dans le Sud-Ouest," *La Révolution française*, LXXXII (1929), 113-132.

Gaston-Martin, "La vie bourgeoise à Nantes sous la Convention, d'après le livre de comptes de Mme Hummel," *La Révolution française*, LXXXVI (1933), 236-258.

Godechot, Jacques, *Les Institutions de la France sous la Révolution et l'Empire* (Paris, 1951).

Guérin, Pierre, "Histoire d'une commune rurale de 1780 à 1800 [Milhaud]," *Mémoires de l'Académie de Nîmes*, VIIe series, XXXII (1910), 100-302.

Guiraud, G.-Edouard, *Le Séminaire de Lausanne et le Pastorat en France pendant la période du Désert, 1715-1787. Thèse présentée à la Faculté de Théologie de l'Université de Genève* (Geneva, 1913).

Haag, Eugène and Emile, *La France Protestante*, 1st edition (Paris, 1846-1859), 2nd edition (Paris, 1877-1888).

Hauser, Henri, *Etudes sur la Réforme française* (Paris, 1909).

Hugues, Edmond, *Antoine Court. Histoire de la restauration du protestantisme en France au XVIII*e *siècle* (Paris, 1872), 2 vols.

Hyslop, Beatrice Frye, *A Guide to the General Cahiers of 1789* (New York, 1936).

Janzé, C. A. de, *Les Huguenots. Cent ans de persécution* (Paris, 1886).

Kuscinski, A., *Dictionnaire des Conventionnels* (Paris, 1916-1919), 4 vols.

Kuscinski, A., *Les Députés au Corps législatif, Conseil des Cinq-Cents, Conseil des Anciens* (Paris, 1905).

Kuscinski, A., *Les Députés à l'Assemblée législative de 1791* (Paris, 1900).

Labat, Léopold, *Le drame de la rue des Filatiers. Jean Calas, son procès, sa mémoire défendue par Voltaire et par la soeur Anne Julie* (Toulouse and Paris, 1910)

La Gorce, Pierre de, *Histoire religieuse de la Révolution française*, 11th edition (Paris, 1912), 5 vols.

La Sicotière, Louis de, *Louis de Frotté et les insurrections normandes, 1793-1832* (Paris, 1889), 2 vols.

Lauze de Peret, P.-J., *Eclaircissemens historiques en réponse aux calomnies dont les Protestans du Gard sont l'objet; et précis des agitations et des troubles de ce Département depuis 1790 jusqu'à nos jours* (Paris, 1818), 5 vols.

Lavisse, Ernest; Carré, Henri; Sagnac, Philippe, *Histoire de France depuis les origines jusqu'à la Révolution*, volume VIII, i, ii; IX (Paris, 1911-1926).

Leflon, Joseph, *La Crise révolutionnaire, 1789-1846*, volume XX of the *Histoire de l'Eglise depuis les origines jusqu'à nos jours*, by Augustin Fliche and Victor Martin (s.l., 1949).

Léonard, Emile-G., *Histoire du Protestantisme* (Paris, 1950).

Léonard, Emile-G., *Histoire ecclésiastique des Réformés français au XVIII*e *siècle* (Paris, 1940).

Léonard, Emile-G., *Mon village sous Louis XV, d'après les Mémoires d'un Paysan* (Paris, 1941).

Léonard, Emile-G., *Problèmes et expériences du Protestantisme français. L'Urbanisation, l'embourgeoisement, les déviations ecclésiastiques, l'attrait catholique* (Paris, 1940).

Léonard, Emile-G., "Le problème du culte public et de l'église dans le Protestantisme français du XVIIIe siècle," *Foi et Vie* (1937), 431-457.

Léonard, Emile-G., *Le Protestant français* (Paris, 1953).

Léonard, Emile-G., "Le Protestantisme français au XVIIe siècle," *Revue historique*, CC (1948), 153-179.

Léonard, Emile-G., "Les protestants français au XVIIIe siècle," *Annales d'histoire sociale*, II (1940), 5-20.

Leroux, Alfred, *Les religionnaires de Bordeaux de 1685 à 1802* (Bordeaux, 1920).

Levasseur, Emile, *La population française. Histoire de la population avant 1789 et démographie de la France* (Paris, 1889), 3 vols.

Lévy-Schneider, Léon, *Le Conventionnel Jeanbon Saint-André, 1749-1813* (Paris, 1901), 2 vols.

Lévy-Schneider, Léon, "Les protestants et la Révolution dans le Sud-Ouest," *La Révolution française*, XXXIX (1900), 11-24.

Lichtenberger, F., ed., *Encyclopédie des sciences religieuses*, volume V, article entitled "La France protestante" (Paris, 1878).

Ligou, Daniel, "Protestants et sans-culottes. La bourgeoisie réformée de Montauban devant la Révolution," *Actes du Xe Congrès des Sociétés Savantes Pyrénées-Languedoc-Gascogne* (1954), 13pp.

Lods, Armand, "L'attitude du clergé catholique à l'égard des protestants en 1789," *La Révolution française*, XXXIII (1897), 128-137.

Lods, Armand, *L'Eglise réformée de Paris pendant la Révolution* (Paris, 1889).

Lods, Armand, *Essai sur la vie de Rabaut Saint-Etienne* (Paris, 1893).

Lods, Armand, *Le Pasteur Rabaut-Pomier, 1744-1820* (Paris, 1893).

Lods, Armand, *Traité de l'administration des cultes protestants* (Paris, 1896).

Marion, Marcel, "Un épisode du mouvement de 1789 à Bordeaux," *Revue d'histoire moderne et contemporaine*, III (1901-1902), 739-753.

Mathiez, Albert, "Protestants et théophilanthropes," *La Révolution française*, XLIV (1903), 385-401.

Mathiez, Albert, *La théophilanthropie et le culte décadaire* (Paris, 1904).

Maury, Léon, *Le réveil religieux dans l'église réformée à Genève et en France* (Paris, 1892), 2 vols.

Mirabaud, Robert, *Un président de la Constituante et de la Convention: Rabaut-Saint-Etienne* (Paris, 1930).

Monod, Albert, *Les Sermons de Paul Rabaut, Pasteur du Désert (1738-1785). Etude sur les manuscrits inédits de Paul Rabaut suivie du texte de trois sermons annotés* (s.l.n.d.).

Nazelle, L.-J., *Le Protestantisme en Saintonge sous le régime de la Révocation* (Paris, 1907).

Noailles, *Histoire de Madame de Maintenon et des principaux événements du régne de Louis XIV* (Paris, 1849-1858).

Peyric, Léon, *Le Rôle religieux des pasteurs dans les assemblées politiques de la Révolution française. Thèse présentée à la Faculté de Théologie protestante de Paris* (Cahors, 1902).

Pouget de Saint-André, *Les Auteurs cachés de la Révolution française* (Paris, 1929)

Pouthas, Charles-H., "Guizot et la tradition du Désert; la vie des protestants du Languedoc au XVIIIe siècle," *Revue historique*, CLXIX (1932), 45-81.

Pouthas, Charles-H., *Une Famille de bourgeoisie française de Louis XIV à Napoléon* (Paris, 1934).

Préclin, E., *Les Jansénistes du XVIIIe siècle et la Constitution civile du Clergé* (Paris, 1929).

Pressensé, Edmond de, *L'Eglise et la Révolution française. Histoire des relations de l'église et de l'état de 1789 à 1814*, 3rd edition (Paris, 1889).

Puaux, Frank, *Histoire de la Réformation française* (Paris, 1868-1869), 7 vols.

Rabaut, Camille, *Lasource, Député à la Législative et à la Convention* (Paris, 1889).

Renauld, Ernest, *Le Péril protestant. Essai d'histoire contemporaine*, 11th edition (Paris, 1899).

Robert, Adolphe, *Dictionnaire des Parlementaires français* (Paris, 1891), 5 vols.

Robinet, J.-F.-E., Adolphe Robert and J. Le Chaplain, *Dictionnaire historique et biographique de la Révolution et de l'Empire* (Paris, 1899), 2 vols.

Robinet, J.-F.-E., *Le Mouvement religieux à Paris pendant la Révolution* (Paris, 1896), 2 vols.

Roschach, Ernest, *Histoire générale de Languedoc*, volume XIII (Toulouse, 1876).

Rouvière, François, *L'Aliénation des biens nationaux dans le Gard* (Nîmes, 1900).

Rouvière, François, *Histoire de la Révolution française dans le Département du Gard* (Nîmes, 1887-1889), 4 vols.

Rouvière, François, *Quatrefages de Laroquete, Constituant du Gard. Etude biographique pour servir à l'histoire de la Révolution française* (Paris, 1886)

Rouvière, François, *Les Religionnaires des diocèses de Nîmes, Alais et Uzès, et la Révolution française* (Paris, 1889).

Schram, Stuart R., *Protestantism and Politics in France* (Alençon, 1954).

Sloan, William Milligan, *The French Revolution and Religious Reform* (New York, 1901).

Sourdat, F. N., *Les Véritables auteurs de la Révolution de France de 1789* (Neufchatel, 1797).

Taillandier, Pierre, *Le mariage des protestants français sous l'ancien régime* (Clermont-Ferrand, 1919).

Vaurigaud, B., *Essai sur l'histoire des Eglises réformées de Bretagne* (Paris, 1870), 3 vols.

Viénot, John, *Histoire de la Réforme française des origines à l'Edit de Nantes* (Paris, 1926-1934), 2 vols.

Young, Arthur, *Travels in France*, ed. Constantia Maxwell (Cambridge, England, 1929).

Periodicals

For printed sources and monographs, the author drew extensively from the periodicals listed below. The most important articles within these periodicals have been listed individually in the appropriate places elsewhere in the bibliography.

The most valuable of the periodicals is the *Bulletin de la Société de l'histoire du Protestantisme français* (cited in the abbreviated form BPF in the footnotes of the text of this work). The Société de l'histoire du Protestantisme français was founded in 1853 with the purpose of "collecting and making available to the public all unedited and printed documents bearing on the history of Protestant churches of the French language." The Society commenced publication of the *Bulletin* on a quarterly basis in 1853 and has continued its work to the present day, with the exception of a brief interruption in the appearance of its *Bulletin* during the Nazi occupation of France during World War II. The thoroughness with which the editors have published materials as they were discovered has made the *Bulletin* an indispensable source of information for all periods of the history of French Protestantism. Because so much of the material for this work was drawn from the *Bulletin*, no attempt has been made to list individual articles or sources taken from it in this bibliography.

Annales d'histoire sociale
Annales historiques de la Révolution française
Annales du Midi
Foi et vie
Mémoires de l'Académie de Nîmes
Mémoires de l'Académie de Toulouse
La Révolution française
Revue d'histoire ecclésiastique
Revue d'histoire moderne et contemporaine
Revue historique
Revue du Midi
Revue des Pyrénées
Société de l'histoire du Protestantisme français; Bulletin historique et littéraire

INDEX

INDEX

INDEX

Lightning Source UK Ltd.
Milton Keynes UK
UKHW02f1450130218
317818UK00004B/235/P

9 780691 626697